Praise for *From Foreclosure to Fair Lending*:

"Realizing the objectives of the 1968 Fair Housing Act has long been considered one of the most critical pieces of unfinished business of the civil rights movement. *From Foreclosure to Fair Lending* shows us what needs to be done to achieve those goals. Hartman and Squires have assembled the nation's leading fair housing advocates and scholars. Given the continuing fallout of the foreclosure debacle, the timing could not be better for this book."
—Ben Jealous, President, NAACP

"Occupy Wall Street's biggest success was its impact on the national conversation. But now, many voices ask, what's next? This book offers some important answers. In *From Foreclosure to Fair Lending*, leading experts and activists in housing and lending practices reflect on how the Occupy spirit revives the historic civil rights and grassroots organizing movements to take on new challenges in a new century."
—Clarence Page, Pulitzer Prize-winning
syndicated columnist for the *Chicago Tribune*

"Housing policies and practices are at the center of the ongoing economic crisis in the United States, and the consequences in lost homes and lost savings have been devastating for many Americans. This collection gives us the essential background to understand these developments and to support the struggle for social justice in housing that is emerging."
—Frances Fox Piven,
City University of New York Graduate School

"Our nation is at a crossroads precipitated by the lending and foreclosure crisis that has the potential of erasing the gains of forty-five years of fair housing/fair lending enforcement. Traditional responses to the current challenges may be reaching the limits of their effectiveness. *From Foreclosure to Fair Lending* demonstrates another way."
—Michael P. Seng, Co-Executive Director,
The John Marshall Law School Fair Housing
Legal Support Center and Clinic

From Foreclosure
TO Fair Lending

From Foreclosure TO Fair Lending

Advocacy, Organizing, Occupy, and

the Pursuit of Equitable Access to Credit

EDITED BY

Chester Hartman

AND

Gregory D. Squires

NEW VILLAGE PRESS • NEW YORK, NY

Published in the United States by
New Village Press
@ Centre for Social Innovation
601 West 26th Street, Suite 325-11
New York, NY 10001
bookorders@newvillagepress.net
www.newvillagepress.net

New Village Press is a public-benefit, not-for-profit publishing venture of Architects/Designers/Planners for Social Responsibility.

In support of the Greenpress Initiative, New Village Press is committed to the preservation of endangered forests globally and advancing best practices within the book and paper industries. The printing papers used in this book are 100% recycled fiber, acid-free (Process Chlorine Free), and have been certified with the Forest Stewardship Council (FSC).

Original paperback ISBN 978-1-61332-013-6
eBook ISBN 978-1-61332-014-3

Publication Date: October 2013

FIRST EDITION

Library of Congress Cataloging-in-Publication Data

From foreclosure to fair lending : advocacy, organizing, occupy, and the pursuit of equitable credit / edited by Chester Hartman and Gregory D. Squires. — First edition.
       pages cm
    Summary: "Twenty-four well-known fair housing and fair lending activists and organizers examine the implications of the new wave of fair housing activism generated by Occupy Wall Street protests and the many successes achieved in fair housing and fair lending over the years. The book reveals the limitations of advocacy efforts and the challenges that remain. Best directions for future action are brought to light by staff of fair housing organizations, fair housing attorneys, community and labor organizers, and scholars who have researched social justice organizing and advocacy movements. The book is written for general interest and academic audiences. Contributors address the foreclosure crisis, access to credit in a changing marketplace, and the immoral hazards of big banks. They examine opportunities in collective bargaining available to home-owners and how low-income and minority households were denied access to historically low home prices and interest rates. Authors question the effectiveness of litigation to uphold the Fair Housing Act's promise of nondiscriminatory home loans and ask how the Consumer Financial Protection Bureau is assuring fair lending. They also look at where immigrants stand, housing as a human right, and methods for building a movement. Chester Hartman is an urban planner, academic, author of more than twenty books, and director of research for the Poverty & Race Research Action Council. Gregory Squires is a professor of sociology and public policy and public administration at George Washington University and advisor to the John Marshall Law School Fair Housing Legal Support Center."— Provided by publisher.
    Includes bibliographical references and index.
    ISBN 978-1-61332-013-6 (pbk.)
    1. Housing—United States. 2. Housing policy—Citizen participation. 3. Mortgage loans—United States. 4. Economic policy—United States—Citizen participation. 5. Occupy movement—United States.
I. Hartman, Chester W. II. Squires, Gregory D..
    HD7293.F756 2013
    332.7'20973—dc23   2013023686

Front cover design by Lynne Elizabeth
Cover photograph by Brennan Cavanaugh
Interior design and composition by Leigh McLellan Design

Contents

Undoing the Bitter Legacy
of Segregation and Discrimination

Douglas S. Massey

I N THE FIRST DECADES of the twentieth century, the United States transformed itself into a racially segregated society in which black and white citizens occupied separate and vastly unequal segments of the urban landscape. As African Americans moved out of the rural South en masse to take factory jobs and service positions in industrializing cities throughout the nation, ever higher levels of racial segregation were imposed by whites (Lieberson 1981). By 1940, the black ghetto had become a standard feature of urban America maintained through institutionalized discrimination in the real estate and lending industries and built into public policies at all levels of government (Katznelson 2005).

From 1940 to 1970, black segregation persisted at extremely high levels across virtually all urban areas. Despite significant changes in the size and geographic distribution of the urban black population, the ghetto remained a constant. The residential color line simply moved in space as the ghetto expanded in size (Massey and Denton 1993). During this period, real estate agents refused to rent or sell homes to blacks within white neighborhoods and systematically steered African American home seekers to black or racially changing neighborhoods. Lenders refused to grant mortgages to black home buyers and denied credit to anyone living in a black or racially changing neighborhood—practices that were built into the US Federal Housing Administration (FHA) and the Department of Veterans Affairs (VA) lending programs. Given these structural constraints, segregation and urban decay were inevitable. Any neighborhood that opened up to black settlement quickly became all-black, and once it became part of the ghetto, it was cut off from capital investment, leading to physical deterioration.

Conditions for African Americans began to improve during the civil rights movement, but the discriminatory supports for housing segregation proved to be intractable. Although early drafts of the Civil Rights Act contained prohibitions on discrimination in housing and mortgage lending, they were dropped as the legislation worked its way toward passage. As a result, the 1964 Civil Rights Act banned racial discrimination in labor markets, retail sales, and public service provisions and the Voting Rights Act of 1965 guaranteed black voting rights and banned practices used to keep blacks from the polls, but discrimination in lending and housing remained perfectly legal. Even Lyndon Johnson's formidable legislative skills were unable to change the status quo when it came to neighborhoods.

As black neighborhoods deteriorated in the face of political isolation and systematic disinvestment, race riots swept through America's urban ghettos despite the Civil Rights Acts. It was only in the wake of the assassination of Martin Luther King, Jr. and a final spasm of racial violence that Congress finally acted to outlaw discrimination in the rental and sale of housing. With National Guard troops stationed in the Capitol to protect it from rioters in adjacent neighborhoods, Congress passed the 1968 Fair Housing Act, which declared discrimination in housing markets to be unlawful but provided weak measures to enforce the law. Congressional action against discrimination in mortgage lending was even later in coming. Not until 1974 did Congress pass the Equal Credit Opportunity Act to outlaw discrimination against black borrowers, and it was not until 1977 that Congress passed the Community Reinvestment Act to ban the practice of redlining by which financial institutions had long channeled funds away from black neighborhoods.

By the late 1970s, of course, much of the damage to urban black America had been done. Decades of isolation and disinvestment had left urban blacks in a very vulnerable position and the stage was set for even more pronounced declines with the rise of income inequality during the 1980s, which drove up the spatial concentration of poverty within black neighborhoods to unprecedented levels (Wilson 1987; Massey and Denton 1993). The concentration of poverty, in turn, only served to exacerbate the disadvantage that African Americans experienced because of their race and class, isolating them from societal resources and exposing them to uniquely high levels of violence and disorder (Peterson and Krivo 2010) that would have grave consequences for well-being on a variety of dimensions (Sampson 2012; Massey et al. 2013).

At present, the principal mechanism for the perpetuation of low socio-economic status among African Americans is the intergenerational transmission of neighborhood disadvantage (Harding 2010; Sharkey 2013). Poor urban blacks routinely experience concentrations of poverty not experienced by any other group in the United States, a condition determined primarily by the persistence of black segregation at uniquely high levels (Massey and Fischer 2000; Quillian 2012; Massey and Rugh, forthcoming). Despite the Fair Housing Act, the Equal Credit Opportunity Act, and the Community Reinvestment Act, black segregation has been slow to change. At the same time, levels of segregation and isolation have risen for Hispanics as their share of the population grew from 4.7 percent in 1970 to 16.3 percent in 2010 (Massey, Rothwell, and Domina 2009). As of 2010, 60 percent of blacks and 50 percent of Hispanics would have to exchange neighborhoods with non-Hispanic whites to achieve an even distribution across neighborhoods. The average urban African American lives in a neighborhood that is 45 percent black, while the average urban Latino lives in a neighborhood that is 47 percent Hispanic (Massey and Rugh, forthcoming).

Trends and levels of segregation and isolation are conditioned by the size of the minority community, however, and in those metropolitan areas where a majority of blacks live, an extreme form of separation known as hypersegregation continues to prevail. Likewise, in those metropolitan areas housing a majority of Hispanics, segregation levels are rising and hypersegregation has emerged (Wilkes and Iceland 2004). Segregation persists because of the weak enforcement measures authorized by civil rights legislation and weak actions on the part of public authorities to implement those statutory provisions for enforcement that do exist.

What legislation did accomplish was an end to overt discrimination in housing and lending. Although minorities are no longer openly denied access to homes and credit, audit studies reveal that discriminatory practices still continue surreptitiously (Squires 1994; Turner et al. 2002; Ross and Turner 2004). At the same time, new and more subtle forms of discrimination have been invented (Massey 2005), such as name discrimination (Bertrand and Mullainathan 2004), linguistic profiling (Massey and Lundy 2001; Squires and Chadwick 2006), predatory lending (Squires 2004), and reverse redlining (Friedman and Squires 2005; Brescia 2009). Density zoning has also emerged as a powerful force promoting racial segregation, since limits on the density of residential construction drive up the cost of suburban housing and make it unaffordable to low- and moderate-income households, which are disproportionately minority (Rothwell and Massey 2009).

In the twenty-first century, predatory lending and reverse redlining have been particularly vicious in affecting African Americans. Predatory lending occurs when black households are targeted for subprime mortgages and other exploitive lending products. Reverse redlining occurs when such products are systematically targeted to black neighborhoods. Both forms of discrimination played an outsized role in the recent housing bust, heaping the pain of foreclosure disproportionately on already vulnerable black communities. The disproportion occurred because ongoing segregation had concentrated black home owners spatially, enabling unscrupulous mortgage brokers to target them for exploitation easily and efficiently. Indeed, the degree of black segregation was the strongest single predictor of the number and rate of home foreclosures across US metropolitan areas between 2006 and 2008 (Rugh and Massey 2010).

Reverse redlining and predatory lending emerged as new forms of discrimination in the 1990s with the rise of securitized mortgages. Securitized mortgages are not held by banks but pooled together to back bonds known as collateralized debt obligations (CDOs) that are then sold to private investors. The advent of CDOs transformed mortgage lending from a bank-based to a securities-based system, vastly expanding the pool of money available for lending (Rugh and Massey 2010). Because virtually any mortgage, however shaky, could be bundled and sold as a CDO, borrowers in ghettos and barrios who were formerly shunned by lenders became very attractive, initiating a new wave of predatory lending and reverse redlining in which independent brokers generated as many high-risk mortgages as they could and immediately sold them to financial institutions, which then capitalized the shaky loans as securities and sold them to third party investors who bore the loss when the housing bubble burst and foreclosures spread.

In the course of the boom and bust cycle, housing wealth was created and then sucked out of black communities throughout the United States. As a result, median black wealth fell from $14,000 in 2007 to $4,800 in 2009, well below its value two decades earlier. While the ratio of black-to-white wealth was 10 percent in 1990, the figures stood at 4 percent in 2010 (Massey, forthcoming). In essence, what little housing wealth black households had been able to accumulate in cities around the nation before 2006 was transferred into the pockets of white investors in and around New York.

In sum, discrimination in lending does much more than simply deny black families access to housing and capital. Indeed, these discriminatory practices played a central role in extracting what little wealth existed in black communities and reducing black assets to their lowest level in decades, both absolutely and relative to whites. Discrimination in lending actively promotes the perpetuation of socioeconomic deprivation among African Americans, underscoring the critical importance of equal access to credit for racial equality in the United States and the urgent need for advocacy, organizing, and occupying to achieve it.

References

Bertrand, Marriane, and Sendhil Mullainathan. 2004. "Are Emily and Greg More Employable Than Lakisha and Jamal? A Field Experiment on Labor Market Discrimination." *American Economic Review* 94: 991–1013.

Brescia, Raymond H. 2009. "Subprime Communities: Reverse Redlining, the Fair Housing Act and Emerging Issues in Litigation Regarding the Subprime Mortgage Crisis." *Albany Government Law Review* 2: 164–216.

Friedman, Samantha, and Gregory D. Squires. 2005. "Does the Community Reinvestment Act Help Minorities Access Traditionally Inaccessible Neighborhoods?" *Social Problems* 52: 209–231.

Harding, David J. 2010. *Living the Drama: Community, Conflict, and Culture among Inner-City Boys*. Chicago: University of Chicago Press.

Katznelson, Ira. 2005. *When Affirmative Action Was White: An Untold History of Racial Inequality in Twentieth-Century America*. New York: W. W. Norton.

Lieberson, Stanley. 1981. *A Piece of the Pie: Blacks and White Immigrants Since 1880*. Berkeley: University of California Press.

Massey, Douglas S. 2005. "Racial Discrimination in Housing: A Moving Target." *Social Problems* 52: 148–51.

———. Forthcoming. "The New Latino Underclass: Immigration Enforcement as a Race-Making Institution." In *Immigration, Poverty, and Socioeconomic Inequality*, edited by David Card and Steven Raphael. New York: Russell Sage Foundation.

Massey, Douglas S., and Nancy A. Denton. 1993. *American Apartheid: Segregation and the Making of the Underclass*. Cambridge, MA: Harvard University Press.

Massey, Douglas S., and Mary J. Fischer. 2000. "How Segregation Concentrates Poverty." *Ethnic and Racial Studies* 23: 670–91.

Massey, Douglas S., and Garvey Lundy. 2001. "Use of Black English and Racial Discrimination in Urban Housing Markets: New Methods and Findings." *Urban Affairs Review* 36: 470–96.

Massey, Douglas S., and Jacob S. Rugh. Forthcoming. "Segregation in Post-Civil Rights America: Stalled Integration or End of the Segregated Century?" *The DuBois Review: Social Science Research on Race*.

Massey, Douglas S., Jonathan Rothwell, and Thurston Domina. 2009. "Changing Bases of Segregation in the United States." *Annals of the American Academy of Political and Social Science* 626: 74–90.

Massey, Douglas S., Len Albright, Rebecca Casciano, Elizabeth Derickson, and David Kinsey. 2013. *Climbing Mount Laurel: The Struggle for Affordable Housing and Social Mobility in an American Suburb*. Princeton, NJ: Princeton University Press.

Peterson, Ruth D., and Lauren J. Krivo. 2010. *Divergent Social Worlds: Neighborhood Crime and the Racial-Spatial Divide*. New York: Russell Sage Foundation.

Quillian, Lincoln. 2012. "Segregation and Poverty Concentration: The Role of Three Segregations." *American Sociological Review* 77: 354–379.

Ross, Stephen L., and Margery A. Turner. 2004. "Other Things Being Equal: A Paired Testing Study of Discrimination in Mortgage Lending." *Journal of Urban Economics* 55: 278–97.

Rothwell, Jonathan, and Douglas S. Massey. 2009. "The Effect of Density Zoning on Racial Segregation in U.S. Urban Areas." *Urban Affairs Review* 44: 799–806.

Rugh, Jacob S., and Douglas S. Massey. 2010. "Racial Segregation and the American Foreclosure Crisis." *American Sociological Review* 75 (5): 629–51.

Sampson, Robert J. 2012. *Great American City: Chicago and the Enduring Neighborhood Effect.* Chicago: University of Chicago Press.

Sharkey, Patrick. 2013. *Stuck in Place: Urban Neighborhoods and the End of Progress Toward Racial Equality.* Chicago: University of Chicago Press.

Squires, Gregory D. 1994. *Capital and Communities in Black and White: The Intersections of Race, Class, and Uneven Development.* Albany, NY: State University of New York Press.

———. 2004. *Why The Poor Pay More: How to Stop Predatory Lending.* Westport, CT: Praeger/Greenwood Publishing Group.

Squires, Gregory D., and Jan Chadwick. 2006. "Linguistic Profiling: A Tradition of the Property Insurance Industry." *Urban Affairs Review* 41 (3): 400–415.

Turner, Margery A., Fred Freiberg, Eerin B. Godfrey, Carla Herbig, Diane K. Levy, and Robert E. Smith. 2002. *All Other Things Being Equal: A Paired Testing Study of Mortgage Lending Institution.* Washington, DC: US Department of Housing and Urban Development.

Wilkes, Rima, and John Iceland. 2004. "Hypersegregation in the Twenty-First Century: An Update and Analysis." *Demography* 41: 23–36.

Wilson, William Julius. 1987. *The Truly Disadvantaged: The Inner City, the Underclass, and Public Policy.* Chicago: University of Chicago Press.

1

INTRODUCTION

Occupy Wall Street

A New Wave of Fair Housing Activism?

Gregory D. Squires and Chester Hartman

A rising tide lifts all boats, sinks all rafts and drowns the people treading water! —VERNELLIA R. RANDALL (2011)

F ORTY YEARS AGO, Gale Cincotta, affectionately known in the community organizing world as the mother of community reinvestment, led her troops into bank lobbies, effectively shutting them down for the day, held barbeques on the front yards of bank executives, and threatened Federal Reserve Chairman Paul Volker that she would hang a "Loan Shark" sign over the Federal Reserve Board office in Washington, DC (Westgate 2011). Since that time, a fair housing/fair lending/community reinvestment infrastructure has emerged, changing the way the nation's financial institutions and housing providers do business. With the passage of fair housing and fair lending laws, lawsuits and administrative complaints to enforce them, community reinvestment agreements, and other tactics, a tradition of redlining and disinvestment slowly evolved into a commitment to fair housing and reinvestment (Squires 2003). But has this movement run its course? And do the Occupy Wall Street protests, which are reminiscent of what Cincotta was doing in the 1970s and for several years after, portend the next wave?

Going back at least to the creation of the Federal Housing Administration (FHA) in 1934, virtually all branches of the housing industry, along with the government agencies that regulated it, practiced explicit, overt racial discrimination (Jackson 1985; Massey and Denton 1993; Meyer 2000). Early FHA underwriting manuals stated that "if a neighborhood is to retain stability, it is necessary that properties shall continue to be occupied by the same social and racial classes" (FHA 1938, par. 937). Racially restrictive covenants assured that properties in the more desirable neighborhoods would stay in white hands until the Supreme Court prohibited enforcement of such agreements in the 1948 case *Shelley v. Kraemer* (Gotham 2002; Satter 2009). Until 1950, the National Association of Realtors stated in its code of ethics, "a realtor should never be instrumental in introducing into a neighborhood . . . members of any race, nationality or any individuals whose presence will clearly be detrimental to property values in that neighborhood" (Judd 1984, 284). Training materials used until the 1970s by the American Institute of Real Estate Appraisers included the following example to illustrate sound neighborhood analysis: "The neighborhood is entirely Caucasian. It appears that there is no adverse effect by minority groups" (Greene 1980, 9). Public housing has long been a linchpin for racial segregation (Hirsch 1983; Polikoff 2006). Redlining by insurance companies and mortgage lenders, and, more recently, the wave of reverse redlining from predatory lending practices sealed the doom of many urban communities (Squires 1997; Immergluck 2004, 2009).

The civil rights movement eliminated virtually all the explicitly discriminatory rules of real estate agents, mortgage lenders, and other housing providers, though discriminatory practices persisted. A host of community organizations, consumer advocacy groups, fair housing agencies, sympathetic attorneys, supportive foundations, some elected officials, and others developed a range of skills (e.g., research, litigation, communication, advocacy) to change the way housing and related services were normally provided. The better-known names that have constituted this community reinvestment infrastructure include National People's Action and National Training and Information Center (both started by Cincotta), National Fair Housing Alliance (NFHA), National Community Reinvestment Coalition (NCRC), Association of Community Organizations for Reform Now (ACORN), Center for Responsible Lending, Center for Community Change, Consumer Federation of America, and, more recently, Americans for Financial Reform.

This community reinvestment movement, consisting of a range of initiatives to increase access to financial services in traditionally underserved low-income and minority communities, has had many successes. Key federal laws include the 1968 Fair Housing Act and subsequent amendments, the Equal Credit Opportunity Act (ECOA), and the Community Reinvestment Act (CRA)—basically, a federal law prohibiting redlining. These and other statutes put the federal government and many state and local governments, which had been explicitly enforcing discriminatory rules for decades, on the side of fair housing. The CRA has generated $6 trillion in new loans in traditionally underserved communities (Community-Wealth.org, 2013). NFHA (2010) reports that since 1999, fair housing organizations have assisted in lawsuits that have generated more than $380 million for victims of housing discrimination through various enforcement activities.

In recent years, government agencies have become more active, particularly in response to the foreclosure crises confronting many families and communities. For example, Goldman Sachs Group, Inc. and the Securities and Exchange Commission (SEC) reached a $550 million settlement over charges that the firm had misled investors in a mortgage-backed investment. Agreements were reached with JPMorgan Chase & Co. ($269.9 million) and Credit Suisse Group AG ($120 million) for similar practices. The Bank of America Corporation, which bought Countrywide Financial in 2008, reached a $335 million settlement with the Department of Justice (DOJ) in response to Countrywide's practice of steering black and Hispanic borrowers to subprime loans while giving better terms to similarly qualified white borrowers ("On the Trail of Mortgage Fraud" 2012; Silver-Greenberg 2012). DOJ also reached a $175 million settlement with Wells Fargo & Company that set aside $125 million in compensation to African American and Hispanic borrowers who were steered to subprime mortgages or charged higher fees and rates than comparable white borrowers and $50 million for down payment assistance to borrowers in communities where the DOJ identified large numbers of discrimination victims (DOJ 2012b). There have been several other settlements involving Citibank, Barclays, and other lenders. But in some cases, judges have stepped in and blocked the settlements, criticizing the enforcement agency for accepting too weak of a deal (New 2011).

More significantly, the DOJ and Department of Housing and Urban Development (HUD), along with forty-nine state attorneys general, announced a $25 billion agreement with five of the nation's largest mortgage servicers (Bank of America Corporation, JPMorgan Chase & Co., Wells Fargo & Company, Citigroup Inc., and Ally Financial Inc.). The settlement involves payment of $20 million to mortgage borrowers and $5 million to federal and state agencies in response to past abuses in the servicing of borrowers, including robo-signing, improper documentation, and lost paperwork. President Obama also appointed a Residential Mortgage-Backed Securities Working Group to investigate wrongful securitization and other fraudulent mortgage-related practices (DOJ 2012a). But it is generally recognized that all of these initiatives are not sufficient to address the wide range of illegal activities and other challenges posed by the financial crisis, as well as related fair housing and fair lending barriers. Tom Perez (2012), assistant attorney general for civil rights, acknowledged in the spring of 2012 that while his office has accomplished a lot, there is a lot more to do. More bluntly, former bank regulator William K. Black, who teaches economics and law at the University of Missouri, dismissed recent federal actions by asserting, "Prosecutors can't argue that these cases will serve as a deterrence when there are no criminal indictments of senior executives" (Douglas 2012).

For example, NFHA (2012, 5, 6) has estimated that there are approximately four million incidents of housing discrimination that occur each year, but just over twenty-seven thousand complaints were filed with fair housing enforcement agencies in 2011. When subprime lending peaked in 2006, 53.7 percent of blacks, 46.6 percent of Hispanics, and just 17.7 percent of whites received high-priced loans. In minority neighborhoods, 46.6 percent received such loans compared to 21.7 percent of borrowers in white areas. These gaps did not close when various credit and financial characteristics of borrowers were taken into consideration (Avery, Brevoort, and Canner 2007). Not surprisingly, the foreclosures that followed reflected these racial disparities. Among borrowers who received loans between 2004 and 2008, 11 percent of African Americans and 14 percent of Hispanics have lost their homes compared to 8 percent of Asians and 6 percent of non-Hispanic whites (Bocian et al. 2012, 39). While levels of segregation have been reduced modestly since the 1970s, black/white segregation in large cities where the black population is highly concentrated (e.g., New York City, Chicago, Detroit, Cleveland, Milwaukee) persists and still amounts to what Douglas Massey and Nancy Denton (1993) refer to as hypersegregation in their classic book *American Apartheid*. To illustrate, in 2010, the typical white resident lived in a neighborhood that was 75 percent white compared to 35 percent for the typical black resident—approximately the same share of white neighbors that black families had in 1940. At the same time, Hispanic and Asian segregation has not been reduced (Logan and Stults 2011). Noting the persistence of housing discrimination despite increased enforcement efforts, Robert Schwemm, one of the nation's leading fair housing legal scholars, asserted, "*something new must be tried*" (2007, 464, emphasis in original).

In describing the success of community reinvestment organizing efforts, Peter Dreier (2003, 344), former director of housing for the Boston Redevelopment Authority and currently a sociologist at Occidental College, referred to CRA-related initiatives as "the most successful example of grassroots community organizing since the mid-1970s." But he also noted that "this is sort of like being the tallest building in Topeka; there's not much competition." He went on to describe challenges that confront this movement, including the increasing concentration and power of the financial services industry. If the community reinvestment movement is to build on its success in the latter decades of the twentieth century and meet emerging twenty-first century challenges, he argued that fair housing and fair lending groups will have to form stronger coalitions with labor unions, environmental groups, progressive elected officials, and others who are struggling with their own versions of uneven and inequitable development. Here is where Occupy Wall Street comes in.

The Meaning of Occupy

The Occupy Wall Street protest movement can trace its beginnings to September 17, 2011, when a group of activists set up camp in Zuccotti Park, in the heart of New York City's financial district. This was not totally spontaneous—organizers had been planning the protest for months. But the creation of the camp and the "We are the 99 percent" slogan set off a wave of protest activity around the world (Hazen, Lohan, and Parramore 2011). Within a month, protest activity had taken place in more than 1,500 cities, according to one account (OccupyWallSt 2011). Most of the encampments that were created in many communities were gone by the winter months, but protest activity persisted and picked up again in the spring with May Day events and others that followed, including several during the first-year anniversary in mid-September of 2012. What may have started as a protest of Wall Street financial institutions and particularly their involvement in creating the foreclosure crisis and the economic chaos that followed has subsequently spread out to many other issues (sometimes for, sometimes against), including, but certainly not limited to, climate change, environmental degradation, sustainability, immigration, student loans, hunger, universal health care, education, and war. It appears that the September 17 moment has truly become a movement.

All of the issues that the Occupy Wall Street movement has called attention to have long been the subject of political debate, academic research, consumer advocacy, and organizing of various stripes. But what has captured the attention of most observers (or at least the media) is the set of tactics. Rejecting traditional approaches to social change, the Occupy movement has employed a range of direct actions, enabling ordinary people to confront powerful individuals and institutions.

In November 2011, thousands of Occupy Oakland protesters marched through downtown, picketed banks, and "visited" the port, effectively shutting it down (Wollan 2011). Hundreds of protesters moved into the lobbies of five Atlanta branches of JPMorgan Chase, shutting down operations for a day in March 2012 (Gottesdiener 2012a). Over one thousand protesters rallied outside a Wells Fargo stockholders meeting in April 2012, with thirty gaining entry to the meeting and demanding changes in some of the bank's investment practices—approximately a dozen were arrested (Scherr 2012). Similar actions followed in cities across the country. A sixty-five-year-old woman lay down on the floor of the Bank of New York Mellon Corporation, refusing to leave until the bank agreed to renegotiate her eviction. She was able to stay in her home. A seventy-eight-year-old woman occupied her home in Nashville and, along with neighborhood support, was able to stop Chase's eviction. Front lawn occupations in San Diego and Los Angeles saved the homes of two families. Occupiers blocked home auctions via two related actions; first, by singing in a courtroom and second, by moving furniture into a Bank of America branch, claiming that the $230 billion bailout taxpayers provided gave them the right to fight the eviction and to live inside the bank itself (Gottesdiener 2012b). Violence has occasionally broken out. Students at the University of California, Davis, were pepper sprayed, a Marine veteran in Oakland was shot, and other incidents have been reported (Van Buren 2011). And some arrests have been made—a total of 7,435 in 120 cities during Occupy's first year (OccupyArrests.com 2012). But this has been a generally peaceful protest movement.

If many issues have been the focus of direct action, financial industry practices and institutions have been the prime target, as the demonstrations noted above indicate. The names of new organizations that have emerged in recent years are illustrative: MakeWallStreetPay, New Bottom Line (with its Move Our Money campaign), Right to the City Alliance, Occupy Our Homes, and Take Back the Land. The overarching issues that tie these actions together are growing concerns with the levels of economic inequality that have not existed since the Great Depression, along with a rising anger at the perceived unfairness in the way income and wealth are distributed (Collins 2012).

A few numbers reveal the surge in inequality since the early 1970s and particularly since the foreclosure crisis hit in 2008. After trending toward greater equality for almost three decades, in 1972, household income in the top 10 percent grew from 8.99 times that of those in the bottom 10 percent to a ratio of 10.58 by 2010 (DeNavas-Walt, Proctor, and Smith 2011, 41, 44). More telling, the top 1 percent increased their income by 275 percent between 1979 and 2007 compared to a 65 percent increase for others in the top 20 percent and just an 18 percent increase for those in the bottom 20 percent (Kneebone, Nadeau, and Berube 2011). The racial impact of the recent foreclosure and related crises is demonstrated by the following pattern. Between 2005 and 2009, median white household wealth declined by 16 percent compared to 53 percent for blacks and 66 percent for Hispanics. This reflected declines in home equity—from $115,364 to $95,000 for whites, from $76,910 to $59,000 for blacks, and from $99,983 to $49,145 for Hispanics. Overall, as of 2009, white households held twenty times the wealth of the typical black household and eighteen times that of an Hispanic household (Kochhar, Fry, and Taylor 2011, 1–3). To the extent that there has been any recovery from the recession that began in 2008, once again, it is the top earners who gained by far the most. Between 2009 and 2010, the income of the top 1 percent of families grew by 11.6 percent compared to 0.2 percent for the bottom 99 percent. In other words, the top 1 percent received 93 percent of the income gains during the first year of recovery (Saez 2012, 1). As the Census Bureau reported, income inequality continued to grow in 2011 (DeNavas-Walt, Proctor, and Smith 2012).

Wealth has long been more unequally distributed than income, and wealth disparities have increased in recent years as well. The ratio of the wealth controlled by the top 1 percent of families compared to the median grew from 125 to 225 between 1962 and 2009 (Economic Policy Institute 2013). During the first two years of the recent economic recovery, the wealthiest 7 percent experienced a 28 percent increase in their net worth compared to a drop of 4 percent for the remaining 93 percent. Consequently, the top group saw their share of the nation's overall household wealth increase from 56 percent in 2009 to 63 percent in 2011 (Fry and Taylor 2013).

Whether the Occupy protests will alter these patterns remains to be seen. But this movement has already changed national attitudes and political debates. In January 2012, the Pew Research Center reported that 66 percent of adults believe there are "very strong" or "strong" conflicts between the rich and the poor, an increase of 19 percentage points since 2009 (Morin 2012). These conflicts now rank ahead of three other long-standing sources of conflict—between immigrants and native born, between blacks and whites, and between young and old. According to Rich Morin (2012) with the Pew Center, "These changes in attitudes over a relatively short period of time may reflect the income and wealth inequality message conveyed by Occupy Wall Street protesters across the country in late 2011 that led to a spike in media attention to the topic." And the media certainly were paying more attention. In a search of the LexisNexis Group database, Peter Dreier (2011) found 409 stories with the word "inequality" in October 2010, with little variation through September 2011, but the number jumped to 1,269 in October 2011. He found the phrase "richest one percent" in between 11 and 32 stories each month from October 2010 to September 2011, but 174 times in October 2011. Perhaps more revealing is a survey showing that confidence in Wall Street reached a forty-year low subsequent to the bailouts of 2008. The lack of confidence in

Wall Street may well be connected to a perceived unfairness with which many are treated in today's economy. A *USA Today*/Gallup Poll taken in early October of 2011 found that 44 percent of Americans say the economic system is personally unfair to them (Stiglitz 2012, xiv; Hampson 2011). A perfect storm of growing economic insecurity coupled with a sense of injustice has created a significant loss of confidence in the nation's financial institutions (Owens 2012). Inequality and unfairness appear to be nurturing protest activity, which, in turn, raises awareness of that same inequality and sense of unfairness in the allocation of income and wealth. As Joseph E. Stiglitz (2012, xxi), Columbia University's Nobel Prize-winning economist, concluded, "these young protesters have already altered public discourse and the consciousness of ordinary citizens and politicians alike."

Despite the obvious racial implications of these trajectories of inequality, there has been some debate regarding the participation, or lack thereof, of racial minorities and particularly African Americans in Occupy protests. One fall 2011 survey found that just 1.6 percent of Occupy Wall Street protesters were African American. Several explanations have been offered. Perhaps leading civil rights organizations that receive financial support from some of the Occupy targets are hesitant to confront their benefactors. It may be that racial minorities simply have more concrete and pressing issues than what is perceived to be an amorphous battle between the 1 percent and the 99 percent, like forced eviction, police brutality, and neighborhood crime (Patton 2011). At a fall 2011 discussion of Occupy DC at a Washington, DC, bookstore that one of us attended, several members of an integrated audience expressed concerns that the Occupy movement was led almost exclusively by whites, with whites being the most active participants. Others disagreed, claiming there were more nonwhite participants than the critics suggested, but most acknowledged this was an ongoing issue. Organizations like Occupy the Dream (led by the veteran civil rights activist Ben Chavis), Occupy Harlem, Occupy the Hood, and other similar organizations indicate there is a concrete nonwhite presence in the Occupy movement. The role of such entities and their relationship to the broader Occupy movement, however, will likely be a continuing topic of discussion. Racial divisions permeate American life. It should not be surprising that they are part of the Occupy movement.

Despite some internal divisions, the Occupy movement has met with some significant success. Whether its activities to date amount to what Noam Chomsky (2012, 54), noted Massachusetts Institute of Technology linguist, has referred to as "the first major public response, in fact, to about thirty years of a really bitter class war" remains to be seen. If this is the case, and the movement is to have a lasting impact, it will be due, in part, to the reality that there is in fact some heterogeneity within both the 1 percent and the 99 percent. Some in the 99 percent are lawyers, accountants, lobbyists, large and small business people, and other professionals who support and nurture current patterns of inequality. But some members of the 1 percent (basically, three million people in 1.5 million households who earn more than $500,000 annually with a net worth of $5 million or more) support many of the objectives of the 99 percent. Warren Buffett famously called for the rich to pay more in taxes, noting he pays a smaller percentage of his income in taxes than his secretary (Buffett 2011). And two-thirds of those at the top share his belief that they should pay more taxes (Collins 2012, 20–23, 81)

Several of the 1 percent are actively working to reform financial institutions and achieve fairer tax policies. For example, Wealth for the Common Good is a network of more than five hundred people with incomes above $250,000 that has petitioned to end the Bush-era tax cuts and to close other tax loopholes (Collins 2012, 81–82). And several Wall Street veterans are entering the fray on behalf of the 99 percent. Some former traders have formed Occupy the SEC to advise the Securities and Exchange Commission on regulations to implement the Volcker Rule, a provision of the Dodd-Frank Wall Street Reform and Consumer Protection Act passed in 2010, which limits a bank's ability to make speculative investments in which deposits are used primarily for the benefit of the bank rather than its customers. Occupy the SEC's objective is to serve as a counterweight to industry lobbyists who are seeking to weaken these provisions of the law. Other former bank executives have created the Occupy Bank Group to explore the creation of an alternative national bank that will serve the interests of the poor and others underserved by traditional financial institutions. The Alternative Banking Group, or Alt. Banking, is a group of financial industry professionals that is trying to educate consumers, including Occupy protesters, on the inner workings of Wall Street and how it can be reformed (Khimm 2012).

Still, major social change has long been primarily the outcome of lengthy, patient, but persistent organizing and advocacy from below (Warren 2001). As Chomsky (2012, 18) noted, quoting the historian Howard Zinn, "Where progress has been made, wherever any kind of injustice has been overturned, it's been because people acted as citizens, and not as politicians. They didn't just moan. They worked, they acted, they organized." Again in tribute to Zinn, Chomsky (2012, 105) wrote that it was "the countless small actions of unknown people that lie at the roots of those great moments." More specifically, he argued, referencing the black feminist poet June Jordan, "We are the ones we have been waiting for" (Chomsky 2012, 17). But as University of Pennsylvania urban historian Thomas J. Sugrue (2009, 136) observed,

"Whenever the arc of history has bent toward justice, this development has been the consequence of a synergy between grassroots activism and political leadership." This brings us back to fair housing.

Occupy, Fair Housing, and the Organization of This Book

The following chapters illustrate the actions of many of those citizens who have long been engaged in fair housing, fair lending, and related social movements. Among the contributors are members of the nation's leading fair housing and fair lending advocacy organizations, labor and community organizers, and scholars who have made significant contributions to the many victories that have been won in recent decades. Their contributions to this volume inform the next steps, including the lessons of Occupy and for building on their victories.

We have organized the book's remaining chapters into three (in some cases, overlapping) segments: the Activists, the Organizers, and the Scholars. The Activists clearly demonstrate that market forces alone will not resolve or self-correct prevailing economic- and housing-related challenges. The dual credit market that keeps many borrowers of color out of the mainstream, reinforcing wealth disparities and violating common notions of fairness, is the subject of Debby Goldberg and Lisa Rice's chapter, which follows this Introduction. The discriminatory lending practices, the complex role of the Federal Housing Administration, the need for constant vigilance by civil rights activists, the changing behavior of regulators and the industry, and the impact of the Occupy Wall Street movement are examined in the subsequent chapter by David Berenbaum and Katrina Forrest. James Carr and Katrin Anacker then lay out the impact of the foreclosure crisis on the broader problems of the US economy and, in turn, how those larger problems damage the housing market. How low-income and minority households were denied access to historically low home prices and interest rates, and why we should take advantage of the current situation to foster wealth accumulation for such households, is the focus of M William Sermons's chapter. Next, John Relman draws lessons from his experience as a lawyer suing Wells Fargo in Memphis and Baltimore for discriminatory lending practices, concluding with recommendations for how Occupy and fair housing activists can more effectively work together. This section concludes with an analysis by Shanna Smith and Shanti Abedin of discrimination in the maintenance and marketing of real estate owned (REO) properties in African American and Latino neighborhoods.

The Organizers build on the analyses of the Activists to delineate strategic next steps. George Goehl and Sandra Hinson call for expanding the goals and techniques of community organizations and offer specific steps for doing so. The opportunity to advocate, campaign for, and win transformational political and economic changes, stressing in detail how relations between banks and communities can be turned around, is what Stephen Lerner and Saqib Bhatti put forward in the subsequent chapter. The case for a right to housing, specifically as it applies to immigrants, is then made by Janis Bowdler, Donald Kahl, and José García.

The Scholars put current advocacy initiatives in broader historical and political contexts. Robert Schwemm identifies the limitations of antidiscrimination litigation around Fair Housing Act (FHA) issues and suggests more effective routes, along with how-to steps, to realize the broader objectives of that 1968 law. The links between housing policy and social policy, via a social justice lens that pays particular attention to race and the country's racial hierarchy, is the theme of john powell's chapter. Community organizing is noted by virtually all as a key component of future advocacy. Mike Miller explores the limitations, along with the potential, of advocacy initiatives. Peter Dreier concludes with a call for building a progressive movement that goes beyond single-issue campaigns and creates powerful coalitions linking local and national struggles.

Towards Justice

The arc of the moral universe is long but it bends towards justice
—MARTIN LUTHER KING, JR. (1965)

Many still ask what the Occupy protesters want. The recommendations just among these friends of fair housing suggest wide-ranging "next steps." But what protesters are calling for is not as amorphous as is often claimed, particularly by those trying to discredit the movement. Shortly after the September 17, 2011 occupation of Zuccotti Park, the following Declaration of the Occupation of New York City was adopted by the occupiers' General Assembly. It provides a fairly clear vision and framework for next steps and is worth quoting in full:

Declaration of the Occupation of New York City

As we gather together in solidarity to express a feeling of mass injustice, we must not lose sight of what brought us together. We write so that all people who feel wronged by the corporate forces of the world can know that we are your allies.

As one people, united, we acknowledge the reality: that the future of the human race requires the cooperation of its members; that our system must protect our rights, and upon corruption of that system, it is up to the individuals to protect their own rights, and those of their neighbors; that a democratic government derives its just power from the people, but corporations do not seek consent to extract wealth from the people and the Earth; and that no true democracy is attainable when the process is determined by economic power. We come to you at a time when corporations, which place profit over people, self-interest over justice, and oppression over equality, run our governments. We have peaceably assembled here, as is our right, to let these facts be known.

- They have taken our houses through an illegal foreclosure process, despite not having the original mortgage.
- They have taken bailouts from taxpayers with impunity, and continue to give Executives exorbitant bonuses.
- They have perpetuated inequality and discrimination in the workplace based on age, the color of one's skin, sex, gender identity and sexual orientation.
- They have poisoned the food supply through negligence, and undermined the farming system through monopolization.
- They have profited off of the torture, confinement, and cruel treatment of countless animals, and actively hide these practices.
- They have continuously sought to strip employees of the right to negotiate for better pay and safer working conditions.
- They have held students hostage with tens of thousands of dollars of debt on education, which is itself a human right.
- They have consistently outsourced labor and used that outsourcing as leverage to cut workers' healthcare and pay.
- They have influenced the courts to achieve the same rights as people, with none of the culpability or responsibility.
- They have spent millions of dollars on legal teams that look for ways to get them out of contracts in regards to health insurance.
- They have sold our privacy as a commodity.
- They have used the military and police force to prevent freedom of the press.
- They have deliberately declined to recall faulty products endangering lives in pursuit of profit.

- They determine economic policy, despite the catastrophic failures their policies have produced and continue to produce.
- They have donated large sums of money to politicians, who are responsible for regulating them.
- They continue to block alternate forms of energy to keep us dependent on oil.
- They continue to block generic forms of medicine that could save people's lives or provide relief in order to protect investments that have already turned a substantial profit.
- They have purposely covered up oil spills, accidents, faulty book-keeping, and inactive ingredients in pursuit of profit.
- They purposefully keep people misinformed and fearful through their control of the media.
- They have accepted private contracts to murder prisoners even when presented with serious doubts about their guilt.
- They have perpetuated colonialism at home and abroad.
- They have participated in the torture and murder of innocent civilians overseas.
- They continue to create weapons of mass destruction in order to receive government contracts.*

To the people of the world,

We, the New York City General Assembly occupying Wall Street in Liberty Square, urge you to assert your power.

Exercise your right to peaceably assemble; occupy public space; create a process to address the problems we face, and generate solutions accessible to everyone.

To all communities that take action and form groups in the spirit of direct democracy, we offer support, documentation, and all of the resources at our disposal.

Join us and make your voices heard!

These grievances are not all-inclusive. (New York City General Assembly 2011)

In responding to the demand for demands, *New York Times* columnist and Nobel laureate in economics Paul Krugman (2011) observed, "It's clear what kinds of things the Occupy Wall Street demonstrators want, and it's really the job of policy intellectuals and politicians to fill in the details." Todd Gitlin (2012), professor of journalism and sociology at Columbia University and cofounder of Students for a Democratic Society, observed that the Occupy movement has created an environment that will make it easier for those intellectuals and politicians, along with unions, civil rights groups, nonprofit advocacy groups, and others, to push their specific demands and achieve their goals. In the following chapters, some of the intellectuals and advocates Krugman and Gitlin refer to do just that. One of their critical messages is to call on all of us to remember and re-embrace many of the tactics, demands, and values of the civil rights movement generally and in particular those that led to Gale Cincotta's triumphs over housing and housing finance industries. In their capacity as policy intellectuals as well as citizens, the authors featured in the following chapters may well be leading a new wave in fair housing activism and achievement.

References

Avery, Robert B., Kenneth P. Brevoort, and Glenn B. Canner. 2007. "The 2006 HMDA Data," *Federal Reserve Bulletin* 93: A73–A101.

Bocian, Debbie, Delvin Davis, Sonia Garrison, and Bill Sermons. 2012. *The State of Lending in America & Its Impact on U.S. Households.* Durham, NC: Center for Responsible Lending. http://www.responsiblelending.org/state-of-lending/state-of-lending.html.

Buffett, Warren E. 2011. "Stop Coddling the Super-Rich." *New York Times*, August 14. http://www.nytimes.com/2011/08/15/opinion/stop-coddling-the-super-rich.html.

Chomsky, Noam. 2012. *Occupy.* Brooklyn: Zuccotti Park Press.

Collins, Chuck. 2012. *99 to 1: How Wealth Inequality is Wrecking the World and What We Can Do About It.* San Francisco: Berrett-Koehler Publishers Inc.

Community-Wealth.org. 2013. "Policy Guide: Community Reinvestment Act." Democracy Collaborative. Accessed April 23. http://community-wealth.org/strategies/policy-guide/cra.html.

DeNavas-Walt, Carmen, Bernadete D. Proctor, and Jessica C. Smith. 2011. *Income, Poverty, and Health Insurance Coverage in the United States: 2010.* Washington, DC: US Census Bureau.

_____. 2012. *Income, Poverty, and Health Insurance Coverage in the United States: 2011.* Washington, DC: US Census Bureau.

DOJ (Department of Justice). 2012a. "$25 Billion Mortgage Servicing Agreement Filed in Federal Court." Office of Public Affairs, March 12. http://www.justice.gov/opa/pr/2012/March/12-asg-306.html.

_____. 2012b. "Justice Department Reaches Settlement with Wells Fargo Resulting in More Than $175 Million in Relief for Homeowners to Resolve Fair Lending Claims." Office of Public Affairs, July 12. http://www.justice.gov/opa/pr/2012/July/12-dag-869.html.

Douglas, Danielle. 2012. "Government Crusade against Mortgage Lenders." *The Washington Post*, October 24. http://articles.washingtonpost.com/2012-10-24/business/35501935_1_repurchase-loans-fannie-and-freddie-issue-loans.

Dreier, Peter. 2003. "The Future of Community Reinvestment: Challenges and Opportunities in a Changing Environment." *Journal of the American Planning Association* 69 (4): 341–353.

____. 2011. "Occupy Wall Street: Changing the Topic." *Huffington Post*, November 1. http://
www.huffingtonpost.com/peter-dreier/occupy-wall-street-media_b_1069250.html.

Economic Policy Institute. 2013. *State of Working America Preview: The Rich Get Richer*.
Washington, DC: Economic Policy Institute. http://www.epi.org/publication/the_rich
_get_richer/.

FHA (Federal Housing Administration). 1938. *Underwriting Manual*. Washington, DC: US
Government Printing Office.

Fry, Richard, and Paul Taylor. 2013. *A Rise in Wealth for the Wealthy; Declines for the Lower
93%: An Uneven Recovery, 2009–2011*. Washington, DC: Pew Research Center.

Gitlin, Todd. 2012. *Occupy Nation: The Roots, the Spirit, and the Promise of Occupy Wall
Street*. New York: ITBooks.

Gotham, Kevin Fox. 2002. *Race, Real Estate, and Uneven Development: The Kansas City
Experience, 1900-2000*. Albany: State University of New York Press.

Gottesdiener, Laura. 2012a. "Occupy's Front Line Moves to the Front Lawn." *Nation of
Change*, March 20. http://www.nationofchange.org/occupy-s-front-line-moves-front
-lawn-1332236487.

____. 2012b. "We Win When We Live Here: Occupying Homes in Detroit and Beyond."
Waging Nonviolence, March 28. http://wagingnonviolence.org/2012/03/we-win-when
-we-live-here-occupying-homes-in-detroit-and-beyond/.

Greene, Zina G. 1980. *Lender's Guide to Fair Mortgage Policies*. Washington, DC: The Poto-
mac Institute.

Hampson, Rick. 2011. "Poll: Washington to Blame More than Wall Street for Economy."
USA Today, October 18. http://www.usatoday.com/news/nation/story/2011-10-17/poll
-wall-street-protests/50804978/1.

Hazen, Don, Tara Lohan, and Lynn Parramore. 2011. *The 99%: How the Occupy Wall Street
Movement Is Changing America*. San Francisco: Alternet Books.

Hirsch, Arnold. 1983: *Making the Second Ghetto: Race and Housing in Chicago 1940-1960*.
Chicago: University of Chicago Press.

Immergluck, Dan. 2004. *Credit to the Community: Community Reinvestment and Fair Lending Policy in the United States*. Armonk, NY: M. E. Sharpe.

____. 2009. *Foreclosed: High-Risk Lending, Deregulation, and the Undermining of America's
Mortgage Market*. Ithaca, NY: Cornell University Press.

Jackson, Kenneth T. 1985. *Crabgrass Frontier: The Suburbanization of the United States*.
New York: Oxford University Press.

Judd, Dennis R. 1984. *The Politics of American Cities: Private Power and Public Policy*.
Boston: Little, Brown, & Co.

Khimm, Suzy. 2012. "Occupy the Regulatory System." *The Washington Post*, April 29.
http://www.washingtonpost.com/blogs/wonkblog/post/occupy-the-regulatory-system
/2012/04/27/gIQAjo2ilT_blog.html.

King, Jr., Martin Luther. 1965. "Martin Luther King, Speech in Montgomery, AL, 1965."
YouTube video, 2:00. Uploaded October 25, 2008. http://www.youtube.com/watch?v
=IITora9-mTc.

Kneebone Elizabeth, Carey Nadeau, and Alan Berube. 2011. *The Re-Emergence of Concentrated Poverty: Metropolitan Trends in the 2000s*. Washington, DC: Metropolitan Policy
Program at Brookings.

Kochhar, Rakesh, Richard Fry, and Paul Taylor. 2011. *Twenty-to-One: Wealth Gaps Rise to
Record Highs Between Whites, Blacks and Hispanics*. Washington, DC: Pew Research

Center. http://www.pewsocialtrends.org/files/2011/07/SDT-Wealth-Report_7-26-11
_FINAL.pdf.

Krugman, Paul. 2011. "Confronting the Malefactors." *New York Times*, October 6. http://
www.nytimes.com/2011/10/07/opinion/krugman-confronting-the-malefactors.html.

Logan, John R., and Brian J. Stults. 2011. "The Persistence of Segregation in the Metropolis: New Findings from the 2010 Census." Census Brief prepared for Project US2010.
http://www.s4.brown.edu/us2010/Data/Report/report2.pdf.

Massey, Douglas S., and Nancy A. Denton. 1993. *American Apartheid: Segregation and the
Making of the Underclass*. Cambridge, MA: Harvard University Press.

Meyer, Stephen Grant. 2000. *As Long as They Don't Move Next Door: Segregation and
Racial Conflict in American Neighborhoods*. Lanham, MD: Rowman & Littlefield
Publishers, Inc.

Morin, Rich. 2012. "Rising Share of Americans See Conflict Between Rich and Poor." *Pew
Research Center*, January 11. http://www.pewsocialtrends.org/2012/01/11/rising-share-of
-americans-see-conflict-between-rich-and-poor/.

NCRC (National Community Reinvestment Coalition). 2007. *CRA Commitments*. Washington, DC: National Community Reinvestment Coalition.

New, Catherine. 2011. "Federal Judge Questions SEC Settlement." *Huffington Post*, December 22. http://www.huffingtonpost.com/2011/12/22/sec-settlement-judge-koss_n
_1165792.html.

New York City General Assembly. 2011. *Declaration of the Occupation of New York City*.
http://www.nycga.net/resources/declaration/.

NFHA (National Fair Housing Alliance). 2010. *$380,000 and Counting*. Washington, DC:
National Fair Housing Alliance.

———. 2012. *Fair Housing in a Changing Nation: 2012 Fair Housing Trends Report*. Washington,
D.C.: National Fair Housing Alliance.

OccupyArrests.com. 2012. "A Running Total of the Number of Occupy Protestors Arrested
around the U.S. since Occupy Wall Street Began on Sep. 19, 2011." OccupyArrests.com.
http://occupyarrests.moonfruit.com/.

OccupyWallSt. 2011. "From Tahrir Square to Times Square: Demonstrations Erupt in
Over 1,500 Cities Worldwide." *OccupyWallStreet*, October 16. http://occupywallst.org
/article/tahrir-square-times-square-protests-erupt-over-150/.

"On the Trail of Mortgage Fraud." 2012. *New York Times*, January 15. http://www.nytimes
.com/2012/01/16/opinion/on-the-trail-of-mortgage-fraud.html.

Owens, Lindsay A. 2012. "The Polls-Trends, Confidence in Banks, Financial Institutions,
and Wall Street, 1971-2011." *Public Opinion Quarterly* 76 (1): 142–162.

Patton, Stacey. 2011. "Why African Americans Aren't Embracing Occupy Wall Street."
Washington Post, November 25. http://articles.washingtonpost.com/2011-11-25/opinions
/35282541_1_black-churches-black-press-black-households.

Perez, Tom. 2012. Remarks delivered to forum on "Fair Lending and Economic Fairness for
All Americans." Center for American Progress, May 3.

Polikoff, Alexander. 2006. *Waiting for Gautreaux: A Story of Segregation, Housing, and the
Black Ghetto*. Evanston, IL: Northwestern University Press.

Randall, Vernellia R. 2011. "Messages." Racism and Health Listserv. Accessed May 9, 2012.
http://health.groups.yahoo.com/group/racism_and_health_listserv/message/1339.

Saez, Emmanuel. 2012. *Striking It Richer: The Evolution of Top Incomes in the United States (Updated with 2009 and 2010 Estimates)*. http://elsa.berkeley.edu/~saez/saez-UStop incomes-2010.pdf.

Satter, Beryl. 2009. *Family Properties: Race, Real Estate, and the Exploitation of Black Urban America*. New York: Metropolitan Books.

Scherr, Judith. 2012. "Occupiers Confront Wells Fargo Shareholders." *Nation of Change*, April 26. http://www.nationofchange.org/occupiers-confront-wells-fargo-shareholders -1335447556.

Schwemm, Robert G. 2007. "Why Do Landlords Still Discriminate (And What Can Be Done About It)?" *The John Marshall Law Review* 40: 463–519.

Silver-Greenberg, Jessica. 2012. "2 Banks to Settle Case for $417 Million." *New York Times*, November 16. http://www.nytimes.com/2012/11/17/business/jpmorgan-and-credit -suisse-to-pay-417-million-in-mortgage-settlement.html.

Squires, Gregory D., ed. 1997. *Insurance Redlining: Disinvestment, Reinvestment, and the Evolving Role of Financial Institutions*. Washington, DC: Urban Institute Press.

——. 2003. *Organizing Access to Capital: Advocacy and the Democratization of Financial Institutions*. Philadelphia: Temple University Press.

Stiglitz, Joseph E. 2012. *The Price of Inequality: How Today's Divided Society Endangers Our Future*. New York: W. W. Norton & Company, Inc.

Sugrue, Thomas J. 2009. *Not Even Past: Barack Obama and the Burden of Race*. Princeton: Princeton University Press.

Van Buren, Peter. 2011. "No Free Speech at Mr. Jefferson's Library." *Huffington Post*, November 28. http://www.huffingtonpost.com/peter-van-buren/no-free-speech-at -mr-jeff_b_1116884.html.

Warren, Mark R. 2001. *Dry Bones Rattling: Community Building to Revitalize American Democracy*. Princeton: Princeton University Press.

Westgate, Michael. 2011. *Gale Force: Gale Cincotta: The Battles for Disclosure and Community Reinvestment*. Cambridge, MA: Education & Resources Group, Inc.

Wollan, Malia. 2011. "Oakland's Port Shuts Down as Protesters March on Waterfront." *New York Times*, November 2. http://www.nytimes.com/2011/11/03/us/occupy -oakland-protesters-set-sights-on-closing-port.html.

The Activists

2

The More Things Change, the More They Stay the Same

Race, Risk, and Access to Credit in a Changing Market

Debby Goldberg and Lisa Rice

THE OCCUPY WALL STREET movement reflects a deep anger and frustration on the part of many Americans over the economic havoc wreaked by the financial services industry and the failure of the federal government to take significant steps to aid "Main Street"—homeowners and others harmed by the foreclosure crisis and subsequent economic meltdown—while taking rapid, unprecedented steps to bail out the banks, or "Wall Street." Occupy Wall Street's slogan, "We are the 99%," recognizes the deep and growing income and wealth divide in the United States. Those at the top of the economic ladder, the 1%, have garnered the lion's share of America's economic growth, while the other 99% have seen their incomes stagnate or decline and their wealth evaporate. This image takes the economic statistics from the abstract to the personal, and Occupy Wall Street activists have shown their dissatisfaction with this state of affairs and their economic prospects with direct action of the most public sort: physically occupying public spaces at the heart of financial and political power.

Deconstructing the Economic Divide

If one drills beneath the surface of the economic divide, it quickly becomes apparent that the divide has a significant racial and ethnic dimension. While people of all races and national origins have suffered in the current economic upheaval, the crisis has hit people of color particularly hard. These disparities are not just the result of the recent foreclosure crisis. They have been in place for many decades; sometimes the result of policies and practices put in place by the federal government, and are reflected in gaps in income, unemployment, homeownership, and wealth.

Housing, and in particular homeownership, plays a major role in wealth inequality in the United States since homeownership has been a traditional path to building wealth. For many generations, families have built up equity in their homes through a combination of regular payments on affordable mortgages and modest but steady increases in home values. Families have relied on that home equity for many purposes. They have tapped into it to send their children to college, start or expand small businesses, weather tough economic times, pay for retirement, and pass along wealth to the next generation.

The Income Gap

The incomes of African American and Latino families have been consistently lower than those of white families, and this gap has only widened in recent years. In 2000, the median income of African American families was approximately $44,000, 63.5 percent of the median for white families. By 2010, the median income of African American families had dropped to $39,715, or 61 percent of the median income for white families. The pattern was similar for Latinos. In 2000, median Latino family income was about $45,000, 64.9 percent of that for white families. In 2010, the median Latino family income, at $40,785, had dropped to 62.6 percent of the median income that white families received (Economic Policy Institute 2012).

The Unemployment Gap

According to research from the Economic Policy Institute, the July 2012 unemployment rate for black workers over sixteen years of age, at 14 percent, was twice that of white workers in the same age range, at 7 percent. The 10 percent unemployment rate experienced by Latino workers over sixteen years of age was 1.5 times that of white workers. Unemployment statistics going back to 1973 indicate that similar disparities have existed consistently over the last four decades (Economic Policy Institute 2012).

The Homeownership Gap

African American and Latino households have long lagged behind white households in homeownership. In 2007, 74.9 percent of white households owned their own homes compared to 48.5 percent of Latino households and

47.7 percent of African American households, a gap of 26.4 percentage points and 27.2 percentage points, respectively. By the end of 2011, the homeownership rates for all groups had dropped: only 45.1 percent of African American households, 46.6 percent of Latino households, and 73.7 percent of white households owned their homes (Weller, Ajinkya, and Farrell 2012). While homeownership rates decreased across the board, the decrease was greater for Latino and African American households, which increased the gap to 27.1 and 28.6 percentage points, respectively, compared to their white counterparts.

The Wealth Gap

A 2011 study by the Pew Research Center compared the wealth held by white households to that held by black and Hispanic households in the United States from 1984 through 2009. In 1984, the median household wealth for white households was twelve times greater than the median wealth of black households and eight times greater than that of Hispanic households. This wealth gap reached its narrowest point in 1995. In that year, the median wealth of white households was seven times greater than that of both black and Hispanic households. As noted in the Introduction, by 2009, the median household wealth of white households was twenty times greater than that of black households, and eighteen times greater than that of Hispanic households (Taylor et al. 2011).

   The Federal Reserve Board (2012) reports that between 2008 and 2011, Americans collectively lost $7 trillion in wealth due to the precipitous decline in home values caused by widespread foreclosures and the resulting economic downturn. The loss of wealth has hit African American and Latino families particularly hard, as traditionally they have relied heavily on home equity as a source of wealth. According to the Pew Research Center, between 2005 and 2009, African American and Latino families experienced, respectively, a 53 percent and 66 percent loss of wealth compared to only 12 percent for white families. The loss was driven largely by declining home values (Taylor et al. 2011).

Communities of Color Targeted for Risky Lending

The links between homeownership and wealth, and the racial and ethnic disparities in each, have been brought into sharp focus by the current meltdown in the mortgage market. Over the last decade, communities of color have been heavily targeted for risky and unsustainable loans, including subprime hybrid adjustable rate mortgages and other toxic products. Such loans were concentrated in older urban neighborhoods, particularly neighborhoods of color, and in new suburban communities, in housing markets experiencing rapid home price increases, where moderate- and middle-income households that could not afford homes elsewhere, including many African American and Latino households, sought to buy homes (Bocian et al. 2011, 10). During 2005 and 2006, the peak subprime lending years, African American and Latino borrowers were, respectively, three times more likely and two-and-a-half times more likely than white borrowers to receive a subprime home purchase loan (Avery, Brevoort, and Canner 2006, 2007).

Predatory lending patterns were not a function of the creditworthiness of nonwhite borrowers, however. In 2005 and 2006, more than 60 percent of the borrowers who received subprime loans had credit scores that qualified them for prime loans ("Subprime Debacle Traps Even Very Creditworthy" 2007). Among mortgages made between 2004 and 2008, African American and Latino borrowers with good credit scores (FICO scores above 660) received subprime loans more than three times as often as white borrowers (Bocian et al. 2011). Since 2012, settlement agreements between the US Department of Justice and a number of lenders, including subprime giants Countrywide (now part of the Bank of America Corporation) and Wells Fargo & Company, document the fact that tens of thousands of African American and Latino borrowers who were qualified for prime loans were steered instead into higher-cost, higher-risk subprime loans. (See Chapter 6 for a discussion of the lending practices of Wells Fargo.) The investigations conducted for these and other private lawsuits uncovered the business strategies by which these lenders targeted communities of color for risky loans, as well as the high profits that fueled these practices.

Subprime and other exotic loan products, such as Option ARMs (adjustable rate mortgages) and Interest Only, or IO ARMs, carry much higher foreclosure rates than traditional thirty-year, fixed-rate mortgages. Because nonwhite borrowers and communities of color were so heavily targeted for such loans, they experienced much higher rates of foreclosure than others. Between 2007 and 2009, 8 percent of African American and Latino borrowers who had purchased a home between 2005 and 2008 lost that home to foreclosure compared to only 4.5 percent of white borrowers (Bocian, Li, and Ernst 2010).

Communities in which foreclosures are concentrated experience many types of harm. The presence of foreclosures drives down prices on nearby homes, and vacant properties can become eyesores, health and safety hazards, and magnets for crime. The decline in property values contributes directly to a decline in tax revenues, leaving local governments starved for the resources needed to pay for schools, parks, libraries, and other essential services. The impact on the social fabric of the community may be just as severe. When families lose their homes to foreclosures and are forced to move, not only do they suffer, but so do the communities and institutions they leave behind: churches lose congregants, schools lose students, civic associations lose members, and the vitality of the community is diminished.

The damage can extend long beyond the moment at which the foreclosure is completed. The manner in which some lenders maintain and market the foreclosed homes under their control has exacerbated the harm caused to communities. Investigations by the National Fair Housing Alliance (NFHA) and a number of its members (described in more detail in Chapter 7) have found that some lenders handle so-called REO (real estate owned) properties much better in white communities than in communities of color. In the latter, foreclosed properties are much more likely to have multiple problems, such as broken windows, unsecured doors, sagging or missing gutters, significant amounts of trash in the yard, and the like. Further, lenders are more likely to market these properties as foreclosures or distressed sales, or not to market them at all. The result is that they languish on the market much longer and are more likely to be purchased by investors than by owner-occupants (NFHA 2012).

Risky lending practices and the chain of events that follow have fueled the racial and ethnic disparities in wealth and income that have long characterized American society. And it is toward these disparities that the Occupy Wall Street movement has been so effective in directing public attention.

The Dual Market for Credit

While the Occupy Wall Street movement helped to focus public attention on the gaping divide between the "haves" and the "have-nots" in American society and the public policies that have contributed to that divide, disparities in wealth and income have existed for decades. The United States has long had a dual credit market, supported and perpetuated by governmental action. People of color have been prevented from gaining access to the best forms of credit at the best price and on the best terms. Instead, they have been relegated to the fringe market, where products are riskier and prices are higher.

It was not so long ago that the federal government and private industry both used race and national origin explicitly as factors in assessing borrower risk. This practice was perfected by the Home Owners' Loan Corporation (HOLC), a federal agency established in 1933 in response to the foreclosure crisis associated with the Great Depression. The HOLC used a discriminatory risk rating system that favored prospective borrowers if the neighborhood in which they wanted to purchase a home was "new, homogeneous, and in demand in good times and bad" (Massey 2008, 69). Properties would be ranked low (and thus judged high risk) if they were "within such a low price or rent range as to attract an undesirable element," which often meant that they were located near an African American neighborhood (Massey 2008, 70). On the so-called residential security maps used to make these classifications, the lowest ranking (riskiest) neighborhoods were labeled "fourth grade" and shaded in red. According to housing scholars William Collins and Robert Margo (2000, 11–12), "the agency's revisions were unprecedented." Private financial institutions incorporated the new rating system in their own appraisals, thereby beginning the widespread institutionalization of the practice known as redlining. These discriminatory policies and practices spread within the real estate sector as private banks began to adopt the underwriting guidelines established by the federal government in the HOLC program.

In the 1940s and 1950s, the HOLC risk rating system came to inform the Federal Housing Administration (FHA) and Veterans Administration (VA) loan programs. The FHA made it possible to purchase a house with just a 10 percent down payment, as compared to the customary 33 percent down payment required before its establishment. Loan terms were also extended for up to thirty years. The VA program provided similar benefits, all while following the FHA in rating properties in large part on the basis of the "stability" and "harmoniousness" of neighborhoods (Massey 2008, 72).

As a result, the increased access to mortgage credit and homeownership made possible through a reduced down payment and better loan terms was available to only some Americans. According to the FHA's policy, "If a neighborhood is to remain stable, it is necessary that properties shall continue to be occupied by the same racial and social classes. Changes in social or racial occupancy contribute to neighborhood instability and the decline of value levels" (Babcock 1938, 137). To implement this policy, the FHA even went so far as to *recommend* the use of restrictive covenants to ensure neighborhood stability and racial homogeneity (Massey 2008).

The home appraisal industry adopted the notion that race had a direct impact on property values, and appraisers were trained to evaluate properties using race as a factor. Lists that ranked race and nationality in order of preference would remain in appraisal manuals long after the Fair Housing Act was passed in 1968. *McMichael's Appraising Manual* by Stanley McMichael

(1951), for example, provided the following ranking of race and nationality by impact on real estate values (in order of preference):

1. English, Germans, Scotch.
2. North Italians.
3. Bohemians or Czechs.
4. Poles.
5. Lithuanians.
6. Greeks.
7. Russians, Jews (lower-class).
8. South Italians.
9. Negroes.
10. Mexicans.

Similar policies were employed in the insurance industry as well. Homeowners' insurance companies adopted policies that resulted in either the outright denial of insurance in communities of color or the availability only of policies that provided inadequate protection at excessive costs to consumers (Squires 1997).

Even after the passage of the 1968 Fair Housing Act, discriminatory practices received tacit approval from the federal banking regulatory agencies. It was not until *National Urban League et al. v. Office of the Comptroller of the Currency et al.*, the lawsuit filed in 1976 by a coalition of civil rights groups against federal bank regulators for failing to enforce the Fair Housing Act, that the federal banking regulatory agencies even acknowledged that they had any enforcement responsibilities under the act. The settlement required the agencies to collect information on the mortgage lending practices of the institutions they regulated and to establish and implement fair lending examination procedures.

The history of discrimination and redlining practices has had long-lasting consequences in the United States. Because borrowers of color could not access credit in the mainstream market, a dual credit market developed—a market that was separate and unequal. White borrowers have had ready access to more regulated, lower-cost, affordable, and sustainable credit products in the mainstream market. Borrowers of color have been relegated to the fringe market, which offers credit products that are largely unregulated, higher cost, and less sustainable. This fringe market was—and, in some cases, still is—the primary source of credit for communities of color.

The Relationship between the Dual Market and Credit Scoring

While race and ethnicity are no longer used as explicit factors in assessing lending risk and controlling access to credit, the discriminatory practices of the past laid the foundation for the current system. Where one lives affects a great many aspects of one's life: access to schools, jobs, transportation, health care, healthy food, parks and recreation, and financial services. Given the racial segregation common in many communities across the US, people of color have less access to mainstream financial services than whites.

Communities of color have fewer branches of federally insured and regulated depository institutions—banks—than white communities. An analysis of the location of bank branches in twenty-five major metropolitan areas found that, on average, white communities had twice as many branches as communities of color. Households of color are more likely to be "unbanked"—that is, not to have an account in a bank, savings and loan, or credit union. A 2003 survey found that 52.4 percent of the unbanked respondents were African American, 35.3 percent were Latino, and only 7 percent were white (National Community Reinvestment Coalition 2007). This is consistent with 2005 research conducted by the Federal Reserve Bank of San Francisco, which found that approximately half of African Americans and Latinos in its region did not have a checking or savings account (Reid and Weiner, n.d.).

On the other hand, residents of communities of color are more likely to have access to so-called fringe banking institutions: check-cashers, payday lenders, and the like. For example, a 2009 study in California found that payday lenders in that state were nearly eight times as concentrated in neighborhoods with the largest share of African Americans and Latinos as white neighborhoods. Even after controlling for the income level of neighborhood residents, payday lenders were 2.4 times more concentrated in communities of color (Li et al. 2009).

The lack of access to a bank account and higher utilization of fringe banking sources experienced by people of color, in part a function of the types of credit providers available in their communities, has an impact on how risky they are perceived to be by mainstream financial institutions. They do not fare as well in the risk analysis that such lenders use to determine whether to offer credit, what type of credit to offer, and at what price. This can be seen in the credit scoring models that lenders use as risk assessment tools in the underwriting process.

Credit scoring systems use mathematical models to analyze information about a borrower's credit history and assess the likelihood that a borrower will become delinquent and/or default on a loan. The credit score is said to be a measurement of borrower risk—that is, the risk of default that the lender assumes by extending credit to a particular borrower.

Although race, gender, national origin, or similar characteristics are not used to evaluate risk, nonetheless, credit scoring systems may have a significant disparate impact on people of color and other underserved consumers because some of their components, which seem neutral on their face, actually have discriminatory effects.

The FICO credit scoring system, for example, is widely known and often viewed as the industry standard for use in mortgage lending. Some of the factors it uses, however, illustrate the problem of how a seemingly neutral system can be discriminatory. Although many of the specific FICO score variables and the weights assigned to them are proprietary and not publicly available, several broad categories that affect the score, such as payment history, amounts owed, length of credit history, new credit, and types of credit used, are public. All of these categories pose potential problems of disparate impact and unintended discriminatory outcomes and affect access to sustainable, affordable, and fair credit. Three factors raise particular concerns: payment history, amounts owed, and types of credit used.

Payment history, which accounts for 35 percent of the FICO score, includes information about whether borrowers make timely debt payments. Among the types of debt included are subprime and other exotic mortgage loans, which have much higher default and delinquency rates than traditional thirty-year, fixed-rate mortgages. Research suggests that these default rates are the result of risky features in the loans themselves, not risky behavior on the part of the borrowers placed in them.

One study by Ding et al. (2011) compared two similar groups of low- and moderate-income borrowers and demonstrated that the product rather than the borrower was the problem. Comparing two mortgage loan portfolios, the study found that both had borrowers with similar credit profiles. However, while one loan portfolio comprised fully documented, low-cost, fixed-rate loans, the other consisted of subprime loans with very different loan terms and conditions, including origination through mortgage brokers, higher origination costs, prepayment penalties, and adjustable interest rates that allowed for large and rapid payment increases. While the traits of both groups of borrowers were similar, the loan performance outcomes were not. The default rate for the subprime portfolio was *four times higher*.

African Americans and Latinos have been targeted for unsustainable subprime loans. The higher rates of poor payment history they experience, however, are not necessarily a reflection of poor credit habits, but rather a function of the types of credit to which they have access and the terms and conditions of the loans available to them. Unfortunately, the credit scoring models used to assess borrowers do not account for the risk associated with the loans themselves.

In addition, the payday lenders that are concentrated in communities of color do not report positive payment history to the credit bureaus whose data are used in credit scoring systems. Timely payment of payday loans does not help improve the credit score of borrowers who use this type of credit. Payday loans only appear in credit records if the borrower has defaulted and the loan has been sent to a collection agency. Borrowers get the downside, but not the upside, of using this type of credit.

Thirty percent of the FICO score is based on the "amounts owed" by the borrower on each trade line or credit account. This category considers the amount of credit available to a borrower on certain types of revolving and installment loan accounts. To the extent that underserved communities have restricted access to credit, and, in particular, the type of credit that will likely be reported in a positive fashion to credit repositories, this category can pose a disparate discriminatory impact. For example, the lack of access to mainstream lenders may mean that underserved consumers have greater difficulty obtaining revolving or installment lines of credit. As a result, they may suffer a lower credit score from a system that considers how much "extra" credit they have available in certain revolving and installment accounts.

The length of the borrower's credit history—how long particular accounts have been open—represents 15 percent of that borrower's FICO score, with longer-standing accounts contributing to a higher score. This component will penalize borrowers who have little access to the type of credit that is reported to the credit repositories. For borrowers of color, restricted access to mainstream financial institutions will lead to fewer trade lines with a significant amount of history. In particular, this factor penalizes recent immigrants and other borrowers who operate on a cash basis, access credit outside of the financial mainstream, have been shut out from traditional sources of credit, or obtain credit from lenders that do not report positive data. Borrowers with these circumstances are disproportionately persons of color.

The "types of credit used" contributes to 10 percent of a borrower's FICO score. While FICO does not reveal exactly how it measures this factor, there is evidence that certain types of credit, such as the credit provided by finance companies, are treated less favorably than credit provided by mainstream lenders, such as insured depository institutions (banks). According to the Federal Reserve Board (2010), "Many credit-scoring models consider the number and type of credit accounts you have. A mix of installment loans and credit cards may improve your score. However, too many finance company accounts or credit cards might hurt your score."

FICO itself suggests that consumers who have installment loans, such as car loans, and credit cards that are reported to the credit repositories will receive more favorable treatment in the FICO credit scoring system. This has dangerous implications for borrowers of color who rely on finance companies as a source of credit because they lack access to mainstream sources.

The redlining of the past, established and institutionalized by the federal government and widely adopted by the private sector, has helped to create banking wastelands. The fact that people use the fringe financial institutions located in their communities works against their efforts to get into the financial mainstream.

Credit Scores, Risk Assessment, and the Foreclosure Crisis

Fair housing advocates are concerned about the interplay between foreclosures and credit scores and its implication for future access to credit. There is a very real prospect that borrowers of color who have been through foreclosure will find their credit scores severely damaged and their access to mainstream credit further restricted.

Depending on the status of other credit accounts (trade lines), a foreclosure can lower a borrower's credit score by anywhere from 10 to 140 points (VantageScore 2009). A large drop in a credit score has a big impact on the borrower's cost of credit. According to FICO, "a 100 point difference in a borrower's credit score can mean over $40,000 in extra interest payments over the life of a 30 year mortgage on a $300,000 loan" (myFICO.com 2012).

A 100 point drop in credit score has profound implications because credit scores affect much more than just the availability and affordability of mortgage loans. Credit and other scoring mechanisms are used by employers to evaluate job applicants, landlords to screen tenants, and insurers to determine auto, life, and homeowners insurance. Credit scoring modelers and companies are also finding even more creative ways to broaden the use of these systems. Credit scores are being used to predict which patients are more likely to take their medication as prescribed (Parker-Pope 2011), and a proposal in Texas suggested using credit scores to determine utility rates (Stillman 2007).

The impact of foreclosure-related declines in credit scores is likely to be very broad. An estimated five million homes have been lost to foreclosure since 2006 (Gopal and Gittelsohn 2012). Many of these homeowners were sold unsustainable subprime loans with high fees, rapidly escalating interest rates, built-in payment shock, and prepayment penalties or other risky loan products. Others found themselves caught between un- or underemployment and falling home prices. Historically, borrowers who lost their jobs or whose income suffered other disruptions that made it difficult for them to keep up with their mortgage payments could sell their homes and use the proceeds of the sale pay off their mortgages. This might be a big financial setback, but it was less harmful to their credit record than a foreclosure. However, as home prices plummeted in recent years, borrowers in this situation often found that they were "underwater," that is, their homes were worth less than their outstanding mortgage balance and a sale would not bring in enough money to pay off the mortgage. Many of these borrowers ended up in foreclosure.

In the face of millions of foreclosures, and with knowledge of the factors causing this level of foreclosure, fair housing advocates are raising questions about the predictive value of credit scores for future credit decisions. Current scoring models attribute foreclosure to the borrower's behavior and do not account for the type of loan available or for the widespread economic disloca-tion experienced in the United States. Yet, unless the credit scoring industry adjusts its models to account for these factors, which is something it has not shown any inclination to do, the discriminatory practices that caused such high rates of foreclosure among borrowers of color will continue to haunt those borrowers for many years. The dual credit market will drag on.

Will Changes Underway Eliminate or Reinforce the Dual Credit Market?

The crisis that sparked the Occupy Wall Street movement also prompted Congress to pass legislation to address some of the policies, practices, and regulatory gaps that contributed to the near-collapse of the financial services industry. The Dodd-Frank Wall Street Reform and Consumer Protection Act prohibits mortgage loans with certain risky features and calls for federal regula-tors to adopt new rules to eliminate risky mortgage lending. One of these new rules is the qualified residential mortgage (QRM) rule, which will determine which mortgage loans will be exempted from the act's risk retention rules for securities. Another major public policy question, not addressed in Dodd-Frank but subject to much debate, is what the future of the secondary mortgage market should look like and what role in it, if any, the federal government should play. Policymakers of all stripes have called for the winding down of Fannie Mae and Freddie Mac, the two government-sponsored enterprises (GSEs) that have formed the backbone of America's housing finance system for many decades. While no consensus has yet emerged about what should replace the GSEs, much attention has focused on how to prevent future secondary market entities from engaging in risky practices that could prove costly for American taxpayers.

What constitutes a risky (or relatively risk-free) mortgage for the purposes of securitization and how much exposure the taxpayer should have to mortgage-lending risk hinges on an analysis of what makes a loan risky and how best to minimize the risk of exposure to borrowers, lenders, investors, and the government. A misreading of the factors that contributed to the meltdown of the nation's housing finance system may lead policymakers to answer these questions in ways that perpetuate, rather than eliminate, the dual credit market. Unfortunately, too often policymakers focus on how to keep banks solvent and markets stable rather than on how to repair the damage communities have suffered in the crisis. The result could be a mortgage system that makes it more difficult for people of color and other underserved borrower segments to obtain affordable, sustainable credit. This, in turn, would only increase the divide between the 99% and the 1%.

The Qualified Residential Mortgage (QRM) Rule

Dodd-Frank requires sponsors of most asset-backed securities to retain 5 percent of the risk associated with the assets backing the securities. By aligning the interests of the sponsors of the securities and their investors, the goal is to make it in everyone's best interest for the assets to perform well over the long term. However, the Dodd-Frank statute provides an exemption from risk retention requirements for securities composed entirely of qualified residential mortgages, or QRMs. These are mortgages with product and underwriting features which historical data indicate result in a lower risk of default. The statute enumerates a list of such features, including loans that do not contain balloon payments, negative amortization, prepayment penalties, or interest-only payments, among others. Notably, the statute does *not* mention down payment as a factor for use in defining QRM.

The federal agencies charged with defining QRM have promulgated a proposed rule, but have postponed finalizing the rule until other rule-making is completed. Fair housing advocates have identified a number of aspects of the proposed QRM rule that may disadvantage borrowers of color and other underserved groups. Chief among these is down payment.

Down Payment

Despite the fact that Congress considered and rejected the use of down payment for QRM, the federal agencies writing the rule have proposed to include a requirement that QRM loans have a down payment of 20 percent, or in the alternative, 10 percent. Fair housing and civil rights advocates have voiced strong opposition to this approach. Down payment size is not a strong indicator of loan performance, and it may have a tremendous negative impact on the ability of borrowers of color and those of low- and moderate-income levels to become homeowners or to refinance existing mortgage loans. Further, if down payment is used as an element of the QRM definition, it may well become the *de facto* government standard for mortgage underwriting and be adopted much more widely, which was not the intention of the QRM provision of Dodd-Frank. This could be the modern version of the HOLC's discriminatory risk assessment standards.

Considerable evidence indicates that the size of the down payment is not a key factor in determining loan performance. This is not to say that there is no relationship between down payment and performance, but rather that as an isolated factor, it is not a good indicator and that its impact on risk can be readily predicted and managed. In the current crisis, widespread mortgage defaults were the result of the layering of risk—piling up such features as rapidly increasing interest rates and monthly payments, prepayment penalties, negative amortization, high points and fees, lax underwriting, and poor servicing—in combination with falling house prices.

Take, for example, a portfolio of loans originated in 2006 and 2007 and insured by MGIC, a private mortgage insurance company. These loans would be considered very safe and sound. They were thirty-year, fully amortizing, fixed-rate mortgages for owner-occupied properties, fully documented and fully underwritten, made to borrowers who had prime credit (a FICO score of 660 or higher), and a debt-to-income ratio of 45 percent or less. Down payments ranged from 20 percent to 3 percent. The foreclosure rates ranged from 1.3 percent for loans with a 20 percent down payment to 3.3 percent for loans with a 10 percent down payment and 4.7 percent for loans with a 3 percent down payment (Zandi 2011). All of these foreclosure rates are far below the double-digit rates seen on subprime loans with multiple layers of risk.

Analysis of the factors contributing to loan performance shows that the size of a down payment is not a leading indicator of risk. According to MGIC, when all other factors are held constant, loans with negative amortization are three to four times more likely to default, loans with reduced documentation are three times more likely to default, loans to borrowers with credit scores below 660 are two to three times more likely to default, and loans to investors are two to three times more likely to default. These, not down payment, are the features most closely associated with default risk (Zandi 2011).

Fair housing advocates are concerned that including down payment in the QRM standards will close the door to affordable mortgages for many families in America, particularly families of color. While it has minimal impact on loan performance, down payment is effectively a measure of wealth, and we have already described America's enormous—and growing—wealth gap based on race and national origin. Using a wealth-based measure as a standard for access to the most affordable, and likely most available, mortgage credit is a cause for grave concern, especially when there are other, more effective measures that do not have the same negative impact based on race and ethnicity.

. In practical terms, this disparity in wealth makes it more difficult for households of color to come up with the 20 percent down payment contemplated in the proposed rule. According to the National Association of Realtors, the median house price in the US in 2010 was $172,900 (Center for Responsible Lending 2011b). A 20 percent down payment for a house of this price would be $34,580. If one assumes an additional 5 percent in closing costs, the cash a borrower would have to bring to closing in order to purchase a house at the median price would be $43,225. The average American household would have to save at an annual rate of 7.5 percent for more than fourteen years to accumulate enough cash for such a purchase, and that assumes that all of their savings is for a home purchase and none is for retirement, college, or other purposes (Center for Responsible Lending 2011a).

For households of color, the time frame for saving enough money to purchase a home is generally much longer. Based on 2009 median household incomes, Hispanic households would have to save for nineteen years to accumulate a 20 percent down payment and closing costs for a median-priced house, and African American households would have to save for twenty-two years (Center for Responsible Lending 2011b). These time frames—which are based on the assumption that households save only for home purchase and no other contingencies—are simply unrealistic. The 20 percent down payment requirement would make access to QRMs out of reach for many households of color.

The picture does not improve much with a 10 percent down payment rather than 20 percent. Using the assumptions described above, home buyers would need to bring $25,071 in cash to the closing table. The average African American family would have to save for fifteen years to accumulate this cash, and the average Latino family would have to save for twelve years. Such a standard would do little to eliminate risk from the mortgage lending transaction, but would effectively put homeownership and the wealth accumulation it offers out of the reach of families of color (Center for Responsible Lending 2011b).

Credit History

The proposed Dodd-Frank QRM rule also seeks to account for the borrower's credit history. Fair housing advocates applauded the regulators' decision not to incorporate into the rule any individual credit scoring system. However, advocates remain concerned about the proposed credit standards, which are very stringent. The standards fail to account for the widespread abuses that have occurred in the mortgage market in recent years and thereby disadvantage borrowers of color who have been disproportionately affected by abusive lending practices.

Borrowers whose loans did not include risky and abusive terms have found themselves squeezed by the dual forces of un- or underemployment and falling house prices as well. Because the value of their homes has declined, borrowers have been unable to refinance to take advantage of lower rates and obtain lower mortgage payments, tap their equity to carry them through their period of financial stress, and sell their homes to prevent foreclosure or move to seek employment. These borrowers, subject to economic forces far beyond their control, have also had difficulty paying bills on time and, in too many cases, have faced foreclosure and bankruptcy. Many borrowers of color have been caught in the squeeze of the recession and declining home values.

The adoption of overly restrictive standards that fail to consider adequately the widespread impact of abusive lending practices and the recession is likely to have a disproportionate impact on borrowers of color. These standards will serve to misclassify risk and reinforce the dual credit market.

Who Will Get the Best Loans?

There are real consequences to the decision about which loans will qualify for Dodd-Frank's QRM exemption. Some, including the agencies writing the rule, believe that a QRM rule that exempts a very narrow slice of the market from the risk retention rules will ensure a robust and competitive market for non-QRM loans, promoting liquidity and affordability for these mortgages. Fair housing advocates do not have confidence in this outcome. The subprime mortgage market was highly competitive and quite robust before the foreclosure crisis hit. Yet, these characteristics of success did not result in cost savings or better products for consumers and did result in devastating consequences for the entire economy.

The National Association of Realtors has estimated the additional cost for non-QRM mortgages at anywhere between 80 and 185 basis points (a basis point is one one-hundredth of a percent, so an 80 basis point increase in the interest rate is equivalent to an increase of eight-tenths of a percent) (Coalition for Sensible Housing Policy 2011, 8). Mark Zandi and Cristian deRitis (2011), of Moody's Analytics, have put the increased cost at 75 to 100 basis points. According to the National Association of Home Builders, every 1 percent increase in interest rates makes the median-priced home unaffordable for 4 million households (Coalition for Sensible Housing Policy 2011, 8). Given the wealth disparities in the US, it is likely that a great many of these would be households of color.

Secondary Market or Dual Market?

In addition to Dodd-Frank's QRM rule, another major policy debate whose outcome will help determine how America's housing finance system will work is the discussion about what to do with Fannie Mae and Freddie Mac. Since September 2008, these companies have operated under federal government conservatorship and have been stuck in a kind of limbo. While policymakers agree that this situation cannot go on indefinitely, they do not agree about what should happen next. The question of the GSEs' future is regarded by some as the unfinished business of Dodd-Frank, as it was not addressed in that legislation. It is a question with significant fair housing implications.

Fannie Mae, Freddie Mac, and other secondary mortgage market players, through their ability to set the terms and conditions of loans they will purchase and hence the terms and conditions of most mortgage loans originated, have had a tremendous impact on access to homeownership broadly, including access for members of protected classes. All of the questions that are being debated in other contexts also come up in the debate about the future of the secondary market: What caused the foreclosure crisis? What are the characteristics of a safe loan? What is the relationship between risk and race? How can we strike a fair balance between eliminating risky lending and providing broad access to affordable, sustainable mortgage loans? How important is homeownership? The answers to these questions will likely inform the shape and operations of any new secondary market institution that may be created to replace Fannie Mae and Freddie Mac.

A number of fair housing and civil rights groups have come together to articulate a set of principles that should guide decision making on the future of the secondary market. These principles fall into three broad areas: the first is to ensure that the housing finance system furthers America's fair housing goals; the second is to avoid overreliance on FHA mortgage insurance; and the third is to support diverse, inclusive neighborhoods and equal home-ownership opportunities. Implementation of each of these requires a deliberate effort to eliminate discriminatory policies and practices from mortgage lending, monitor the activities of lenders and secondary market institutions, and create an effective and robust regulatory structure to oversee the housing finance system.

Conclusion

The United States is still haunted by a dual credit market that leaves too many borrowers of color out of the mainstream. Federal and private market policies and practices have created a system in which borrowers of color pay more for inferior and riskier products and services. That history is threatening to repeat itself in existing credit scoring systems and pending policy proposals that do little to dismantle the dual credit system or to formulate a fair and equitable system that provides equal access to quality, affordable credit. The Occupy Wall Street movement seeks to eliminate policies and practices that perpetuate inequities, unduly enrich the wealthiest citizens, force more Americans out of the middle class, and deepen the roots of poverty in the nation. Whether we associate ourselves with the Occupy Wall Street movement or not, we must all protest policies that reinforce wealth disparities and advocate for policies and practices that promote fairness, equality, and opportunity.

References
Avery, Robert B., Kenneth P. Brevoort, and Glenn B. Canner. 2006. "Higher Priced Home Lending and the 2005 HMDA Data." *Federal Reserve Bulletin* 92 (September): A123–A166.
———. 2007. "The 2006 HMDA Data." *Federal Reserve Bulletin* 93 (December): A73–A109.
Babcock, Frederick. 1938. "Techniques of Residential Location Rating." *Journal of the American Institute of Real Estate Appraisers of the National Association of Real Estate Boards* 6 (2): 137.

Bocian, Debbie Gruenstein, Wei Li, and Keith S. Ernst. 2010. "Foreclosures by Race and Ethnicity: The Demographics of a Crisis." *CRL Research Report*, June 18.

Bocian, Debbie Gruenstein, Wei Li, Carolina Reid, and Roberto Quercia. 2011. *Lost Ground, 2011: Disparities in Mortgage Lending and Foreclosures*. Durham, NC: Center for Responsible Lending.

Center for Responsible Lending. 2011a. "Don't Mandate Large Down Payments on Home Loans; Proposal Would Harm the Economy, Housing Market, and Middle-Class Families." *CRL Brief*, February 25.

———. 2011b. "Locked out of a Home: The Impact of a 10% Down Payment Requirement on Prospective Home Buyers." *CRL Issue Brief*, June.

Coalition for Sensible Housing Policy. 2011. "Proposed Qualified Residential Mortgage Definition Harms Creditworthy Borrowers While Frustrating Housing Recovery." Coalition for Sensible Housing Policy white paper submitted on July 11. http://www .sensiblehousingpolicy.org/uploads/Coalition_for_Sensible_Housing_Policy_-_QRM _White_Paper.pdf.

Collins, William J., and Robert A. Margo. 2000. "Race and Homeownership: A Century-Long View." Working paper number 00-W12, Vanderbilt University, May. http:// www.vanderbilt.edu/econ/wparchive/workpaper/vu00-w12.pdf.

Ding, Lei , Roberto G. Quercia, Janneke Ratcliff, and Wei Li. 2011. "Risky Borrowers or Risky Mortgages: Disaggregating Effects Using Propensity Score Models." *Journal of Real Estate Research* 33: 245–78.

Economic Policy Institute. 2012. "The State of Working America" Economic Policy Institute. Accessed September 27. http://stateofworkingamerica.org/.

Federal Reserve Board. 2010. "5 Tips: Improving Your Credit Score." Board of Governors of the Federal Reserve System. Last updated on June 17. http://www.federalreserve.gov /consumerinfo/fivetips_creditscore.htm.

———. 2012. "The US Housing Market: Current Conditions and Policy Considerations." Board of Governors of the Federal Reserve System white paper submitted on January 4. http://www.federalreserve.gov/publications/other-reports/files/housing-white-paper -20120104.pdf.

Gopal, Prashant, and John Gittelsohn. 2012. "Foreclosures to Climb Before Bank Deal Helps US Housing Market." *Bloomberg Businessweek*, February 21.

Li, Wei, Leslie Parish, Keith Ernst, and Delvin Davis. 2009. "Predatory Profiling: The Role of Race and Ethnicity in the Location of Payday Lenders in California." Durham, NC: Center for Responsible Lending. http://www.responsiblelending.org/payday-lending /research-analysis/predatory-profiling.pdf.

Massey, Douglas S. 2008. "Origins of Economic Disparities: The Historical Role of Housing Segregation." In *Segregation: The Rising Costs for America*, edited by James H. Carr and Nandinee K. Kutty, 39–80. New York: Routledge.

McMichael, Stanley L. 1951. *McMichael's Appraising Manual*. New York: Prentice Hall Press.

myFICO.com. 2012. "Get Credit Reports and FICO Scores Online: Shop for myFico Products." Fair Isaac Corporation. Accessed September 1. http://www.myfico.com /Products/Products.aspx?cm_sp=GuestHome-_-CompareProducts-_-ProdOverview2/.

National Community Reinvestment Coalition. 2007. *Are Banks on the Map? An Analysis of Bank Branch Location in Working Class and Minority Neighborhoods*. Washington, DC: National Community Reinvestment Coalition. http://www.ncrc.org/images/stories /mediaCenter_reports/ncrc%20bank%20branch%20study.pdf.

NFHA (National Fair Housing Alliance). 2012. *The Banks are Back, Our Neighborhoods Are Not: Discrimination in the Maintenance and Marketing of REO Properties.* Washington, DC: National Fair Housing Alliance. http://www.nationalfairhousing.org/Portals/33/the_banks_are_back_web.pdf/.

Parker-Pope, Tara. 2011. "Keeping Score on How You Take Your Medicine." *New York Times*, June 20.

Reid, Carolina, and Alisa Weiner. n.d. *Understanding the Unbanked Market in San Francisco: A Preliminary Analysis.* San Francisco: Federal Reserve Bank of San Francisco. http://www.frbsf.org/community/resources/banksfpresentation.pdf/.

Squires, Gregory D., ed. 1997. *Insurance Redlining: Disinvestment, Reinvestment, and the Evolving Role of Financial Institutions.* Washington, DC: The Urban Institute Press.

Stillman, Jim. 2007. "Your Credit Score Determines the Availability of Credit . . . and the Cost." *Yahoo! Voices*, June 20.

"Subprime Debacle Traps Even Very Creditworthy." 2007. *Wall Street Journal*, December 3.

Taylor, Paul, Rakesh Kochhar, Richard Fry, Gabriel Velasco, and Seth Motel. 2011. *Twenty to One: Wealth Gaps Rise to Record Highs between Whites, Blacks and Hispanics.* Washington, DC: Pew Research Center.

VantageScore. 2009. Unpublished PowerPoint presentation provided to authors with permission.

Weller, Christian, Julie Ajinkya, and Jane Farrell. 2012. "The State of Communities of Color in the U.S. Economy, Still Feeling the Pain Three Years into the Recovery." Washington, DC: Center for American Progress.

Zandi, Mark. 2011. "The Skinny on Skin in the Game." *Moody's Analytics*, March 8.

Zandi, Mark, and Cristian deRitis. 2011. "Reworking Risk Retention." *Moody's Analytics Special Report*, June 20.

3

Onward and Upward

The Fight to Ensure Equal Access to Credit via the Federal Housing Administration

David Berenbaum and Katrina S. Forrest

I N THE INTRODUCTORY CHAPTER, the question was posed: Has the fair lending, fair housing movement run its course? And, are the Occupy Wall Street protests the next wave? The answer to the first question is a resounding "no" and to the second question, the answer is, "stay tuned." On September 17, 2011, a group of frustrated and disappointed organizers assembled in Zuccotti Park in New York City's Wall Street financial district. Their goal was to initiate a protest against social and economic inequality, greed and corporate corruption. The efforts of this group, which became known as the Occupy Wall Street (OWS) movement, were galvanizing, spurring the creation of similar movements across the country. Despite its early ubiquity, however, the OWS movement in 2012 is far less visible than it was just two years ago, but it remains active as a "leaderless movement" working for social change and corporate responsibility—most recently, by assisting victims of Hurricane Sandy. As the adage goes, "Rome was not built in a day." For that reason, the OWS movement should not be viewed as the primary example for effecting political change, but rather a partner for change in the broader civil rights movement. There is much that we can learn from OWS and the organic network of citizens who were inspired to action by its leadership. Similarly, OWS could realize so much more of its agenda if it embraced the strategic model of the civil rights movement coupled with individual political action. The approach of the National Community Reinvestment Coalition (NCRC) and similar community organizations are a positive example of what can happen when people or a group, with clear ideas and focus, come together to harness their collective synergies.

Major social change has long been primarily the outcome of lengthy, patient, but persistent organizing and advocacy on the grassroots level. This fact alone does not negate the impact of the OWS movement. The OWS movement placed perpetual issues into mainstream consciousness during the "Great Recession," on the heels of an important election year. The efforts of the OWS organizers sparked national debate and raised awareness of many issues, including those affecting lending and banking services as a whole. OWS is to be commended for driving increased national dialogue on important issues on behalf of working families and the "99%." To date, its leaderless assemblies have not expanded the movement adequately to bring long-term social or political change, though they have certainly influenced the dialogue. The time has come for greater strategic collaboration between both constituencies so that a mutual goal of fair and sustainable lending by responsible Wall Street and corporate citizens can be realized.

Though the civil rights movement worked to eradicate overt discrimination in housing and lending, more subtle forms of discrimination are still prevalent. For that reason, the fair lending and fair housing movement remains vibrant, and organizations like NCRC, the National Low Income Housing Coalition, the National Council of La Raza, the National Association for the Advancement of Colored People (NAACP), and other national organizations are continuing to carry the torch and work for social justice and change. Like the OWS movement, NCRC worked to bring awareness, and ultimately change, to a more covert form of discrimination that was pervasive with insidious effects. Prior to and after the beginning of the Great Recession, the dual lending marketplace was creating one standard of access for qualified white applicants and another for equally qualified African American and Latino borrowers. This dual lending continues to smear America's housing finance markets while creating a double standard in violation of the federal Fair Housing Act and the Equal Credit Opportunity Act. The remainder of this chapter will explore how NCRC and its member organizations utilized their collective strengths to bring about meaningful change in the lending marketplace.

When the mortgage finance and housing market collapsed in 2008, private lenders reacted by tightening standards to the point of significantly constricting credit opportunities for many borrowers, even those with good credit. Out of necessity, the federal government remained one of the few sources of credit. This, along with other critical government actions, helped bring the economy back from the brink of total collapse.

It is important to note the critical, countercyclical role the Federal Housing Administration (FHA) has played in the housing market during these difficult economic times. When the market began its slow collapse, the FHA comprised only about two-to-three percent of the housing market. When private capital vanished at the end of 2008, it was the FHA that stepped in, insuring over 30 percent of purchases and 20 percent of refinances in the housing market (HUD 2010a, 6). Since January 2009, the agency has helped millions of Americans either purchase a home or refinance into more stable, affordable mortgages. While the work of the Obama administration had been successful at preventing a full-blown economic depression, its ability to rebuild and strengthen the economy had been hampered by the continual refusal of financial institutions to lend to creditworthy African American, Latino, and low- to moderate-income consumers of all races and backgrounds.

Even after former Chairman of the Federal Reserve Board Alan Greenspan warned of "infectious greed" and "malfeasance" during a July 2002 testimony, the financial industry continued to operate irresponsibly, pursuing arbitrary polices and practices that were detrimental to consumers and the economy. Leading up to the economic crisis, many financial institutions pushed products that stripped consumers of their wealth rather than building and improving their economic security or otherwise serving their financial interest. During this time, mortgage lenders originated irresponsible, risky, and complicated financial products. This greed and malfeasance spread throughout the financial system and directly led to the foreclosure crisis, which continues to undermine the economy and destabilize tax bases in cities and states nationwide.

Further, during this time, large banks and independent mortgage companies were refusing to lend to a sizable segment of the population, disproportionately working-class families who had lower credit scores resulting from a temporary situation, such as job loss, illness, or other factors that did not accurately reflect an ongoing credit risk. Those practices froze efforts to revitalize the economy and create jobs. Specifically, the nation's largest lenders had arbitrarily cut off access to one of the last remaining sources of credit: FHA loans.

One of the major challenges that the Obama administration faced when it took over was to ensure that the FHA loan program remained solvent. FHA Commissioner David Stevens successfully navigated the rough tides that were threatening the program in 2009. Wide-scale fraud, weak underwriting by FHA lenders, and increasing defaults plagued the portfolio. Some in Congress were calling for much more restrictive underwriting, for example, 20 percent down payments coupled with consumer credit scores of 720 or above, at a time when the FHA loan program was playing a critical role in the damaged economy.

NCRC spearheaded a collaborative effort with the FHA to establish a balanced approach to ensure that the loan program continued to realize its core mission of ensuring access to credit for working families. The FHA then amended its underwriting to require a minimum credit score of 580 for the 3.5 percent down product and implemented a 10 percent down payment requirement for consumers with credit scores between 500 and 579. This rational approach, coupled with enhanced antifraud and lender oversight as well as FHA's commitment to ensuring equal access to responsible and sustainable credit, in theory, ensured that Americans seeking to purchase a home or refinance out of a subprime or nontraditional loan could do so. In truth, the reality was quite different. In fact, the housing counseling agencies certified by the Department of Housing and Urban Development (HUD) and affiliated with NCRC during the summer of 2010 began to complain that lenders had implemented so-called credit overlays and were denying qualified consumers access to the FHA loan product. A lender overlay is an augmentation to established lender guidelines and can include, but is certainly not limited to, items like debt ratio, amount of assets and the type of assets, minimum down payment, property seasoning, and other attributes. Most common is the credit score overlay. FHA, as previously noted, amended their underwriting guidelines to require a minimum credit score of 580, yet most banks require a minimum credit score of 620 or higher to approve the loan. Some, especially some larger regional banks, require a minimum score of 660 to qualify for an FHA loan.

Based on the agency and consumer complaints, NCRC (2010) began an investigation and discovered that a majority of the top fifty FHA lenders had instituted policies that limited access to credit to working families in low- and moderate-income communities and communities of color—the very same communities that had been most harmed by the greed and malfeasance of Wall Street and the financial industry. The findings of NCRC's investigation were confirmed in consultation with FHA officials, best practice discussions with industry professionals, and by NCRC's direct work with consumers and member organizations around the US.

NCRC's (2010) investigation revealed that far too many of America's largest and leading financial institutions were refusing to lend under the FHA loan program to consumers with credit scores between 580 and 640. Widespread use of credit overlays, which are intended to protect the lender against default risk, was allowing lenders to systematically choose which consumers they would lend to in violation of the Fair Housing Act. Even though the government insured the loans, Ginnie Mae and the FHA could still make the lender indemnify the FHA against losses if underwriting errors were discovered. However, as the investigation revealed, these lenders could not document a business justification, and it was NCRC's contention that they discriminated against minorities and the poor by reducing their access to credit. This practice was taking place despite the fact that the FHA policy established a 100 percent guarantee for refinance and home purchase loans to a credit score of 580 for borrowers with a 3.5 percent down payment. NCRC's investigations showed that the majority of top lenders had a minimum credit score requirement of 620 or 640.

These across-the-board restrictions imposed by various lenders had no legitimate business defense considering that the loans were 100 percent guaranteed against losses, except in cases where the lender fraudulently or improperly originated the loan. Notably, the FHA had put into place more stringent lending standards to ensure that taxpayers were not on the hook for losses. In response to these unfair and pervasive practices that were taking place, NCRC, as the sole advocate in this space, called upon the Department of Justice, the HUD, the Federal Reserve, the Federal Deposit Insurance Corporation, the Office of Thrift Supervision, the Office of the Comptroller of the Currency, and the Consumer Financial Protection Bureau to investigate and end these discriminatory practices. In addition, NCRC called upon the nation's lenders to voluntarily revise their policies and to extend credit, in a safe and sound manner, to all hardworking Americans based on their ability to pay and other strong underwriting standards.

The widespread policy that was in place had profound consequences for consumers, their families, and the economy. Nearly one-third of all Americans had credit scores below 620, and thus, a significant segment of the American public was being denied access to credit. To make matters worse, NCRC had discovered through various news outlets that many lenders were moving to increase their minimum credit score requirements. This shift would have effectively denied credit opportunities to millions of potential homeowners.

Not only did the policies in place deny access to credit to qualified individuals seeking to purchase or refinance a home under the FHA loan program, but they also restricted the availability of credit and the ability of the economy to recover. Ultimately, the policies were in contradiction of the purpose and intent of the FHA loan program, which was created during the Great Depression to help working-class Americans secure access to credit in order to realize or sustain homeownership at a time when the private lending market was nearly frozen. By the end of 2008, almost one-half of the home purchase loans and one-quarter of the refinance loans were FHA—or Veterans Affairs (VA)—insured (Avery et al. 2009).

Investigation Findings

During the course of NCRC's (2010) investigation, it sought to determine if the nation's largest FHA lenders had instituted arbitrary and restrictive policies and practices, and whether those policies had an adverse and disparate impact on African American and Latino consumers. Lenders were chosen according to their market share and the volume of FHA loans, as well as through discussions with community leaders. The initial results of the investigation of FHA-approved lenders were staggering. Of the 50 lenders tested, forty-four did not lend at a 580 credit score. Thirty-two lenders, or 65 percent, refused to lend to consumers with credit scores below 620. An additional eleven lenders, or 22 percent, refused to extend credit to consumers with credit scores below 640. One lender refused to lend to consumers with credit scores below 600. Only five lenders, or 10 percent, had policies in place that served the needs of consumers with credit scores between 580 and 620, in accordance with FHA policy and in compliance with fair lending laws (NCRC 2010) (See Figure 1).

The total number of lenders investigated that did not make FHA loans at a 580 credit score represented roughly 67 percent of the entire FHA market share (NCRC 2010), leaving many consumers without any other alternative to access credit. Because of this arbitrary restriction on credit, millions of Americans were affected. Further, these policies had a particularly devastating impact on low- and moderate-income communities and communities of color by constricting their ability to access credit. These communities were experiencing "double jeopardy," having first been targeted for risky, toxic loans that lead to a tsunami of home foreclosures.

Based on the nefarious practices being employed by lenders, NCRC began filing complaints with HUD, seeking an end to the arbitrary and restrictive minimum credit score requirements. Due to the nature of this space, NCRC was at the forefront of this movement and the only community-organizing group actively working to overturn these practices. In December 2010, HUD launched an investigation to determine whether twenty-two mortgage lenders had been discriminating against qualified African American and Latino borrowers by denying them government-insured loans. The inquiry was a direct result of the complaints filed by NCRC. Moreover, of the forty-four lenders

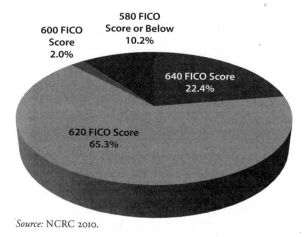

Source: NCRC 2010.

Figure 1. Investigation results: Minimum credit score
requirements of lenders investigated.

that NCRC filed complaints or challenged, sixteen have abandoned the practice. In addition to HUD, NCRC also asked other regulators to investigate
possible violations of the Equal Credit Opportunity Act and the Community
Reinvestment Act (CRA).

While investigating the practices of FHA-approved lenders, NCRC (2010)
encountered vapid justifications from lenders as to why they chose not to lend
to borrowers with credit scores below 620. The justifications offered did not
document actual risk to the financial institution if they originated the loans
in a safe and sound manner. Further, the business defenses also did not justify
the disproportionate and adverse impact the policies had on African American and Latino borrowers and communities. Based on discussions between
NCRC and the various lenders investigated, the following are some of the
most common "justifications":

1. Unable to originate loans in full compliance with FHA policy because originators faced a substantial risk of liability for the indem-
   nification of loans within the FHA loan program and that risk was
   particularly high for loans originated to consumers with credit scores
   between 580 and 620.

2. Lenders argued that consumers with credit scores between 580 and
   620 were not qualified to own a home and were a bad risk.

3. Some lenders argued that they would be unable to sell FHA loans
   on the secondary market.

4. Lenders claimed that they had the authority to use their own credit
   score minimum requirements, or credit overlays. (NCRC 2010)

Though facially valid, these justifications could not be substantiated because originators and investors had a 100 percent loan guarantee from the FHA for all responsibly and appropriately underwritten loans. Further, the risk was not borne by the lender unless the loan was fraudulently or improperly originated. Similarly, FHA loan products were only supposed to be originated to qualified consumers who met all of the program's safety and soundness and its responsible loan underwriting standards. In addition, Ginnie Mae, a government-sponsored enterprise (GSE) within HUD, insured, securitized, and sold FHA loans on behalf of FHA-approved lenders, so the argument that lenders would be unable to sell on the secondary market was a fallacy. Lastly, FHA-approved lenders had only limited discretion to use their own credit score minimum requirements in order to address actual risk documented within their portfolio. Lenders could not and cannot establish pricing or credit overlay policies that violate the federal Fair Housing Act or the Equal Credit Opportunity Act.

The Increased Role of FHA Lending in Our Communities

The FHA was created in 1934 to serve an important counter-cyclical role in America's housing market. As previously noted, prior to the financial crisis, FHA lending constituted less than 3 percent of the housing market; however, when the credit markets froze in 2008, the FHA filled a void. In this role, they insured approximately 30 percent of purchases and 20 percent of refinances in the housing market. Beginning in January 2009, the agency helped nearly three million Americans either purchase a home or refinance into more stable affordable mortgages, according to HUD (McDonald and McDonald 2012).

When mortgage lenders raise the minimum credit score on FHA-insured loans that they will originate or buy to 640 from 620, it impacts over 6.3 million people who fall within that range. Further, according to Zillow, an online real estate database, 29.3 percent of the American public had a credit score below 620 in 2010 (Curnutte 2010). These higher hurdles for FHA loans added to challenges for a housing market that was already struggling with record-low sales and surging foreclosures. While lax underwriting and problematic and often discriminatory lending fueled the bust that led the US into recession, the new requirements stifled the real estate recovery needed to revive the economy.

When HUD (2010b) released its quarterly report to Congress, FHA loans accounted for nearly 40 percent of all purchase mortgages for the period of

November 2009 to November 2010. Overall, government-backed loans, which included FHA, Veterans Affairs (VA), and loans backed by the GSEs—accounted for 38 percent of home purchase loans in 2006, but rose to nearly 82 percent by 2009. Meanwhile, government-backed (government-insured or backed by the GSEs) refinance lending surged from 27 percent of loans in 2006 to 76 percent in 2009, while the share of nonconventional (or just government-insured) loans grew from 3 percent to 19 percent over the same time period (HUD 2010b).

According to the Federal Reserve, the principal reason why FHA's share of the market increased so dramatically was because borrowers had reduced options since the private sector, including lenders and private mortgage insurance companies, reduced acceptable loan-to-value ratios and raised minimum credit score requirements (NCRC 2010). While FHA lending affected Americans of all demographics, it was and continues to be one of the most vital tools available for helping low- and moderate income and minority families purchase homes. Among home buyers, low- and moderate-income individuals, as well as African American and Latino homeowners, used nonconventional loans to a much greater extent than their white counterparts. For example, in 2009, 78 percent of home purchase loans taken out by African American homeowners were nonconventional compared to 47 percent for white consumers (Avery et al. 2010). The crux of the issue then is that policies that may seem neutral on their face may in fact have a disparate impact in violation of the FHA (Figure 2).

Further, when lending institutions refuse to offer government-insured loans to borrowers with credit scores above 580 but below 620, they are neglecting their CRA obligation to affirmatively serve all communities, including low- and moderate-income communities, consistent with safety and soundness. HUD has determined that responsibly underwritten FHA loans can be made to borrowers in this credit score range, and low- and moderate-income borrowers have relied upon FHA loans in the years since the foreclosure crisis (Figure 3). Cutting off these modest-income borrowers in the 580 to 620 credit score range has violated CRA's affirmative mandate to serve communities.

An analysis of FHA loans conducted by NCRC using the Lender Processing Services (LPS) database revealed that loans disproportionately served borrowers with credit scores between 580 and 620 (Immergluck 2009). In addition, NCRC's (2010) analysis found that zip codes with concentrations of minorities contained a disproportionate percentage of consumers with credit scores between 580 and 620. Therefore, financial institutions that adopted policies of not offering FHA loans to borrowers with credit scores between

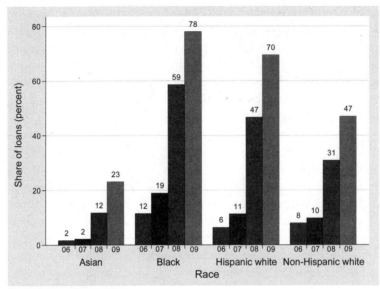

Source: Avery et al. 2010.

Figure 2. Incidence of nonconventional loan originations
      by borrower race, 2006–2009.

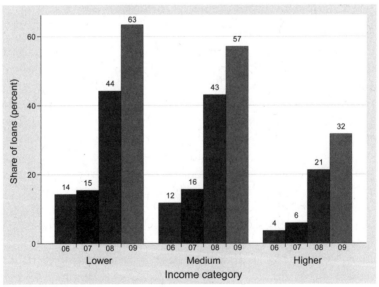

Source: Avery et al. 2010.

Figure 3. Incidence of nonconventional loan originations
      by borrower income, 2006–2009.

580 and 620 disproportionately and adversely affected access to FHA loans for predominantly minority neighborhoods. Since FHA is a market niche for borrowers with credit scores between 580 and 620, a disparate impact—giving rise to a possible violation of federal fair housing laws—occurred when financial institutions did not adopt FHA's policy of offering FHA loans to borrowers with credit scores of 580 and above.

According to HUD (2010b, 5), "Nearly 58 percent of borrowers (of FHA loans) had credit scores of 680 or better, while only 4 percent had credit scores below 620. As recently as the last half of 2008, less than 20 percent of borrowers had credit scores of 680 or better and 45 percent had credit scores below 620." A significant factor contributing to this dramatic shift in credit score distribution was lender policies refusing to lend to borrowers with credit scores below 640. By denying access to FHA loans for qualified, creditworthy individuals without valid justification for the actual risk posed by the loan to the financial institutions, lenders discouraged the flow of credit and capital into communities of color and modest-income neighborhoods. Their policies amounted to discrimination in violation of the FHA, the Equal Credit Opportunity Act, and the CRA.

Conclusion

In the March 2012, the FHA published "The Facts on FHA" on the *HUDdle*, the official blog for HUD. Listed among a series of changes implemented since January 2009 by the FHA were new standards required for FHA loans in regards to FICO score requirements and down payments (Galante 2012). According to HUD and David Stevens, assistant secretary of housing and FHA commissioner, "new borrowers will now be required to have a minimum FICO score of 580 to qualify for FHA's 3.5 percent down payment program. New borrowers with less than a 580 FICO score will be required to put down at least 10 percent. This allows the FHA to better balance its risk and continue to provide access for those borrowers who have historically performed well" (Roussell 2010).

Despite this well-intentioned change, borrowers with credit scores at or near 580 may still find it challenging to get a home loan in spite of the fact that, technically, they do meet the FHA 580-or-higher FICO requirement. This is because many participating FHA lenders require a FICO score of at least 620 in order to qualify for an FHA home loan. Just because the FHA minimum is 580 does not mean a particular bank is willing to issue credit to those with that score—the FHA loan program is a voluntary one, lenders are not required to participate, and the FHA cannot force the bank to lower its FICO requirements. This remains an open CRA issue for the prudential regulators and the Consumer Financial Protection Bureau.

Further, it is also important to acknowledge that some lenders in the VA loan program use credit overlays and the pricing matrixes of the GSEs demand strict fair lending scrutiny. While all consumers deserve access to the FHA loan program, under no circumstances should consumers be steered to the program based upon being a member of a protected class or the demographics of the community where they reside.

The July 2012 report, *Paying More for the American Dream VI—Racial Disparities in FHA/VA Lending*, published by a collaborative project of seven NCRC member organizations, dramatized the importance of the return of and access to the conventional loan market from a fair pricing perspective. The report notes that FHA and VA loans accounted for three out of every four home-purchase loans made to black borrowers and two out of every three loans made to Latino borrowers compared to approximately one out of every three loans made to white borrowers. Further, the report showed that borrowers who purchased homes in communities of color received government-backed loans twice as often as did borrowers in predominantly white communities. Similarly, black and Latino homeowners received government-backed refinance loans 3.5 and 2.1 times more often than did white homeowners, respectively. Homeowners in communities of color received government-backed refinance loans more than three times as often as did homeowners in predominantly white neighborhoods (California Reinvestment Coalition et al. 2012).

Continued vigilance by civil rights advocates, regulators, and industry remains critical. Still, with the passage of the Dodd-Frank Act and other legislation to overhaul the financial industry as a whole, efforts have been made to revitalize and stabilize the economy. In this way, we can ensure that credit overlays are only used when there is a legitimate business justification and that all Americans, regardless of race, color, religion, disability, national origin, age, gender, and familial status, are able to access credit and the window to prosperity that it can provide.

NCRC's (2010) investigation was cutting edge and revealed detrimental and pervasive discrimination in FHA lending practices. The policies presented had no reasonable business justification and had a disparate impact on the basis of race and national origin. The discovery that the majority of the country's largest FHA lenders were refusing to lend under the FHA loan program to consumers with credit scores between 580 and 640, despite the fact that FHA policy was for approved lenders to extend credit to consumers with credit scores at 580 and above, was disheartening. Like those involved with the OWS movement, NCRC recognized a damaging problem and took swift action and, as previously mentioned, directly challenged over forty FHA lenders. Unlike the OWS movement, however, due to constant research, persistence, and the collective focused efforts of NCRC staff and member groups, the organization was able to bring about positive and concrete change in the economic climate. As of 2012, eighteen national and regional mortgage originators have abandoned the credit overlay practice, permitting tens of thousands of new loans to be originated or refinanced.

The fair housing and fair lending movement is still very much alive, and the continued commitment of all community organizations to social and economic justice will continue to bring about much needed change to ensure that minorities and low- to moderate-income families have access to credit and financial services. NCRC will continue to fight for equality to help communities and families to create and sustain affordable housing.

References

Avery, Robert B., Neil Bhutta, Kenneth P. Brevoort, and Glenn B. Canner. 2010. "The 2009 HMDA Data: The Mortgage Market in a Time of Low Interest Rate Economic Distress." *Federal Reserve Bulletin*, December 22. http://www.federalreserve.gov/pubs/bulletin/2010/articles/2009HMDA/default.htm.

California Reinvestment Coalition, Empire Justice Center, Massachusetts Affordable Housing Alliance, Neighborhood Economic Development Advocacy Project, Ohio Fair Lending Coalition, Reinvestment Partners, and Woodstock Institute. 2012. *Paying More for the American Dream VI: Racial Disparities in FHA/VA Lending.* July 19. http://www.empirejustice.org/assets/pdf/publications/reports/paying-more-for-the-american.pdf.

Curnutte, Katie. 2010. "Low Credit Scores Keep Homeownership Out of Reach for 1/3 of Americans." *ZillowBlog*, September 27. http://www.zillowblog.com/2010-09-27/low-credit-scores-keep-homeownership-out-of-reach-for-13-of-americans/.

Galante, Carol. 2012. "The Facts of FHA." *The HUDdle*, March 27. http://blog.hud.gov/index.php/2012/03/27/the-facts-on-fha/.

HUD (Department of Housing and Urban Development). 2010a. *Annual Report to Congress Regarding the Financial Status of the FHA Mutual Mortgage Insurance Fund: Fiscal Year 2010.* Washington, DC: US Department of Housing and Urban Development. http://www.hud.gov/offices/hsg/rmra/oe/rpts/actr/2010actr_subltr.pdf.

———. 2010b. "FHA Single Family Mutual Mortgage Insurance Fund Programs." *Quarterly Report to Congress Q4.* http://portal.hud.gov/hudportal/documents/h uddoc?id=DOC_16565.pdf.

Immergluck, Dan. 2009. "Intrametropolitan Patterns of Foreclosed Homes: ZIP-Code Level Distributions of Real Estate-Owned (REO) Properties during the U.S. Mortgage Crisis." Community affairs discussion paper, no. 01–09, *Federal Reserve Bank of Atlanta*, April 21.

McDonald, Oonagh, and Lynn McDonald. 2012. *Fannie Mae & Freddie Mac: Turning the American Dream into a Nightmare*. New York: Bloomsbury Publishing.

NCRC (National Community Reinvestment Coalition). 2010. *Working-Class Families Arbitrarily Blocked from Accessing Credit*. Washington, DC: National Community Reinvestment Coalition.

Roussell, Melanie. 2010. "FHA Announces Policy Changes to Address Risk and Strengthen Finances." US Department of Housing and Urban Development press release, no. 10-016, January 20. http://portal.hud.gov/hudportal/HUD?src=/press/press _releases_media_advisories/2010/HUDNo.10-016.

4

Five Lessons Offered by but Not Learned from the Recent Collapse of the US Economy and the Housing Market

James H. Carr and Katrin B. Anacker

I N THIS CHAPTER, we discuss five lessons that the recent collapse of the US economy and the housing market has offered, but which have not necessarily been learned by key policymakers as demonstrated through their policy responses. The collapse of the US economy was triggered when the supply of new homes began to outstrip demand in early 2006 (Roubini and Mihm 2011). The growing housing glut led to a slowdown and ultimate collapse of home prices beginning in April 2006 (CoreLogic 2012), which, in turn, prevented borrowers with subprime mortgages from refinancing their loans when their rates reset upward in 2006 and early 2007 (Schwartz 2012). America has since been struggling with a foreclosure crisis (Carr, Anacker, and Mulcahy 2011).

The total equity lost by families with foreclosed properties is estimated at more than $7 trillion (Raskin 2012; see also Kelleher, Hall, and Bradley 2012). The effect of the economic crisis has been enormous, both nationally and globally, and the confidence Americans once had in homeownership as a path to wealth has been shaken. Generations will be impacted for decades to come.

While much has been written about the collapse of the US economy and the housing market, we argue that not many sources have focused on the lessons that can be taken away from this crisis. More specifically, we identify five lessons offered by the recent collapse of the US economy and the housing market that are not reflected in most policy responses. The five lessons are the following:

1. The struggling US economy and financial and housing markets are not self-regulating.

2. Subprime and unsustainable mortgage products caused the collapse of the housing market.

3. Failure to address the worsening wealth inequality is negatively impacting the US economy.

4. A healthy housing market is essential to a strong US economy.

5. The economy will not self-correct.

1. The Struggling US Economy and the Financial and Housing Markets Are Not Self-Regulating

In *The Wealth of Nations,* published at the end of the eighteenth century, Adam Smith advanced the metaphor of the invisible hand "to capture the seemingly miraculous process by which the selfish and divergent interests of individual economic actors somehow coalesce into a stable self-regulating economic system" (Roubini and Mihm 2011, 40; Okun 1975). At the end of the twentieth century, the Federal Reserve and many other federal and state authorities still agreed with Smith's observations and supported self-regulation and free market fundamentalism (Barlett and Steele 2012; Greenspan 2005). Support for self-regulation and free market fundamentalism has had enormous consequences since the subprime crisis has evolved (discussed in the next section).

Interestingly, Lloyd Blankfein stated in April 2009, "self-regulation has its limits. At the very least, fixing a system-wide problem, elevating standards or driving the industry to a collective response requires effective central regulation and the convening power of regulators" (Blankfein 2009). We think he was correct. Indeed, the Dodd-Frank Wall Street Reform and Consumer Protection Act of 2010 dismisses the idea that markets can be self-regulating, requiring "lenders to ensure home owners have the ability to repay their mortgages" (Erickson, Fucile, and Lutton 2012, 11) and prohibiting the use of financial incentives that encourage lenders to steer borrowers into more costly loans, among many other aspects (US Senate Committee on Banking, Housing, and Urban Affairs 2010). Interestingly, Mitt Romney, Newt Gingrich, and others would like to repeal the Dodd-Frank Act (Wyatt 2011). In a perfect world of self-regulating markets, lenders would not originate loans that they know could not be repaid. Lenders would not provide incentives to independent mortgage brokers who ignore borrower qualifications.

The myth of self-regulation is also obvious in the underpricing of risk for many borrowers during the lending boom that coincided with the house price bubble from 2000 until mid-2006. The underpricing of risk was aided by many lending industry practices that were widespread during the lending boom in the early 2000s—for example, originating low-documentation, no-documentation, stated income, or NINJA (no-income, no-job, or no-assets) loans (Engel and McCoy 2011; Roubini and Mihm 2011). The underpricing of risk was also aided by securitization through Wall Street as well as government-sponsored enterprises (GSEs). While securitization worked for several decades, it worked less well after deregulation through the Financial Services Modernization Act of 1999, when financial innovations in the form of toxic mortgage products were introduced (Barlett and Steele 2012).

In the meantime, regulation has addressed the underpricing of risk (i.e., both Dodd-Frank's requirement that borrowers should have the ability to repay their mortgage and its suggested risk retention rules that would require mortgage lenders to retain capital in the amount of 5 percent of the loans they sell into the secondary market are disincentives to irresponsible lending). This is popularly referred to as "skin in the game" (Carr, Anacker, and Mulcahy 2011). Beyond risk retention, Roubini and Mihm (2011) suggest reforming securitization through greater transparency, standardization, regulation, and scrutiny of mortgages that are packaged for the securitization pipeline.

Self-regulation of the markets also does not accommodate mistakes and misjudgment. For example, JPMorgan Chase & Co.'s $5.8 billion loss in May and June 2012 due to a trading strategy was "flawed, complex, poorly reviewed, poorly executed and poorly monitored" (Summers 2012). As JPMorgan Chase & Co. CEO Jamie Dimon stated, "So we've had audit, legal, risk, compliance, some of our best people looking over that. We know we were sloppy. We know we were stupid. We know there was bad judgment. We don't know if any of that's true yet" (Summers 2012). If the Volcker Rule, which protects taxpayers from excessive risk taking by financial institutions (US Senate Committee on Banking, Housing, and Urban Affairs 2010; Erickson, Fucile, and Lutton 2012; Rizzuto 2012), had been implemented before the trade that led to the $5.8 billion loss (which might actually be higher), the transaction may never have occurred. This particular transaction, however, has not yet resulted in financial consequences beyond the bank's ability to manage. But colossal mistakes of this type can and do happen, and effective regulation works to limit the impacts of private decisions on the public purse.

In sum, we argue that the struggling US economy and financial and housing markets are not self-regulating, agreeing with Alan Greenspan (2008), who conceded that he was partially wrong about his previous statement that "government regulators were no better than markets at imposing discipline." Indeed, Ben Bernanke (2010, 21) suggests that the execution of financial regulation and supervision "must be better and smarter." We argue that regulation is needed. However, having a good degree of regulation is vital. Too much regulation might stifle the flow of credit, and too little regulation might lead to continuing practices like those illustrated above that occurred during the house price bubble and lending boom.

While positive statements about the need for improved regulation by Blankfein, Dimon, Greenspan, and Bernanke might lead many to conclude that the need for better regulation of the financial system is universally accepted, statements by key members of Congress and other influential policymakers make it clear that this is not a correct conclusion. The Consumer Financial Protection Bureau (CFPB), for example, has been under assault by lawmakers who have expressed a desire to repeal or significantly reduce the authority of that new agency (Kavoussi 2012).

2. Subprime and Unsustainable Mortgage Products Caused the Collapse of the Housing Market

Before the 1980s, mortgage applicants, based on then-current mortgage underwriting practices and standards, either qualified for a mortgage or did not. At that point in time, mortgages were either conventional or a Federal Housing Administration (FHA) or Veterans Administration (VA) mortgage (Schwartz 2010). This situation changed in the early 1980s when the Depository Institutions Deregulation and Monetary Control Act gave banks the flexibility to set rates and fees for mortgages beginning in 1980 and the Alternative Mortgage Transaction Parity Act allowed banks to make variable rate mortgages with balloon payments beginning in 1982 (Ludwig, Kamihachi, and Toh 2009). Thus, in the mid-1980s, lenders introduced risk-based pricing (i.e., in exchange for higher risk of predicted default, borrowers would pay higher interest and fees) (Immergluck 2009).

Loans originated in the shadow banking system (i.e., subprime mortgages) would become more common in the 1990s and especially the 2000s. Originations in subprime loans increased rapidly near the beginning of the national house price bubble in 2002 (with 6.9 percent subprime loans of all originated loans) until just after the peak of the national house price bubble in the third quarter of 2006 (with 21.2 percent subprime loans of all originated loans) (Joint Center for Housing Studies of Harvard University 2008).

Numerous reasons have been offered to explain the increase in the absolute number and the proportion of subprime loans. We will discuss these reasons, differentiating between the financial sector and public policy. One reason for the increase was that "Wall Street paid the most for these most dangerous mortgages" (Stein 2008, 3). Lenders were being paid more for delivering higher-risk loans to the secondary markets than lower-risk, fixed-rate loans, which allowed lenders to pay higher fees to brokers who were also being handsomely compensated for peddling defective loan products instead of low-risk, sustainable, conventional, and fixed-rate products.

Another reason for the increase in the absolute number and the proportion of subprime loans was that the financial sector had utilized technological advances in terms of automated underwriting and predictive default models, which not only allowed for faster processing of loan originations but, over time, probably led to relaxed lending and underwriting standards (Engel and McCoy 2011; Roubini and Mihm 2011). These technological advances led not only to cost savings for lenders but also to credit that was relatively easy for borrowers to obtain quickly, which, in turn, led to greater demand for mortgages, including subprime mortgages, which drove up house prices. While increased house prices are seen as an affordability issue for first-time home buyers, they are also seen as an increase in equity by homeowners (although the house price bubble showed that the increase in equity was inflated), especially in times of stagnant or declining real wages for most workers (Peck 2011).

The financial sector also took advantage of agency and private securitization, established in the early 1970s, which not only provided liquidity but also a relatively risk-free tool to keep (risky) loans out of their portfolios (Johnson and Kwak 2010). As Engel and McCoy (2011, 43) state:

> If lenders had kept their subprime loans on their books, they probably would have made fewer loans and taken greater care with the ones they made. With securitization, however, they could write risky loans and shed them quickly for cash. The buyers, mostly Wall Street banks, converted the loans into securities and passed the risk onto investors. That risk then "went viral" with the creation of trillions of dollars in complex credit derivatives built on subprime loans. Commercial banks, investment banks, insurance companies, hedge funds, pension plans, and governments around the world bought subprime derivatives, which depended on one thing: the timely payment of U.S. subprime mortgages. When that edifice cracked, the structure of private-label securitization came tumbling down.

These developments happened during a global investment glut, but were spurred on by financing from China, Brazil, India, Russia, Saudi Arabia, and other countries (Pozen 2010; Roubini and Mihm 2011). Low interest rate policies by the Federal Reserve have also been blamed for the subprime crisis (Schwartz 2012). While these policies resulted in low interest rates of prime loans, subprime loans typically carried high interest rates.

Some have blamed public policy in the form of GSEs for the subprime crisis. For example, Wallison (2011) argues that, as of June 30, 2008, there were 26.7 million subprime and Alternative-A (Alt-A) mortgages—between prime and subprime mortgages in terms of risk—outstanding (out of 55 million total mortgages). He claims that of those 26.7 million mortgages, 19.25 million (72.10 percent) were the responsibility of Fannie Mae, Freddie Mac, the Community Reinvestment Act, and other federal programs designed to boost affordable housing (see also Pinto 2008). However, many experts and independent federal agencies have dismissed Pinto and Wallison's work. For example, Min (2011) clarifies that Wallison's estimate of 26.7 million subprime and Alt-A mortgages outstanding uses a definition of subprime loans that is contradictory to industry norms, citing estimates of the nonpartisan Government Accountability Office of only 4.58 million outstanding subprime and Alt-A loans out of roughly 55 million total loans (see also Shear et al. 2010). Min (2011) also points out that Wall Street securitized 85 percent of subprime loans as defined by industry norms and that private label securitizations had a default rate that was more than six times that of the GSEs.

Public policy did play a significant and definitive role in promoting reckless subprime lending until after the flood in subprime lending had been well over. For example, the government's unwillingness to ban toxic mortgage products until the adoption of new rules under the Home Ownership and Equity Protection Act (HOEPA) in 2008 played a profound role in allowing the subprime market to thrive. While the HOEPA Act of 1994 required certain disclosures and placed restrictions on lenders of high-cost loans, the new rules passed in 2008 curbed the "abuses about which consumer groups had raised red flags for years—including a requirement that borrowers have the ability to repay loans made to them" (Financial Crisis Inquiry Commission 2011, 22).

Moreover, the federal government actually opposed actions by states to protect the financial interests of their citizens. For example, in 1999, North Carolina took the lead in the state movement for antipredatory lending laws by passing the first comprehensive state antipredatory lending statute. Many anticipated that other states would follow North Carolina's efforts and pass similar antipredatory lending laws. However, in 2004, the Office of the Comptroller of the Currency (OCC) passed a rule exempting national banks and their mortgage-lending subsidiaries from most state lending laws protecting consumers, which was similar to a previously issued rule by the

Office of Thrift Supervision (OTS) that exempted federal thrifts from state lending laws (Berner and Grow 2008; Hawke 2003; OCC 2004a, 2004b; Williams 2003). Therefore, the OCC and OTS rules created an incentive for many subprime lenders to become subsidiaries of national banks or federal thrifts, thus avoiding state restrictions on subprime mortgages, during a time of consolidation in the banking industry and during the lending boom in the mid-2000s (Engel and McCoy 2011).

While many studies on racial and ethnic inequality in the mortgage market have shown that subprime mortgages are more heavily concentrated in neighborhoods of color even after controlling for many demographic, socio-economic, and mortgage-related factors (Bocian, Ernst, and Li 2006; Calem, Gillen, and Wachter 2004; Calem, Hershaff, and Wachter 2004; Center for Responsible Lending 2007; Mayer and Pence 2008), we argue that subprime mortgages (i.e., the products) and not the borrowers of subprime mortgages caused the housing market collapse. Many of these products were toxic in the first place and should have been better regulated, as we hope to witness under the future efforts of the newly established CFPB.

3. Failure to Address the Worsening Wealth Inequality Is Negatively Impacting the US Economy

In the United States, the past several decades have been characterized by the loss of blue-collar jobs that paid well and that came with good benefits, and the creation of new jobs in the service industry characterized by low wages with little or no benefits (Barlett and Steele 2012; Florida 2002) and by stagnant wages (Barlett and Steele 2012; Warren 2007). The reasons for this development are, among others, offshoring, automation, and the "lack of public and private investment in the United States, both in infrastructure and in new productive facilities" (Dolbeare and Hubbell 1996, 37; see also Barlett and Steele 2012). The dramatic decline in worker unionization since the turn of the last century has also resulted in the loss of worker wages and benefits (Mishel et al. 2012). These global and domestic economic and social changes have coincided with domestic policies starting in the 1990s that have resulted in a redistribution of wealth from the middle class towards the top 1 percent through tax cuts for the top 1 percent and reduced benefits for the middle class (Dolbeare and Hubbell 1996; Noah 2012; Schumer 2008; Stiglitz 2012). While some have pointed out supply-side or "trickle-down" economics, others argue that this approach has not worked (Ettlinger and Linden 2012; Ettlinger 2012).

Ettlinger (2012) and Madland (2011, 2012) have focused on the middle class, pointing out that: (a) middle-class customers patronize businesses, creating stability and investment in the economy; (b) middle-class employees provide skills to the economy; and (c) middle-class people are disproportionately found among entrepreneurs. In other words, "it isn't the rich that lead the way to growth and prosperity. Instead, it is a thriving and vibrant middle class that shows us the path" (Madland 2011, 16).

The longer-term economic and social changes combined with the recent crises starting in 2007 have had vast reverberating effects on the opportunities, well-being, and wealth-building potential of generations and have exacerbated the nation's inequality. Interestingly, wealth inequality had been tolerated in the past because most Americans believe in upward economic mobility, which is tied to American exceptionalism, which, in turn, is connected to the American Dream. While many still believe in upward economic mobility, it has become more of a myth, exacerbated by the "Great Recession" (Mazumder 2012; Noah 2012).

Inequality has been discussed in connection with entrepreneurship, risk-taking, and innovation (Siebert 1998), more work effort (Bell and Freeman 2001; Siebert 1998), efficiency, and notions of fairness (Okun 1975). America's current level of inequality, however, was greater than most other developed nations and even its own recent past (Stiglitz 2012). While many point out that inequality in America should be addressed (as we discuss below), Conard (2012, 80) and others think that inequality should be celebrated:

> The commercialization of the Internet and email has increased the value of innovation relative to the everyday jobs common to the economy. As innovation has grown relatively more valuable, the share of pretax income produced by successful innovators has grown relatively more valuable, the share of pretax income produced by successful innovators has naturally risen. . . . It's not as though the outsized success of the top 1 percent has lowered median wages in the United States relative to those of Europe or Japan. Quite the contrary; rather than bemoaning unequal distribution of income, we should be celebrating the extraordinary success of U.S. innovation relative to the rest of the world and its beneficial effect on domestic employment.

Median and mean real incomes will probably not increase due to the current jobless recovery. In June 2009, the National Bureau of Economic Research (2012) declared the recession to be technically over. While the national unemployment rate had decreased to 8.2 percent in 2012 from its peak of 9.9 percent in April 2010 (Bureau of Labor Statistics 2012), the unemployment rate has not reached pre-crisis levels yet and is not expected to do so for many years (Shierholz 2012). The national unemployment rate in 2011 of Blacks/African Americans,[1] at 15.9 percent, and of Hispanics/Latinos, at 11.5 percent, was much higher, however, which has a severe impact on their opportunities and economic mobility (Austin 2012a and 2012b).

The declines in median and mean family incomes have primarily affected middle-class families, which have been under economic strains for several decades (Harkin 2011; Newman 1993; Warren 2007; Warren and Tyagi 2005; see also De Graaf et al. 2005; Frank 1999; and Schor 1998 for alternative opinions), while top earners have seen an increase (Piketty and Saez 2003; Urahn et al. 2012).

The income declines for the middle class occurred while many of their expenses went up. Warren (2007), using Consumer Expenditure Survey data, found that between 1972 and 2004, the biggest items in the family budget were fixed items (i.e., items that cannot be saved upon), such as a mortgage, health care, cars, child care, and taxes, and all had dramatically increased in cost (see also Newman 1993; Harkin 2011). As Barlett and Steele (2012) point out, in the early 1950s, the top tax rate was 92 percent. Although not many paid the 92 percent, top earners paid a much higher percentage than they did in 2012. Flexible items in the family budget (i.e., items that can be saved upon to some degree or even postponed for a short period of time), such as clothing, food, appliances, and expenditures per car, on the other hand, had decreased in cost (Warren 2007).

Given the dramatic increases in health care costs in the early twenty-first century, fixed expenditures are assumed to have increased even further. As Warren (2007, 44) points out,

> the family of the 1970s had about half its income committed to big fixed expenses. Moreover, it had a stay-at-home parent, someone who could go to work to earn extra income if something went wrong. By contrast, the family of 2004 has already put everyone to work, so there is no extra income to draw on if trouble hits. Worse yet, even with two people in the workforce, after they pay their basic expenses, today's two-income family has less cash left over than its one-income parents had a generation ago.

While it is important to discuss income inequality, it is even more important to discuss wealth inequality. Assets often expand choices, horizons,

---

1. For this chapter, the established race and ethnicity categories of the US Census Bureau will be used. These include non-Hispanic Whites, Blacks/African Americans, and Hispanics/Latinos.

and opportunities—such as access to good schools, protection from crime, and proximity to good employment—and thus offer freedom from worrying about the basic necessities of life, allowing individuals to focus on longer-term economic opportunity. A lack of assets, however, typically limits opportunities and contributes to racial and ethnic inequality (Logan and Molotch 1987; Oliver and Shapiro 2006; Weller and Helburn 2009).

The Great Recession has also had a negative effect on median and mean family net worth, the difference between families' gross assets and their liabilities. While changes were negative in 1992, reflecting the recession from July 1990 to March 1991, they were positive from 1995 to 2007, and then negative from 2007 to 2010. From 2007 to 2010, family median net worth fell 38.84 percent, family mean net worth fell 14.68 percent, and the mean-to-median ratio increased to 6.5 (after a low point of 3.7 in 1995). The increase in the mean-to-median ratio indicates that wealth is increasingly located at the top of the wealth distribution, as the mean is influenced by outliers (Levine 2012; Bricker et al. 2012).

Racial, ethnic, and class wealth inequality, which has been much more uneven than income inequality, has been well researched (Blau and Graham 1990; Chang 2010; Conley 2001; Keister 2005, 2008; Lupton and Smith 1999; Oliver and Shapiro 2006; Sherraden 1991; Smith 1995; Spilerman 2000; Wolff 1998). Indeed, as the Great Recession has increased wealth inequality, this topic has entered into the public discussion to an even greater extent.

Kochhar, Fry, and Taylor (2011) point out that 35 percent of Black/African American, 31 percent of Hispanic/Latino, and 19 percent of Asian households had zero or negative net worth in 2009 compared with 15 percent of non-Hispanic White households. In 2005, these proportions were 29 percent for Blacks/African Americans, 16 percent for Hispanics/Latinos, 12 percent for Asians, and 11 percent for non-Hispanic Whites. Even after excluding home equity, wealth losses are disconcerting. Kochhar, Fry, and Taylor (2011) analyzed the median net worth of households with and without home equity and found that losses were most severe for households of color (37.35 percent for Blacks/African Americans, 25.19 percent for Asians, and 14.58 percent for Hispanics/Latinos). Net worth does not only depend on housing equity (discussed in the next section) but also on other forms, as illustrated by Bricker et al. (2012) and Kochhar, Fry, and Taylor (2011). While some people invest directly in the stock market—19 percent in 1989, but 51 percent in 2007 (Levine 2012)—others invest indirectly through their retirement accounts. Between September 2007 and March 2009, major stock market indexes fell nearly 50 percent, although they had recouped to some degree by September 2010

(Bricker et al. 2012). This loss affected non-Hispanic Whites as a group to a higher degree than others, as a higher proportion of non-Hispanic Whites participates in employer-sponsored retirement plans. Butrica and Johnson (2010) show that 55.1 percent of non-Hispanic Whites participated in retirement plans in 2009, basing their research on the March 2009 Current Population Survey (CPS). In contrast, only 44.5 percent of Blacks/African Americans and 30.2 percent of Hispanics/Latinos participated in this form of saving. The lower participation rates reflect that a disproportionate share of Blacks/African Americans (26.6 percent compared to 25.4 percent of non-Hispanic Whites) work part time and that a disproportionate share of Hispanics/Latinos work for employers with fewer than one hundred employees (47.7 percent compared to 35.2 of non-Hispanic Whites and 27.7 percent of Blacks/African Americans) and for the public sector (11.4 percent compared to 17.3 percent of non-Hispanic Whites and 21.1 percent of Blacks/African Americans).

Much has been written about the reasons for wealth inequality, including racial and ethnic wealth inequality. Reasons that have been discussed and analyzed are income inequality, gender, marital status, and discrimination, among others (Blau and Graham 1990; Chang 2010; Conley 2001; Keister 2005, 2008; Lupton and Smith 1999; Oliver and Shapiro 2006; Sherraden 1991; Smith 1995; Spilerman 2000; Wolff 1998).

Observing trends in wealth inequality, Hacker (2008, xv) suggests a "Great Risk Shift," where, over time, "more and more economic risk has been off-loaded by government and corporations onto the increasingly fragile balance sheets of workers and their families," which "has affected Americans of every walk of life, class standing and political persuasion." Boushey and Hersh (2012, 42) have proposed rent-seeking, which occurs when "individuals (or corporations) seek to obtain economic gain by manipulating politics rather than by making new investments in productive activities," to be another reason for wealth inequality.

As Stiglitz (2012, 28) points out, "much of the inequality that exists today is a result of government policy, both what the government does and what it does not do." The federal government is primarily concerned with profits, executive compensation, and tax and expenditure policies and continues to provide the resources, modify the distribution of income, and change the dynamics of wealth through its policies. Stiglitz (2012) also points out that technology, scarcity, and political and economic forces all help to shape inequality.

In the United States, there is a misperception between the actual and perceived wealth distribution. Norton and Ariely (2011) revealed that in one survey completed in December 2005, respondents vastly underestimated the actual level of wealth inequality, erroneously assuming that the top quintile held only 59 percent of the wealth (instead of 84 percent). Interestingly, the wealth distribution preferred by the respondents has the top quintile holding 32 percent of the wealth. Whereas all groups in this particular study desired a more equal distribution, including the wealthiest respondents, Norton and Ariely (2011, 12) stated that "Americans may remain unlikely to advocate for policies that would narrow this gap" because they (still) optimistically believe in social mobility, which has become increasingly a myth (Benabou and Ok 2001; Charles and Hurst 2003; Keister 2005).

While some embrace redistribution as a way to solve America's wealth inequality, others oppose it. Conard (2012, 88) argues,

> Opponents of income redistribution believe that leaving income and wealth in the hands of successful risk-takers through lower marginal tax rates and unequal distribution of income, rather than redistribution to poor consumers, increases the willingness of investors to bear risk. This drives up the demand for assets, which increase their price. This increases the payout for risky investments that produce increases in future profits. Higher payouts lead to increased risk taking. Again, consumers and wage earners are chief beneficiaries of increased investment.

A substantial amount of economics literature has analyzed the link between inequality and economic growth for developing (Barro 2000; Deininger and Squire 1998; Rodriguez 2000) and developed countries. In regard to the latter, some find a presence of a positive relationship between inequality and economic growth (Panizza 2002; Partridge 2005), others find a negative relationship (Frank 2005; Frank and Freeman 2002; Furman and Stiglitz 1998; Persson and Tabellini 1994), while yet others have either inconsistent or inconclusive results (Barro 2000; Quah 2011). In regard to the former, Voitchovsky (2005), for example, finds that inequality at the top end of the distribution is positively associated with growth, while inequality at the bottom end of the distribution is negatively associated with growth. Nevertheless, most scholars who worked on this topic point out data and methods issues that influence results. Given the timeliness of the topic and the impact of the recession on the middle class (Leonhardt 2012), we suggest studying the link between inequality and economic growth based on the most recent national data.

In terms of the consequences of inequality on individuals, some point out that inequality may limit the ability of low- and moderate-income households to make investments in human or physical capital, thus reducing economic growth (Aghion, Caroli, and Garcia-Penalosa 1999; Stiglitz 2012).

As Boushey and Hersh (2012, 4) point out, "human capital, and the higher incomes that go along with it, are increasingly passed from parents to off-spring through social (not biological) channels. This means that individuals are being rewarded for privileges conveyed by their parents' socioeconomic status, not just their productivity characteristics, which will pull U.S. economic growth down." (See Pew Economic Mobility Project (2011) for an international comparison.) Others point out the connection between higher inequality and voter participation, trust in the political system, corruption, crime, and upheaval, with the latter possibly increasing pressure for distortionary government redistribution (Persson and Tabellini 1994; Stiglitz 2012).

Income and wealth inequality grew and accelerated during the two decades leading up to the Great Recession. Over time, well-paid, blue-collar jobs with benefits have been replaced by low-pay, service sector jobs without benefits due to an increase in offshoring, automation, decrease in unionization, and millions of additional low-wage workers entering the global labor markets. Over the past several decades, real incomes have declined while expenses, especially fixed expenses that cannot be reduced by much, have increased. These and other reasons have resulted in income and wealth inequality that had been tolerated before the Great Recession due to a belief in upward mobility and trickle-down effects.

Income and wealth inequality, which have become especially pronounced for people of color, make it difficult to invest in human or physical capital and thus hamper upward mobility at the individual level. At the societal level, income and wealth inequality translate in reduced economic growth and trust in the political system. If policymakers do not act, the negative effects of income and wealth inequality will continue to increase, especially for people of color, thus restricting economic recovery.

While globalization and technological advancements have occurred in other developed countries, many of these countries pursued public policies that differed from those in the US. For example, since the mid-1990s, Germany has experienced an increase in real incomes and trade surpluses, partly due to a higher proportion of employees working in manufacturing, partly due to shortened work weeks (to prevent or decrease mass layoffs), and partly due to a "social contract that brings together business, labor, and government working for the nation's benefit.... Trade union leaders sit on the supervisory boards of major firms..., positioned to persuade management to keep the highest value-added work in Germany. As a trade-off, unions have eased demands for pay increases" (Smith 2012, 387). We encourage the US to pursue a similar social contract.

4. A Healthy Housing Market Is Essential to a Strong US Economy

At the national level, housing contributes to the gross domestic product (GDP) through private residential investment (i.e., the construction of new single-family and multifamily structures, residential remodeling, production of manufactured homes, and brokers' fees) and through consumption spending on housing services (i.e., gross rents, including utilities paid by renters, owners' imputed rents, and utility payments) (NAHB 2012a). Since the 1990s, private residential investment was about 5 percent of the real GDP, although there have been variations. Over the same time frame, housing services made up about 12 or 13 percent of the real GDP (NAHB 2012a). The proportion of residential fixed investment was highest (6.1 percent) at the peak of the national house price bubble in 2005 and lowest (2.5 percent) after the Great Recession was technically over (in both 2010 and 2011). Interestingly, housing services have been steadier, possibly indicating housing affordability issues for renters (Anacker and Li, in progress).

The National Association of Home Builders (NAHB) (2012b) also estimates that for each new single-family home that is constructed, three jobs are created, half of them in the construction industry and the other half in the lumber, concrete, lighting fixtures, and heating and cooling equipment sectors, most of which are produced in the United States. Furthermore, the NAHB (2012b) estimates that for each new single-family home that is constructed, $90,000 in government revenues are generated (i.e., $67,000 in federal taxes and $23,000 in state and local taxes). Finally, the NAHB (2012b) estimates that there is a gap between production and potential housing construction of about one million homes and, thus, that there are more than three million untapped American jobs.

At the individual level, homeownership has historically translated into wealth building, at least before the Great Recession. The national house price crash has had a profound effect on the portfolio of many homeowners. As Bricker et al. (2012, 1) point out, "although declines in the values of financial assets or business were important factors for some families, the decreases in median net worth appear to have been driven most strongly by a broad collapse in house prices."

The national decline in house prices disproportionately affected those families that had a larger share of their portfolios invested in homeownership. These tend to be primarily families with low- and middle-income levels and families of color (Belsky and Retsinas 2005). However, there are vast differences among the racial and ethnic groups. Wolff (2010) found that the overall projected proportion of homeowners with negative home equity in 2009 was 16.4 percent. Using the 2007 Survey of Consumer Finances (SCF) and the 2009 Panel Study of Income Dynamics (PSID), both of which were national in scope, the racial and ethnic groups were compared: the proportion of non-Hispanic Whites with negative home equity was 14.5 percent, the proportion of Blacks/African Americans was 27.9 percent, and the proportion of Hispanics/Latinos was 23.2 percent. These findings indicate not only that borrowers purchased properties in metropolitan areas and neighborhoods that disproportionately lost value due to the foreclosure crisis but also that some home values might have been inflated upon origination (NAHB 2012c). In addition to the lost equity, an underwater home typically means that a borrower is not able to leverage the house for investments in post-secondary education or starting or expanding a small business, or for expenditures on home maintenance and repairs, medical bills, or extracurricular activities.

Decreased house prices and underwater homes have had a significant negative impact on consumer spending and consumer confidence (Bankrate.com 2012). The Bureau of Labor Statistics (BLS) found that average annual expenditures per consumer unit fell 2 percent in 2010 following a decrease of 2.8 percent in 2009. While consumer spending fell in 2010, prices for goods and services increased 1.6 percent from 2009 to 2010, as measured by the Consumer Price Index (Bureau of Labor Statistics 2011).

5. The Economy Will Not Self-Correct

The national foreclosure crisis started in early 2007, and gradual fallout of the financial system and the broader economy followed, although the stock market continued to rally, reaching its peak in October 2007. The annual unemployment rate remained low in 2007 (4.6 percent), but started to increase in 2008 (5.8 percent) (Bureau of Labor Statistics 2012). Nevertheless, in 2007 and 2008, hundreds of banks and mortgage lenders went bankrupt, among them Countrywide Financial, Bear Stearns Companies, Inc., Lehman Brothers Holding Inc., Merrill Lynch, Washington Mutual, Inc., Wachovia, Citigroup Inc., and American International Group, Inc. (Immergluck 2011).

During this time, many economists and some policymakers and government officials argued that the housing market should be allowed to work itself out of its crisis and that the government should not intervene (Calmes 2009; Jackson 2007). Over time, however, many realized that the Great Recession was more severe than previously assumed, and that government intervention was essential to prevent the complete collapse of the US financial system and, potentially, the US economy (Calmes 2009).

Government intervention for the financial sector occurred through the Emergency Economic Stabilization Act (EESA), passed in October 2008, which included the Troubled Assets Relief Program (TARP) for an initial price tag of $700 billion (although, in 2012, only $431 billion had been disbursed, according to Lerner et al. (2012)). Originally, TARP was designed to buy up toxic assets, but ended up as a program that disbursed funds to banks in exchange for dividend-paying preferred stock. Thanks to TARP, the banking system survived the crisis (as banks were unable to sustain themselves without significant government intervention) (Carr 2012). In 2008, the Federal Deposit Insurance Corporation (FDIC) launched an initiative that mass modified loans in the portfolio of the failed thrift institution IndyMac, which resulted in a projected 1.5 million in avoided foreclosures (FDIC 2012).

Government intervention for consumers occurred through the Economic Stimulus Act of 2008, which was signed into law in February 2008. This $152 billion stimulus provided tax rebates to low- and middle-income US taxpayers, tax incentives to stimulate business investment, and increased limits on conforming mortgages eligible for government insurance and GSE purchase to stimulate the economy (Broda and Parker 2008). Later, the Housing and Economic Recovery Act (HERA), passed in July 2008, provided a tax credit for eligible first-time home buyers of up to $8,000 from 2008 to 2010 (Immergluck 2011).

Another massive public policy response in the form of an economic stimulus was the American Recovery and Reinvestment Act (ARRA) that was signed into law in February 2009 and for which $831 billion (revised amount) was allocated. This economic recovery program was among the biggest in US history. ARRA purchased goods and services by funding construction and other investment activities that could take several years to complete; it provided funds to states and localities and increased aid for education and transportation projects; it supported people in need by extending and expanding unemployment benefits and increasing benefits under the Supplemental Nutrition Assistance Program (formerly the Food Stamp program); and it provided temporary tax relief for individuals and businesses by raising exemption amounts for the alternative minimum tax, adding a new Making Work Pay tax credit, and creating enhanced deductions for depreciation of business equipment (Reichling et al. 2012).

The nonpartisan Congressional Budget Office estimated that the macroeconomic effects have been modest and pointed out sluggish GDP growth

	Real GDP (%) Low Estimate	Real GDP (%) High Estimate	Unemployment Rate (Percentage Points) Low Estimate	Unemployment Rate (Percentage Points) High Estimate	Employment Rate (Millions of People) Low Estimate	Employment Rate (Millions of People) High Estimate	Full-Time Equivalent Employment (Millions) Low Estimate	Full-Time Equivalent Employment (Millions) High Estimate
2009	0.4	1.8	−0.1	−0.5	0.2	0.9	0.3	1.3
2010	0.7	4.1	−0.4	−1.8	0.7	3.3	0.9	4.7
2011	0.4	2.3	−0.2	−1.4	0.4	2.6	0.6	3.6
2012	0.1	0.8	−0.1	−0.6	0.2	1.1	0.2	1.3
2013	0.1	0.4	*	−0.3	0.1	0.5	*	0.3

Note: For cells containing an asterisk (*), values range between -0.05 to 0.05.
Source: Reichling et al. 2012.

Figure 1. Calendar year average of estimated macroeconomic impact of the American Recovery and Reinvestment Act, 2009–2013.

and a high unemployment rate (see Figure 1), but we think that without the stimulus package, the economic situation would have been much worse. As ARRA was only a temporary program, its impacts are already waning as of 2012. While Representative Eric Cantor of Virginia called the package "a spending bill beyond anyone's imagination" (Calmes 2009), Stiglitz argued that the stimulus bill was "an anemic and insufficient response to the recession" (National Public Radio 2010) and Krugman (2011) found that the stimulus was "clearly inadequate to the task."

Government interventions for foreclosed homeowners and communities consisted of several initiatives and programs, although many economists and politicians have been critical of the impacts. The first program was the FHA Secure program, announced in August 2007, through which the FHA refinanced delinquent homeowners into more affordable loans to prevent foreclosure (131,881 conventional loans refinanced from October 2007 until the end of March 2008, but "fewer than 2,000 homeowners at risk of foreclosure . . . helped" (Swarns 2008). FHA Secure was followed by the Hope Now Alliance, announced in October 2007, which was an alliance of lenders, NeighborWorks, and nonprofit organizations that provided foreclosure prevention counseling to homeowners over the phone free of charge.

In December 2007, the National Foreclosure Mitigation Counseling (NFMC) program was launched and funded by over $500 million, which was awarded to local housing counseling organizations to advise homeowners in or at risk of foreclosure. Mayer et al. (2012) found that after the Home Affordable Modification Program was established, a loan modification through NFMC resulted in an average additional reduction of $176 in monthly payment and a reduction of 36 percent in foreclosure completions, among many other findings.

HERA, passed in July 2008, provided $7 billion of funding for local governments and nonprofit organizations to buy and renovate foreclosed properties through the Neighborhood Stabilization Programs (NSP1, NSP2, NSP3) to stabilize communities ravaged by the foreclosure crisis (Schwartz 2012; Department of Housing and Urban Development 2011). HERA also established the Hope for Homeowners (H4H) program, which resulted in only 340 originated loans (Immergluck 2011).

The passing of the Financial Stability Act of 2009 resulted in the Making Home Affordable (MHA) initiative, for which $29.9 billion was allocated (Carr, Anacker, and Mulcahy 2011). MHA has many components, among them the Home Affordable Modification Program (HAMP) and the Home Affordable Refinance Program (HARP). While HAMP seeks to reduce the debt-service costs of eligible homeowners at risk of foreclosure, HARP is intended to help eligible homeowners refinance their mortgages under more affordable terms through the GSEs (Schwartz 2012).

From early 2011 until the end of the first quarter of 2012, servicers conducted almost 2.3 million home retention actions through the HAMP program (OCC 2012). From April 1, 2009 to May 31, 2012, HARP refinanced 1,318,954 loans (Federal Housing Finance Agency 2012). While both programs have significant design and implementation issues, they have nevertheless prevented many foreclosures and refinances. Immergluck (2011) argues that federal programs should be substantially revised and better executed and that the bankruptcy law should be changed to have a larger number of prevented foreclosures. Working on these aspects will be necessary, as Bocian et al. (2011, 3) found that the "nation is not even halfway through the foreclosure crisis."

To solve the foreclosure crisis, Smith (2012) suggests a domestic Marshall Plan with the following eight criteria:

- Create infrastructure jobs to compete better;
- Push innovation, science, and high-tech research;
- Generate a manufacturing renaissance;
- Make the US tax code fairer;
- Fix the corporate tax code to promote job creation at home;

- Push China to live up to fair trade to generate four million jobs in the United States;
- Save on war and weapons;
- Fix housing and protect the safety net.

President Barack Obama has asked Congress numerous times to join him in passing legislation that invests in America's infrastructure and green technologies and creates jobs for working Americans. In response, Congress has been heading in the opposite direction—towards a fiscal cliff of automatic spending cuts and tax increases that could propel the economy back into recession.

The Policy Road Ahead

In this chapter, we discussed five lessons that the recent collapse of the US economy and the housing market has offered, but that have not, necessarily, been learned. The first lesson is that markets are not self-regulating. While self-regulation and free-market fundamentalism had been embraced by the economic elites for decades, the subprime and the ensuing foreclosure and economic crises have shown that self-regulation does not work, and the most well-known free-market champions, including Lloyd Blankfein, Alan Greenspan, and Jamie Dimon, have acknowledged this. The Dodd-Frank Act of 2010 provides a framework that, if implemented properly, reins in the kinds of practices during the house price bubble that proved to be disastrous to the financial system and the US economy. But with the crisis fading in the memories of many corporate executives, the push to undermine market regulation, including repealing or significantly weakening Dodd-Frank, has been strong.

The second lesson is that subprime and unsustainable mortgage products caused the collapse of the housing market. While gradual deregulation had taken place since the early 1980s amidst preemption and the resistance to banning toxic mortgages, Wall Street, aided by low interest rates, continued to reward risk, took advantage of securitization, and introduced subprime loans in the late 1990s. Arguments that the crisis was caused by a legitimate attempt to expand homeownership are without merit. Research to demonstrate that the crisis was the result of the GSEs is flawed. The newly established Consumer Financial Protection Bureau (CFPB) is tasked to regulate subprime and unsustainable mortgage products, preventing a potential future collapse of the housing market due to these products.

The third lesson is that the failure to address the worsening wealth inequality is negatively impacting the US economy. Wealth serves critical economic security functions in an economy that primarily relies on individual initiative. Interestingly, tax policies favor asset building through homeownership and investment, both of which disproportionately favor high-income earners who are disproportionately non-Hispanic White. Conversations on the future of mortgage finance threaten to further limit homeownership for low- and moderate-income households and people of color. Future policy discussions could lead to significant consequences with respect to the role of public policy in promoting a more equitable distribution of federal subsidies and, consequently, economic equality.

The fourth lesson is that a healthy housing market is essential to a strong US economy. In spite of somewhat positive housing market news in 2012, the housing market remains troubled. Ignoring the continuing foreclosure crisis, for example, is a mistake. Failing to address the millions of vacant and abandoned properties that litter the landscapes of communities across the US where foreclosures have been concentrated is also a mistake. Moreover, public policy has strongly supported homeownership as a key national policy goal and the most broadly accessible means to wealth building. The national house price crash, the foreclosure and economic crises, the lending freeze, and discussions about a potential 20 percent down payment have put a damper on this goal. As of this writing, numerous authors have discussed the GSE reform, which will most likely negatively impact homeownership, especially for people of color. Because of housing's unique characteristics—the high leverage used to purchase it and its ability to serve as a household's principal residence—it is an irreplaceable asset builder. Policies that push America to a rental society will have major, long-term, and damaging consequences for family wealth accumulation, household economic mobility, and overall national economic output.

The final lesson is that the economy will not self-correct. While a series of economic stimuli have been passed, they have been insufficient in the context of the magnitude of the crisis. Moreover, many subsidies have disproportionately aided major corporations and, by extension, their executives and shareholders. The result is that public policy has contributed to an increase in economic and social inequality while failing to address fundamental challenges facing the economy. The unwillingness of Congress to pass legislation that invests in America's infrastructure and green technologies will leave the US economy struggling for years. Attempts to achieve a massive deficit reduction without a view toward investments in the economy threaten to put the nation back on the road towards another recession. The middle class deserves an equivalent set of consistent and generous stimulus programs to those that are currently reserved for the wealthy.

References

Aghion, Philippe, Eve Caroli, and Cecilia Garcia-Penalosa. 1999. "Inequality and Economic Growth: The Perspective of the New Growth Theories." *Journal of Economic Literature* 37: 1615–60.

Anacker, Katrin B., and Yanmei Li. In progress. "Analyzing Housing Affordability of Renters during the Great Recession, 2007 to 2009."

Austin, Algernon. 2012a. *Black Metropolitan Unemployment in 2011: Las Vegas's Rate Rises Significantly.* Economic Policy Institute, Issue Brief no. 337, July 2. http://www.epi .org/files/2012/ib337-black-metropolitan-unemployment.pdf.

———. 2012b. *Hispanic Metropolitan Unemployment in 2011: Providence, RI, Again Tops the List.* Economic Policy Institute, Issue Brief no. 336, July 2. http://www.epi.org/files/2012 /ib336-hispanic-metropolitan-unemployment.pdf.

Bankrate.com. 2012. "Feelings of Financial Security Sag in July." *Bankrate.com*, July 25 http://www.bankrate.com/finance/consumer-index/financial-security-poll-0712.aspx.

Barlett, Donald L., and James B. Steele. 2012. *The Betrayal of the American Dream.* New York: PublicAffairs.

Barro, Robert J. 2000. "Inequality and Growth in a Panel of Countries." *Journal of Economic Growth* 5: 5–32.

Bell, Linda A., and Richard B. Freeman. 2001. "The Incentive for Working Hard: Explaining Hours Worked Differences in the US and Germany." *Labour Economics* 8: 181–202.

Belsky, Eric S., and Nicolas P. Retsinas. 2005. "New Paths to Building Assets for the Poor." In *Building Assets, Building Credit: Creating Wealth in Low-Income Communities*, edited by Nicolas P. Retsinas and Eric S. Belsky, 1–9. Cambridge, MA: Joint Center for Housing Studies and Brookings Institution Press.

Benabou, Roland, and Efe A. Ok. 2001. "Social Mobility and the Demand for Redistribution: The POUM Hypothesis." *The Quarterly Journal of Economics*, May: 447–87.

Bernanke, Ben S. 2010. "Monetary Policy and the Housing Bubble." Remarks at the Annual Meeting of the American Economic Association, Atlanta, Georgia, January 3. http://www.federalreserve.gov/newsevents/speech/bernanke20100103a.pdf.

Berner, Robert, and Brian Grow. 2008. "They Warned Us About the Mortgage Crisis." *Bloomberg Businessweek*, October 8. http://www.businessweek.com/stories/2008-10-08 /they-warned-us-about-the-mortgage-crisis.

Blankfein, Lloyd. 2009. "It's Time to Rethink Financial Services Regulation." Remarks at the Meeting of the Council of Institutional Investors, New York, April.

Blau, Francine D., and John W. Graham. 1990. "Black-White Differences in Wealth and Asset Composition." *The Quarterly Journal of Economics*, May: 321–39.

Bocian, Debbie Gruenstein, Keith S. Ernst, and Wei Li. 2006. *Unfair Lending: The Effect of Race and Ethnicity on the Price of Subprime Mortgages.* Durham, NC: Center for Responsible Lending. http://www.responsiblelending.org/mortgage-lending/research -analysis/rr011-Unfair_Lending-0506.pdf.

Bocian, Debbie Gruenstein, Wei Li, Carolina Reid, and Roberto Quercia. 2011. *Lost Ground, 2011: Disparities in Mortgage Lending and Foreclosures.* Durham, NC: Center

for Responsible Lending. http://www.responsiblelending.org/mortgage-lending
/research-analysis/Lost-Ground-2011.pdf.

Boushey, Heather, and Adam S. Hersh. 2012. *The American Middle Class, Income Inequality,
and the Strength of Our Economy.* Washington, DC: Center for American Progress.
http://www.americanprogress.org/issues/2012/05/pdf/middleclass_growth.pdf.

Bricker, Jesse, Arthur B. Kennickell, Kevin B. Moore, and John Sabelhaus. 2012. Changes
in U.S. Family Finances from 2007 to 2010: Evidence from the Survey of Consumer
Finance. *Federal Reserve Bulletin* 98 (2): 1–80. http://www.federalreserve.gov/pubs
/bulletin/2012/PDF/scf12.pdf.

Broda, Christian, and Jonathan A. Parker. 2008. "The Impact of the 2008 Rebate." *VoxEU.
org*, August 15. http://www.voxeu.org/article/did-2008-us-tax-rebates-work.

Bureau of Labor Statistics. 2011. "Consumer Expenditures—2010." Bureau of Labor Statistics news release, September 27. http://www.bls.gov/news.release/archives/cesan
_09272011.pdf.

———. 2012. "Labor Force Statistics from the Current Population Survey." US Department
of Labor, Bureau of Labor Statistics. Accessed July 18. http://data.bls.gov/timeseries
/LNS14000000.

Butrica, Barbara A., and Richard W. Johnson. 2010. *Racial, Ethnic, and Gender Differen-
tials in Employer-Sponsored Pensions.* Statement of Barbara A. Butrica and Richard W.
Johnson, the Urban Institute, before the ERISA Advisory Council, US Department
of Labor, June 30. Washington, DC: The Urban Institute. http://www.urban.org
/UploadedPDF/901357-racial-ethnic-gender-differentials.pdf.

Calem, Paul S., Kevin Gillen, and Susan Wachter. 2004. "The Neighborhood Distribution
of Subprime Mortgage Lending." *Journal of Real Estate Finance and Economics* 29:
393–410.

Calem, Paul S., Jonathan E. Hershaff, and Susan M. Wachter. 2004. "Neighborhood Patterns of Subprime Lending: Evidence from Disparate Cities." *Housing Policy Debate* 15:
603–22.

Calmes, Jackie. 2009. "House Passes Stimulus Plan with no G.O.P. Votes." *New York Times*,
January 28. http://www.nytimes.com/2009/01/29/us/politics/29obama.html.

Carr, James H. 2012. "A Stimulus for the Middle Class." *PBS*, July 13. http://www.pbs.org
/wnet/need-to-know/opinion/a-stimulus-for-the-middle-class/14233/.

Carr, James H., Katrin B. Anacker, and Michelle L. Mulcahy. 2011. *The Foreclosure Crisis
and Its Impact on Communities of Color: Research and Solutions.* Washington, DC:
National Community Reinvestment Coalition.

Center for Responsible Lending. 2007. *Subprime Lending: A Net Drain on Homeownership.*
Durham, NC: Center for Responsible Lending. http://www.responsiblelending.org
/mortgage-lending/research-analysis/Net-Drain-in-Home-Ownership.pdf.

Chang, Mariko Lin. 2010. *Shortchanged: Why Women Have Less Wealth and What Can Be
Done about It.* Oxford: Oxford University Press.

Charles, Kerwin Kofi, and Erik Hurst. 2003. "The Correlation of Wealth across Generations." *Journal of Political Economy* 111: 1155–82.

Conard, Edward. 2012. *Unintended Consequences: Why Everything You've Been Told About the
Economy Is Wrong.* New York: Portfolio/Penguin.

Conley, Dalton. 2001. "Decomposing the Black-White Wealth Gap: The Role of Parental
Resources, Inheritance, and Investment Dynamics." *Sociological Inquiry* 71: 39–66.

CoreLogic. 2012. *House Price Index May 2012.* Santa Ana, CA: CoreLogic. http://www
.corelogic.com/about-us/researchtrends/asset_upload_file765_15538.pdf.

De Graaf, John, David Wann, and Thomas H. Naylor. 2005. *Affluenza: The All-Consuming Epidemic*. San Francisco: Berrett-Koehler Publishers, Inc.

Deininger, Klaus, and Lyn Squire. 1998. "New Ways of Looking at Old Issues: Inequality and Growth." *Journal of Development Economics* 57: 259–87.

Department of Housing and Urban Development. 2011. "Neighborhood Stabilization Program Grants." US Department of Housing and Urban Development. http://portal .hud.gov/hudportal/HUD?src=/program_offices/comm_planning/community development/programs/neighborhoodspg.

Dolbeare, Kenneth M., and Janette Kay Hubbell. 1996. *U.S.A. 2012: After the Middle-Class Revolution*. London, United Kingdom: Chatham House Publishers.

Engel, Kathleen C., and Patricia A. McCoy. 2011. *The Subprime Virus: Reckless Credit, Regulatory Failure, and Next Steps*. New York: Routledge.

Erickson, Jennifer, Tamara Fucile, and David J. Lutton. 2012. *Dodd-Frank Financial Reform After Two Years: 5 Successes and 5 Things That Will Make Our Markets Stronger*. Washington, DC: Center for American Progress. http://www.americanprogress.org/issues /2012/07/pdf/dodd_frank.pdf.

Ettlinger, Michael. 2012. *The Middle Class and Economic Growth: A Project of the Center for American Progress*. Washington, DC: Center for American Progress. http://www .americanprogress.org/issues/2012/08/middle_class_growth.html.

Ettlinger, Michael, and Michael Linden. 2012. *The Failure of Supply-side Economics: Three Decades of Empirical Economic Data Shows that Supply-Side Economics Doesn't Work*. Washington, DC: Center for American Progress. http://www.americanprogress.org /issues/2012/08/failure_supply_side_econ.html.

FDIC (Federal Deposit Insurance Corporation). 2012. *FDIC Loss Sharing Proposal to Promote Affordable Loan Modifications*. Washington, DC: Federal Deposit Insurance Corporation.

Federal Housing Finance Agency. 2012. *Refinance Report May 2012*. Washington, DC: Federal Housing Finance Agency. http://www.fhfa.gov/webfiles/24058/May12RefiReport 71112.pdf.

Financial Crisis Inquiry Commission. 2011. *The Financial Crisis Inquiry Report: Final Report of the National Commission on the Causes of the Financial and Economic Crisis in the United States*. New York: PublicAffairs.

Florida, Richard. 2002. *The Rise of the Creative Class: And How It's Transforming Work, Leisure, Community and Everyday Life*. New York: Basic Books.

Frank, Mark W. 2005. "Income Inequality and Economic Growth in the U.S.: A Panel Cointegration Approach." Working Paper from Sam Houston State University, Department of Economics and International Business. http://www.shsu.edu/~eco _www/resources/documents/IncomeInequalityandEconomicGrowth.pdf.

Frank, Mark W., and Donald G. Freeman. 2002. "Relationship of Inequality to Economic Growth: Evidence from U.S. State-Level Data." *Pennsylvania Economic Review* 11: 24–36.

Frank, Robert H. 1999. *Luxury Fever: Money and Happiness in an Era of Excess*. Princeton: Princeton University Press.

Furman, Jason, and Joseph E. Stiglitz. 1998. "Economic Consequences of Income Inequality." Paper presented at the Symposium on Income Inequality Issues and Policy Options sponsored by the Federal Reserve Bank of Kansas City, Jackson Hole, Wyoming, August 27–29. http://www.kc.frb.org/publicat/sympos/1998/s98stiglitz.pdf.

Greenspan, Alan. 2005. "Testimony of Chairman Alan Greenspan." *Federal Reserve Board's Semiannual Monetary Policy Report to the Congress*, testimony before the Committee on Financial Services, US House of Representatives, Washington, DC, July 20. http:// www.federalreserve.gov/boarddocs/hh/2005/july/testimony.htm.

———. 2008. "Testimony of Dr. Alan Greenspan." Testimony before the Committee of Government Oversight and Reform, Washington, DC, October 23. http://democrats .oversight.house.gov/images/stories/documents/20081023100438.pdf.

Hacker, Jacob S. 2008. *The Great Risk Shift: The New Economic Insecurity and the Decline of the American Dream.* Oxford: Oxford University Press.

Harkin, Tom. 2011. *Saving the American Dream: The Past, Present, and Uncertain Future of America's Middle Class.* Washington, DC: United States Senate: Health, Education, Labor and Pensions Committee. http://harkin.senate.gov/documents/pdf/4e5fa704 f2533.pdf.

Hawke, John D. 2003. "Remarks by John D. Hawke, Jr., Comptroller of the Currency before the American Bankers Association." Waikoloa, Hawaii, September 22. http:// www.occ.gov/static/news-issuances/speeches/2003/pub-speech-2003-75.pdf.

Immergluck, Dan. 2009. *Foreclosed: High-Risk Lending, Deregulation, and the Undermining of America's Mortgage Market.* Ithaca, NY: Cornell University Press.

———. 2011. "Too Little, Too Late and Too Timid: The Federal Response to the Foreclosure Crisis at the 5-Year Mark." Working Paper, School of City and Regional Planning, Georgia Institute of Technology, September 19. http://papers.ssrn.com/sol3/papers .cfm?abstract_id=1930686.

Jackson, Alphonso. 2007. "Remarks at International Housing Finance Policy Roundtable at the U.S. Department of Housing and Urban Development." Washington, DC, November 28.

Johnson, Simon, and James Kwak. 2010. *13 Bankers: The Wall Street Takeover and the Next Financial Meltdown.* New York: Pantheon Books.

Joint Center for Housing Studies of Harvard University. 2008. *The State of the Nation's Housing 2008.* Cambridge, MA: Joint Center for Housing Studies of Harvard University. http://www.jchs.harvard.edu/sites/jchs.harvard.edu/files/son2008_bw.pdf.

Kavoussi, Bonnie. 2012. "On CFPB's First Birthday, Watchdog Is Still Vulnerable to Possible Dodd-Frank Repeal." *The Huffington Post*, July 20. http://www.huffingtonpost.com /2012/07/20/cfpb-first-birthday_n_1690412.html?view=screen.

Keister, Lisa. 2005. *Getting Rich: America's New Rich and How They Got That Way.* Cambridge, United Kingdom: Cambridge University Press.

———. 2008. "Conservative Protestants and Wealth: How Religion Perpetuates Asset Poverty." *American Journal of Sociology* 113: 1237–71.

Kelleher, Dennis, Stephen Hall, and Katelynn Bradley. 2012. *The Cost of the Wall Street-Caused Financial Collapse and Ongoing Economic Crisis Is More than $12.8 Trillion.* Washington, DC: Better Markets. http://www.bettermarkets.com/sites/default/files /Cost%20Of%20The%20Crisis.pdf.

Kochhar, Rakesh, Richard Fry, and Paul Taylor. 2011. *Wealth Gaps Rise to Record Highs between Whites, Blacks, and Hispanics.* Washington, DC: Pew Research Center. http:// www.pewsocialtrends.org/files/2011/07/SDT-Wealth-Report_7-26-11_FINAL.pdf.

Krugman, Paul. 2011. "On the Inadequacy of the Stimulus." *New York Times*, September 5. http://krugman.blogs.nytimes.com/2011/09/05/on-the-inadequacy-of-the-stimulus/.

Leonhardt, David. 2012. "A Closer Look at Middle Class Decline." *New York Times*, July 23. http://economix.blogs.nytimes.com/2012/07/23/a-closer-look-at-middle-class-decline/.

Lerner, Avi, Peter Fontaine, Theresa Gullo, and Jeffrey Holland. 2012. *Report on the Troubled Asset Relief Program—March 2012*. Washington, DC: Congressional Budget Office. http://www.cbo.gov/publication/43139.

Levine, Linda. 2012. *An Analysis of the Distribution of Wealth across Households, 1989-2010*. Washington, DC: Congressional Research Service. http://www.fas.org/sgp/crs/misc /RL33433.pdf.

Logan, John R., and Harvey Molotch. 1987. *Urban Fortunes: The Political Economy of Place*. Los Angeles: University of California Press.

Ludwig, Eugene A., James Kamihachi, and Laura Toh. 2009. "The CRA: Past Successes and Future Opportunities." In *Revisiting the CRA: Perspectives on the Future of the Community Reinvestment Act*, edited by Prabal Chakrabarti, David Erickson, Ren S. Essene, Ian Galloway, and John Olson, 84–104. Boston and San Francisco: Federal Reserve Bank of Boston and Federal Reserve Bank of San Francisco.

Lupton, Joseph, and James P. Smith. 1999. *Marriage, Assets, and Savings*. Santa Monica, CA: RAND. http://www.rand.org/pubs/drafts/2008/DRU2215.pdf.

Madland, David. 2011. "Growth and the Middle Class." *Democracy: A Journal of Ideas*, Spring: 16–22.

———. 2012. *Making Our Middle Class Stronger: 35 Policies to Revitalize America's Middle Class*. Washington, DC: Center for American Progress. http://www.americanprogress.org /issues/2012/08/middle_class_policies.html.

Mayer, Chris, and Karen Pence. 2008. *Subprime Mortgages: What, Where, and to Whom?* Washington, DC: Federal Reserve Board. http://www.federalreserve.gov/pubs/feds /2008/200829/200829pap.pdf.

Mayer, Neil, Peter A. Tatian, Kenneth Temkin, and Charles A. Calhoun. 2012. "Has Foreclosure Counseling Helped Troubled Homeowners? Evidence from the Evaluation of the National Foreclosure Mitigation Counseling Program." The Urban Institute, Brief no. 1, January: 1–9. http://www.urban.org/UploadedPDF/412492-Has-Foreclosure -Counseling-Helped-Troubled-Homeowners.pdf.

Mazumder, Bhashkar. 2012. "Is Intergenerational Economic Mobility Lower Now than in the Past?" *Chicago Fed Letter*, no. 297 (April). http://www.chicagofed.org/digital _assets/publications/chicago_fed_letter/2012/cflapril2012_297.pdf.

Min, David. 2011. *Faulty Conclusions Based on Shoddy Foundations: FCIC Commissioner Peter Wallison and Other Commentators Rely on Flawed Data from Edward Pinto to Misplace the Causes of the 2008 Financial Crisis*. Washington, DC: Center for American Progress. http://www.americanprogress.org/wp-content/uploads/issues/2011/02/pdf /pinto.pdf.

Mishel, Lawrence, Josh Bivens, Elise Gould, and Heidi Shierholz. 2012. *The State of Working America*. Ithaca, NY: Cornell University Press.

NAHB (National Association of Home Builders). 2012a. "Housing's Contribution to Gross Domestic Product (GDP)." National Association of Home Builders. Accessed July 12. http://www.nahb.org/generic.aspx?sectionID=784&genericContentID=66226.

———. 2012b. *Economic Benefits of New Home Construction*. Washington, DC: National Association of Home Builders. Accessed July 12. http://www.nahb.org/fileUpload_details .aspx?contentID=155811.

———. 2012c. *A Comprehensive Framework for Housing Finance System Reform*. Washington, DC: National Association of Home Builders. https://www.nahb.org/assets/docs/files /NAHBHousingFinanceWhitePaperFeb2012_20120302094029.pdf.

National Bureau of Economic Research. 2012. "U.S. Business Cycle Expansions and Contractions." National Bureau of Economic Research. Accessed July 18. http://www.nber.org/cycles.html.

National Public Radio. 2010. "Stiglitz Says Government Misses Mark on Economy." *NPR*, January 15. http://www.npr.org/templates/story/story.php?storyId=122620894.

Newman, Katherine S. 1993. *Declining Fortunes: The Withering of the American Dream.* New York: BasicBooks.

Noah, Timothy. 2012. *The Great Divergence: America's Growing Inequality Crisis and What We Can Do about It.* New York: Bloomsbury Press.

Norton, Michael I., and Dan Ariely. 2011 "Building a Better America—One Wealth Quintile at a Time." *Perspectives on Psychological Science* 6: 9–12.

OCC (Office of the Comptroller of the Currency). 2004a. "Bank Activities and Operations: Final Rule." *Federal Register* 69: 1895–904.

———. 2004b. "Bank Activities and Operations; Real Estate Lending and Appraisals: Final Rule." *Federal Register* 69: 1904–17.

———. 2012. *OCC Mortgage Metrics Report: Disclosure of National Bank and Federal Savings Association Mortgage Loan Data, First Quarter 2012.* Washington, DC: Office of the Comptroller of the Currency. http://www.occ.treas.gov/publications/publications-by-type/other-publications-reports/mortgage-metrics-2012/mortgage-metrics-q1-2012.pdf.

Okun, Arthur M. 1975. *Equality and Efficiency: The Big Tradeoff.* Washington, DC: The Brookings Institution.

Oliver, Melvin L., and Thomas M. Shapiro. 2006. *Black Wealth/White Wealth.* New York: Routledge.

Panizza, Ugo. 2002. "Income Inequality and Economic Growth: Evidence from American Data." *Journal of Economic Growth* 7: 25–41.

Partridge, Mark D. 2005. "Does Income Distribution Affect U.S. State Economic Growth?" *Journal of Regional Science* 45: 363–94.

Peck, Don. 2011. *How the Great Recession Has Narrowed Our Futures and What We Can Do About It.* New York: Crown Publishers.

Persson, Torsten and Guido Tabellini. 1994. "Is Inequality Harmful for Growth?" *American Economic Review* 84: 600–21.

Pew Economic Mobility Project. 2011. *Does America Promote Mobility As Well As Other Nations?* Washington, DC: The Pew Charitable Trusts. http://www.pewstates.org/uploadedFiles/PCS_Assets/2011/CRITA_FINAL%281%29.pdf.

Piketty, Thomas, and Emmanuel Saez. 2003. "Income Inequality in the United States, 1913–1998." *The Quarterly Journal of Economics* 118: 1–39.

Pinto, Edward J. 2008. "Statement of Edward J. Pinto before the Committee on Oversight and Government Reform, United States House of Representatives." Washington, DC, December 9.

Pozen, Robert. 2010. *Too Big to Save? How to Fix the U.S. Financial System.* Hoboken, NJ: John Wiley & Sons.

Quah, Danny. 2011. "Some Simple Arithmetic on How Income Inequality and Economic Growth Matter." Working paper, Department of Economics, London School of Economics. http://econ.lse.ac.uk/~dquah/p/0106iieg.pdf.

Raskin, Sarah Bloom. 2012. "Creating and Implementing an Enforcement Response to the Foreclosure Crisis." Speech given at the Annual Meeting of the Association of American Law Schools, Washington, DC, January 7. http://www.federalreserve.gov/newsevents/speech/raskin20120107a.htm.

Reichling, Felix, Wendy Edelberg, William Randolph, Jared Brewster, Mark Lasky, Benjamin Page, and Joshua Shakin. 2012. *Estimated Impact of the American Recovery and Reinvestment Act on Employment and Economic Output from October 2011 through December 2011*. Washington, DC: Congressional Budget Office. http://www.cbo.gov /publication/43013.

Rizzuto, Robert. 2012. "Elizabeth Warren Renews Call for Glass-Steagall Act Following JPMorgan's Announcement That Risky Trading Loss Grew to $5.8 Billion." *MassLive. com*, July 13. http://www.masslive.com/politics/index.ssf/2012/07/elizabeth_warren _renews_call_f.html.

Rodriguez, Francisco C. 2000. "Inequality, Economic Growth and Economic Performance: A Background Note for the World Development Report 2000." Working paper, Department of Economics, the University of Maryland. http://siteresources.worldbank .org/INTPOVERTY/Resources/WDR/Background/rodriguez.pdf.

Roubini, Nouriel, and Stephen Mihm. 2011. *Crisis Economics: A Crash Course in the Future of Finance*. New York: Penguin Books.

Schor, Juliet B. 1998. *The Overspent American: Why We Want What We Don't Need*. New York: Harper.

Schumer, Charles E. 2008. "Opening Statement." In *How Much More Can American Families be Squeezed by Stagnant Wages, Sky-Rocketing Household Costs, and Falling Home Prices?: Hearing before the Joint Economic Committee, One Hundred Tenth Congress, Second Session, July 28*. Washington, DC: US Government Printing Office. http:// www.gpo.gov/fdsys/pkg/CHRG-110shrg45065/html/CHRG-110shrg45065.htm.

Schwartz, Alex. 2010. *Housing Policy in the United States: An Introduction*. New York: Routledge.

———. 2012. "US Housing Policy in the Age of Obama: From Crisis to Stasis." *International Journal of Housing Policy*.

Shear, William, Steve Westley, William Bates, Jan Bauer, Stephen Brown, Julianne Dieterich, DeEwa Kamara, John McGrail, John Mingus, Marc Molino, Bob Pollard, and Jennifer Schwartz. 2010. *Nonprime Mortgages: Analysis of Loan Performance, Factors Associated with Defaults, and Data Sources*. Washington, DC: United States Government Accountability Office. http://www.gao.gov/new.items/d10805.pdf.

Sherraden, Michael. 1991. *Assets and the Poor: A New American Welfare Policy*. Armonk, NY: M. E. Sharpe.

Shierholz, Heidi. 2012. "The Labor Market is Treading Water." *Economic Policy Institute*, July 6. http://www.epi.org/publication/labor-market-treading-water/.

Siebert, Horst. 1998. "Commentary: Economic Consequences of Income Inequality." Paper presented at the Symposium on Income Inequality Issues and Policy Options sponsored by the Federal Reserve Bank of Kansas City, Jackson Hole, Wyoming, August 27–29. http://www.kc.frb.org/publicat/sympos/1998/S98siebert.pdf.

Smith, Hedrick. 2012. *Who Stole the American Dream?* New York: Random House.

Smith, James P. 1995. "Racial and Ethnic Differences in Wealth in the Health and Retirement Study." *The Journal of Human Resources* 30: S158–S183.

Spilerman, Seymour. 2000. "Wealth and Stratification Processes." *Annual Review of Sociology* 26: 497–524.

Stein, Eric. 2008. *Turmoil in the U.S. Credit Markets: The Genesis of the Current Economic Crisis*. Testimony of Eric Stein before the U.S. Senate Committee on Banking, Housing and Urban Affairs, Washington, DC, October 16. http://banking.senate.gov

/public/index.cfm?FuseAction=Files.View&FileStore_id=03d72248-b676-4983-bd3e
-offec936b509.

Stiglitz, Joseph E. 2010. *Freefall: America, Free Markets, and the Sinking of the World Economy.*
New York: Norton.

———. 2012. *The Price of Inequality: How Today's Divided Society Endangers Our Future.* New
York: Norton.

Summers, Juana. 2012. "JPMorgan Chase CEO Jamie Dimon: 'Terrible, egregious mistake.'"
POLITICO, May 13. http://www.politico.com/news/stories/0512/76240.html.

Swarns, Rachel L. 2008. "Federal Mortgage Plan Falls Short, Critics Say." *New York Times*,
April 30. http://www.nytimes.com/2008/04/30/business/30fha.html.

Urahn, Susan K., Erin Currier, Diana Elliott, Lauren Wechsler, Denise Wilson, and Daniel
Colbert. 2012. *Pursuing the American Dream: Economic Mobility across Generations.*
Washington, DC: The Pew Charitable Trusts. http://www.pewstates.org/uploadedFiles
/PCS_Assets/2012/Pursuing_American_Dream.pdf.

US Senate Committee on Banking, Housing, and Urban Affairs. 2010. *Brief Summary of
the Dodd-Frank Wall Street Reform and Consumer Protection Act.* Washington, DC:
US Senate. http://banking.senate.gov/public/_files/070110_Dodd_Frank_Wall_Street
_Reform_comprehensive_summary_Final.pdf.

Voitchovsky, Sarah. 2005. "Does the Profile of Income Inequality Matter for Economic
Growth? Distinguishing between the Effects of Inequality in Different Parts of the
Income Distribution." *Journal of Economic Growth* 10: 273–96.

Warren, Elizabeth. 2007. "The Vanishing Middle Class." In *Ending Poverty in America: How
to Restore the American Dream*, edited by John Edwards, Marion Crain, and Arne L.
Kalleberg, 38–52. New York: The New Press.

Wallison, Peter J. 2011. *Dissent from the Majority Report of the Financial Crisis Inquiry Commission.* Washington, DC: American Enterprise Institute for Public Policy Research.
http://www.aei.org/files/2011/01/26/Wallisondissent.pdf.

Warren, Elizabeth, and Amelia Warren Tyagi. 2005. *All Your Worth: The Ultimate Lifetime
Money Plan.* New York: Free Press.

Weller, Christian E., and Amy Helburn. 2009. "Public Policy Options to Build Wealth for
America's Middle Class." Working paper, Political Economy Research Institute, University of Massachusetts, November. http://scholarworks.umass.edu/cgi/viewcontent
.cgi?article=1178&context=peri_workingpapers.

Williams, Julie L. 2003. "Remarks by Julie L. Williams, Chief Counsel and First Senior
Deputy Comptroller, Office of the Comptroller of the Currency, Before the Consumer Federation of America, 15th Annual Consumer Financial Services Conference."
Washington, DC, December 5. http://www.occ.gov/static/news-issuances/speeches
/2003/pub-speech-2003-97.pdf.

Wolff, Edward N. 1998. "Recent Trends in the Size Distribution of Household Wealth."
Journal of Economic Perspectives 12: 131–50.

———. 2010. "Recent Trends in Household Wealth in the United States: Rising Debt and the
Middle-Class Squeeze—an Update to 2007." Working paper, no. 589, Levy Economics Institute of Bard College, Bard College, March. http://www.levyinstitute.org/pubs
/wp_589.pdf.

Wyatt, Edward. 2011. "Dodd-Frank Act a Favorite Target for Republicans Laying Blame."
New York Times, September 20. http://www.nytimes.com/2011/09/21/business/dodd
-frank-act-is-a-target-on-gop-campaign-trail.html?pagewanted=all&_r=0.

5

Opportunity Lost

How Low-Income and Minority Households Were Denied Access to Historically Low Home Prices and Interest Rates.

M William Sermons

WHILE MUCH HAS been written about the recession of 2007 to 2009, the subprime mortgage crisis that precipitated it, and the impact that new federal regulation will have on the future of the housing market, less attention is paid to the state of the current housing and mortgage markets. This largely makes sense. The impacts of risky lending in the years leading up to the housing crisis were historic, and tens of millions of borrowers are still experiencing the impact of that risky lending. Likewise, the future—when all of the Dodd-Frank mortgage reforms are in place and the fate of the government-sponsored enterprises (GSEs) has been determined—will set the course for the next few generations of homeowners and potential homeowners. However, as this chapter argues, the current period represents a critical time as well, specifically, a lost opportunity for wealth creation for low- and moderate-income African American and Latino households that will exacerbate already historic racial and ethnic wealth disparities.

The "Opportunity"

By many measures, now is the time to buy an affordable home that will deliver wealth in the form of home equity. One of those measures is housing affordability. One common way of measuring affordability is calculating the ratio of home prices to income. Figure 1 shows the home price-to-income

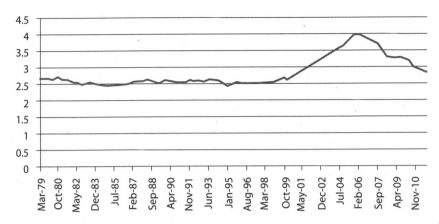

Source: Gudell 2012.

Figure 1. Zillow price index to median income ratio, March 1979–March 2012.

ratio from March 1979 to March 2012 and reveals that the index was steady at around $2.5 in home price per dollar of annual income from 1979 up until the beginning of the last decade, when it began to rise to unprecedented levels. Since peaking in March 2006 (at roughly four), the affordability index has declined steadily to levels approaching the prior steady level of 2.5. In other words, housing is becoming affordable again.

In addition to affordability, which is a function of price and income, mortgage rates are at historically low levels, so the real cost of financing a house of a given price is as low as it has ever been. To go along with these historically low mortgage rates, mortgages are safer, as the mortgage reforms of the Dodd-Frank Act largely eliminated the risky mortgage terms and practices that led so many to lose their homes to foreclosure. Finally, projections by housing experts reveal that housing prices are expected to rise steadily, but modestly, from 2013 through 2017 and beyond (Humphries 2012). These factors—affordable prices, predictions of increasing home values, and new protections against abusive mortgage terms—all suggest that now is an optimal time to invest in a home.

Of course, this opportunity is inaccessible to many low- and moderate-income African American and Latino borrowers for a number of reasons that will be addressed in this chapter. First, tens of millions of African American and Latino borrowers were targeted for risky loans in the years leading up to the housing crisis when home prices were historically high. As a result, these borrowers are overrepresented among households that have experienced or will experience foreclosure. Second, the economy of the last decade, with its stagnant wages and high unemployment, has left many households—especially African American and Latino households—without the income necessary to take on a mortgage. Lastly, the tight credit conditions of the current mortgage market is one in which many borrowers who would otherwise be successful homeowners are unable to secure loans.

Lost Ground

In the fallout of the foreclosure crisis, the alphabet soup of harmful lending products and practices is now well known. Many of these features and practices were, at one time, touted as innovations to serve borrowers. As the foreclosure crisis has made plain, such rhetoric has failed to match reality.

Over the last ten years, the Center for Responsible Lending (CRL) has produced research highlighting the increased foreclosure risk posed by abusive lending practices. In 2006, which predated the collapse of the housing market, CRL released a report estimating that abusive and predatory lending would lead to approximately 2.2 million foreclosures among subprime mortgages (Schloemer et al. 2006). As we all now know, the report's projections were actually quite conservative, not just in terms of the number of subprime loans that failed, but in its inability to project the degree to which the crisis would spread throughout the greater housing and financial markets.

At the end of 2011, CRL released a report entitled *Lost Ground* that built on the organization's precrisis research and confirmed the link between risky mortgage features and foreclosure rates (Bocian et al. 2011). For mortgages originated between 2004 and 2008, this research showed that loans originated by a mortgage broker, containing hybrid or option adjustable rate mortgages (ARMs), having prepayment penalties, and featuring high interest rates (i.e., subprime loans) were all significantly more likely to be seriously delinquent or foreclosed upon than a thirty-year fixed-rate mortgage without a prepayment penalty.

CRL's *Lost Ground* research also demonstrates that African American and Latino borrowers were much more likely to receive mortgages with these harmful features. For example, African American and Latino borrowers with FICO scores above 660 were three times more likely to have a higher interest rate mortgage than white borrowers in the same credit range. Although the majority of foreclosures have affected white borrowers, *Lost Ground* confirmed that African American and Latino borrowers have faced a disproportionate number of foreclosures and delinquencies compared to white borrowers within every income range.

The foreclosure crisis could have been prevented, but it was not, and it bears revisiting in more detail the kind of harmful lending practices that fueled the crisis that still affect communities across the United States:

2/28s and Other ARMs: Adjustable rate mortgages (ARMs)—including "2/28s," where starter rates reset after the first two years—were widespread in the years leading up to the foreclosure crisis. These 2/28s and other ARMs led to payment shocks for many households that were unprepared for higher monthly payments once the interest rate increased (Schloemer et al. 2006). As of 2009, subprime mortgages with short-term hybrid ARMs, with an initial fixed rate followed by an adjustable rate, had serious delinquency rates of 48 percent compared to 21 percent for subprime fixed-rate mortgages (US Government Accountability Office 2010). In fact, were it not for the Federal Reserve lowering interest rates to historically low levels following the financial crisis, it is easy to imagine the payment shock from expiring teaser rates leading to an even higher number of foreclosures than has occurred so far.

A related product called interest-only (IO) ARMs let borrowers make interest-only payments during an introductory period, which jeopardized any ability to build equity and led to payment shock for borrowers once the loan started amortizing over a reduced loan life. Even worse, payment-option ARMs (POARMs) allowed borrowers to make monthly payments where the amount paid could vary from month to month, including payment amounts that did not cover the full interest due. This resulted in negative amortization, where the principal balance of the loan actually grew over time. Too many lenders structured these loans so that the payments would substantially increase in five years or less when borrowers hit their negative amortization cap; underwrote the loans only to the very low introductory teaser rate; and failed to document income.

Prepayment Penalties: Many borrowers facing payment shock from increased interest rates once an introductory period ended also faced penalties when trying to refinance into a new mortgage or sell the property. These prepayment penalties are a feature associated with a higher likelihood of default (Ding et al. 2010) and were present in the great majority of subprime mortgages during the mortgage boom (Department of Housing and Urban Development 2010). To avoid default, the typical subprime borrower had to sell or refinance before the rate reset. Because the average borrower did not have the cash on hand sufficient to cover the prepayment penalties and refinancing fees, they had to pay them from the proceeds of the new loan. This produced ever declining equity even when home prices were rising. Once home prices declined, foreclosure risk climbed catastrophically, as these borrowers no longer had the equity needed to refinance and could not afford the higher rates.

No-Doc or Low-Doc Loans: The practice of failing to document a borrower's income and assets was also prevalent in the subprime market (Sengupta 2010). By 2006, so-called no-doc or low-doc loans made up 27 percent of all mortgages (Financial Crisis Inquiry Commission 2011). These loans without adequate documentation were frequently underwritten with inflated statements of the borrower's income (Sharick et al. 2006). Lawyers representing borrowers in predatory lending cases often found the borrower's tax returns included in the file of those who were nevertheless given no-doc or low-doc loans. Unbeknownst to these borrowers, they paid higher interests rates for the "privilege" of receiving a no-doc loan, even when they provided full documentation to the broker.

Yield Spread Premiums: The proliferation of mortgages with harmful features was driven in significant part by the use of yield spread premiums (YSPs) as a way to compensate mortgage brokers. Because YSPs paid mortgage brokers higher payments when a mortgage had a higher interest rate than the borrower qualified for, these YSPs gave mortgage brokers incentives to steer borrowers into loans that were more expensive and less stable than they qualified for. And, by 2006, mortgage brokers accounted for 45 percent of all mortgage originations and 71 percent of all nonprime mortgage originations (Essene and Apgar 2007). In fact, most borrowers who received subprime loans could have qualified for better, more sustainable loans. Many qualified for lower-cost prime loans (Brooks and Simon 2007), and those who did often would not have qualified for sustainable, thirty-year fixed-rate subprime loans with only slightly higher rates than the introductory rate on the ARM loans they were given (Coalition for Fair and Affordable Lending 2007).

No Escrows for Taxes and Insurance: Subprime lenders commonly did not escrow for taxes and insurance, attracting borrowers with the monthly payments that were deceptively low. This practice increased the risk of default when the tax and insurance bills came due and produced further equity-stripping cash-out refinancing in those cases where the borrower had the equity to cover the bills and refinancing fees and penalties. On top of the harmful loan features and lending practices, many lenders also failed to determine whether a borrower had an actual ability to repay their mortgage. Proper underwriting is particularly important for mortgages with resetting interest rates, negative amortization, or interest-only payments (or all of the above) to ensure that borrowers can afford the larger monthly payments when they kick in down the road. However, for many mortgage originators, this straightforward underwriting never happened. For example, when federal regulators proposed that lenders fully underwrite mortgages with ARMs, interest-only, and negative amortization features to the fully indexed rate and payment, Countrywide estimated that 70 percent of their recent borrowers would be unable to meet such a standard (Countrywide Financial Corporation 2007). This type of lender disregard for the borrowers' ability to afford their mortgages set them up for failure and, as a result, caused a foreclosure crisis.

The American Household Balance Sheet

Over the past decade, American families have faced strong headwinds as they have struggled to resist losing economic ground or to get ahead, even slightly. Challenges to economic stability and mobility include, but are not limited to, the precipitous loss of home equity due to a housing crash that was created by the aggressive marketing of high-risk loan products in the years leading up to the crash. The challenges have also come in the form of high unemployment and underemployment, stagnant wages for the employed, increasing nondiscretionary expenses, and limited access to responsible credit. The result is a well-documented loss of net wealth by households of all races and unprecedented wealth disparities between white households and African American or Latino households (Kochhar, Fry, and Taylor 2011).

The impact of these economic circumstances has been devastating for the typical American household. Data from the 2010 Consumer Expenditure Survey and the 2007 and 2010 Survey of Consumer Finances show that the typical American household has very little economic breathing room (Figure 2). After households pay for housing, utilities, food, health care, debt payments, and other expenses, there is just one hundred dollars left each month. Enough, perhaps, to meet expected monthly obligations, but not nearly enough to incur an unexpected expense or to save for college, retirement, or a down payment for a home purchase.

The stagnant finances of American households are no surprise given the dismal performance of the US economy since the middle of the last decade. Figure 3 shows the gross domestic product (GDP), the most commonly used metric for summarizing economic health, from 1970 to 2011 in real (inflation-adjusted) dollars and nominal (not inflation-adjusted) dollars. The

Item	Value ($)
Yearly Income (less taxes and insurance/pension contributions)	**$ 41,516**
Annual nondiscretionary expenses	37,651
• Housing (including upkeep and operation)	11,455
• Transportation	7,160
• Food	5,596
• Utilities	3,603
• Health Care	3,068
• Education (including reading)	594
• Other expenses (excluding alcohol, tobacco, entertainment)	6,175
Debt Payments (excluding mortgage and auto)	2,658
Discretionary Income	1,207
Loss in home value, 2007 to 2010	19,622
Loss in total net worth, 2007 to 2010	21,000

Note: Income, expenses, net worth, and home values from 2010 Consumer Expenditure Survey and 2007 and 2010 Survey of Consumer Finances for households in the middle income quintile in both surveys. Loss in home values is an average for those with and without holdings.

Source: 2010 Consumer Expenditure Survey and 2007 and 2010 Survey of Consumer Finances (Bureau of Labor Statistics 2012a).

Figure 2. Household balance sheet of typical American household.

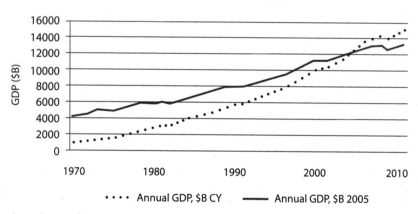

Source: Bureau of Economic Analysis 2012b.

Figure 3. Annual GDP, current year and real dollars, 1970–2011.

flat real GDP growth and slow nominal growth since 2005 stands out from the trend of generally increasing GDP of the last forty years. The 16.5 percent real growth from 2000 to 2010 is less than half the growth rate in each of the prior three decades. The data further reveal that the decline in real and nominal GDP from 2007 and 2008 to 2009 represented the first nominal decline in GDP in sixty years and the largest real decline since the Bureau of Economic Analysis (2012b) began keeping statistics in 1929.

It is no mere coincidence that the economic status of the typical American household and the entire US economy are simultaneously troubled, as 71 percent of GDP is made up of consumer expenditures on goods and services (Bureau of Economic Analysis 2012a). The economic growth in the decades preceding and in the years following the recession of 2007 to 2009 was largely driven by increases in household consumption of goods and services. In order for the US economy to grow again, individual households must find themselves in a position to increase their spending. This will be difficult as long as households continue to face stagnant incomes, increasing expenses, and declining net worth.

Declining Incomes

The wages of one or two workers fuel the economies of the typical American family. Families use their income to pay rent, to pay for food, clothing, child care, and routine and emergency medical care, to get to and from work, and to generally meet their basic needs. Those who can afford it also use their wages to fund the dream of building wealth through homeownership, to save for a retirement without hardship, or to create future opportunity for their children by sending them to college. Having incomes that keep pace with the rising costs of their basic and aspirational needs is essential to the future economic health of the American family.

Though essential to their current and future well-being, income growth and stability did not exist for American families during the last decade. It is true that the typical American household brought in more nominal income in 2010 than it did at the beginning of the last decade (see Figure 4), but all of the income growth was in the years leading up to the recession of 2007 to 2009. As Figure 4 shows, nominal incomes declined throughout the years of the recession and continued to decline as the decade concluded.

Furthermore, looking at nominal income paints too rosy a picture of the income trends American households faced during the last decade because it ignores the impact of increasing prices. When inflation is factored in (see Figure 5), the typical household really had less real income by the end of

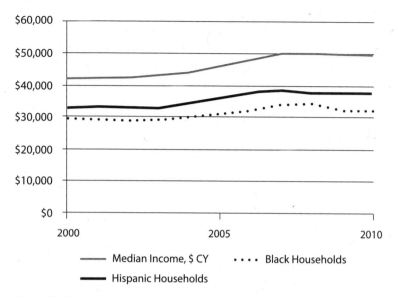

Source: US Census Bureau 2012.

Figure 4. Nominal income, 2000–2010.

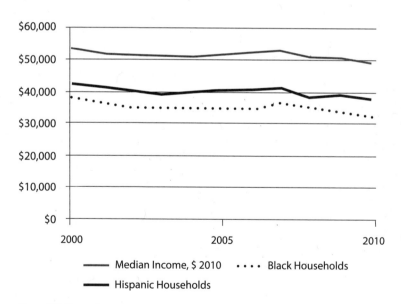

Source: US Census Bureau 2012.

Figure 5. Real income, 2000–2010.

the decade than it did at the beginning. What looked like income "growth" at the beginning of the decade, as measured in nominal dollars, was really a period of stagnant real income, and the declines at the end of the decade were more pronounced. And though workers made less and less money as the decade progressed, they produced more and more as worker productivity increased by 20 percent (Jank and Owens 2012). Thus, business owners and shareholders enjoyed the benefits of increased productivity, but workers responsible for that increased productivity did not.

Declines in wages were particularly pronounced for families of color. The income declines for African American and Latino families during the recession were greater than those of non-Latino whites. One reason is the disproportionate impact of job losses on African American and Latino workers. While, for the overall population, job gains from 2000 to 2007 were erased by the recession, African American workers lost double what they had gained during the prerecession part of the decade (see Figure 5). Industries upon which many African American and Latino workers have relied for well-paying, stable employment—namely manufacturing and construction—suffered job losses of 10 and 20 percent, respectively (see Figure 6). And while the losses in construction followed a boom in the earlier part of the decade, jobs losses in manufacturing began well before the recession.

Increasing Cost of Living and Shifting Expenditures

The flat nominal incomes of the last decade would not have been so hard on families if the cost of maintaining a household had also remained unchanged. While families would not have had resources to improve their standard of living or absorb the costs of raising a newborn or sending an older child to college, they would have at least been able to tread water by continuing to consume at the same level year after year. Instead, families were faced with increases in basic nondiscretionary expenses like food, housing, transportation, medical care, and utilities (Figure 7) with no growth or even decreases in income to pay for these items.

Education was one of the fastest-growing categories of expenses during this period, growing at over 2.5 times the rate of inflation from 2000 to 2010. And education costs are growing at a time when families are placing more and more emphasis on the value of a college degree. Virtually all Americans view a college degree as "absolutely necessary," and the average in-state tuition has doubled in the last twenty-five years, creating an expense that is equal to almost 20 percent of a family's pretax income (Warren 2004).

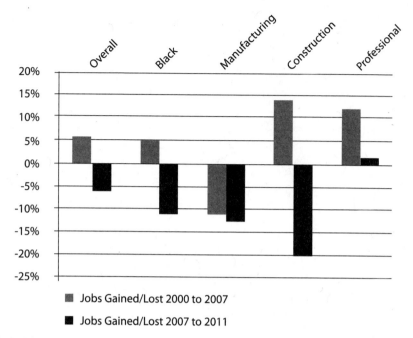

Source: Bureau of Labor Statistics 2012b.

Figure 6. Job gains/losses, 2000–2007 and 2007–2011.

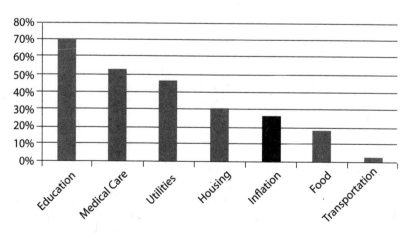

Source: Bureau of Labor Statistics 2012c.

Figure 7. Change in nominal household spending by category,
2000–2010.

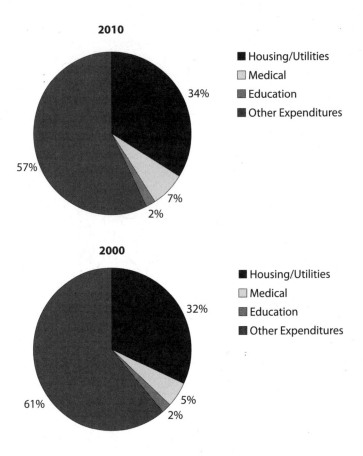

Source: Bureau of Labor Statistics 2012c.

Figure 8. Housing, utilities, medical expenses, and education
as a fraction of expenditures, 2000–2010.

Medical expenses have also increased at twice the rate of inflation. These
expenses often wreak havoc on household finances not only because they
are high but also because most are unplanned and unexpected. Harvard researchers Draut and Garcia (2010) point to evidence that shows that more
than half of all low- and middle-income households attribute a portion of
their credit card debt to medical expenses and that 60 percent of bankruptcies
are medical related.

Together, increases in the costs of medical care, education, and housing
are taking up a larger fraction of household expenses in 2010 than they did

in 2000 (see Figure 8). This has caused households to adjust and reduce their spending in other areas, such as clothing, housewares, entertainment, dining out, and personal care (Bureau of Labor Statistics 2012a).

Declining Assets

While the overwhelming majority of American household expenses are covered by wages (or Social Security or other retirement income for older Americans), households also have varying levels of assets on which to draw to assist in meeting their regular and unexpected financial obligations. These assets can be classified as either financial or nonfinancial. Nonfinancial assets, such as equity in a home or an automobile, must often be sold or liquidated in some other way (e.g., home equity line of credit) in order for the asset to be used to cover household obligations. Financial assets in the form of stock, bonds, checking or savings accounts, and various forms of retirement accounts are usually more readily available.

University of Michigan researchers Stafford, Chen, and Schoeni (2012), using 2009 and 2011 data from the Panel Study of Income Dynamics, found that the recession had the effect of depleting household assets. They found that households lost value in their homes and other financial assets and also used financial assets to deal with income loss. A review of the asset data in the Survey of Consumer Finances shows the same pattern. Figures 9 and 10 show

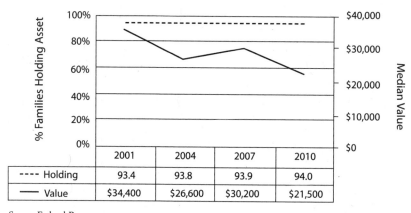

	2001	2004	2007	2010
---- Holding	93.4	93.8	93.9	94.0
—— Value	$34,400	$26,600	$30,200	$21,500

Source: Federal Reserve 2012.

Figure 9. Financial asset holdings and values, 2001–2010.

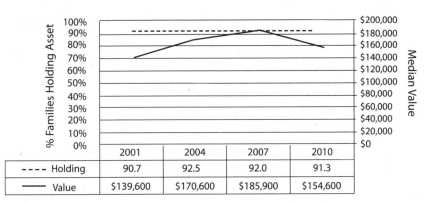

	2001	2004	2007	2010
- - - - Holding	90.7	92.5	92.0	91.3
——— Value	$139,600	$170,600	$185,900	$154,600

Source: Federal Reserve 2012.

Figure 10. Nonfinancial asset holdings and values, 2001–2010.

the trend in asset holdings and median value of held assets for the years 2001, 2004, 2007, and 2010. The data show that inflation-adjusted financial asset values have declined sharply since 2001, from $34,000 to $21,500, with the two declines from 2001 to 2004 and from 2007 to 2010 representing the largest percent and absolute declines in financial asset values since the survey began in 1989. The data also show that while nonfinancial assets increased in value through 2007, values declined sharply from 2007 to 2010.

As Figures 11 and 12 reveal, the rise and fall in nonfinancial assets from 2001 to 2010 was driven by changes in home values. The figures show how home values, in absolute terms and relative to income, increased relative to income in the years leading up to the housing crisis and then fell precipitously beginning in early 2007. In just three years, real home values plummeted by 17 percent, from a high of $185,900 in 2007 to $154,600 in 2012. The impacts have been devastating. Since housing prices began their rapid decline in early 2007, 10.9 million homes have begun or completed the foreclosure process. In addition to families that have faced the displacement and short- and long-term financial devastation that accompanies foreclosure, millions of homeowners have lost some or all of the equity they had in their homes prior to the crisis.

Increasing Debt Burdens

In the face of the combination of stagnant wages, increasing expenses, and declining assets values over the last decade, American households have responded in two ways. One way is by reducing their spending. In real, inflation-adjusted

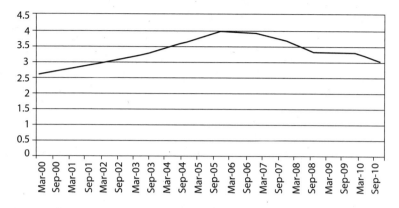

Source: Zillow Real Estate Research 2012.

Figure 11. Home prices relative to income, 2000–2010.

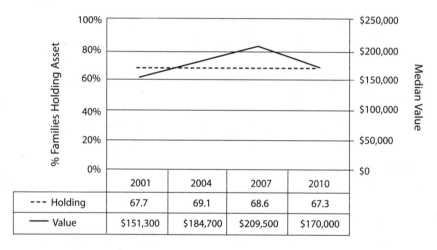

	2001	2004	2007	2010
--- Holding	67.7	69.1	68.6	67.3
— Value	$151,300	$184,700	$209,500	$170,000

Source: Federal Reserve 2012.

Figure 12. Home holdings and values, 2001–2010.

terms, the average spending of households with incomes in the middle quintile of earners declined by 5 percent, from $43,200 in 2000 to $41,200 in 2010 (Bureau of Labor Statistics 2012a). The other way households have compensated is taking on additional debt. Figure 13 shows how median household debt values increased from 2001 to 2007 and then remained flat from 2007 to 2010.

Much of the increase in debt burden came in the form of larger mortgages, as the cost for new homes skyrocketed between 2000 and 2007.

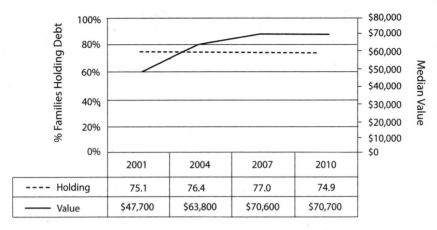

Source: Federal Reserve 2012.

Figure 13. Debt holdings and values, 2001–2010.

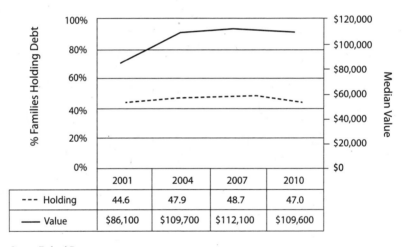

Source: Federal Reserve 2012.

Figure 14. Mortgage debt holdings and values, 2001–2010.

Figure 14 shows the increases in mortgage holdings and the size of those mortgages between 2001 and 2004. The increases from 2001 to 2004, both in the percentage of households with mortgages and the median value of those mortgages, are the largest documented three-year increases since the Survey of Consumer Finances began in 1989. And while home values declined from

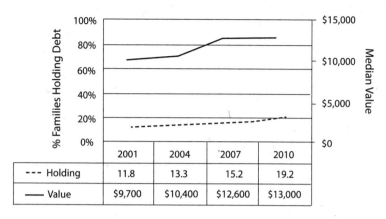

	2001	2004	2007	2010
--- Holding	11.8	13.3	15.2	19.2
—— Value	$9,700	$10,400	$12,600	$13,000

Source: Federal Reserve 2012.

Figure 15. Student loan debt holdings and values, 2001–2010.

2007 to 2010, the balance of the mortgages remained high, eating away at the net worth of American families.

Another area where debt increased dramatically is student loans. In 2001, one in eight households had an educational installment loan. By 2010, one in five had such a loan. As Figure 15 shows, over that same period, the median size of those loans increased by one-third, from $9,700 to $13,000 (Federal Reserve 2012). That student loans and mortgages accounted for much of the rise in debt levels from 2001 to 2010 is unsurprising. Despite, or perhaps because of, the trend in nonincreasing wages, families chose to incur the kinds of debts that they reasonably expected to pay off in the form of increased future earnings for college graduates and increased home values and equity. The ongoing housing and employment crises mean that these investments have yet to pay off for many who made those investments.

While student loans and mortgages are areas where households increased their levels of debt, families reduced their debt load in other areas in the years since the recession of 2007 to 2009. As Figure 16 shows, fewer households had credit card balances in 2010 than in 2001. In fact, fewer households had balances than at any other time since before 1989. The size of consumers' balances also decreased between 2007 and 2010, recording the only decrease in credit card balances since before 1989. While the credit card deleveraging occurred due to the financial crisis, Figure 17 shows how deleveraging on auto loans began earlier in the decade, as households responded to their deteriorating income situations by buying used cars instead of new ones and holding on to their cars for longer periods of time (MarketingCharts 2008).

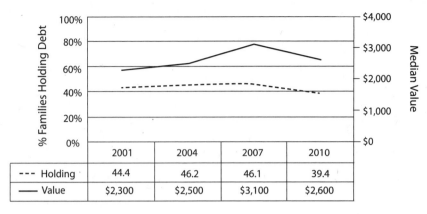

Source: Federal Reserve 2012.

Figure 16. Credit card holdings and values, 2001–2010.

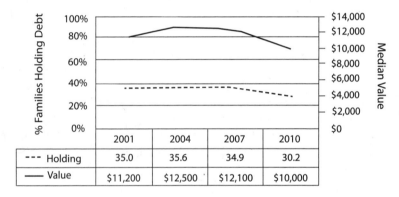

Source: Federal Reserve 2012.

Figure 17. Auto loan holdings and values, 2001–2010.

The Outcome

The result of the pattern of declining real income, increasing expenses, declining asset values, and increased mortgage and student loan debt is that
the financial health of American families deteriorated from 2000 to 2010.
Household net worth is a useful metric for summarizing the overall financial health and capacity of American families. Figure 18 shows that median
family net worth increased for all families each three-year period from 1995
through 2007, and then decreased dramatically in 2010 to pre-1995 levels.

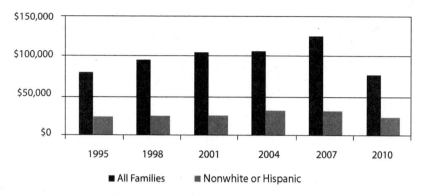

Source: Federal Reserve 2012.

Figure 18. Median family net worth by race/ethnicity.

While the Survey of Consumer Finances (used in Figure 18) provides limited data on which to compare declines for nonwhite households, the Pew Research Center used different data sources and found much larger declines in net worth for African American and Latino households as compared to white households. Pew also found that the decline in wealth from 2005 to 2009 resulted in the largest documented wealth gaps between African American and white households and between Latino and white households (Kochhar, Fry, and Taylor 2011). These net worth data reveal the ultimate outcome of the financial circumstances that households have faced in the past decade—declining net worth for all households and a disproportionate decline for African American and Latino households.

Salvaging the Lost Opportunity

The American Household Balance Sheet section of this chapter details the many reasons why African American and Latino household will struggle in the coming years to take advantage of the wealth-building opportunity presented by the affordability, safe mortgages, and projected future price-appreciation of today's housing market. However, these challenges can be alleviated with policies that promote economic growth and access to safe, affordable mortgages. First, policies that create a robust and sustained economic recovery will greatly enhance the employment and income opportunities for these families. Second, ensuring that all qualified borrowers have access to safe, affordable credit is critical. With both in place—real income gains and access to credit—there is an opportunity to avert the disaster of further-broadening wealth disparities between African American and Latino families and their white counterparts.

References

Bocian, Debbie, Wei Li, Carolina Reid, and Roberto G. Quercia. 2011. *Lost Ground, 2011: Disparities in Mortgage Lending and Foreclosures.* Durham, NC: Center for Responsible Lending. http://www.responsible lending.org/mortgage-lending/research-analysis /Lost-Ground-2011.pdf.

Brooks, Rick, and Ruth Simon. 2007. "Subprime Debacle Traps Even Very Credit-Worthy as Housing Boomed, Industry Pushed Loans to a Broader Market." *Wall Street Journal,* December 3. http://online.wsj.com/article/SB119662974358911035.html#articleTabs% 3Darticle.

Bureau of Economic Analysis. 2012a. "GDP and the Economy: Third Estimates for the First Quarter of 2012." *Survey of Current Business,* July 15. http://www.bea.gov/scb/pdf /2012/07%20July/0712_gdpecon.pdf.

———. 2012b. "GDP and the National Income and Product Account Historical Tables." Bureau of Economic Analysis. Accessed July 30. http://www.bea.gov.

Bureau of Labor Statistics. 2012a. "Consumer Expenditure Survey." Bureau of Labor Statistics. Accessed July 30. http://www.bls.gov/cex/.

———. 2012b. "Labor Force Statistics from the Current Population Survey." Bureau of Labor Statistics. Accessed July 30. http://www.bls.gov/cps/.

———. 2012c. "Current Expenditure Tables, 2000 & 2010." Bureau of Labor Statistics. Accessed July 30. http://www.bls.gov/cex/.

Coalition for Fair and Affordable Lending. 2007. Letter from the Coalition for Fair and Affordable Lending to Ben S. Bernanke, Sheila C. Bair, John C. Dugan, John M. Reich, JoAnn Johnson, and Neil Milner, January 25.

Countrywide Financial Corporation. 2007. "3Q 2007 Earnings Supplemental Presentation." Countrywide Financial Corporation, October 26.

Department of Housing and Urban Development. 2010. *Report to Congress on the Root Causes of the Foreclosure Crisis.* Washington, DC: US Department of Housing and Urban Development. http://www.huduser.org/Publications/PDF/Foreclosure_09.pdf.

Ding, Lei, Roberto G. Quercia, Wei Li, and Janneke Ratcliffe. 2010. "Risky Borrowers or Risky Mortgages: Disaggregating Effects Using Propensity Score Models." Working paper, Center for Community Capital, May 17. http://www.ccc.unc.edu/documents /Risky.Disaggreg.5.17.10.pdf.

Draut, Tamara, and José Garcia. 2010. "Moving Forward: Unfairness in Life and Lending: Credit and Low-Income Americans." Working paper, Joint Center for Housing Studies, Harvard University, August 1. http://www.jchs.harvard.edu/research/publications /moving-forward-unfairness-life-and-lending-credit-and-low-income-americans.

Essene, Ren S., and William Apgar. 2007. "Understanding Mortgage Market Behavior: Creating Good Mortgage Options for All Americans." Joint Center for Housing Studies, Harvard University, April 25. http://www.jchs.harvard.edu/sites/jchs.harvard .edu/files/mm07-1_mortgage_market_behavior.pdf.

Federal Reserve. 2012 "Survey of Consumer Finances Chartbook, 2010." Federal Reserve Bank. Accessed July 21. http://www.federalreserve.gov/econresdata/scf/files/2010_SCF_Chartbook.pdf.

Financial Crisis Inquiry Commission. 2011. *The Financial Crisis Inquiry Report: Final Report of the National Commission on the Causes of the Financial and Economic Crisis in the United States*. Washington, DC: US Government Printing Office.

Gudell, Svenja. 2012. "Comparing Price to Income Affordability across Markets." *Zillow Real Estate Research*, June 29. http://www.zillow.com/blog/research/2012/06/29 comparing-price-to-income-ratios-to-affordability-across-markets/.

Humphries, Stan. 2012. "May Case-Shiller Composite-20 Expected to Show 1% Decline from One Year Ago." *Zillow Real Estate Research*, July 27. http://www.zillow.com/blog /research/2012/07/27/zillow-forecast-may-case-shiller-composite-20-expected-to -show-1-decline-from-one-year-ago/.

Jank, Sharon and Lindsay Owens. 2012. "Inequality in the United States: Understanding Inequality with Data." *Stanford Center on Poverty and Inequality*, May.

Kockhar, Rackesh, Richard Fry, and Paul Taylor. 2011. "Pew Research Center: Wealth Gaps Rise to Record Highs between White, Blacks and Hispanics." *Pew Social Trends*, July 26. http://www.pewsocialtrends.org/2011/07/26/wealth-gaps-rise-to-record-highs -between-whites-blacks-hispanics/.

MarketingCharts. 2008. "Half of Consumers Delaying New Car Purchases, Buying Used." *MarketingCharts*, December 5. http://www.marketingcharts.com/wp/topics/automotive /more-than-half-of-consumers-delaying-new-car-purchases-or-buying-used-7075/.

Schloemer, Ellen, Wei Li, Keith Ernst, and Kathleen Keest. 2006. *Losing Ground: Foreclo-sures in the Subprime Market and Their Costs to Homeowners*. Durham, NC: Center for Responsible Lending. http://www.responsiblelending.org/mortgage-lending/research -analysis/foreclosure-paper-report-2-17.pdf.

Sengupta, Rajdeep. 2010. "Alt-A: The Forgotten Segment of the Mortgage Market." *Federal Reserve Bank of St. Louis Review* 92 (1): 55–71. http://research.stlouisfed.org /publications/review/10/01/Sengupta.pdf.

Sharick, Merle, Erin E. Omba, Nick Larson, and D. James Croft. 2006. *Eighth Periodic Mortgage Fraud Case Report to Mortgage Bankers Association*. Reston, VA: Mortgage Asset Research Institute, Inc. http://www.mortgagebankers.org/files/News/Internal Resource/42175_Final-8thAnnualCaseReporttoMBA.pdf.

Stafford, Frank, Bing Chen, and Robert Schoeni. 2012. "Mortgage Distress and Financial Liquidity: How US Families are Handling Savings, Mortgages and Other Debts Survey." Technical series paper #12-02, Survey Research Center, Institute for Social Research, University of Michigan, May. http://psidonline.isr.umich.edu/Publications /Papers/tsp/2012-02_MortgageDistress.pdf.

US Census Bureau. 2012. "Current Population Survey, Table H-9. Race of Head of House-hold by Median and Mean Income." US Census Bureau. Accessed July 30. http:// www.census.gov/hhes/www/income/data/historical/household/.

US Government Accountability Office. 2010. "Nonprime Mortgages: Analysis of Loan Per-formance, Factors Associated with Defaults, and Data Sources." GAO-10-805, report to the Joint Economic Committee, United States Congress, August. http://www.gao. gov/assets/310/308845.pdf.

Warren, Elizabeth. 2004. *The Two-Income Trap*. New York: Basic Books.

Zillow Real Estate Research. 2012. "Interactive Chart: Historical Home Price to Income Ratio and Affordability Index by Metro." Zillow Real Estate Research. Accessed August 15. http://www.zillowblog.com/research/2012/06/29/comparing-price-to -income-ratios-to-affordability-across-markets/.

6

Finding a Home for the Occupy Movement
Lessons from the Baltimore and Memphis Wells Fargo Litigation

John P. Relman[1]

MUCH HAS BEEN written about the Occupy Wall Street movement. Yet, years after the initial Occupy Wall Street protest in 2011 made headlines around the world, observers are still struggling to understand its import. What makes the task so difficult is that the Occupy movement as a whole appears incapable of definition. Broad themes run through many of the protests that have occurred over the two years since the movement began, but they are so expansive in meaning and scope—the 99% versus the 1%; economic injustice; inequalities created by corporatism and banks—that they leave us no better informed about who or what is behind the movement, the direction it is headed, and what its long-term significance might be.

The problem lies not in the movement itself, but in how we think of it. The movement initially gained prominence as a response to glaring and rapidly growing inequalities in the distribution of economic wealth and power in the United States. But within months of its arrival on the national scene with the gathering of protesters in Manhattan's Zuccotti Park, the Occupy movement had balkanized into a constellation of loosely connected protests covering a wide variety of issues and concerns. Some now describe this as a "franchised" movement, in that the disparate protest cells resemble the loose coalition found in a corporate business operation, where separately owned businesses or "franchises" within a chain enter into a contract with

---

1. The author wishes to thank Jamal Hill and Hannah Kieschnick for their invaluable research assistance in preparing this chapter.

the "franchisor" to use the same name (think of Denny's or McDonalds) for the purpose of creating brand familiarity or building customer loyalty.

One of the franchise movements that has emerged from the initial Occupy Wall Street protest is known as Occupy Our Homes. Comprised of community organizations and Occupy activists, Occupy Our Homes was formed to fight foreclosures and evictions. It has defended at-risk homeowners by pressuring banks to renegotiate mortgages and keep families in their homes. With the foreclosure crisis still unresolved in many cities, housing issues have become a natural rallying point for Occupy activists interested in addressing issues of economic injustice and unequal concentrations of wealth and power. Most important perhaps, the adversary in each of these individual foreclosure battles is the denizen of Wall Street itself—America's banking industry.

A proper understanding of the significant role that Occupy Wall Street could play in the fair housing movement requires a focus not on the Occupy movement writ large, but rather on individual franchise movements like Occupy Our Homes. With this franchise in particular, we find issues and organizing opportunities that have the potential to bring together two historically separate parts of the housing advocacy world: affordable housing activists and fair housing activists.

Since the passage of the federal Fair Housing Act in 1968, housing activists have been largely separated into two branches—those who primarily advocated for the construction and provision of safe and affordable housing for underserved communities; and those interested in removing legal or other barriers to housing for persons protected under the Act. In some cases, the causes of these two camps intersected, but mostly they ran on parallel—albeit sometimes competing—tracks. The foreclosure crisis changed all of this.

The industry behavior that caused the foreclosure crisis in the first instance was not race neutral. Banks like Wells Fargo targeted minority communities for risky, high-cost loans—even when borrowers qualified for better, lower-cost loans—because the practice was lucrative. They unloaded the risk by selling the loans on the secondary market, but kept the profit in the form of points and fees generated at the time the loans were made to consumers. They brought these loans to minority communities because these were the neighborhoods that had historically been starved for credit due to past discrimination, and which they knew would be more likely to say yes to whatever was offered. We know all of this from the litigation that the Cities of Memphis and Baltimore brought against Wells Fargo, and from the similar cases prepared against Wells Fargo by the Civil Rights Division of the Department of Justice and the States of Pennsylvania and Illinois.

The predatory practices, in turn, have resulted in significantly higher rates of foreclosure in minority neighborhoods than in similarly situated white neighborhoods. An issue of economic justice clearly has become one of racial justice. Foreclosures are not just about continued access to safe and affordable housing, but, as Wells Fargo taught us, about racial exploitation and discrimination.

This, of course, is where Occupy Our Homes finds a home in the fair housing movement. In protesting issues of foreclosure in the communities where homeowners are most likely at risk and families are struggling to stay in their homes, Occupy activists find themselves more often than not working in African American and Latino neighborhoods. Individuals who joined the Occupy movement to protest issues of economic justice—the 99% versus the 1%—are now working with, and among, people of color. An issue of economic justice has taken on a different complexion—one that looks increasingly like a civil rights issue.

Occupy Our Homes offers real hope for an infusion of important new community activism into the fair housing movement. It is here—over the critical issue of foreclosures—that the Occupy movement has a unique opportunity to bring together two historically separate camps of the fair housing movement. At the same time, Occupy holds the potential to reenergize the fair housing movement by reminding it of the potency of protests and direct action that gave birth to the modern civil rights movement.

The opportunity to seize this moment and join these movements lies before us. To do this, though, one has to understand the fundamental interconnection between racial justice and economic justice. As explained more fully in the sections below, the Wells Fargo litigation has much to teach us about this interconnection and about the opportunity for coalition building between the Occupy Wall Street and civil rights movements.

Occupy Our Homes

The initial Occupy Wall Street protest movement hit the front pages with a fury in September 2011. Within months, however, it had slumped badly, deflated by the difficulties of maintaining encampments and unified protests in multiple cities in the face of police crackdowns and opposition from local governments. Grievances were many, but a central, defining issue with a simple human story was lacking.

By the end of 2011, the missing piece for many activists involved in the original protests began to emerge: saving homes from foreclosure. George Packer (2011), writing for the *New Yorker*, first noticed the development:

> Today, members of Occupy Wall Street will fan out around Brooklyn, the rest of the city, and the country, to try to prevent foreclosures and take over vacant properties on behalf of homeless families. It seems like the beginning of a new stage in the movement, its first concerted effort since the evictions of occupiers in New York and other cities.

Within four months, saving homes had become its own franchise movement, identified by a website bearing the name "occupyyourhomes." On April 9, 2012, *Reuters* reported that Occupy activists in eleven states across the country had taken up foreclosure fights with rallies, home occupations, and even court appearances. Citing one activist, the article asserted that "more than 100 Occupy groups had taken direct action or formed foreclosure working groups" (Carey 2012).

The reason for the resurgence around saving homes from foreclosure was clear. As one Occupy Los Angeles activist put it, "This cause . . . brings together everything that we are fighting against—corporate greed, bank bail outs, a corrupt judiciary and corrupt government" (Carey 2012). If the movement had lost some of its initial punch, the *Reuters* article noted, "focusing on an issue that affects the working class and leaves people feeling alienated is potentially a good strategy" (Carey 2012).

Many of the protests to save homes were taking place in minority neighborhoods. This should not have been surprising because while millions of Americans lost their homes in the foreclosure crisis that began in 2007, minorities suffered disproportionately. In Chicago, for example, studies showed that 17 percent of homeowners in predominantly white areas were under water, while in mostly black or Hispanic areas that percentage exceeded 40 percent (Carey 2012).

For an Occupy movement that began with a public face that was largely white and middle class, taking up foreclosure as a protest issue in cities across the country necessarily brought diversity to its ranks. In some cases, as with Occupy Homes MN, the approach came from African American housing counselors seeking help for their clients in minority neighborhoods. *Reuters* reported that housing counselor Newby (who would later become a member of Occupy Homes MN) made a conscious decision to approach the Occupy movement: "The African American community has been dealing with hardship for decades. But it was new for those White kids on the plaza who were falling out of the middle class for the first time" (Carey 2012).

Stories like that described by Newby were repeated around the country—in Birmingham, Atlanta, and Southeast Washington, DC. One example from Nashville illustrates the evolving black-white coalition particularly well. In February 2012, Helen Bailey, an African American Nashville resident and former civil rights activist who had marched with Dr. Martin Luther King, Jr., faced foreclosure. Occupy Nashville picked up her cause (Peck 2012). More than 105,000 individuals signed a petition demanding that JPMorgan Chase & Co. modify her loan (Occupy Nashville Housing Protection 2012). Prominent civil rights leaders Cornel West and Gary Flowers lent their support (Peck 2012.), and Occupy Nashville staged large rallies in front of the JPMorgan Chase offices in Nashville, mocking the advertisements that touted the bank's commitment to Dr. King's legacy. The protest resulted in an agreement that allowed Ms. Bailey to stay in her home for the rest of her life.

The organizing gains that the Occupy Our Homes strategy brought to the broader Occupy movement were evident to activists struggling for ways to keep the movement current and topical. What had started as an "impromptu battle" was now becoming a "long-term strategy" (Carey 2012). As Tim Franzen of Occupy Atlanta put it, "This is a strategy to generate tangible wins and build a broader base for the movement. You don't have to go to a park downtown to make a difference. You go two doors down and help your neighbor" (Carey 2012).

The evolution from Occupy Wall Street to Occupy Our Homes was organic. The decision to rally around foreclosures and the racial diversity it brought to the movement was not so much planned, as it just happened. But neither the decision to focus on foreclosures nor the change in demographic support happened without reason. The decision to rally around foreclosures made sense from an organizing perspective. The broadening of the movement as a result of a new focus on foreclosures had to do with the intersection of race and economic injustice; the relationship of segregation to rates of foreclosure; and the continuing effect that structural racism plays in determining where good money is invested and where it is not.

To understand why this is the case—and the broader implications that the Occupy Our Homes movement has for the fair housing and civil rights movements—requires a closer look at the Wells Fargo fair lending litigation and the tensions that have historically existed within the fair housing movement.

The Wells Fargo Fair Lending Litigation

The Divide within the Fair Housing Movement

The connection between poverty and discrimination is both obvious and undeniable. One does not have to look beyond the most basic census data from any major metropolitan statistical area to appreciate this truth. Yet, for many years following passage of the Fair Housing Act in 1968, fair housing advocates focused exclusively on issues of discrimination—striking down legal barriers to housing—while paying little attention to problems surrounding the supply and availability of affordable housing. The latter was left largely to neighborhood Legal Service providers and policy analysts to grapple with. The schism was reflected in the Department of Housing and Urban Development itself, which dealt with issues of discrimination and affordability through entirely separate offices that rarely spoke to each other, let alone collaborated on joint programs or enforcement efforts.

Since the 1990s, a new understanding of the importance of approaching the problems of poverty and discrimination together has emerged. A rethinking began in earnest in 1993 with the publication of Douglas Massey and Nancy Denton's (1993) seminal work, *American Apartheid: Segregation and the Making of the Underclass.* In this book, Massey and Denton chronicled the way in which residential spatial segregation in America's cities had contributed to the growth of an African American underclass that threatened to make urban poverty and racial injustice a permanent fixture of American society. Central to their argument was the evidence that "hypersegregation," or the extreme concentration of poor blacks in inner-city neighborhoods, has left many minority communities vulnerable to a socioeconomic "downward spiral" at the slightest turn in the economy (Massey and Denton 1993, 74–78, 118–30). Relying on empirical data, Massey and Denton (1993, 118–130) convincingly explained the precise manner in which spatial segregation combines negative social and economic conditions to push poor black neighborhoods beyond the threshold of stability.

The connection that Massey and Denton (1993) identified so clearly in *American Apartheid* was not new to some in the fair housing movement. Leading advocates like Chester Hartman and Philip Tegeler have worked hard through their organization, the Poverty & Race Research Action Council (PRRAC), to document the inseparable link between issues of economic and racial justice. And a number of cases, culminating in the 2009 and 2012 litigations in Westchester County, New York, and St. Bernard Parish, Louisiana, respectively, over the refusal to site affordable housing in white communities, have served to further highlight the importance of understanding how and why issues of affordable housing cannot be kept apart from traditional issues of discriminatory access.[2]

No litigation, however, so dramatically illustrated the artifice of the divide between issues of economic justice and racial justice as the fair lending litigation against Wells Fargo that was completed in July 2012. The cases brought by the Department of Justice and the Cities of Baltimore and Memphis graphically demonstrate how historic discrimination in the provision of loans results in economic exploitation. They show how and why foreclosure issues are necessarily issues of economic and racial justice. And they demonstrate how rallying around issues of foreclosure can bring together advocates on both sides of the fair housing movement—those who have focused on traditional enforcement actions in court to strike down racially discriminatory barriers to housing; and those who have focused their advocacy on access to affordable housing through community organizing, direct action, or policy solutions.

Baltimore and Memphis

Foreclosures and Subprime Lending

Like many cities across the country in 2007, Baltimore and Memphis found themselves in the grip of a burgeoning foreclosure crisis, the magnitude of which had never been seen. The crisis was due in significant part to the rapid expansion of subprime lending. Subprime lending developed in the mid-1990s as a result of innovations in risk-based pricing and in response to the demand for credit by borrowers who were denied prime credit by traditional lenders.

Prior to the emergence of subprime lending, most mortgage lenders made only "prime" loans. Prime lending offered uniformly priced loans to borrowers with good credit. Individuals with blemished credit were not eligible for these loans. Although borrowers with blemished credit might still represent a good mortgage risk at the right price, prime lending did not provide the necessary flexibility in price or loan terms to serve these borrowers (Relman 2003, 55, 64–65).

---

2. See U.S. ex rel. Anti-Discrimination Ctr. v. Westchester County, N.Y., 668 F. Supp. 2d 548 (S.D.N.Y. 2009) and Greater New Orleans Fair Hous. Action Ctr., et al. v. St. Bernard Parish, et al., No. 06-7185, 2011 WL 4915524 (E.D. La. Oct. 17, 2011).

In the early 1990s, technological advances in automated underwriting allowed lenders to predict with new accuracy the likelihood that a borrower with blemished credit would successfully repay a loan. This gave lenders the ability to adjust the price of loans to match the different risks presented by borrowers whose credit records did not meet prime standards. Lenders found that they could now accurately price loans to reflect the risks presented by a particular borrower (Senhauser and Relman 2001, 9, 15–18). When done responsibly, this made credit available much more broadly than had been the case with prime lending.

As the technology of risk-based pricing developed rapidly in the 1990s, so did the market in subprime mortgages. Subprime loans accounted for only 10 percent of mortgage loans in 1998, but grew to 23 percent within eight years (Schloemer et al. 2006, 7). By 2007, outstanding subprime mortgage debt stood at $1.3 trillion, up from $65 billion in 1995 and $332 billion in 2003 (Joint Economic Committee 2007, 4). These subprime loans allowed millions of borrowers to obtain mortgages at marginally increased prices even though their credit profiles did not qualify them for lower-cost prime loans. This opened the door to homeownership to many people, especially low-to-moderate-income and minority consumers who otherwise would have been denied mortgages. At the same time, subprime lending created opportunities for unscrupulous lenders to engage in irresponsible lending practices that resulted in loans that borrowers could not afford. This, in turn, led directly to defaults and foreclosures.

Enticed by the prospect of short-term profits resulting from exorbitant origination fees, points, and related pricing schemes, many irresponsible subprime lenders took advantage of a rapidly rising real estate market to convince borrowers to enter into loans that they could not afford. Often, this was accomplished with the help of deceptive practices[3] and promises to refinance at a later date. The abusive subprime lenders did not worry about the consequences of default or foreclosure to their business because, once made, the loans were sold on the secondary market.

As the subprime market grew, the opportunities for abusive practices grew with it. As long as housing prices continued to rise, the deleterious effect of these practices was delayed and hidden. When the real estate bubble burst in 2007, the inevitable occurred, and foreclosure rates began their dramatic rise. Bent on maximizing short-term profits and protected by the ability to sell their loans on the secondary market, irresponsible subprime lenders left

---

3. See Hargraves v. Capital City Mortgage Corp., 140 F. Supp. 2d 7, 16–21 (D.D.C. 2000).

countless homeowners saddled with unaffordable mortgage debts and no way to save their homes in a declining housing market.

Foreclosure Disparities in Minority Neighborhoods

Nationwide, the impact of the foreclosure crisis has been felt most acutely in minority communities. From 2000 to 2008, subprime borrowers of color lost between $164 billion and $213 billion, reflecting the fact that people of color are more than three times as likely as whites to have high-cost, sub-prime loans (Rivera et al. 2008, vii). According to a report released by the Pew Research Center, between 2005 and 2009, foreclosures resulted in a 66 percent and 53 percent loss of median net household worth for Hispanics and African Americans, respectively, compared to a 16 percent loss of median net household worth for whites (Kochhar et al. 2011).

The Cities of Baltimore and Memphis are no exception. In Baltimore, for example, as of the end of 2007, census tracts that were above 80 percent African American accounted for 49 percent of Baltimore's foreclosure filings even though these same tracts accounted for only 37 percent of the City's owner-occupied households.[4] In Memphis, as of the end of 2009, census tracts above 80 percent African American accounted for 40.9 percent of all foreclosure filings although these tracts accounted for only 24.4 percent of owner-occupied households (Powell 2009; Rugh and Massey 2010).[5]

Many housing advocates point to the practice of reverse redlining as a major cause of this nationwide disparity. As used by Congress and the courts, the term "reverse redlining" refers to the practice of targeting residents in certain geographic areas for credit on unfair terms due to the racial or ethnic composition of the area. In contrast to redlining, which is the practice of denying prime credit to specific geographic areas because of the racial or ethnic composition of the area, reverse redlining involves the targeting of an area for the marketing of deceptive, predatory, or otherwise deleterious lending practices because of the race or ethnicity of the area's residents. This practice has repeatedly been held to violate the federal Fair Housing Act.[6]

Reverse redlining typically flourishes in cities where two conditions are met. First, the practice afflicts cities where minorities historically have been

---

4. Complaint at ¶ 34, Mayor & City Council of Baltimore v. Wells Fargo Bank, N.A., No. 1:08-cv-00062 (D. Md., filed Jan. 8, 2008) ("Baltimore Complaint").

5. Am. Complaint at ¶ 54, City of Memphis and Shelby County v. Wells Fargo Bank, N.A., et al., No. 2:09-cv-02857-STA-cgc (W.D. Tenn., filed Apr. 7, 2010) ("Memphis Complaint").

6. See, e.g., Barkley v. Olympia Mortgage Co., 2007 WL 2437810 (E.D.N.Y. Aug. 22, 2007); Hargraves v. Capital City Mortgage Corp., 140 F. Supp. 2d 7 (D.D.C. 2000).

denied access to credit and other banking services. The legacy of historic discrimination, or redlining, often leaves the residents of minority communities desperate for credit and without the knowledge or experience required to identify loan products and lenders offering products with the most advantageous terms for which they might qualify. Instead, residents of underserved minority communities often respond favorably to the first offer of credit made without regard to the fairness of the product. This makes them especially vulnerable to irresponsible subprime lenders who, instead of underwriting carefully to ensure that the loans they offer are appropriate for their customers, engage in unscrupulous lending practices.

Second, reverse redlining arises in cities where there are racially segregated residential living patterns. This means that the people who are most vulnerable to abusive lending practices are geographically concentrated and therefore easily targeted by lenders.

Both of these conditions are present in Baltimore and Memphis. Baltimore's minority communities historically have been victimized by traditional redlining practices. Through much of the twentieth century, the federal government, mortgage lenders, and other private participants in the real estate industry acted to deny homeownership opportunities and choices to the City's African Americans (Power 1983, 319, 322).[7] The practice and effects of widespread redlining in Baltimore persisted for decades. An analysis of data from the 1980s, long after much of the institutionalized governmental and corporate apparatus of discrimination had been dismantled, found that the more African American residents in a Baltimore neighborhood, the fewer mortgage loans and dollars the neighborhood received (Shlay 1987). The same study also found that while 73 percent of majority white census tracts received a medium or high volume of single-family mortgage loans, the same was true of only 5 percent of majority African American tracts (Shlay 1987). The same is true for Memphis.[8]

Both Cities are highly segregated between African Americans and whites. For example, even though Baltimore is 64 percent African American and 32

---

7. The secretary of the Department of Housing and Urban Development admitted in 1970 that the federal government had "refus[ed] to provide insurance in integrated neighborhoods, promot[ed] the use of racially restrictive covenants," and engaged in other methods of redlining. See Thompson v. U.S. H.U.D., 348 F. Supp. 2d 398, 466 (D. Md. 2005). The federal government even published a map in 1937 titled "Residential Security Map for Baltimore" designed to facilitate private redlining by mortgage providers. See id. at 471. Mortgage lenders actively engaged in redlining for decades, treating "black and [the few] integrated neighborhoods as unstable and risky" (Power 1983, 289, 319, 322).

8. Memphis Complaint at ¶ 52.

percent white, many neighborhoods have a much higher concentration of one racial group or the other.[9] The same is also true for Memphis.[10]

The Case against Wells Fargo

Against a backdrop of mounting foreclosures and damage to African American neighborhoods, in 2008 and 2009, respectively, the Cities of Baltimore and Memphis filed suit against one particular lender with a large presence across both Cities—Wells Fargo. At the heart of the complaints rested the allegation that Wells Fargo had engaged in a pattern and practice of unfair, deceptive, and discriminatory lending practices targeted at Baltimore's and Memphis's African American neighborhoods. The complaints alleged that these practices had resulted in disproportionately high rates of foreclosure and consequent financial damage in these communities, as well as direct and continuing financial harm to each City. Wells Fargo, in short, was alleged to have engaged in a practice of reverse redlining that violated the Fair Housing Act.

Statistical Evidence

Initially, the cases were based primarily on statistical evidence. In both Cities, Wells Fargo was one of the leading lenders in terms of loan volume and number of foreclosures. But in each case, most of Wells Fargo's foreclosures were in census tracts that were more than 80 percent or 60 percent African American.[11] When one factored in the relative number of loans originated in African American neighborhoods compared to white neighborhoods, a deeply troubling fact emerged. Although many more loans were made in white areas than in African American neighborhoods, the rate of foreclosure was far higher in African American neighborhoods. These disparities were not small: In Baltimore, a Wells Fargo loan in a predominantly African American neighborhood was nearly four times as likely to result in foreclosure as a Wells

---

9. In its complaint against Wells Fargo, the City of Baltimore alleged, for example, that the African American population exceeded 90 percent in East Baltimore, Pimlico/Arlington/Hilltop, Dorchester/Ashburton, Southern Park Heights, Greater Rosemont, Sandtown-Winchester/Harlem Park, and Greater Govans, and exceeded 75 percent in Waverly and Belair Edison. At the same time, the complaint alleged that the white population exceeded 80 percent in Greater Roland Park/Poplar, Medfield/Hampden/Woodberry, and South Baltimore, and exceeded 70 percent in Cross-Country/Cheswolde, Mt. Washington/Coldspring, and North Baltimore/Guilford/Homeland. Third Am. Complaint at ¶ 34, Mayor & City Council of Baltimore v. Wells Fargo Bank, N.A., No. 1:08-cv-00062-JFM (D. Md., filed Oct. 20, 2010) ("Baltimore TAC").

10. Memphis Complaint at ¶ 51.

11. Baltimore TAC at ¶ 37; Memphis Complaint at ¶ 4.

Fargo loan in a predominantly white neighborhood. In Memphis, the same disparity ratio was closer to seven to one.[12]

Wells Fargo's foreclosure rate disparities were significantly higher than their competitors' and could not be readily explained by responsible underwriting practices. The advent of automated underwriting had, by the early 2000s, brought a science to the underwriting process that had not been seen before. Using sophisticated risk assessment tools and relying on traditional underwriting criteria such as FICO scores, debt-to-income ratios, loan-to-value ratios, and cash reserves, any lender engaged in responsible underwriting practices designed to identify qualified borrowers could predict with statistical certainty the likelihood of default or delinquency. Lenders engaged in marketing loans in a fair and responsible manner should have had no difficulty sifting out unqualified borrowers or borrowers whose loans would likely result in delinquency, default, or foreclosure. If the relevant information about the borrower's qualifications was not available, a lender would not extend credit. The science of underwriting—the ability to predict default and delinquency—is what banks like Wells Fargo pride themselves on. Statistically, therefore, it made no sense why Wells Fargo would be four or seven times more likely to get it wrong in African American neighborhoods than in white neighborhoods.

Foreclosure disparity ratios were consistent with what the statistical evidence showed about the types of loans made in minority and white communities. In each City, Wells Fargo's African American customers were far more likely to receive high-cost or subprime loans. In 2006, for example, 65 percent of Wells Fargo's African American customers in Baltimore received a subprime loan compared to 15 percent for white customers. In 2005, the respective rates were 54 percent and 14 percent. In Memphis, from 2004 to 2008, 63 percent of Wells Fargo's African American borrowers received a high-cost loan compared to 26 percent of white borrowers.[13]

The statistical evidence also showed that a significantly higher percentage of the loans made by Wells Fargo in Baltimore's and Memphis's African American neighborhoods involved the notorious "3/27" or "2/28" product.[14] Regulators have come to learn that these "teaser" products were involved in many foreclosures because lenders used them to entice borrowers into an adjustable rate mortgage with promises of a low, fixed "teaser" rate for the first two or three years of the loan term. (Hence the "3/27" or "2/28"

---

12. Memphis Complaint at ¶ 5.
13. Ibid. at ¶ 120.
14. Baltimore TAC at ¶ 82; Memphis Complaint at ¶ 130.

name—a fixed low rate for two or three years followed by twenty-seven or twenty-eight years at an adjustable rate.) Wells Fargo qualified borrowers at the low teaser rate, with promises to refinance after the teaser term expired based on the expectation of rising property values. No contingency was made for the possibility that property values might flatten or drop (as they did in 2007), refinancing might become impossible, and the borrower might face steep increases in monthly mortgage payments when the teaser rate ended and the loan rate floated with the market.

Ex-Employee Testimony

Shortly after Baltimore and Memphis filed suit, former employees of Wells Fargo came forward with stunning testimony that confirmed exactly what the statistics showed. In Baltimore, long-time Wells Fargo employees Beth Jacobson and Tony Paschal—both loan officers—explained precisely how Wells Fargo targeted African American neighborhoods in Baltimore for predatory, subprime loans. The testimony garnered national attention because it explained in graphic detail how Wells Fargo steered borrowers who qualified for low-cost prime loans into expensive subprime products.

According to Jacobson and Paschal, Wells Fargo deliberately targeted African American zip codes and churches with African American congregations for predatory products and practices. Employees were assigned to marketing teams based on their race. Paschal testified that African American borrowers were referred to as "mud people;" with the "N" word; and as "those people [who] have bad credit" and "don't pay their bills."[15] According to Paschal, loans to African Americans were referred to as "ghetto loans."[16] Paschal produced a copy of a marketing software program that Wells Fargo employees were encouraged to use in marketing products. The program included a drop-down menu with a selection for "language." One of the selections was "African American."[17]

In the early 2000s, Jacobson was one of Wells Fargo's top producing subprime loan agents. Jacobson testified that many African American borrowers who qualified for prime loans were deliberately steered into more costly subprime loans. The reason for this was simple: both Wells Fargo and the loan officers made more money on subprime loans than prime loans because the company's profit was realized at the time the borrower closed on the loan through the payment of higher points and fees. In fact, Jacobson explained,

---

15. Baltimore TAC at ¶ 56.
16. Ibid.
17. Ibid. at ¶ 55.

a prime agent (defined as a loan officer who dealt with prime loan customers) could make more money from the 40 percent commission received by referring one of her customers to a subprime agent (like Beth Jacobson) to be placed into a subprime loan than she could from the 100 percent commission she received if she put her prime customer into a prime loan. This was because the points and fees, upon which the commission was based, were so much higher with a subprime loan than a prime loan. Once the profit was realized, Wells Fargo did not worry about the risk of foreclosures because it sold the loan—and all of the underlying risk—to the secondary market (e.g., Wall Street, Fannie Mae, or Freddie Mac).

Loan officers had substantial discretion to steer customers into subprime loans. Jacobson explained precisely how this was done. African American borrowers were encouraged to submit a "stated income" loan even when they had income documentation. This converted the loan to a higher-priced, subprime loan product. Borrowers were told not to make down payments or to apply for a cash-out home equity loan—factors that also automatically converted the loan into a higher-priced subprime product.

And in many cases, Jacobson testified, borrowers were deliberately deceived. Wells Fargo agents falsified loan applications; told customers loan rates were "locked" when they were not; did not mention lower-cost products; lied about prepayment penalties; and qualified African American borrowers for risky loans based on teaser rates.[18] According to Jacobson, senior managers knew about these practices.[19]

Four former employees from Memphis testified to similar practices. According to Camille Thomas, a former loan processor for Wells Fargo in Memphis, loan agents worked off of lists of "leads" generated by businesses located in African American neighborhoods. Wells Fargo agents "cold-called" these individuals and encouraged them to consolidate car loans or unsecured credit card debt with a Wells Fargo loan, using their house as collateral. This, of course, placed the house at risk should the borrower fail to make a payment.

Managers pressured loan agents to make expensive subprime loans to African American customers who, in some cases, qualified for prime loans and, in other cases, could not afford the loan. Thomas testified that teaser rate loans were made without informing the borrower that the loan had an adjustable rate; documents were falsified and LTV (loan-to-value) calculations manipulated in order to qualify borrowers for loans that were larger than they

---

18. Ibid. at ¶ 67-71.
19. Ibid. at ¶ 78.

could afford; and expensive "extras" were added to loans when the borrower did not need them.[20]

Doris Dancy, a former credit manager for Wells Fargo in Memphis, explained that most of her time was spent calling leads and pressuring them to come into the office to apply for a loan. Eighty percent of the leads she was given to call were African American. Once in the office, the agents engaged in deceptive practices in order to make the loan. According to Dancy,

> We were supposed to try and refinance these individuals into new, expensive subprime loans with high interest rates and lots of fees and costs. The way we were told to sell these loans was to explain that we were eliminating the customer's old debts by consolidating their existing debts into one new one. This was not really true—we were not getting rid of the customer's existing debts; we were actually just giving them a new more expensive loan that put their house at risk.[21]

Dancy testified that she was pressured into putting customers with low credit scores and high debt-to-income ratios into loans she knew they could not afford and would not be able to pay back. These loans, she explained, violated Wells Fargo's own underwriting guidelines.[22] Managers told Dancy that African American customers could be "talked into anything," and that she should conceal the details of the loans. After six months, Dancy found herself "hating to go to work" and "crying at the end of the day." Like other former employees, she decided to leave the company rather than engage in what she considered "unethical" practices.[23]

If there were any question as to how Wells Fargo had ended up with different rates of foreclosure in African American and white neighborhoods, the testimony of these former employees provides the answer.

Procedural History—The Battle over "Standing"

Despite the power of the testimony and the statistical evidence, both cases took a long time to wind their way through the judicial process. This was

---

20. Decl. of Camille Thomas, Attach. to First Am. Compl., City of Memphis and Shelby County v. Wells Fargo Bank, N.A., et al., (Doc. No. 29-4, filed Apr. 7, 2010) at ¶ 22.

21. Decl. of Doris Dancy, Attach. to First Am. Compl., City of Memphis and Shelby County v. Wells Fargo Bank, N.A., et al., Decl. of Doris Dancy (Doc. No. 29-1, filed Apr. 7, 2010) at ¶ 6.

22. Ibid. at ¶ 9.

23. Ibid. at ¶ 16.

due in significant part to what lawyers call issues of "standing," or the right of the plaintiff to assert injury and file suit in court.

The plaintiff in each of these cases was the City itself, not the Wells Fargo borrowers who were ultimately foreclosed on. Once the cases were filed in court, Wells Fargo moved to dismiss, arguing that the Cities were not proper plaintiffs because they could not show that Wells Fargo had "caused" the foreclosures or that anything Wells Fargo had done had directly caused tangible or concrete harm to the Cities themselves, as opposed to the borrowers.

From the beginning, both Baltimore and Memphis argued that they were uniquely positioned to seek relief under the Fair Housing Act for the reverse redlining practices that Wells Fargo had engaged in. Standing to sue under the Fair Housing Act extends as broadly as Article III of the Constitution will allow; Congress and the courts have determined that there are no prudential limitations on standing.[24] The statute itself provides that any "person" aggrieved by conduct made illegal by the Act may bring suit,[25] and defines "person" to include corporations.[26] Many cities, like Baltimore, are incorporated and thus fall directly within the definition of "person" for purposes of standing. Indeed, the plaintiff in one of the Supreme Court's relatively few Fair Housing Act cases was a municipal corporation.[27] This means that where a city claims injury from the reverse redlining practices of a given lender, it has standing to pursue a federal fair housing claim against that entity.

When it comes to remedies, the Fair Housing Act is equally useful to municipal plaintiffs like Baltimore. As originally drafted in 1968, the Fair Housing Act permitted aggrieved persons to recover unlimited compensatory damages, but capped punitive damages at $1,000.[28] In 1988, the Act was amended to

---

24. See Havens Realty Corp., 455 U.S. at 372; Gladstone, Realtors v. Vill. of Bellwood, 441 U.S. 91, 103 n.9, 109 (1979); Trafficante v. Metro. Life Ins. Co., 409 U.S. 205, 209 (1972).

25. 42 U.S.C. § 3613(a)(1)(A).

26. 42 U.S.C. § 3602(d).

27. See Gladstone, Realtors v. Vill. of Bellwood, 441 U.S. 91 (1979). In the decision under review, the Seventh Circuit held that a village, as a municipal corporation, had standing as a "person" under the FHA. See Vill. of Bellwood v. Gladstone Realtors, 569 F.2d 1013, 1020 n.8 (7th Cir. 1978). The Supreme Court noted the Seventh Circuit's holding but did not address the issue because it had been raised belatedly. See *Gladstone, Realtors*, 441 U.S. at 109 n.21; see also City of Chicago v. Matchmaker Real Estate Sales Ctr., Inc., 982 F.2d 1086, 1095 (7th Cir. 1992) (Chicago had standing under FHA); Vill. of Bellwood v. Dwivedi, 895 F.2d 1521, 1525 (7th Cir. 1990) (Village of Bellwood had standing under FHA); Heights Cmty. Congress v. Hilltop Realty, Inc., 774 F.2d 135, 138–39 (6th Cir. 1985) (Cleveland Heights had standing under FHA).

28. See New Jersey Coal. of Rooming & Boarding House Owners v. Mayor & Council of City of Asbury Park, 152 F.3d 217, 223 (3d Cir. 1998) (discussing limitation on punitive damages as FHA was originally enacted).

remove the cap on punitive damages.[29] Any municipality, therefore, that brings a reverse redlining claim may seek unlimited punitive damages against a defendant lender, subject only to constitutional due process limitations having to do with the ratio of the size of punitive to compensatory damages.[30]

Damages, of course, must be proven. But here, too, the empirical and methodological foundation is strong for cities, like Baltimore, that seek to show the precise harm in dollar terms that they have suffered from the wave of foreclosures.

As a general matter, foreclosures caused by discriminatory reverse redlining practices produce multiple types of injuries to a city like Baltimore. Foreclosures result in a dramatic increase in the number of abandoned and vacant homes. Frequently concentrated in compact, clearly defined geographic areas, these abandoned properties become centers for squatting, drug use, drug distribution, prostitution, and other illegal activities. The costs to the city are enormous: increased expenditures to secure the newly abandoned and vacant homes; increased expenditures for police and fire protection; additional expenditures to acquire and rehabilitate vacant properties, where possible; and new outlays of tax dollars to fund social programs to stabilize the affected neighborhoods and deal with the homelessness, job loss, and educational needs that inevitably flow from the displacement and relocation of residents who have lost their primary (and often only) investment.

Foreclosures result in two other forms of financial damage to a city as well. First, abandoned and vacant properties in a neighborhood produce a clearly identifiable decline in the value of nearby homes, resulting in a significant decrease in property tax revenue. Cities also lose revenue from real estate transfer taxes because foreclosures depress the market for home sales. Second, there are large costs to a city associated with the processing of foreclosed properties through the city or county legal or administrative system.

Baltimore and Memphis argued that they had suffered precisely these types of injuries and that these costs were fully capable of empirical quantification. Wells Fargo contended that these injuries were speculative, hypothetical, and incapable of precise measurement.

Both cases sat for many months while judges in Baltimore and Memphis contemplated the legal arguments. In the summer of 2009, the court in Baltimore held an evidentiary hearing to determine whether the evidence

---

29. See *id.*, 223–24 (discussing 1988 amendment whereby "Congress eliminated the $1,000 cap on punitive damages").

30. See, e.g., State Farm Mut. Auto. Ins. Co. v. Campbell, 538 U.S. 408, 424–428 (2003); BMW of N. America, Inc. v. Gore, 517 U.S. 559, 580-83 (1996).

was sufficient to allow the case to establish standing and allow the case to proceed. In early August 2009, the court held that the plaintiffs had met their burden and established standing. But, in an unexpected turn of events, the judge who had presided over the case recused himself from the proceedings and the matter was referred to a different judge who nearly two years (and many motions and briefs) later, in April 2011, ultimately ruled that the City of Baltimore had met its burden with respect to standing and could proceed with the case.

Despite being filed later, the Memphis litigation proved to be on a similar track. Shortly after the court ruled for the City of Baltimore in April 2011, the court in Memphis held in May 2011 that the City of Memphis had established standing and could proceed with its case as well.

The Government Litigation against Wells Fargo

Time did not stand still for Wells Fargo while the Baltimore and Memphis cases sat waiting for a decision. Aware of the evidence in Baltimore and apprised of the testimony given by Wells Fargo's former employees, the Civil Rights Division of the US Department of Justice had opened a fair lending investigation of Wells Fargo by May 2009. Investigations were also underway in the States of Illinois and Pennsylvania, culminating in the filing of suit by both States later in 2009 and 2010. The two state enforcement actions accused Wells Fargo of the very same reverse redlining and discriminatory pricing practices alleged in the Baltimore and Memphis cases.

In the summer of 2011, the Federal Reserve announced that it had concluded a national investigation of Wells Fargo's lending practices, finding that the bank had steered borrowers who qualified for prime loans into more expensive subprime products and falsified loan applications. The Federal Reserve imposed an $85 million fine on Wells Fargo, along with an order for the bank to provide restitution to injured borrowers. The fine itself is the largest the Federal Reserve has ever ordered in a consumer enforcement case. The amount of restitution Wells Fargo may have to pay in addition to the fine could reach $200 million (Federal Reserve 2011).

In the spring of 2012, Wells Fargo revealed that the Justice Department had authorized the filing of a lawsuit against the bank for fair lending violations, and shortly thereafter, in July 2012, the Justice Department, the States of Pennsylvania and Illinois, and the Cities of Baltimore and Memphis reached a global resolution of their fair lending cases against Wells Fargo.

The terms of the resolution are historic in nature. Under the Consent Order resolving the Justice Department case and the two brought by the

States of Pennsylvania and Illinois, Wells Fargo agreed to pay $125 million in compensation to more than thirty-four thousand African American and Hispanic borrowers located in thirty-six states whom the government determined were either qualified for prime loans and steered into subprime loans or otherwise charged higher prices than similarly situated white borrowers.[31] In addition, Wells Fargo agreed to pay $50 million in down payment assistance to residents of eight cities (including Baltimore) where the government concluded Wells Fargo's conduct had resulted in significant harm to minority communities.[32]

The Consent Decree and Complaint filed by the Justice Department lays out the case against Wells Fargo. The Consent Decree reads like a guilty plea. After reviewing thousands of Wells Fargo's loan files, the Justice Department found that highly qualified African American borrowers were four times more likely to receive subprime loans than whites, and Hispanic borrowers were three times more likely to receive subprime loans than whites.[33] Between 2004 and 2009, more than thirty thousand minority borrowers paid higher fees and costs than similarly situated whites.[34] And after controlling for all relevant risk-based borrower credit characteristics, these disparities remained statistically significant.[35]

Consistent with the testimony of Beth Jacobson and other former Wells Fargo employees, the Justice Department's investigation revealed internal documents that showed senior bank officials were aware of the tactics subprime originators used to keep prime-qualified borrowers in subprime loans and to steer qualified borrowers into subprime loans.[36] Controls that had supposedly been put into place by the bank to prevent these abusive practices were manipulated.[37]

If there were any doubt about the nature or extent of Wells Fargo's discriminatory practices and the clear effect they had in contributing to the high foreclosure rate in minority communities like those identified in the Baltimore and Memphis cases, the Justice Department's three-year investigation has put those doubts to rest for all time. Wells Fargo may deny liability, but

---

31. Consent Decree at ¶ 17, United States v. Wells Fargo Bank, N.A., No. 1:12-cv-01150 (D.D.C., filed July 12, 2012) ("Consent Order").

32. Ibid. at ¶ 30.

33. Complaint at ¶ 2, United States v. Wells Fargo Bank, N.A., No. 1:12-cv-01150 (D.D.C., filed July 12, 2012) ("Dep't of Justice Complaint").

34. Ibid. at ¶ 3.

35. Ibid. at ¶ 39.

36. Ibid. at ¶ 7.

37. Ibid.

they offered no answer at the time of settlement, and to date have given none, to explain the factual disparities the Justice Department found.

At the same time that the Justice Department announced its settlement with Wells Fargo, the City of Baltimore reached a separate agreement resolving its suit with Wells Fargo. In addition to the relief that borrowers in the City of Baltimore will receive under the Justice Department settlement, the agreement with Baltimore provided the City with $7.5 million in funds for down payment assistance and other programs, as well as a commitment to make $425 million in prime loans to Baltimore borrowers, $125 million of which will be earmarked for low- and moderate-income neighborhoods. This term of the settlement is particularly important because in the years following the mortgage foreclosure crisis, the pendulum has swung far in the opposite direction; credit has dried up in minority communities. Prime loans in particular are difficult for those in minority neighborhoods to obtain.

A few weeks before the Baltimore settlement, Wells Fargo reached agreement with the City of Memphis to resolve its litigation against the bank. The terms of that settlement are similar in virtually all respects to the Baltimore settlement.

In fitting fashion, what began in Baltimore ended in Baltimore. On July 12, 2012, the day that the Attorney General announced the filing of the Consent Decree and the terms of the government's settlement with Wells Fargo, Assistant Attorney General for Civil Rights Tom Perez traveled to Baltimore to join the City's mayor in announcing the resolution of the Baltimore case. In a gracious nod to the City, the Assistant Attorney General acknowledged the important role that Baltimore had played in righting an injustice and helping the nation understand the mortgage and foreclosure crisis as a civil rights issue. Referring to the government's investigation, Perez said:

> It all started here in Baltimore City. The lawsuit filed by Baltimore City in 2008 was the catalytic force, plain and simple. When you filed this lawsuit to call attention to the devastating consequences of this crisis, you got the attention of the federal government and you got the attention of the nation. (Broadwater 2012)

Lessons for the Fair Housing and Occupy Movements

The Wells Fargo fair lending litigation offers a number of important lessons for the Occupy and fair housing movements. First, the cases underscore the connection between issues of racial justice and economic justice; segregation and exploitation; race and poverty. Wells Fargo's exploitation of the African

American neighborhoods of Baltimore and Memphis was possible only because of the legacy of discrimination in those communities. Wells Fargo was able to target those communities because of the segregated living patterns; and the bank succeeded in convincing African American borrowers to pay higher prices and accept risky loan products in significant part because they had no other option and had faced years of discrimination in the provision of prime loans. In short, economic exploitation was made possible by years of racial discrimination in lending and housing.

Second, the litigation demonstrates the potency of foreclosures as a rallying point for both Occupy and the fair housing movement. Foreclosures represent the inevitable result of the economic exploitation that Wells Fargo engaged in. But they ravaged Memphis's and Baltimore's African American communities in out-sized numbers because of racial targeting. Foreclosures, therefore, represent the injury suffered as a result of the confluence of economic exploitation and racial discrimination. They symbolize how race and poverty, segregation and exploitation, work together to compound an injury on a minority population. Foreclosures, therefore, are a perfect issue to bring the Occupy and fair housing movements together: Each has a reason to point to foreclosures as the symbol of the injury they are trying to redress or the result of a wrong (economic exploitation for Occupy, discrimination for fair housing) that they seek to remedy.

The Wells Fargo cases show that it is not just an issue that the movements now share; foreclosures mean working on the same turf. The harm from foreclosures is local. It is felt in neighborhoods and working communities. That is the reason cities like Memphis and Baltimore became plaintiffs and decided to sue Wells Fargo. But it is also the very place where Occupy Our Homes is now engaged and fair housing advocates have traditionally done their work. Occupy activists are engaged in community organizing and direct action in minority neighborhoods because that is where foreclosures are happening; fair housing advocates are involved in client work and legal action in minority communities because that is where discrimination occurs. Whether they realize it or not, the fair housing and Occupy movements will literally need to work side by side if they are serious about the issue of foreclosure.

It should also be clear from the litigation and the settlements that legal remedies have as much to do with the supply of affordable housing as with integration. New equity—in the form of down payment assistance programs or prime loans—means an increase in the supply of affordable housing and the opportunity for mobility. Returning equity to underserved communities is as much about creating housing as it is about creating hope for new investment, new renters and home buyers, new businesses, and housing choice. These are the building blocks necessary for the growth of integrated communities and lowered levels of segregation.

These twin goals—an increase in affordable housing and the promotion of integrated communities—bring together both sides of the fair housing movement. The Wells Fargo litigation shows that fair housing advocates should care about foreclosure as much as affordable housing advocates. For the same reason that Occupy Our Homes has found itself squarely involved in a civil rights issue, the cases have taught us that foreclosure is an issue that can and should be a rallying point for two sides of the fair housing movement that have not always worked together.

The lesson of Wells Fargo, then, boils down to this: Occupy Wall Street has a home in the fair housing movement. They are neighbors now, both on the issues and in the community. Foreclosure is not just an issue of equity stripping. Baltimore and Memphis teach us that it is an issue of stripping equity out of minority communities. That makes it a civil rights issue. And that is what can, and should, bring the Occupy movement and both sides of the fair housing movement together.

Moving Forward Together

Where do we go from here? There is much to be gained for both movements by working together on the issue of foreclosure. The problem is certainly not going away anytime soon. Millions of Americans remain underwater with their mortgages and are threatened by foreclosure and the prospect of losing their home. There is much to do, and too few to do it. Joining forces makes sense for many reasons.

The Occupy Wall Street movement has been criticized for losing focus and momentum since its inception in September 2011. The fair housing movement has kept its focus and its momentum intact for more than forty years. One reason is its reliance on enforcement actions in the courts—a trademark of the civil rights movement. Litigation demands focus. It rights specific wrongs. It delivers money in the form of damages. And it brings public attention and support. These are all things that Occupy could benefit and learn from. An alliance with fair housing activists would teach Occupy much about how to focus its actions in ways that will help build identity for the movement and grassroots support. It would also help to diversify its base of support, both in terms of the advocates it reaches and the strategic capital it will be able to tap.

At the same time, the fair housing movement can learn from Occupy. The civil rights movement was born in a crucible that combined protests and direct actions with a shrewd litigation strategy. Birmingham in 1964 was a battle fought on two fronts—Dr. King in the streets, Thurgood Marshall and the NAACP Legal Defense Fund in the courts. The fair housing movement has had many legal victories since, but it would benefit by remembering and reexperiencing the potency of protests and direct action. That is something Occupy can help with. Occupy Our Homes has the foot soldiers, the energy, and the physical presence in local neighborhoods to allow the fair housing movement to return to a "two-front" strategy.

If advocacy on foreclosure issues is going to be effective, joint action is necessary. Occupy activists and fair housing advocates are stronger together than apart. Occupy will learn from litigation, and the fair housing movement will benefit from a return to its roots in direct action. Both need to reach across the advocacy divide to work together in formulating strategy to protect homeowners and rebuild minority communities. Commenting on a stirring, high- profile Occupy Our Homes protest action in Minnesota on behalf of an African American homeowner, Congressman Keith Ellison said it well: "We need each other to be successful" (Dean 2012). Energetic but inexperienced activists need the wisdom and networks of established civil rights leaders and organizations. Fair housing advocates need the enthusiasm, front-line action, and attention that come with a movement like Occupy Our Homes.

There is much work to be done in building an effective coalition around the issue of foreclosures. The leading national fair housing and civil rights organizations, such as the National Fair Housing Alliance, the NAACP Legal Defense Fund, and the Leadership Conference on Civil and Human Rights, however, are no strangers to this work. Coalitions have been the key to their survival and success since the days of Dr. King.

This is an alliance whose time has come. Occupy is hard at work in communities where the fair housing movement has been for many years. Like it or not, the two movements are neighbors. It is time for each to open their doors and welcome the other in. They share a common interest and have an important issue to talk about.

References

Broadwater, Luke. 2012. "Wells Fargo Agrees to Pay $175M Settlement in Pricing Discrimination Suit." *The Baltimore Sun*, July 12.

Carey, Nick. 2012. "Occupy Wall Street Groups United Over Foreclosures." *Reuters*, April 9.

Dean, Amy. 2012. "Can Occupy Our Homes Move Congress?" *The American Prospect*, April 13.

Federal Reserve. 2011. "Press Release." *Board of Governors of the Federal Reserve*, July 20.

Joint Economic Committee. 2007. *Sheltering Neighborhoods from the Subprime Foreclosure Storm*. 110th Congress, Special Report.

Kochhar, Rakesh, Richard Fry, and Paul Taylor. 2011. *Wealth Gaps Rise to Record Highs between Whites, Blacks, and Hispanics*. Washington, DC: Pew Research Center.

Massey, Douglas S., and Nancy A. Denton. 1993. *American Apartheid: Segregation and the Making of the Underclass*. Cambridge, MA: Harvard University Press.

Occupy Nashville Housing Protection. 2012. "Chase: Don't foreclose on Helen Bailey." *Change.org*, January 9.

Packer, George. 2011. "Foreclosed Futures." *The New Yorker*, December 6.

Peck, Adam. 2012. "Occupy Our Homes Saves Former Civil Rights Activist Helen Bailey from Foreclosure." *Think Progress*, February 14.

Powell, Michael. 2009. "Minorities Affected Most as New York Foreclosures Rise." *New York Times*, May 15.

Power, Garrett. 1983. "Apartheid Baltimore Style: The Residential Segregation Ordinances of 1910–1913." *Maryland Law Review* 42: 289–328.

Relman, John P. 2003. "Taking It to the Courts; Litigation and the Reform of Financial Institutions." In *Organizing Access to Capital: Advocacy and the Democratization of Financial Institutions*, edited by Gregory D. Squires, 55–71. Philadelphia: Temple University Press.

Rivera, Amaad, Brenda Cotto-Escalera, Anisha Desai, Jeannette Huezo, and Dedrick Muhammad. 2008. *State of the Dream 2008*. Boston: United for a Fair Economy.

Rugh, Jacob S., and Douglas S. Massey. 2010. "Racial Segregation and the American Foreclosure Crisis." *American Sociological Review* 75 (5): 629–51.

Schloemer, Ellen, Wei Li, Keith Ernst, and Kathleen Keest. 2006. *Losing Ground: Foreclosures in the Subprime Market and Their Cost to Homeowners*. Durham, NC: Center for Responsible Lending.

Senhauser, William B., and John P. Relman. 2001. "Reflections on the Airlie Conference." In *The Role of Automated Underwriting in Expanding Minority Homeownership: Conference Proceedings*, edited by Fannie Mae, 9–21. Warrenton, VA: Fannie Mae.

Shlay, Anne B. 1987. *Maintaining the Divided City: Residential Lending Patterns in the Baltimore SMSA*. Baltimore: Maryland Alliance for Responsible Investment.

7

A Tale of Two Recoveries

Discrimination in the Maintenance and Marketing of REO Properties in African American and Latino Neighborhoods across America

Shanti Abedin and Shanna L. Smith

T HE FORECLOSURE CRISIS resulted in a myriad of tragedies—families lost their homes, neighborhoods became blighted by vacant and too often boarded bank-owned properties, and municipalities and boards of education became unable to rely on property tax revenues to provide basic services and opportunities for residents. Wall Street and bankers collaborated in creating and pushing high-cost predatory lending products on home buyers by providing financial incentives to loan originators and mortgage brokers to close on these toxic loan products. While millions of homeowners were subject to these types of lending schemes, African American and Latino homeowners and neighborhoods of color were targeted disproportionately.

Banks have had a long and sordid history of denying credit—especially conventional home mortgage loans—to African Americans, Latinos, and female-headed households. The mortgage redlining of the past has been replaced with a new kind of discriminatory conduct—pushing unsustainable loan products such as exploding adjustable rate mortgages and interest-only loans, and providing no documentation loans to home buyers who were actually qualified for thirty-year fixed-rate loans.

The Occupy Wall Street movement repeatedly made the point that one individual is not more important than another, that each person deserves equal respect. In the context of the ongoing foreclosure recovery, it is important for the banks and the trusts that own the homes to respect every home in every neighborhood, regardless of its racial, ethnic, or economic composition. However, the quality of life and accumulation of wealth for homeowners remaining in neighborhoods of color with foreclosures has suffered dramatically. One of the major effects of the foreclosure debacle is the disproportionate concentration of vacant, bank-owned, or real estate owned (REO) properties in these communities of color. When the banks fail to do routine maintenance and professionally market REO properties, they result in an additional set of negative effects on the surrounding neighborhoods, further inhibiting revitalization of the community and exacerbating various trajectories of inequality. A vicious cycle then plays out in which those patterns of inequality create even more problems for those neighborhoods and more challenges to their recovery. The Occupy movement protesters focused on inequality for good reason.

The National Fair Housing Alliance (NFHA) has undertaken a deep and extensive investigation of the current practices shaping the REO market today. With mortgage default and foreclosure numbers only projected to increase by millions over the coming years, civil rights concerns are more important than ever in order to help reestablish homeownership in African American and Latino neighborhoods across the United States.

NFHA's nationwide investigation has uncovered deeply troubling patterns of neglect and mistreatment of REO homes in communities of color. Consistently, homes in predominantly white communities are clean, well-presented with manicured lawns, and marketed with professional "For Sale" signs and flattering photos on the multiple listing services or the bank's website. By contrast, the REO properties in predominantly nonwhite neighborhoods have missing "For Sale" signs, overgrown lawns and shrubs, and unsecured or broken doors and windows, creating a condition that attracts vandalism and dumping of trash. This not only creates blight in once vibrant homeowner communities but also deters families from purchasing REO homes in communities that desperately need new homeowners to recover. The poor maintenance and marketing also makes the REOs targets for investor purchases, resulting in absentee landlords that further harms recovery. One result of this investigation and research has been the resolution of NFHA's housing discrimination complaint against Wells Fargo Bank. As part of a US Department of Housing and Urban Development (HUD) conciliation agreement, Wells Fargo Bank made a commitment to more equitably and more aggressively maintain and market its REO properties.

This chapter will outline NFHA's (2012) findings of an investigation of over one thousand REO properties in nine metropolitan regions and will provide concrete actions that banks, regulators, local governments, and other community stakeholders must undertake in order to ensure real and concrete changes in the disposition of REO properties. Discrimination in lending and foreclosure practices defined the housing crisis and devastated neighborhoods and communities all over the country; we must eliminate discrimination in REO maintenance and marketing in order to prevent it from shaping our recovery as well. The Fair Housing Act is the perfect legal tool to address the differential treatment of REO homes because of the racial or ethnic composition of the neighborhood in which the REO is located. Mirroring the way the Occupy movement took root in cities across the country to highlight inequity, NFHA invited other fair housing centers working at the local level to collaborate in a widespread effort to identify the nature and extent of the problem and develop strategies to help neighborhoods recover.

It's the Law: REO Maintenance and the Application of the Fair Housing Act

Senators Walter Mondale (D-MN) and Edward Brooke (R-MA) first introduced a fair housing bill in 1965, but there was little support for promoting residential integration and even less support for challenging rental or real estate companies that denied apartments or homes for sales to African Americans. In fact, the Fair Housing Act was only revived in 1968 because of the civil unrest following the assassination of Dr. Martin Luther King, Jr. on April 4, 1968. President Lyndon B. Johnson reached out to Mondale and Brooke to resurrect their open housing legislation, but the administrative enforcement mechanism in the legislation was watered down in compromises to get it passed quickly. Seven days later, President Johnson signed the Civil Rights Act of 1968, commonly referred to as the Fair Housing Act (FHA).

In 1988, Congress amended the law to give HUD and the Department of Justice (DOJ) a much-needed federal enforcement mechanism. The Fair Housing Amendments Act supported the funding for both private fair housing agencies and state and local government human rights agencies to enforce access to housing regardless of a person's race, color, religion, sex, religion, familial status, or disability.

The FHA has two goals: to eliminate housing discrimination and to promote residential integration. HUD's regulations interpreting the Fair Housing Act state:

> It shall be unlawful because of race, color, religion, national origin, sex, familial status or disability to restrict or attempt to restrict the choices of a person by word or conduct in seeking, negotiating for, buying or

renting a dwelling so as to perpetuate segregated housing patterns, or to discourage or obstruct choices in a community, neighborhood or development.[1]

The differing maintenance of REO properties based on the racial composition of neighborhoods is a violation of the FHA.

- HUD's regulations clearly state that "failing or delaying maintenance or repairs of sale or rental dwellings because of race" is a prohibited action under the FHA.[2]

- Steering by real estate agents based on neighborhood racial composition is illegal and other behavior in the housing sale or rental market that operates to discourage potential buyers from purchasing or renting homes in minority neighborhoods, such as by failing adequately to maintain properties in minority neighborhoods, can also violate the act.

- In addition, the FHA makes it unlawful to "make unavailable or deny" housing to any person because of race.[3] If the poor maintenance of an REO property in a minority neighborhood makes it difficult for a potential purchaser to obtain a mortgage loan for the property, the poor maintenance has made the housing "unavailable" within the meaning of the act.[4]

If the federal government, especially the financial regulators, had responded to the foreclosure crisis promptly and provided the necessary oversight and regulation of Wall Street, it is likely that some of these fair housing concerns could have been mitigated. Civil rights advocates tried to alert the Federal Reserve and bankers to the looming crisis in April 2007 when they called for an immediate six-month moratorium on foreclosures of single-family homes in order to devise programs to modify unsustainable and toxic loans. However, the request for a moratorium fell upon deaf ears: regulators and the banking industry said advocates were exaggerating the potential for

---

1. 4 CFR 100.70 (a)
2. 24 CFR 100.65(b)(2)
3. 42 USC § 3604.
4. See N.A.A.C.P. v. American Family Mutual Insurance Co., 978 F.2d 287, 297 (7th Cir. 1992) (discriminatory insurance practices can violate § 3604 because "no insurance, no loan; no loan, no house; lack of insurance thus makes housing unavailable"). It is important to note that municipalities and neighborhood residents have standing under the act to challenge discriminatory behavior occurring in their cities and neighborhoods. Gladstone Realtors v. City of Bellwood, 441 U.S.91 (1979).

deep economic harm, and Federal Reserve Chairman Ben Bernanke argued the crisis would be limited to the subprime market.[5]

Devastating Wealth Loss in Communities of Color

The Center for Responsible Lending (CRL) reported that for mortgages originated between 2004 and 2008, African American and Latino borrowers were over twice as likely as white borrowers to have one or more "high risk" features or conditions in their loans. Such features included higher interest rates, option adjustable rate mortgages (ARMs), or prepayment penalties (Bocian, Li, and Ernst 2010, 8).

Latinos and African Americans have seen their net worth plummet. According to a 2011 study by the Pew Research Center, the foreclosure crisis has had a larger effect on African Americans and Latinos. Between 2005 and 2009, Latino families and African American families lost 66 percent and 53 percent of their household wealth, respectively. This compares to a 16 percent drop in wealth for white households. The bulk of this decline in net worth is attributed to the loss of home equity (Kochhar, Fry, and Taylor 2011, 4).

But the resulting disproportionate concentration of REO properties is detrimental even to those who have been able to make mortgage payments and stay in their homes. Substantial research exists documenting the spill-over effects of foreclosures on nearby properties—a field of research that has become increasingly important as the foreclosure crisis worsens. This body of research as a whole strongly suggests that visible deterioration, maintenance, and vandalism often paired with vacant REO properties is linked to a decline in neighborhood property values and declines in investment in the neighborhood by those still in their homes (Immergluck and Smith, 2005a).

The drastic decline in the housing market has ushered in a loss of home-ownership among people of color in particular; and with this comes the loss of billions of dollars of wealth in the form of home equity. Not only do individuals of color suffer from major losses by way of lower credit scores, higher costs, and limited availability of future credit and the major disruption of

---

5. On April 4, 2007, NFHA and other national civil rights groups, including the Leadership Conference on Civil and Human Rights, the NAACP, the National Council of La Raza, and the Center for Responsible Lending held a news conference and called for mortgage lenders, loan servicers, and loan investors to institute an immediate six month moratorium on subprime home foreclosures resulting from reckless and unaffordable loans in the subprime market.

losing a home, their neighbors and communities at large suffer as well, many of whom may be underwater in their mortgages.

Conservative estimates of property value decline for properties within the same block as an REO property are around 0.9 percent. This increases in low- and moderate-income areas, where this decline averages around 1.44 percent (Immergluck and Smith 2005a, 3). CRL estimates that 1.95 trillion dollars in property value has been or will be lost by homeowners in neighborhoods where foreclosures have occurred and that over one-half of this lost wealth is associated with communities of color (Bocian, Smith, and Li 2012, 2). In communities where there are two or more REO properties on one block, a common occurrence in the wake of the foreclosure boom, this wealth loss is only amplified.

Erosion of the Property Tax Base and High Costs to Municipalities

Additionally, local municipalities must bear heavy costs to handle poorly maintained REO properties. The neglect of REO properties results in direct increased expenditures for municipalities, which are burdened with the expenses incurred from increased policing and firefighting services, demolition contracts, building inspections, legal fees, and other expenses associated with nuisance abatement.[6] Often, municipalities also provide lawn maintenance and other time-consuming and costly property care. One Chicago-based study calculated the concrete costs to municipalities of five distinct foreclosed properties. The least expensive case cost the municipality $430 to secure the house in the short term until it was sold. However, on the other extreme, a fire-damaged abandoned property cost the municipality $34,199 (Apgar and Duda 2005, 24–28). Even when costs to municipalities are on the lower end of the spectrum, they quickly become unsustainable as the number and concentration of REO properties grow.

As municipalities struggle to cover these additional costs, they are also constrained by a corresponding lack of resources. High numbers of REO properties erode their property tax bases, reducing local government revenue that is normally available not only to address the problems presented by the poorly maintained vacant homes but also to provide the city with other valuable services.

---

6. See complaint, People of the State of California v. U.S. Bank Natl. Assoc., et al., No. BC488436, Cal. Super. (2012).

Neighborhoods that were once stable are also seeing an increase in safety concerns as the number of poorly maintained REO properties that sit vacant increases. Boarded and badly maintained REO properties become targets for vandalism, theft, and looting, and the neighborhoods in which they are located see increases in dumping, rodents, squatters, and criminal and drug-related activities. Poorly maintained, unsecured homes are more likely to attract increased criminal activity and require more policing and nuisance abatement (Immergluck and Smith 2005b, 5–6).

Municipalities, neighbors, and neighborhood organizations have standing to file administrative or legal complaints under the FHA because they can document economic injury as a result of the failure of banks to maintain and market the REOs owned or serviced by them.

REO Maintenance Overview

During the foreclosure process, properties that are unoccupied and not located in states with redemption laws are generally maintained by the servicer of the loan to a standard outlined by the lender or owning entity. These standards require keeping the home in compliance with local ordinances to protect its value and include actions such as mowing lawns and removing trash at a minimum. The servicer is also responsible for paying taxes, holding a valid homeowners insurance policy, and paying homeowners association fees and related expenses.

Once foreclosure proceedings are completed, the home becomes real estate owned by a bank, the Federal Housing Administration, or a government-sponsored enterprise (GSE) such as Fannie Mae or Freddie Mac. Each institution utilizes its own particular system for maintaining an REO. Many companies contract with a real estate broker who is responsible for marketing and selling the home and either a local, regional, or national vendor who is tasked with the maintenance of the home. The broker or vendor may be required to oversee securing the property, assessing the value of property, subcontracting with a preservation maintenance provider, and developing a marketing strategy for selling the property.

In many models, the real estate broker or vendor is also responsible for requesting interior and exterior repairs and providing the bank with a list of items that need repair or replacement to increase the market value for the home. Too often, these brokers and maintenance vendors are not local and are unfamiliar with the community, community organizations, and local government redevelopment programs where the REO is located. This may be problematic when it comes to determining the proper pricing, marketing strategies, and maintenance of the REO. In other models, the decision to make further repairs or other investments in the property above that which is necessary to meet public safety and health guidelines is executed within the bank. There exists no documentation or internal analysis of the difference in quality and number of repairs made based on the racial or ethnic economic composition of the neighborhood in which the REO is located.

Though the specific models of maintenance and marketing may vary, routine yard maintenance, property protection, trash removal, and general upkeep are generally contracted to a property maintenance and preservation company or asset management company. This contractor may be a national company that subcontracts at the regional, state, or local level, or—in some limited situations—may be a local small business that works directly within the lender's network of vendors. Typically, these vendors are expected to visit the property weekly and conduct maintenance to ensure that the REO property complies with local building and public safety standards. Lenders *repeatedly* state that they expect their REO to look as good or better than the other homes in the neighborhood.

Homes that appear vacant and look unsightly due to poor maintenance will often deter real estate agents from showing the REO to home buyers, but creates an investor market demand and a decline in home prices.

Banks May Fail to Maintain REOs Based on Faulty Principles

A bank's failure to adequately maintain an REO property may be due to a false perception of the home's actual value or the bank's erroneous assumptions about a potential return on its investment. Such assumptions could be based upon an inaccurate appraisal of the property's market value or biased perceptions about the neighborhood because of its racial composition. The stigma suffered by neighborhoods of color from banks, real estate agents, and preservation maintenance workers contributes to the lowering of sales prices and pushing homes to investors for cash sales.

Banks select real estate companies to sell the REOs, and the real estate agents receive REO listings based in large part on the time it takes them to sell the home. The shorter the time span, the more REOs the real estate agents receive from the bank. This practice creates a strong incentive for the agent to find an investor who will pay cash and close a deal quickly rather than working with community development corporations, housing counseling agencies, local community groups, and the government to identify owner-occupant buyers.

Incentive structures for real estate agents to prioritize the REOs time listed on the market over its actual sales price and sale to an owner-occupant have an extremely detrimental impact on the values of the surrounding homes. Additionally, an agent typically recommends price reductions twenty days after listing and more reductions each week until the price brings in an investor. Since REOs are not professionally marketed in the same manner in communities of color, owner-occupant buyers lose a competitive edge to purchase. Moreover, these practices may have extremely harmful outcomes for communities of color

Methodology

To date, NFHA and its members have investigated REO maintenance practices in twenty metropolitan areas; selecting neighborhoods with either predominantly white residents or neighborhoods that were predominantly Latino, African American, or a combination of both (NFHA 2012). These neighborhoods were also selected because their recent foreclosure rates were high in comparison to other neighborhoods in the same metropolitan area. Because this was an enforcement-based investigation and not a research study, data collection was not limited to a random sampling of the REO properties in each neighborhood. Rather, *all* target lender-owned properties within zip codes selected based on their racial makeup and foreclosure rates were visited and, when vacant, evaluated. Thus, in the targeted zip codes, all REOs listed in public records as owned by the bank were evaluated.

Once the target neighborhoods were identified, data providing the addresses of REO homes, as well as the banks listed as the owners of the homes, were collected in each of the areas. These lists were compiled using county property records, records kept by the clerk of courts, RealtyTrac, and other database sources. Several banks were identified as the major owners of REO properties in the subject communities and thus became the focus of the investigation.

Upon visiting the property, staff evaluated each property using an evaluation form that included over thirty factors under seven major categories: curb appeal, structure, signage and occupancy, paint and siding, gutters, water damage, and utilities. Evaluators answered "yes" or "no" to indicate whether each of these factors was or was not present on the property, and took pictures of the property and surrounding area. For example, next to "Trash" on the score sheet, the evaluator would mark "yes" if there was a visible amount of trash on the REO property, which would then translate into a deduction from the overall score. A lack of certain criteria, like a missing "For Sale" sign, also would constitute a deduction.

To ensure consistency, evaluators were trained extensively on-site and utilized a glossary of terminology developed by NFHA and its partners using pictures and descriptions to illustrate various examples that would constitute a "yes" answer for each of the components needed to score the properties. The data and pictures were uploaded into a central database that was used to assign a score and document deficiencies to the REO property. Each property was assigned a neighborhood designation based on the racial or ethnic makeup of the area, or Census Block Group,[7] in which the address was located. REO properties could fall into one of four neighborhood designations: (1) African American, (2) Latino, (3) white, or (4) predominantly nonwhite.[8] Both the overall maintenance of each property and the occurrence of deficiency or problem with a property were compared against one other.

In its first round of investigations, neighbors of the REO properties often approached staff members evaluating homes. The neighbors provided staff with accounts of their experiences and concerns regarding the REO property. In an attempt to capture some of this information, a short survey was developed that asked a few key questions about the care, maintenance, and marketing of the REO property and mailed to neighbors on either side of the REO, as well as the neighbor across the street (NFHA 2012).

Disparities in Maintenance: Overall Trends

REO Properties in White Communities Were More Likely to Be Marketed with Professional Signage than Communities of Color

The NFHA (2012) investigation found that properties in communities of color were marketed in a substandard fashion, a practice that extends the

---

7. The US Census Bureau defines a block group as a cluster of census blocks within a census tract, generally containing between 600 and 3,000 people, with an optimum size of 1,500 people.

8. Neighborhoods were defined as white if the surrounding block group was greater than 50 percent white, African American if the surrounding block group was greater than 50 percent African American, Latino if the block group contained 50 percent or more Hispanic residents, and predominantly nonwhite if the white population of the surrounding block group was less than 50 percent and no other race comprised more than 50 percent of the population alone.

amount of time REO properties remain vacant and for sale. This has extremely harmful effects on local property markets. Investigators routinely found that REO properties in communities of color were far less likely to have a functional, attractive "For Sale" sign out front. Instead, these properties often had cardboard signs reading "Bank-Owned," "Auction," or "Foreclosure." Overall, homes in white neighborhoods were 32.2 percent more likely than African American properties and 37.5 percent more likely than REO properties in Latino neighborhoods to have been properly marketed with a "For Sale" sign (S. Smith and S. Abedin, unpublished data).

In the Majority of the Regions Investigated, the Banks Owned Significantly Fewer REO Properties in White Neighborhoods than in Communities of Color

The majority of the REO properties that NFHA staff identified and visited in nearly every market were located in predominantly African American and Latino neighborhoods. Only 21.2 percent of properties surveyed for this investigation were located in predominantly white neighborhoods (NFHA 2012, 20). Although NFHA and its partners investigated the same number of zip codes containing predominantly white neighborhoods as it did for neighborhoods of color, it consistently found fewer REO properties in predominantly white communities. This could be attributed to superior maintenance and marketing leading to faster sales in white neighborhoods and, in some metropolitan regions, to the fact that fewer homes went in to foreclosure in white neighborhoods to begin with.

Newer Homes Were Subject to Fewer Maintenance and Marketing Problems when Compared to Older Homes, but Racial Disparities Persisted with Nonstructural Factors Such As Curb Appeal and Signage

The NFHA (2012) investigation considered whether racial disparities in maintenance and marketing existed in newer properties in the same way they did in neighborhoods with older housing stock. To this end, NFHA staff examined maintenance and marketing trends of REO properties built after 1990 in all racial or ethnic neighborhoods and found that disparities in maintenance scores between newer properties (built after 1990) and older ones were essentially the same.

NFHA (2012) also found that maintenance and marketing were consistently superior for newer REO properties in white neighborhoods than newer

REO properties in communities of color by isolating elements of maintenance that were nonstructural such as trash and signage. Among newer homes, REO properties in communities of color were 32 percent more likely to have trash on the premises (NFHA 2012, 21). This sort of disparity is detrimental to the curb appeal of the house and is a clear indicator of neglect by the banks.

Newer REO properties in white communities were also found to be approximately 37 percent more likely to have a "For Sale" sign posted on the property than those in African American or Latino neighborhoods (NFHA 2012, 21). This trend indicates that newer properties in neighborhoods of color are not being advertised as available to potential homeowners at the same rate as properties in predominantly white neighborhoods. By not marketing REO properties as for sale in an equal manner in nonwhite neighborhoods, banks are engaging in a form of racial steering and are restricting housing choice for all prospective purchasers seeking to buy a home.

REOs that Were Maintained and Marketed Well Were More Likely to Be Purchased by Owner-Occupants, while Those that Were Maintained and Marketed Poorly Were More Frequently Purchased by Investors

In order to measure how poor maintenance affects the sale of REO properties, NFHA (2012) analyzed the property records of ninety REOs in the Washington, DC, metropolitan area that were evaluated prior to August 2011 to observe the disposition outcomes after six months or more under bank ownership. Each of these ninety homes was documented as purchased by either (1) a primary resident, presumably by an owner-occupant, (2) an investor or purchaser who did not list the home as a primary residence, or (3) remained a bank-owned property.

The results of this inquiry can be seen in Figures 1 and 2. Alarmingly, poorly maintained REOs were much less likely to be sold after at least six months had passed, and if they were purchased, these poorly maintained REO properties were far more likely to be purchased by an investor rather than an owner-occupant. Specifically, REO properties that were well maintained were nearly four times more likely to be purchased by owner-occupants than REO properties that scored below sixty points on the property evaluation form. Similarly, 59 percent of REO properties that were poorly maintained were purchased by investors rather than owner-occupants, while only 36 percent of REO properties receiving high scores were purchased by investors (NFHA 2012, 22).

Well-Maintained Properties (A or B)

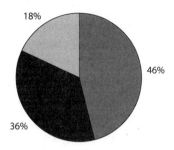

Poorly Maintained Properties (D or F)

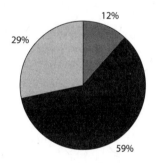

■ Purchased by Owner-Occupant   ■ Purchased by Investor   ▨ REO

Source: NFHA 2012.

Figure 1. Disposition outcome for REO properties based on maintenance score.

The sales patterns are extremely troubling when coupled with the findings that homes in communities of color are more likely to be subject to poor maintenance and marketing practices in regional markets across the nation. In fact, the NFHA (2012, 22) investigation also revealed that REO properties in white neighborhoods were nearly two times as likely to be sold to owner-occupants as REO properties in communities of color. Moreover, investors purchased 52 percent of the REO properties in African American neighborhoods in Prince George's County, Maryland, and only 33 percent of

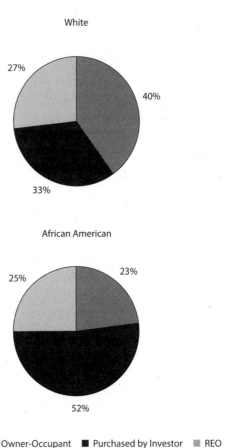

White

27%

40%

33%

African American

25%

23%

52%

■ Purchased by Owner-Occupant   ■ Purchased by Investor   ▨ REO

Source: NFHA 2012.

Figure 2. REO disposition outcome for REO properties
based on race of neighborhood.

REO properties in white neighborhoods in Montgomery County, Maryland (NFHA 2012, 22). See Figures 3 and 4 to see this breakdown.

Investor purchases can be detrimental to the overall health of a community and thwart would-be owner-occupants from purchasing homes. A study by PolicyLink notes that investors are purchasing 20 percent of REOs and short sales in the US, and this number jumps to 60 percent when focused on REOs that have been damaged (Treuhaft, Rose, and Black 2011, 19). Therefore, the patterns of neglect and poor maintenance in communities of color that NFHA (2012) has documented have only led to investors

Figure 3. REO property located in the predominantly African American suburb of Capitol Heights, Maryland. *Photo credit:* Shanti Abedin.

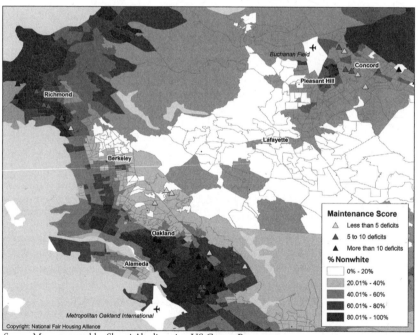

Source: Map generated by Shanti Abedin using US Census Bureau 2010 race data and unpublished REO maintenance and marketing data.

Figure 4. Number of maintenance and marketing deficiencies documented at REO properties owned by one major lender in Oakland, Richmond, and Concord, California.

representing a disproportionately large share of property owners in those same communities.

Predatory investor ownership occurs most often in low-income communities of color and can include bulk purchasing of homes with the intention of renting them out with little or no maintenance or rehabilitation (Treuhaft, Rose, and Black 2010, 3). These harmful practices by investors can deeply affect the character of the neighborhood and drive down the prices of neighboring homes. The troubling trend in investor purchases in communities of color documented by the NFHA (2012) investigation will make it even more difficult for these communities to recover, particularly as the REO inventory increases in years to come. This is not to condemn all investors, for among them are nonprofit organizations that buy REOs, take on the task of renovating them to transition them fairly back on the owner-occupied market, and resell them to owner-occupants and investors (Treuhaft, Rose, and Black 2010, 8).

Disparities in Maintenance: Regional Findings

Although disparities in maintenance and marketing practices by banks between white communities and communities of color were documented consistently across the country, disparities differed region by region. The following section outlines a sample of findings in several cities with particularly striking maintenance and marketing disparities.

Oakland and East Bay, California

REO properties in the Oakland and East Bay Area were evaluated in communities that were predominantly white, Latino, and African American, as well as some diverse communities with an Asian population of up to 33 percent. Seventy-six percent of REOs in African American neighborhoods, 75 percent of REOs in Latino neighborhoods, and 77 percent of REOs in neighborhoods with a majority of nonwhite residents had more than five deficits, whereas only 46 percent of homes in white communities had comparable numbers (NFHA 2012, 26).

When examining the number of properties with more than ten deficits, only 5 percent of homes in white neighborhoods were affected. This compared to 42 percent of REO properties in Latino neighborhoods, 15 percent of REO properties in African American neighborhoods, and 23 percent of REO properties in communities with a nonwhite majority (NFHA 2012, 26).

REOs in the African American neighborhoods in the East Bay region were 3.45 times more likely to not have a "For Sale" sign than their white counterparts. Similarly, Latino homes were 92 percent less likely to be marketed with a "For Sale" sign. Communities of color also experienced a higher number of curb appeal problems. For example, 55 percent of REOs in African American neighborhoods had overgrown shrubs and 60 percent had trash on their lawns, while only 18 percent of REOs in white neighborhoods had overgrown or dead shrubbery and only 36 percent were littered with trash (NFHA 2012, 26). (See Figures 5 through 8.)

Dayton, Ohio

In Dayton, 44 percent of homes in African American neighborhoods reviewed had more than ten maintenance deficits, while none of the homes in white areas had over ten problems. NFHA and the Miami Valley Fair Housing Center's investigation of REO maintenance and marketing revealed a particularly large disparity in Dayton with respect to structural and security issues. Sixty percent of REOs in African American neighborhoods had broken or unsecured doors, while only 18 percent of REOs in white neighborhoods

Figure 5. This property (Property 1) located in an African American neighborhood in Oakland, California, was documented with substantial trash, dead grass, boarded-up windows and doors, and no "For Sale" signage. The neighboring house, pictured in Figure 8, in contrast, is maintained extremely well. *Photo credit:* Shanna L. Smith.

Figure 6. Trash on side of Property 1. *Photo credit:* Shanna L. Smith.

Figure 7. Back view of Property 1. *Photo credit:* Shanna L. Smith.

Figure 8. The well-maintained property neighboring Property 1.
Photo credit: Shanna L. Smith.

suffered from this problem. And 40 percent of REOs in African American neighborhoods had broken or boarded windows, while only 21 percent of the REO homes in white areas had their windows broken or boarded. Disparities with regard to signage were also consistent in this area. An alarming 84 percent of homes in African American neighborhoods had no "For Sale" sign out front, while only 64 percent of homes in white areas had the same problem (NFHA 2012, 27). (See Figures 9 and 10.)

Atlanta, Georgia

It comes as no surprise that Atlanta, a metropolitan region in which foreclosed homes make up 24 percent of all home sales (Rich 2012), is home to an exorbitant number of REO properties. Metro Fair Housing in Atlanta and NFHA staff found striking racial disparities across all maintenance categories. Seventy-four percent of REOs in African American neighborhoods were documented to have more than five maintenance deficits, while this was the case for only 57 percent of REO properties in white neighborhoods. This disparity increased substantially when considering properties with more than ten problems. Thirty-two percent of REOs in African American neighborhoods had more than ten deficits, while not a single property in a white

Figure 9. This REO property (Property 2) located in an African American neighborhood in Charleston, South Carolina, was listed on the bank's Web site as for sale, but it did not have a "For Sale" sign, the majority of the windows were boarded up, and trash was lying around on the property.
Photo Credit: Shanti Abedin.

Figure 10. This REO property (Property 3) located in an African American neighborhood in Atlanta, Georgia, had no "For Sale" sign and was covered in leaves even though investigators had visited it in February. The property had broken doors and wide open holes in the back walls that exposed the inside of the structure to damage from rain and wild animals.
Photo credit: Shanna L. Smith.

neighborhood was subject to such poor maintenance. REO properties in African American neighborhoods were nearly 4.65 times more likely than homes in predominantly white neighborhoods to be missing a "For Sale" sign on the property. Curb appeal issues were also a huge problem in communities of color: 31 percent of homes in all communities of color had overgrown lawns, while less than 10 percent of REOs in white neighborhoods had poorly maintained lawns; and 31 percent of REOs in African American neighborhoods had unsecured or broken doors, while only 14 percent of REOs in white areas had the same problem (NFHA 2012, 25–28).

Neighbor Survey Findings

Homeowners whose properties neighbored an REO property received surveys in the mail requesting their input on a variety of topics related to the REO. The results of these surveys provided some insight into the experiences of residents living next to or across from a bank-owned property. Overall, the feedback from neighbors in the surveys confirmed what staff observed while visiting and evaluating REO properties: lenders are *not* maintaining the properties in communities of color in the same way they are maintaining properties in communities where residents are predominantly white. Of the 165 surveys received by NFHA prior to its report in 2012, slightly more than 60 percent were received from neighbors in communities of color, and the remainder were from residents in predominantly white neighborhoods.

While neighbors of the REO properties in all neighborhoods reported that they often took it upon themselves to pick up trash, mow lawns, and secure the vacant properties next door, residents of neighborhoods of color disproportionately faced other issues brought about by the inferior care of REO properties in their communities. Only 30 percent of those surveyed in communities of color stated that they had observed routine and consistent maintenance of their neighboring REO properties; nearly 54 percent of the surveys from residents in predominantly white communities reported observing this sort of routine maintenance. Similarly, only 20 percent of residents in communities of color reported seeing home improvement contractors working on the neighboring REO property, while nearly 40 percent of neighbors in predominantly white areas stated they had seen home improvement contractors at the property (NFHA 2012, 23).

The discriminatory treatment of REO properties is clearly a fact of life. But, at least, the beginnings of a resolution of these issues are in sight. In June 2013, the NFHA, along with thirteen of its member organizations, settled a fair housing complaint filed with HUD against Wells Fargo Bank.

At the same time, HUD resolved a Secretary Initiated Complaint with Wells Fargo using NFHA's evidence. In the NFHA settlement, the bank agreed to provide $27 million to NFHA and thirteen members to use in nineteen cities to promote neighborhood stabilization and homeownership in communities of color. The HUD complaint included $11.5 million in twenty-five cities to be used to promote homeownership, neighborhood stabilization, property rehabilitation, and development of communities of color. Among its commitments, Wells Fargo will implement a set of best practices to assure the equitable maintenance and marketing of all REO properties, with a third party retained to monitor compliance with the standards of the agreement. A significant point in the agreement includes the bank not only extending priority to owner-occupants in the first days the REO is for sale but also giving this priority each and every time the price is reduced on the REO. By extending the owner-occupant priority in this fashion, real estate agents will have a better opportunity to help home buyers compete with investors and a cash offer will not be treated as a better offer by the bank. Along with NFHA, Wells Fargo will develop a fair housing training program for bank employees who deal with REO properties. The agreement also provided $3 million to the complainants for their diversion of resources and attorneys' fees.[9] Hopefully, this settlement will send a message to other lenders that it is imperative to maintain and market REOs in communities of color in the same manner as those in predominantly white communities if they do not want to face costly consequences.

Policy Implications and Conclusions

The findings outlined in this chapter point to a disconcerting pattern of discriminatory practices in communities of color across the country. There are a number of sound actions that the various key players in the REO disposition practice can undertake to ensure that REO properties are maintained without regard to the racial or ethnic composition of the neighborhood, as outlined in the rest of this section. Additionally, fair housing agencies, municipalities, and neighborhood organizations can work together to bring complaints against banks that do not maintain REOs because of the racial or ethnic composition in which the homes are located.

---

9. National Fair Housing Alliance, et al. v. Wells Fargo Bank, N.A., et al., HUD Case No. 09-12-0708-8. (June 5, 2013).

Banks must have a comprehensive understanding of the Fair Housing Act—which protects people and neighborhoods on the basis of race, color, religion, national origin, familial status, disability, and sex—as well as state and local fair housing laws—which may include protections for sexual orientation, gender identity, and source of income. The Fair Housing Act also prohibits discrimination because of race or national origin of the residents in a neighborhood. The process of REO disposition has many key players and many stages in which housing discrimination can occur. It is the responsibility of the banks to make sure that all parties involved, including their subcontractors, are trained in the Fair Housing Act and that strict adherence to the law is enforced. All vendors selected to work on the disposition of REOs should receive high-quality fair housing training, not be the subject of pending complaints of discrimination, and have successfully resolved any past complaints of discrimination.

The banks have an obligation to implement sound quality control practices to guarantee REOs are maintained and marketed without regard to the racial or ethnic composition of the neighborhoods in which REOs are located.

Selection of Vendors by the Banks

Some banks hire national companies to dispose of their REOs in specific regions of the country. This often results in money trickling down to subcontractors at a local level to address the maintenance and marketing of REOs. NFHA (2012) has observed that banks with direct contracts with local vendors typically have better on-site maintenance of REOs.

An REO listing broker's local expertise and connection to the neighborhood is vital to the proper treatment and marketing of REOs, and banks must enact policies to ensure that the agent assigned to an REO property (a) has an office that is located in close proximity to the home, (b) has the capacity to closely manage and oversee the treatment of the REO, and (c) has community contacts and understands the revitalization efforts directed in the neighborhood. Using this type of selection criteria will ensure that REO agents are familiar with the community and are committed to its recovery. Banks should also maintain and routinely train a network of diverse and multilingual agents who can work to provide equal access for non-English speaking buyers and promote residential integration.

Equally important in the fair treatment of REO properties is the selection of the preservation and maintenance companies. These companies should be selected using geographic parameters similar to those used to select sales agents. This will ensure that companies with local offices are hired, which will support small businesses.

Detailed Expectations and Oversight of All Vendors in the REO Disposition Process

Banks should provide clear guidelines for all vendors that include detailed agreements, policies, and procedures to ensure high-quality property maintenance regardless of the racial or ethnic composition of a neighborhood. These documents should clearly outline expectations for the speedy and thorough processing of properties—from the time they become bank owned through the point of sale. For example, Freddie Mac (unpublished data) implements a policy that requires properties be secured, any trash and debris cleaned out, and the yard brought up to an acceptable standard within seventy-two hours of the REO becoming vacant.

Preservation maintenance vendors ought to have a certain amount of financial leeway to address emergency issues arising at the REO. For example, a vendor ought to have authority to immediately repair leaking water pipes, running toilets, and broken gutters, doors, or windows without having to go through a lengthy administrative process for approval of expenditures. Access to an emergency repair fund with guidelines for what constitutes an emergency would be a good practice.

Maintenance practices should be reinforced with a vigorous system of quality control. Banks should hire inspectors that visit a substantial percentage of properties—especially homes located in integrated and predominantly African American and Latino neighborhoods, as well as REOs in modestly priced neighborhoods—to check overall quality in maintenance and whether or not professional "For Sale" signs are posted. For example, Freddie Mac (unpublished data) implements a monthly inspection of 25 percent of its REOs using a thirteen-point checklist. NFHA (2012) observed that Freddie Mac properties in all neighborhoods appeared to be properly maintained and professionally marketed. High-quality maintenance can be due, in part, to Freddie Mac's practice of posting a 1-800 hotline number so neighbors can report issues requiring immediate action. Additionally, disciplinary procedures should be in place to take regular action against any vendor with performance problems—including terminating the contract with that vendor or broker.

Marketing and Sale of the Property

Banks must utilize robust valuation practices and price homes at fair market value in order to promote recovery and rebuild wealth. All appraisals of any

REO properties must be completed without any consideration of the race and ethnicity of the residents of its neighborhood. In the case of a bank using a Broker Price Opinion (BPO)—a tool used to value properties—in place of a full appraisal, the BPO should take into account a fair assessment of the interior, including photographs.

REO properties should also be advertised broadly. The real estate company listing the home should reach out to people living inside and outside the neighborhood in which the REO is located. Expansive free advertising on the Internet, including local blogs, listservs, and other online social media, can tap into a market segment that may not be familiar with the neighborhood and its opportunities for homeownership. This method of marketing promotes residential integration. Brokers should have standardized signage to use in all communities.

Make REO Data Transparent and Publicly Accessible

Each bank should have an online publicly accessible, regularly updated database of its REO listings, including the name of the asset manager or vendor(s) responsible for listing, maintaining, and selling the property and an emergency 1-800 number serviced 24/7. The availability of these data in real time would empower communities to monitor REO disposition practices and enable them to contact the bank's representative when problems are identified. Publicly accessible data about REOs will also facilitate purchase of these properties by prospective owner-occupants rather than investors.

Conduct a Major Investigation of Bank Policies and Practices

Federally regulated banks play a major role with respect to REOs, both as owners of these foreclosed properties and as servicers or trustees of other institutions' REO portfolios. Federal banking regulators, including the Consumer Financial Protection Bureau and federal law enforcement agencies such as the DOJ, should use their authority to conduct a major, nationwide investigation of bank and servicer policies and practices with regard to REO properties, similar to NFHA's (2012) nine-city investigation. The federal investigation should look especially for any discriminatory policies and practices in the management and marketing of REOs, including policies or practices that may have a disparate impact on members of protected classes. In addition to the issues specifically addressed in this chapter, a larger investigation should examine whether and to what extent vendor contracts are made available to minority and women-owned enterprises.

Congress should also investigate discrimination in the REO arena. While Congress has held extensive hearings on the housing crisis, REO discrimination and its implications on the national debt and America's economic health have not been sufficiently addressed.

Make Provisions for Local Guidance and Assistance

The vision for rebuilding communities affected by the foreclosure crisis rests at the local level, with agencies and institutions whose mission is to create healthy and vibrant neighborhoods of opportunity. Investors who pursue bulk purchases of REOs may not share or be guided by that same vision. By making sure that some of the foreclosed homes are put into the hands of nonprofit community development organizations, community land trusts, and other community-based and community-minded institutions, the federal government and banks can facilitate the realization of a vision to help rebuild vibrant communities.

One way to ensure that neighborhoods of opportunity are created is to give prospective owner-occupants and nonprofit community organizations greater opportunities to purchase foreclosed homes. Some banks offer a "first look" program for a fifteen-day period for such buyers to have exclusive rights to purchase the REO. We recommend that banks reinstate this "first look" program for five more days every time the list price for the REO is reduced.

In addition, communities that have been hard hit by foreclosures are struggling to devise ways to help neighborhoods recover from the damage they have suffered. Many have developed revitalization plans using federal funds under the Neighborhood Stabilization Program, Community Development Block Grant, and the HOME program, as well as other sources. The disposition of REO properties, both at the point of sale to investors and at the point when investors resell the homes, should be coordinated with these local plans so as to leverage a positive impact on the community rather than undermine it.

Bulk sales of REOs to private equity firms also must be evaluated because too many homes that used to be owner-occupied end up as permanent rental properties. Additionally, private equity firms are flush with cash from foreign investors and are buying up REOs in bulk. A recent *Wall Street Journal* article described firms attending bulk sales auctions in the ballrooms of hotels with brief cases full of cashier checks worth $3 million to pay for single-family homes in Atlanta, Georgia (Whelan 2012). Once these portfolios are created as rental properties, it is unlikely that these homes will return to the homeownership market. This can result in former owner-occupied neighborhoods becoming investor-owned, rental neighborhoods. Auctioning the homes at the foreclosure sale prevents them from ever entering the REO market.

Use REOs to Expand Housing Opportunities

Many REO properties are located in communities that offer access to quality education, jobs, transportation, parks and recreation facilities, grocery stores, and other such amenities. Yet, many of these communities are largely segregated, with few families of color among their residents. This is, in part, a function of the discriminatory practices that persist in the real estate and banking industries. Banks and investors purchasing these properties must be required to take affirmative steps to market these homes to a wide range of households, including families of color, families with children, people with disabilities, and others, to expand the range of housing options available to all families and begin to make a dent in the patterns of segregation that have marred the US.

Create a Path Back to Homeownership

Over four million families have lost their homes to foreclosure since 2007. Evidence from a variety of federal enforcement actions tells us that, in many cases, families were steered into loans more risky and more expensive than their financial qualifications should have dictated.[10] In other cases, people have been caught between record high levels of sustained unemployment and falling home prices that have made it impossible for them to sell or refinance their homes. Offering families a path back to homeownership is an important component of rebuilding stable, vibrant communities and stabilizing the economy.

When an REO property is acquired at a price below the previous mortgage balance, the new owner can set a new sales price that is based on the property's market value, eliminating the burden of excess debt that was fueled by unsustainable mortgage products. Many REO properties become rentals, with some remaining as rental properties for the foreseeable future and others

---

10. One example is the recent settlement between the US Department of Justice (DOJ) and Countrywide Financial, in which the government found that some ten thousand African American and Latino borrowers who qualified for prime loans were steered into subprime loans (DOJ 2011).

being resold within a few years. The first group may help address America's growing need for rental units, while the second group may offer a path to homeownership for families who have been through foreclosure and those who have difficulty qualifying for a mortgage in the current mortgage market.

Nonprofit, community-based development organizations and community development financial institutions are exploring the use of lease-purchase programs for REO properties that become rentals. Under such programs, a portion of each month's rent is set aside to build a down payment, and the rental period gives the tenant (who may even be the previous owner) time to repair a poor credit rating, with the goal of ultimately purchasing the home. With the proper protections built in for the tenant or potential purchaser, this may be a promising path to rebuilding financial security for families knocked low by foreclosure. NFHA (2012) recommends that banks and other investors that hold REO portfolios work with appropriate nonprofit or local government agencies to make some REO properties available through such lease-purchase programs.

Conclusion

If left unaddressed, discrimination in the maintenance and marketing of REO properties will continue to perpetuate residential segregation, impede America's economic recovery, and perpetuate what has been a thirty-year spike in economic inequality. As noted previously, the surge in inequality in turn reinforces segregation and further undermines revitalization efforts. As the Occupy movement reminds us, those broader patterns of inequality should be a focal point of fair housing, fair lending, and virtually all social justice movements. The nationwide investigation of REO properties by NFHA constitutes just one example of the types of innovative and aggressive advocacy tactics suggested—sometimes explicitly, sometimes implicitly—by the Occupy movement.

As banks and their vendors continue to fail to maintain properties in African American and Latino neighborhoods, this pattern and practice will continue to compound the discriminatory impact that the foreclosure crisis has had on communities of color. The rash of vacant REO properties in these communities was created by predatory and discriminatory lending practices, and the harm continues to deepen each day these REOs are poorly maintained and marketed. Looking forward, residents of *all* communities must be able to count on banks to be good—albeit temporary—neighbors in order to facilitate a sound recovery.

References

Apgar, William, and Mark Duda. 2005. *Collateral Damage: The Municipal Impact of Today's Mortgage Foreclosure Boom.* Minneapolis, MN: Homeownership Preservation Foundation.

Bocian, Debbie Gruenstein, Wei Li, and Keith Ernst. 2010. *Foreclosures by Race and Ethnicity: Demographics of a Crisis.* Durham, NC: Center for Responsible Lending.

Bocian, Debbie Gruenstein, Peter Smith, and Wei Li. 2012. *Collateral Damage: The Spillover Costs of Foreclosure.* Durham, NC: Center for Responsible Lending.

DOJ (Department of Justice). 2011. "Justice Department Reaches $335 Million Settlement to Resolve Allegations of Lending Discrimination by Countrywide Financial Corporation." Press release from the US Department of Justice, Office of Public Affairs, December 21. http://www.justice.gov/opa/pr/2011/December/11-ag-1694.html.

Immergluck, Daniel, and Geoff Smith. 2005a. *There Goes the Neighborhood: The Effect of Single-Family Mortgage Foreclosures on Property Values.* Chicago: Woodstock Institute.

———. 2005b. *The Impact of Single-Family Mortgage Foreclosures on Neighborhood Crime.* Chicago: Woodstock Institute.

Kochhar, Rakesh, Richard Fry, and Paul Taylor. 2011. *Twenty to One: Wealth Gaps Rise to Record Highs between Whites, Blacks, Hispanics.* Washington, DC: Pew Research Center.

NFHA (National Fair Housing Alliance). 2012. *The Banks Are Back—Our Neighborhoods Are Not.* Washington, DC: National Fair Housing Alliance.

Rich, Mokoto. 2012. "In Atlanta, Housing Woes Reflect Nation's Pain." *New York Times,* January 31.

Treuhaft, Sarah, Kalima Rose, and Karen Black. 2010. *When Investors Buy Up the Neighborhood: Preventing Investor Ownership from Causing Neighborhood Decline.* Oakland, CA: PolicyLink. http://www.policylink.org/BuyUp.

———. 2011. "When Investors Buy Up the Neighborhood: Preventing Investor Ownership from Causing Neighborhood Decline." *Community Investments* 23 (1): 19–33. http://www.frbsf.org/publications/community/investments/1104/CI_Treuhaft_et_al.pdf

Whelan, Robbie. 2012. "Firms Flock to Foreclosure Auctions." *Wall Street Journal,* September 12.

The Organizers

8

Building the Power to Win the Battle of Big Ideas and Advance a Long-Term Agenda

George Goehl and Sandra Hinson

G REG SQUIRES AND Chester Hartman open this book with a description of Gale Cincotta, the founder of National People's Action (NPA) and mother of the community reinvestment movement, taking over bank lobbies and holding barbecues on the front lawns of bank executives. George had the good fortune to work with Cincotta during the 1990s. Cincotta was a visionary who was fearless about conflict and capable of inspiring people to think big about what we might accomplish. As a result, she led the charge to advance some of the most significant and people-friendly reforms to the banking system since the Great Depression. Sadly, many of the reforms she championed have been rolled back or worked around. The same working-class and poor people she cared about and led are bearing the brunt of the recent financial crisis and America's winner-take-all politics.

Advancing the next set of structural reforms to the banking and housing systems will not happen in a vacuum. Housing and reinvestment activists must operate within, and help shape, a broader political context. We should be deliberate in building a new banking and housing movement in America that is embedded in a broader effort to shift the nation's political headwinds and the structure of the overall economy. This means engaging in multiple fields of struggle and rethinking community organizing.

In this chapter, we want to name some specific ways in which we need to act differently to advance a steady stream of reforms that move us toward a new economy—an economy that advances racial justice, significantly narrows the inequality gap, is sustainable, and moves more and more capital toward democratic forms of control. For this to happen, we must create a political context much different from the one in which we currently operate.

The Corporate-Conservative Movement

With corporate influence stronger than ever in the United States government, the two political parties as they exist bear little resemblance to the ones that Gale Cincotta dealt with. While the degrees vary, members of both parties are beholden to Wall Street and the corporate sector. Cincotta worked with both Republicans and Democrats. For example, in 1975, Gerald Ford signed into the law the Home Mortgage Disclosure Act (HMDA), which made banks disclose to whom they were making and denying loans. During the George H. W. Bush administration, Republican Department of Housing and Urban Development (HUD) Secretary Jack Kemp worked with low-income housing advocates on policies to allow for cooperative buy-outs of subsidized housing. This brand of Republican is in scarce supply today. Instead, we live in an era in which a Republican presidential candidate dismissed 47 percent of the population as deadbeat dependents who "want stuff."

Meanwhile, many in the Democratic Party continue to cozy up with Wall Street. While Democrats have certainly sought to rein in Wall Street to a greater degree than Republicans, the Democratic Party has also shifted to the right, particularly when it comes to regulating corporate behavior or pushing back against deficit hawks. Some Democrats come into office with center-right politics, while others have adapted as a means of retaining office within the political constraints of their states or districts and national politics.

Since the early 1980s, both parties have been in thrall to neoliberalism. The neoliberal "commonsense" holds that corporations and markets reign supreme. Government exists to serve the market, and the interests of individuals (who are on their own) naturally align with what is good for markets. Government interference (and the demands of organized groups like workers, communities, people of color, etc.) upsets this natural order.

To understand how and why national politics and the two parties have shifted so far to the right, we turn to the rise of a corporate-conservative movement. This takes us back forty years to the birth of an infrastructure that brought together corporate interests and wealthy elites, along with deep-pocketed funders, intellectual idea makers, and alternative (now mainstream) media. This far-thinking infrastructure fostered a political and economic system that is highly responsive to the organized economic interests of its constituents at the expense of everyone else. These constituents have consolidated their power through an infrastructure that coordinates around a long-term agenda, dominates the battle of ideas, and that eventually has taken over government.

Aggregating Corporate-Conservative Power

Conservatives have developed a deeply interconnected infrastructure, with its disparate parts and unlikely allies held together by long-term strategic goals and a conservative ideology, along with more immediate incentives and rewards for many of the conservatives' constituencies. They were able to do this in spite of the many differences between the various strands of the movement: libertarians, evangelicals, corporatists, etc.—all have a unifying interest in gaining governing power.

Through this infrastructure, corporate conservatives developed a long-term agenda that has guided them since the 1970s. They have been advancing the agenda in a systematic way. While they have sought to win on issues and expand profits, the heart of their agenda has been about power: more power to run our society, and less power for the rest of us. The most often mentioned blueprint for this work has become known as the "Powell Memo," referring to a memorandum crafted by Lewis F. Powell, dated August 23, 1971. Powell, who would soon be confirmed as a US Supreme Court justice, addressed his memo to Eugene B. Sydnor, chairman of the Education Committee of the US Chamber of Commerce.

While Powell's memo named multiple ways in which he thought corporations needed to be more strategic, he was particularly clear about two. First, he advocated for a strategy focused on the expansion and consolidation of power in the political arena. Second, he named the need to advance ideas and worldview that favored deregulation and privatization. He named specific strategies to make this happen, including wielding power within universities and investing in their own set of public thinkers and public thought institutions (Moyers 2012).

The long-term agenda that Powell laid out and others built upon is very clear as we look back on the forty years that followed the memo:

- Corporate conservatives gaining control of the government.
- Deregulation.
- Privatization.
- The use of taxes to redistribute wealth to the top.

Key strategies for advancing the corporate-conservative agenda have in-cluded explicitly and implicitly using race to divide people, undermining the role of government, and weakening the power of unions, community organizations, and voters of color. When analyzing the corporate-conservative agenda, we often lose track of the fact that there has been an incredible em-phasis not only on expanding profits but also on the expansion of power. Gaining control of the government, taking control of public functions, and freeing themselves from rules that limit their ability to create larger and less restrained corporations has allowed for the consolidation of power in the market place as well as in the political life for corporate conservatives.

In the field of community organizing, we have historically looked at potential campaigns and asked how a given campaign can improve people's lives and help build power for our organizations. Typical criteria for selecting a campaign or organizing effort have been: will it bring it more members, more money, or more power relationships? Meanwhile, corporate conserva-tives focused on structural reforms that often codified, or legalized, a shift in political or financial power in the US, not just for one company or another, but for an entire sector or big corporations writ large. One result is that, whether Republicans or Democrats are in control of federal policy, corporate conservatives have incredible influence over what ultimately emerges.

Using the Power of Ideas

The long-term agenda of the corporate-conservative movement has succeeded in working a set of ideas into an understandable and dynamic narrative, and moving this story into the center of American life. That narrative says we are a society of rugged individuals, that unfettered markets in a capitalist economy lift all boats, creating equal opportunity and building wealth for those that work hard and play by the rules, and that government undermines the power of markets and is simply a means to take away from winners and give to losers. It also says we already live in a racially just society. The same people who make this last point also send out coded signals that use race to undermine support for government programs that are meant to address historical disparities and growing inequality.

Using race to stigmatize government has been a central part of their worldview strategy. In *Progressive Politics: The Strategic Importance of Race*, john powell notes how public programs have been racialized over time (powell and Menendian 2006). It dovetails with the construction of the middle class. After World War II, thanks in large part to government initiatives, US society became "middle class"—an artificially homogenized category that includes white working class and well-paid professionals, blue and white collar. "Middle class" became synonymous with "white." In this construct, the middle class does not depend on the government (long forgotten are the ways that government programs lifted people into the middle class in the first place). The making of the middle class helped shape a radically individualist worldview: the white working class moved from seeing themselves as part of a collective struggle to improve conditions for the class as a whole to being individuals who strive (alone) for their piece of the American Dream. We saw this in the 2012 election, as both parties obsessively appealed to an elusive middle class while failing to address the deepening economic crisis that engulfs African American, Latino, and white working-class communities (Hahn 2012).

What has been particularly powerful about the corporate-conservative worldview and agenda is the ways in which specific strategies support and feed off of each other. Using race to undermine the role of government helps build the case for privatization. Privatization allows for an elite few to consolidate economic and political power. Undermining the efficacy of government also shields abusive corporations from responsibility and weakens the case for regulation. This exact strategy was on display as conservatives unleashed attacks on the Community Reinvestment Act (CRA) and government-sponsored entities (GSEs), such as Fannie Mae and Freddie Mac, following the financial crisis. It was used to protect Wall Street and divert attention from deregulatory disasters and pin the blame instead on programs that helped low- and moderate-income families, disproportionately families of color, to obtain affordable housing and access to credit.

Rethinking Organizing: The Next Forty Years

We believe that we are a good five years into a rethinking and reorganization of the larger progressive sector. A key place where this rethinking is happening is in community organizing, the craft in which Cincotta and the organization she led were central. While these changes are in their early stages, the groundwork is being laid for a new kind of organizing that could have the power to advance a transformative change agenda.

Forty years ago, the world of community organizing was absorbing many of the people, and the lessons learned, from the civil rights movement, the antipoverty and fair housing movements, and the New Left of the mid-to-late-1960s. By the mid-1970s, many social justice activists, trade unionists, environmentalists, and community organizers had become wary of big challenges to the status quo and about the ways in which ideological struggles could make it harder to reach mainstream Americans. These new leaders had a series of ideas about how to make change. Key features of community organizing at the time included organizing that was issue focused, nonelectoral, less ideological, and that discouraged forming permanent alliances. What this period of community organizing was very good at was engaging poor and working-class people, developing leadership, and winning on specific issue campaigns. What it did not succeed in doing was shifting the larger political and ideological environment in which this engagement and campaign work took place.

NPA came onto the organizing scene in the midst of these developments in the 1970s. We bucked some of these trends; we may have reinforced others. NPA was formed when the community groups from dozens of cities that were fighting an onslaught of foreclosures across the US got together to do something proactive and saw a need to project national power to address the issues impacting working-class neighborhoods. Interestingly, Cincotta was not a trained organizer, and had little buy-in around hard and fast rules of what was organizing and what was not. NPA's founding as a national organization was questioned by some of the most prominent community organizers of the day, including Tom Gaudette of the Industrial Areas Foundation, who groomed NPA cofounder Shel Trapp. Despite these critiques from peers, Cincotta, Trapp, and NPA seized a movement moment and went on to spearhead passage of the Home Mortgage Disclosure Act of 1975 (HMDA) and the Community Reinvestment Act (CRA) of 1977. Yet, as time went on, NPA was not quick to break with community organizing orthodoxies that were preventing us from building the kind of collective power needed to shift the context in which we organized. We certainly perpetuated the "no permanent allies" maxim, had limited engagement in elections, and were not engaged in deep ideological work.

Stepping back and looking at the forty years that followed, we see some impressive developments. But we also see a lot of unevenness. Popular and progressive groups have been fragmented and siloed, lacking cross-sector coordination and any sense of cohesion. We have nothing that compares with the powerful corporate-conservative infrastructure that propelled their plutocratic, class-biased, racially divisive, and antigovernment agenda into the mainstream. As we noted earlier, the progressive sector is in the early stages of rethinking the vision, strategy, and integration of our broader work. This is thanks in part to new leadership that is willing to question the old verities. This level of inquiry into questions of strategy for the future is also driven in part by the absolute necessity of figuring out how to aggregate our power—by taking on the battle of big ideas, putting forward a bold, long-term agenda, and building a new electoral bloc in America.

In April of 2013, NPA held its fortieth annual convention. We used the occasion to celebrate and carry forward the best of what we've been able to do in the past forty years, while also reflecting on shifts in our work: our investments in new formations and alliances, our work on the battle of big ideas, our use of old and new tactics to confront corporate power, our emerging approaches to civic engagement, and our focus on developing a long-term agenda. These shifts have opened up new possibilities that move us beyond tinkering with a broken economy, pushing forward an agenda for a new, morally grounded and community-centered economy. In the rest of this chapter, we describe promising new developments and talk about how we can take them even further to build the power needed to advance an agenda for a new economy.

Our Long-Term Agenda for a New Economy

To create an America in which all communities are brimming with opportunity, we must take up the fight for a new economy. Lessons from the 1970s to the present suggest that the time for tinkering with housing, banking, and other systems has passed. We've run out of options within the current context. We need to transform it.

As we seek to build a long-term agenda, we must acknowledge that we are at a crossroads. We can try to revive the past. We can work to improve what we've got. Or we can choose to completely reimagine what is possible; to refuse to let the challenges of the moment limit our ability to think big about the kind of society we want to live in. Considering the dismal realities that surround us today, this kind of big thinking is not easy. But if we allow current prospects to lower our expectations of what is possible, then we have already lost. This is why it is critical that we develop a long-term vision that has the power to inspire millions of people to join the fight and put skin in the game. A good strategy will incorporate elements of defending the safety net and reclaiming past gains and also have an eye toward a total rethinking of what our economy should look and feel like.

Starting with Core Principles

NPA's work on worldview, which we will discuss in some detail in the next section, has intersected with its campaigns to rein in Wall Street, creating energy for network-wide conversations about transforming, instead of tinkering with, the economy. NPA members have identified principles that provide the foundation for the kind of economy and society that America needs. These principles for a new economy include the following five elements:

1. Democratic Control of Capital. Significant sums of capital must be moved toward collective control and accountability. In the current system, too much money is controlled by too few people and is concentrated into large, unaccountable business and financial institutions. Therefore, we support varied means for shifting trillions of dollars of capital into more democratic forms of control. This could take many forms, such as creating pools of capital through a federal infrastructure bank and through "new economy" block grants from federal agencies, like HUD, state banks, and transfers of capital from big banks to local community banks. We need new economic rules that favor local economic growth and keep wealth in local communities. These rules should also favor more cooperative structures (for housing, for worker management and ownership, etc.) as well as more democratically managed public structures.

2. Racial Justice. The fight for an economy that puts people first and that gives people greater control over their economic lives is an opportunity to address persistent structural barriers to racial equity and opportunity in society. These barriers have expanded since the 1970s in spite of reform efforts in housing, lending, and antidiscrimination in employment. As part of building toward a new economy, we must advance policy reforms that not only include universal improvements in people's lives but that also specifically ensure additional resources are targeted to communities of color as a means of addressing long-standing racial disparities. Beyond this, efforts to support more local control should tap into cooperative economic traditions in communities of color that go back to Reconstruction. A new economy must lead to greater economic self-determination for communities of color as well as social inclusion.

Cross-race solidarity will be critical in the struggle for a new economy. This will not happen unless racism is explicitly addressed and achieving racial justice is understood to be in our collective best interest.

3. Reduce the Power of Corporations and Reinstate the Need for a Public Purpose. Thanks to Wall Street and corporate domination of both the government and economy, the US political system creates a handful of very big winners that have captured most of the economic gains since the 1970s. To change things, America needs a new bottom line—one that includes the health, well-being, and happiness of the entire population. To do so, we need to restructure corporations and our relationship with them. We often forget that corporations are the creation of the laws of the government. In the late eighteenth and early nineteenth centuries, corporations were expected to demonstrate a public service in order to receive a charter. Corporations in the twenty-first century should be smaller, accountable to, and governed by the public. More importantly, they should be accountable to people in ways that are hard to imagine today.

4. Renewing Democracy. The new economy cannot happen without more popular control over the federal and state governments than there has been before. We must pursue openings to gain greater control over agenda setting on economic and social issues. A few pathways toward more popular and democratic control include a "people-in, money-out" agenda that reverses trends like Citizens United, the 2010 Supreme Court decision that allows for unlimited independent expenditures on elections by corporations and others. We need to reform an electoral system that makes voting harder than it needs to be and right-wing attempts (funded by the corporate-conservative infrastructure) to suppress voting in communities of color. But democratic renewal is much bigger than voting. It also must include new means to increase civic engagement such as participatory budgeting, shareholder activism, greater community control of service provision, and more. A living, breathing democracy in our communities is about exercising power through institutions we control and having access to the resources that are necessary for sustained and effective decision making.

5. Ecological Sustainability. The reality of climate change has made the issue of protecting the environment not only an ecological issue, but a social justice issue as well. An economic and racial justice agenda that does not include an eye toward sustainability will run into trouble down the road. Transforming the economy provides an opportunity to rethink growth and redirect investments into green alternatives. Climate change compels us to prepare for its effects, such as more dramatic storms, rising sea levels, and more drought conditions, in ways that are just and equitable.

Corporations have powerful interests in unlimited growth and in avoiding responsibility for the consequences and environmental costs of their actions. The government has been subservient to corporations on this, which has meant, among other things, that the costs of large-scale environmental degradation have been borne by communities, not corporations. This must change; indeed, this must be a major element of a new economy strategy—no more externalities.

All of these changes should be made with an eye toward the steady accumulation of power by everyday people and a reduction of the power held by a set of corporate boards and CEOs. An agenda without a strategy to move power into the hands of more people might result in some policy wins along the margins, but it will lack the potential for building something truly transformative.

Crafting and Working from a Long-Term Agenda

As part of an inquiry into a larger set of questions, hundreds of members of NPA are currently engaged in a yearlong process to develop a forty-year agenda. The purpose is to attract more people to participate in building a long-term agenda, developing a deeper understanding of structural reforms, and inspiring more thoughtful approaches to how NPA sequences campaigns as part of a long-term strategy.

An effective long-term agenda needs to name where a successful forty-year economic and racial justice movement would end up. The five principles described earlier have been used to carve out pathways along which our movements can advance structural reforms that shift economic and political power from corporate elites to communities and workers. To move along these pathways toward our long-term goals, we need range of structural reforms that serve as stepping-stones. The specific stepping-stones will shift based on political opportunities (moving between local, state, and national governments), different issue priorities, and different points of intervention (whether corporate, regulatory, legal, or legislative). The agenda also will include a set of tools for choosing campaigns. In the field of community organizing, organizers have historically looked at potential campaigns and asked: how will this campaign improve people's lives and help us build power for our organizations? The criteria for taking on a campaign or organizing effort have included whether it will bring more members, more money, or more power relationships.

With a long-term agenda to work from and greater clarity about what structural reforms are and why they are critical, we can assess campaigns with a clearer lens in terms of how specific efforts improve people's lives and codify a structural shift in power that stands us on stronger ground for future battles. We would then be able to sequence campaigns that take advantage of political openings to do multiple things at once—improve people's lives, create shifts in power, shift worldview, and grow organizations.

Engaging the Battle of Big Ideas

One of the most powerful shifts taking place in community organizing is the recognition that we must actively shape the ideas at the center of American life. If we do not, we will continue to lose on the issue front. This awareness is a big shift; especially since multiple generations of community organizers have been trained with a focus on building organizations and winning issues, but have had little preparation or education about how the broader ideological landscape impacts their ability to move those issues and how campaigns could play a role in shifting the larger political environment. While often unstated, for many organizers, this has meant trying to win the best possible outcome within the existing issue environment. As a result, most organizers make limited investments in structuring organizing drives or campaigns in order to play a role in shifting the realm of what is possible. This often means winning in the present at the expense of the long-term idea battle. It means framing campaigns in the most expedient way possible, even if it reinforces the conservative worldview and thereby limits our abilities to move beyond what is currently possible.

In 2008, NPA began partnering with the Grassroots Policy Project (GPP) to more fully engage in what it called the "battle of big ideas." The battle of big ideas is a struggle to challenge the dominance of a corporate-conservative worldview. Corporate-conservative power is often hidden. It masks the causes of inequality and subordination in society and demobilizes people who otherwise would be clamoring for change.

An important step in the battle of big ideas has been in understanding the corporate-conservative worldview that plays a dominant role in some of the biggest debates taking place in the US and abroad. Earlier in this chapter, we noted the core ideas that bolster the corporate-conservative agenda. At the 2008 NPA convention, members took these core ideas on and began fleshing out their own ideas about the role of markets, corporations, government, and communities in creating conditions for shared prosperity, equity, and racial justice. Over time, NPA and community organizers have affirmed their beliefs in a positive role for a government that is of, by, and for the people. They put forward ideas about how markets should operate in ways that serve the people and not the other way around, putting people and the planet above profits. Because structural racism is real and creates disparities in housing, education, health care, criminal justice, and employment that harm all of us, NPA's big ideas emphasize taking action to ensure racial justice in all social and economic systems.

NPA is not alone in taking up the battle of big ideas. For example, faith-based organizations have been digging more deeply into the connections between faith and worldview. GPP has worked with ISAIAH in Minnesota on worldview and narrative since the early 2000s. ISAIAH describes its work on big ideas as "pursuing a deep and authentic exploration by real people about their faith, values and beliefs and how they connect with economic and racial justice" (Cryan 2011). On a parallel track, ISAIAH's statewide ally TakeAction Minnesota is also using worldview to build progressive power in the state. Their issue campaigns are linked together through a shared vision for a more prosperous and democratic Minnesota. TakeAction and other progressive groups in Minnesota coordinate on campaigns that are changing the political landscape, such as the ReNew MN effort in 2010 that challenged gubernatorial candidates around values instead of issues, and, in 2012, the successful effort to defeat a voter ID ballot initiative.

The battle of big ideas compels us to deepen our analysis and to understand the role of worldview in politics and culture. Our ideas tie all of our issues together into one narrative that can compete directly with the dominant ideas about the economy and the role of the government. Our ideas challenge current power relations and ongoing conditions of subordination that are based on class, race, and gender. And yet, our worldview does more than counter the corporate-conservative worldview: it taps into and reflects our deeply held beliefs and our aspirations for what the world could be—a world where every person and every community is respected; where economic and social relationships reflect our interconnectedness; where differences in culture, language, and experience are honored and treated as sources of collective strength; and where we all have a say in what happens in both our economy and our government.

Understanding the need to engage in the battle of big ideas is one thing. Acting on it is another. It calls for a significant shift in how we operate. The Occupy Wall Street movement provides helpful lessons as we seek to advance narratives that shift worldview toward more people- and planet-friendly politics. Absent funding, pollsters, or a communications war room, Occupy Wall Street put forward an analysis and public story that captured the nation's attention. This narrative, as spelled out in the "Declaration of the Occupation of New York City," had more political impact than those crafted by some of the most well-financed progressive organizations in the country (Occupy Wall Street 2011).

The analysis was powerful in large part because of its honesty. No punches were pulled in terms of naming the sins of Wall Street and the damage created by corporate power. Too often key progressive institutions focus only on speaking to where people are versus speaking to where we want them to go. If too much emphasis is placed on speaking to the middle, and not enough on shifting where the middle resides, our movements will lose the larger struggle.

Engaging in deep political analysis and strategy development to challenge the dominant worldview, and move our ideas to the center of American life, is not extra credit. It should move from the periphery toward the center of work. This means that political education that helps organizers and community leaders understand the role of worldview, and how that understanding informs strategies, campaigns, and communications, should be engrained in our training and leadership development programs. Strategic plans should demonstrate how our work not only helps us win campaigns and build organization now but also positions ideas to shift the realm of what is possible. This is new territory for many, but the potential for significant advances in using organizing to move people and ideas is a powerful development that we should foster and grow.

A New Political Bloc to Advance Our Long-Term Agenda

One of the verities community organizers inherited from the 1970s was, with a few exceptions, an aversion to electoral politics. The thinking was that getting involved with elections could compromise the ability to be oppositional. Many community organizers saw liberal and progressive groups in other sectors get too caught up in the inside game where Democratic Party operatives called the shots. It may have made sense at the time, but this approach is no longer sufficient if organizations are serious about building power to move a transformational agenda. As we build relationships and alliances and foster a powerful infrastructure, we need a strategy for exercising power in the electoral arena—critically independent power, with an inside-outside strategy. This calls for increased focus on building 501c4 and 527 organizations with significant and independent sources of financing.

An imperative we face today is the need to break open the narrowness of the current political debate. The limits we see in electoral and legislative arenas reflect how leaders in both parties are unwilling to rein in abusive corporations. This spells the need for a new political force that can pull politics in a new direction, creating space for candidates who want to lead us toward a new economy. Eventually, this independent electoral force would be sizable enough to actually inform the politics and decisions of both parties. It would reward elected officials who are willing to put principles over party and it would take on corporatist Democrats. This is one of the ways in which the forces we have in mind would be independent, for this electoral force would bring repercussions to bear against anyone who continued to favor the consolidation of financial power in the hands of the few at the expense of shared prosperity, opportunity, and inclusion for the rest of us.

Creating an independent force does require dealing with the tension between two hard realities. On the one hand, we are far from a moment that will give way to an alternative progressive or populist party. On the other, neither the Republican Party nor the Democratic Party is likely to become the party we need or want anytime soon. Which means that we have to work both outside of as well as within the current two-party structure, and make it work for us.

Everything we do on the inside must be linked to democratic organization that is deeply rooted in independent community, labor, and faith-based movements. Because we have not been so good at navigating these tensions over the past forty years, it's been bit of an either-or strategy. We either tend to get drawn into the inside game, losing our critical independence, or we have opted out of electoral politics altogether and largely have been an oppositional force. Neither is sufficient.

There are many historic models of independent political organizing that we can draw upon for inspiration: from the white abolitionists and black political leaders who came together in the 1840s and 1850s to the suffragists and the Niagara Movement in the early twentieth century; from the populists of the late nineteenth century to the nonpartisan leagues and the multiracial coalitions that worked both inside and outside of the Roosevelt administration for New Deal reforms and helped seed the leadership and infrastructure for the civil rights movement. Each effort in its way had to address similar challenges around their relationship to party politics, possibilities for creating progressive wings within existing parties versus creating third party alternatives, how to leverage voting power among disenfranchised groups (African Americans, farmers, workers, women, etc.), and how to work in coalition with other sectors.

A number of promising developments are taking place today across community, labor, and other sectors. A growing number of leaders around the country are creating state models for building independent political organizations that are multiracial, class-oriented, durable, and competent political organizations. An effort to build on and network these developments is described by Daniel Cantor and Anthony Thigpenn (2012) in their contribution to the *American Prospect's* issue exploring a progressive version of the Powell Memo. The idea is to strengthen existing electorally oriented organizations in key states, expanding carefully into other states, and knitting these together through a national network. As the momentum builds, these independent political efforts would be able to bring this organized power to bear in the struggle to move the Democratic Party in a progressive direction, including a readiness to challenge corporate-friendly Democrats in primaries.

We must remember that corporate-conservative thinkers did not see their goal as electing Republicans to state and federal office. They saw the Republican Party as a tool to achieve their long-term agenda. Taking over the party helped them turn the country toward the right on all the crucial issues affecting their interests. They didn't stop there. They also developed the power to control parts of, and inform much of, the Democratic Party. Progressive activists could apply a similar approach and do so in a way that is truly multiracial, with leadership from communities of color, articulating race-conscious and class-conscious politics.

The 2012 elections demonstrated how demographic shifts and strong on-the-ground voter engagement efforts can provide the opportunity to build a new electoral bloc that could shift the politics of the nation in powerful ways. And yet, shifting demographics alone will not automatically yield policy that advances racial and gender justice or rein in the power of abusive corporations. Instead, we will need to construct an effort specifically designed to make both happen.

In a *Nation* article calling for a "neo-rainbow" formation, Bill Fletcher and Danny Glover (2005) share lessons learned from the Jesse Jackson-led National Rainbow Coalition in the 1980s. Fletcher and Glover (2005) very clearly name the imperative of weaving together progressive populist traditions with a core emphasis on racial and gender justice:

> The politics of a neo-Rainbow initiative must be pro-equality populist. This means having more than an anti-corporate message, as important as that is. It must be about more than class, though rooted among working people and seeking the support of labor unions. A movement that links the fights for racial, gender and economic justice will resonate particularly, though not exclusively, with communities of color.

Knitting together this kind of multiracial electoral bloc will not be easy and it will require a lot of attention to relationship and trust building. But it is essential if we are to succeed.

Concluding

We are in a moment that is ripe with opportunity for building a movement that can create a long-term shift in our political economy. There are signs that community organizers and others are ready to think and act differently to make this happen. While there are a number of things that must shift, we feel certain that having a long-term agenda focused on structural reforms, winning the battle of big ideas, and adding political muscle and nuance to the work should be central to our strategy moving forward. If housing and banking activists and community organizers are able to integrate this kind of thinking and practice into our efforts, and do so in partnership with other key sectors and functions of the progressive movement, we could go a long way toward a new economy—one in which families, communities, and the environment are priorities for a new national bottom line.

References

Cantor, Daniel, and Anthony Thigpenn. 2012. "Build An Independent Political Organiza-tion (But Not Quite a Party)." *The American Prospect*, November 28. http://prospect.org/article/build-independent-political-organization-not-quite-party.

Cryan, Phillip. 2011. *Strategic Practice for Social Transformation.* Cambridge, MA: Grassroots Policy Project. http://www.strategicpractice.org/system/files/isaiah_report.pdf.

Fletcher, Bill, and Danny Glover. 2005. "Visualizing a Neo-Rainbow." *The Nation*, February 14. http://www.thenation.com/article/visualizing-neo-rainbow.

Hahn, Steven. 2012. "Political Racism in the Age of Obama." *New York Times*, November 11. http://www.nytimes.com/2012/11/11/opinion/sunday/political-racism-in-the-age-of-obama.html?_r=0.

Moyers, Bill. 2012. "The Powell Memo: A Call-to-Arms for Corporations." *Moyers & Company*, September 14. http://billmoyers.com/content/the-powell-memo-a-call-to-arms-for-corporations/.

Occupy Wall Street. 2011. "Forum Post: First Official Release from Occupy Wall Street." *OccupyWallStreet*, September 30. http://occupywallst.org/forum/first-official-release-from-occupy-wall-street/.

powell, john a., and Steve Menendian. 2006. *Progressive Politics: The Strategic Importance of Race.* Columbus, OH: Kirwan Institute for the Study of Race and Ethnicity, the Ohio State University. http://roadmapconsulting.org/latest-resources/item/51-progressive-politics-the-strategic-importance-of-race.

9

Forcing Banks to the Bargaining Table

Renegotiating Wall Street's Relationship with Our Communities

Stephen Lerner and Saqib Bhatti

T HE WORLD CHANGED in 2008 when the American financial crisis
cratered the United States and global economy. The scale of the devastation is overwhelming. Americans lost $17 trillion in household wealth as a result of the financial crash (Erickson, Fucile, and Lutton 2012), including more than $6 trillion in homeowner equity (Allegretto 2011, 1). Communities of color bore the brunt of the impact. According to a 2011 report by the Pew Research Center, Latinos lost 66 percent of their household wealth after the housing bubble burst and African American households lost 53 percent (Kochhar, Fry, and Taylor 2011, 1–2). RealtyTrac Staff (2013) reported that at the end of 2012, nearly twelve million families either had lost their homes to foreclosure or were in the process of foreclosure. Another sixteen million are underwater on their mortgages according to Zillow (2012), an online resource for real estate information. Chronic unemployment and underemployment has cost millions their livelihoods. Food stamp use is at an all-time high, with one out of every seven Americans dependent on the program (USDA 2012, 2). Data from the American Bankruptcy Institute (2013) show that personal bankruptcies have risen back to the levels they were once at before the Bankruptcy Abuse Prevention and Consumer Protection Act of 2005 made it more difficult to discharge debt through bankruptcy.

Meanwhile, the very people who caused the collapse have seen their wealth and power grow even greater. At the end of 2012, the top six banks controlled a larger swath of the American economy than ever before. According to the

Federal Reserve's National Information Center (2012), they held 73 percent of the total assets in the US banking sector. A report by the New Bottom Line (2012, 3) showed that bankers at those six firms have taken home more than half a trillion dollars in bonuses and compensation since the bailout.

However, the very concentration of financial and corporate power that led to the economic collapse is also creating the conditions that make it possible to build a broad-based movement dedicated to redistributing wealth and power in the US. Because wealth and power in America have become concentrated in the hands of a very small group of corporations and wealthy individuals, it is becoming increasingly clear who the villains are that are responsible for the growing inequality and suffering in America. Even though the wealthiest people and corporations are richer and more powerful than ever before, the economy they have created is increasingly unstable and their personal fortunes are increasingly vulnerable. The global financial system continues to teeter, and any one of the growing economic implosions around the world could knock the system into a global recession or depression.

At this moment in history, we have the greatest opportunity in generations to advocate for, campaign for, and win transformational political and economic change. Looking backward and trying to recapture the golden era of the housing justice movement in the 1970s when the Community Reinvestment Act was passed will not achieve this, however. Instead, we need to offer an analysis of why the system is broken, a vision of what we can win, and a concrete set of strategies and tactics that rise to both the perils and opportunities of our time.

Sadly, many groups and people are sleepwalking through a changed landscape, using the same set of tools, tactics, and strategies that were designed for a different political and economic time. If community groups, unions, organizers, advocates, lawyers, and others involved in fighting for fair housing and a more just society are approaching their work in the same way after the financial crisis as they did before, it is, at best, insufficient and, at worst, counterproductive. People know their world has been turned upside down and there is no evidence that the traditional set of legal, political, and regulatory tools offer any real hope of regaining what has been lost, much less creating greater opportunities for the future.

Because wealth and power are so concentrated in the United States and Wall Street banks are so dominant, it is impossible to develop a strategy to address the housing crisis by focusing on the need for fair housing, access to credit, and an end to discriminatory practices alone. Wall Street has developed an economic model that is based on burdening every aspect of people's lives with debt, and the housing crisis is just one symptom of the larger disease.

We are struggling with a myriad of other types of debt as well—education debt, credit card debt, and the public debt that is strangling state and local governments. We cannot relieve any of these individual symptoms without treating the larger disease. To do that, we need to fundamentally change the way that big Wall Street banks relate to communities.

By connecting the issues of community indebtedness with the larger question of out-of-control corporate political power, the defunding of social services, and the increasingly inefficient and ineffective ways that Wall Street lends, allocates, and directs capital, we can start to develop a movement that both engages the majority of the people in the country and challenges how the economy is organized.

In order to create an effective movement to combat corporate power, we need to be crystal clear in our analysis and thinking. The top bankers on Wall Street are unreformed, unrepentant, and unpunished. They literally pay billions of dollars in fines and legal settlements out of shareholders' money without batting an eye or suffering any drop in their stock prices or bonuses. They will clog up, dilute, and ultimately undermine any attempt to regulate them unless there is an organized political movement to hold them accountable.

Only by challenging, threatening, and disrupting banks' abilities to make money can we have any hope of changing how they operate. We need to force the banks to look into the economic abyss and feel the same panic that homeowners feel when they are about to be evicted. We need to make them understand the helplessness of cities as they sink into bankruptcy because of a declining tax base precipitated by the economic crash. We need to make them experience the anxiety of unemployed college graduates about to default on tens of thousands in student loans because they cannot find jobs.

However, there are two things we need to recognize: the global financial system is more interconnected than ever before and the big Wall Street banks are as weak, unstable, and vulnerable as they have ever been. In order to force banks to fundamentally change the way they operate and relate to communities, we need to bring the crisis on Main Street to their doorstep on Wall Street. But because of the banks' size and reach, any crisis that could force them to change their behavior also has the potential to impact the entire global economic system. In fact, just having to pay back the money they have stolen from communities through fraud, toxic interest rate swaps, and other schemes would likely cause some of them to go bankrupt. That is why any movement to transform Wall Street and rein in its control over society has to include breaking up the banks.

This chapter lays out some ideas of how we can start to make Wall Street banks feel the political and economic pain necessary to create an environment that forces them to bargain with homeowners, students, and municipalities about renegotiating existing debt and getting fair access to reasonable credit in the future.

Forcing Banks to the Bargaining Table

Wall Street has us under its thumb. Elected officials are accountable to the guy in the suit in a corner office in Manhattan rather than the constituents who elected them. In order to force banks to the bargaining table, we need to understand where their power comes from and devise a campaign to turn that power on its head. We need to build a movement supported by real leverage and power that forces the banks to renegotiate their relationship with Main Street.

There are two key ways that banks assert their dominance over society: debt and size. Wall Street banks are suffocating communities under mountains of unsustainable debt. We are being crushed with housing debt, consumer debt, and education debt, and state and local governments are slashing essential services in order to cope with their public debt. We have become slaves to our collective debt, with important decisions about when to start a family, where to live, where to work, and which services to fund being dictated by our debt load rather than the needs of our families and communities.

The big banks' second means of control over society is their size and their reach. The sheer size of the banks and the concentration of unfathomable wealth on Wall Street have distorted democracy and the economy in the US. Not only are the banks too big to fail, they are too big to regulate, too big to prosecute, and too big to jail. Big banks use their size to cheat and defraud consumers and taxpayers alike, and rest easy that they will be shielded from any real accountability because of their importance to the broader financial system. Their very size is central to America's economic problems, and they effectively use their size to hold the country hostage.

If debt and size are the weapons that banks use to control society, then we need a campaign that directly challenges the toxic debt deals with Wall Street and exploits the vulnerabilities inherent in the banks' unwieldy and unmanageable size. We need to use our leverage with the banks as both their customers and their debtors to create intense economic pressure. We need to challenge and chip away at their standing and power in order to weaken them enough politically to make real regulatory and legal action possible. Ultimately, this will help us create the conditions necessary to make it possible to break up the big banks and force them to renegotiate their relationship with our communities.

Immoral Hazard

In the United States, we are trained to believe that the credit-debtor relationship is a one-way street. The creditor holds all the power, and the debtor is at his mercy. In reality though, this relationship is much more equal than appears at first blush. After all, the debtor has the creditor's money and if he does not pay it back, then the creditor is out of luck. Corporate America understands this, and there are many examples of major multinational companies walking away from bad debt deals. In fact, Morgan Stanley walked away from its mortgage on five office towers in San Francisco in 2009 because it was too far underwater (Levy 2009).

But banks have gone to great lengths to make borrowers feel powerless. They use credit scores and, in the case of municipal borrowers, credit ratings to make borrowers feel trapped. Credit card companies like MBNA, now owned by Bank of America Corporation, led the charge in lobbying for the bankruptcy "reform" law of 2005 that made it difficult to discharge credit card debt through bankruptcy (Walker 2005). Reports from the US Senate Lobbying Disclosure Act Database (2013) show that, in 2009, banks lobbied heavily against laws that would have allowed judges to reset mortgage principal during bankruptcy proceedings, once again, to take away borrowers' leverage. When San Bernardino County in California announced a proposal to use eminent domain to reset mortgages, the banks immediately tried to nip the idea in the bud (Lazo 2012). Perhaps most powerful of all, banks have created a culture of shame around debt. They have even given it a name: moral hazard. Society looks down on people with debt and especially those who default on their debt. But this morality around debt is a Wall Street construct that only applies to Main Street, and it is a key tool that banks use to take away our leverage as debtors.

If we want to loosen Wall Street's debt grip over our communities, then we need to overcome the morality that the banks created and reactivate debtors' leverage. We need debtors of all stripes to understand their power in the creditor-debtor relationship and to be ready to use it. Figure 1 illustrates some of the strategies and tactics for doing this. It shows ways that we can fight back against housing debt, education debt, consumer debt, and public debt, and how they start to fit together as one campaign.

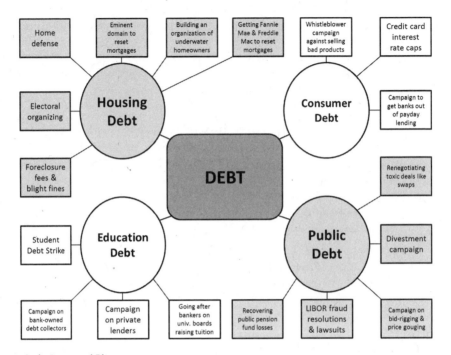

Credit: Lerner and Bhatti.

Figure 1. Organizing against debt.

A campaign to directly engage and challenge Wall Street power must address each of the four forms of debt featured in Figure 1 with a set of interrelated strategies and tactics. This campaign would provide us with the opportunity to directly organize millions of people across the country, all of whom have been negatively impacted by Wall Street banks. Data at the end of 2012 show us that nearly the entire population of the United States is impacted by these four types of debt:

- Housing debt: Twenty-eight million families (seventy-two million people) are either underwater on their homes (Zillow 2012), facing foreclosure, or have already lost their homes to foreclosure (RealtyTrac Staff 2013). Underwater homeowners owe $1.2 trillion more on their mortgages than their homes are worth.

- Education debt: Thirty-seven million students, graduates, parents, and grandparents owe $1 trillion in education debt (Johnson, Van Ostern, and White 2012, 10).

- Public debt: Approximately 150 million people live in the twelve states where there are plans to campaign around renegotiating public debt. These states have been forced to slash essential services to close $33 billion in budget gaps for fiscal year 2013 (Oliff, Mai, and Palacios 2012, 5).
- Consumer debt: According to the Federal Reserve's (2013) G.19 report on consumer credit, American families had $2.8 trillion in consumer debt as of November 2012, of which approximately $860 billion was credit card debt. A 2007 study by Demos found that nearly six in ten households in the United States with credit cards carry a balance (Garcia 2007, 5), and therefore have to pay high interest rates.

With nearly all Americans impacted by one or more of these four types of debt, we are given a massive constituency to organize, a common analysis of what is wrong with the economy, and common villains for building a campaign that calls for renegotiating debt. In so doing, it also lays the groundwork for addressing the crisis in housing, as well as broader questions of inequality and lack of opportunity in American society.

Housing Debt

Since the beginning of the economic crisis, the campaigns to stop foreclosures and make banks reset mortgages to fair market value have seen some of the most robust organizing work in the country. The housing work has offered some of the greatest opportunities to expand the number of people involved in building a broader movement and to achieve initial victories while setting the stage for bigger battles. While there are literally hundreds of groups and approaches to housing, we want to summarize the work of a couple of key players, the issues they are focused on, and the tactics they have adopted to start to paint a picture of the existing work to date.

Home Defenders League: Expanding Our Base

Underwater homeowners have lacked representation as a constituency. Many within the ranks of the sixteen million families that have seen their hard-earned wealth stripped away are angry and would like to fight for a solution, but they have not had the vehicle to do so. Now they do. The Home Defenders League (HDL), which was launched in May 2012 in nineteen cities and seventeen states, is a national membership-based organization of underwater and struggling homeowners. HDL creates a way for underwater homeowners to organize and speak with one voice about their needs and demands and to use their collective voting power to force a response to their issues. Through a sophisticated phone bank system, online organizing, and advertising, HDL is conducting mass outreach efforts inviting underwater homeowners to join. New members pledge to be Home Defender Voters who will look for the candidates willing to stand up for homeowners over Wall Street and champion their issues. Additionally, HDL members commit to engaging in campaign activities and working to recruit others into the league.

Operating simultaneously at the national and local levels is at the heart of the HDL strategy. Nationally, HDL is casting a wide net and offering itself as a vehicle for representing the interests of underwater homeowners broadly. These homeowners are then being mobilized into campaign activities in their communities locally. HDL tactics range from online actions to coordinated days of action across the country.

Underwater Voters: Creating an Electoral Constituency

Underwater homeowners emerged as an important voting bloc in the 2012 election. For the first time, a political action committee (PAC) specifically advocating for underwater homeowners was established—the Defend Our Homes PAC. A study by the Analyst Institute found that underwater homeowners who had received two mailers and two phone calls about a candidate's poor record on the housing crisis were 6.5 percent more likely to view that candidate as being "on the side of Wall Street and the big banks" rather than on "my side and the side of my family" (Defend Our Homes PAC Memorandum 2012). In future elections, the millions of underwater homeowners could be a key electoral constituency that fights for fairer housing policies as part of a broader electoral economic justice agenda.

Occupy Our Homes: Defending Homeowners

Occupy Our Homes is part of the Occupy Wall Street movement and helps connect Occupy members to traditional community organizing groups. It has led nonviolent resistance to foreclosure around the country through "home defense" actions. Members of Occupy Our Homes have successfully stopped many families from being evicted from their homes and have directly engaged Fannie Mae, Freddie Mac, and the big banks around the need to modify loans to keep people in their homes. Through direct action, they have both put a boot in the wheel of foreclosures and motivated and organized a new generation of organizers.

Resetting Mortgages to Fair Market Value: Creating Jobs by Fixing the Housing Crisis

Experts agree that the overhang of underwater mortgage debt is one of the primary drags on the economy and is a key cause of the jobs crisis. According to Zillow (2012), sixteen million families across the country owe $1.2 trillion more on their mortgages than their homes are worth. Even as Americans have seen their hours slashed and wages cut amid the recession, they are stuck paying the banks inflated boom-era mortgages. A study by the New Bottom Line (2011) found that if their mortgages were reset to fair market value, it would save the average underwater homeowners $543 per month on their mortgage bills. Spread across sixteen million families, this would pump $104 billion into the national economy every year. This would create 1.5 million jobs annually.

The research that has established that the housing crisis is a drag on the broader economy is an important part of creating a consensus that fixing housing has an importance far beyond the impact on struggling homeowners.

Using Eminent Domain to Reset Mortgages: Forcing Banks to the Table

Even though resetting mortgages is in the best interest of struggling home-owners, the investors that own the affected mortgages, families living in neighboring homes, and local governments, broad-based mortgage principal reduction has remained off the table. This is because the banks that service the loans and often own the second-lien mortgages have different incentives, and the decision is currently in their hands. Those banks refuse to reset mortgages because it is more profitable for them to let a loan go into foreclosure than to write down principal. However, there is a growing movement to take that decision out of their hands by using eminent domain.

If banks will not do the right thing and reset mortgages, then many cities are considering seizing the mortgages through eminent domain and doing it for them. Under a proposal first introduced in San Bernardino County, California, homeowners would stay in their homes, but the local government would buy the underlying mortgage notes at market value and refinance the homeowners into new fixed-rate mortgages with reduced principal (Ross

2012). Cities have never had a problem using eminent domain to seize homes to make room for stadiums and highways. Using eminent domain to seize mortgages to save neighborhoods, fix city budgets, and reset mortgages to fair market value would help jumpstart economic recoveries at the local level in every city that did this.

Writing down mortgages through eminent domain would immediately cost the banks billions of dollars, and it would set a precedent that could have broader implications for them. That is why the banks are pulling out all the stops to try to stop this from happening, raising legal challenges and trying to delegitimize it in the press. If the five most severely underwater US cities did this, they could seize $140 billion worth of underwater homes from the banks. In just those five cities, the banks would be forced to take a $30 billion haircut on the underwater loans.

Public Debt

Debt service is one of the biggest drains on public budgets, and banks have found numerous ways to nickel-and-dime municipalities on fees and interest rates. According to the Securities Industry and Financial Markets Association (2013), states, cities, counties, and other public entities have $3.8 trillion in outstanding bond debt and pay billions of dollars in interest each year. While banks have received money at zero or near zero interest rates from the Federal Reserve, they have continued to grow their profits by trapping cities in toxic debt deals. This has become an unsustainable crisis for America's cities and states.

Forty-eight states have been forced to close nearly $600 billion in budget gaps between fiscal years 2009 and 2013 (Oliff, Mai, and Palacios 2012, 5–11). They did this by slashing services and raising taxes. In the summer of 2012, three California cities filed for bankruptcy (Luhby 2012), and Scranton, Pennsylvania, was forced to cut nearly every city worker's pay down to minimum wage because it almost ran out of money (Cooper and Walsh 2012). But even as many other cities teeter on the verge of insolvency, banks are gouging them on deals like interest rate swaps, letters of credit, and predatory short-term loans.

In the past, there was little that people could do about these bad Wall Street deals, but a new scandal in the banking industry has allowed for new opportunities for cities and states looking to get a fair shake from Wall Street by giving them real leverage to force banks to renegotiate—LIBOR fraud.

LIBOR Interest Rate Fraud

Some of the world's biggest banks illegally rigged an interest rate index called the London Inter-Bank Offered Rate, or LIBOR, to pad their own profits, and taxpayers lost billions as a result. LIBOR is the interest rate that the world's largest banks charge each other for short-term borrowing, and is widely used as a benchmark for financial transactions as simple as credit cards and as complex as derivatives. It is self-reported by those banks and is compiled by the British Bankers Association (BBA). Globally, up to $800 trillion worth of securities and loans is tied to LIBOR, including investments held by cities, states, and public pension funds, which lost billions of dollars when banks colluded to drive down LIBOR. A slew of lawsuits is coming (Popper 2012), and the banks are potentially on the hook for trillions of dollars in damages (Rickards 2012)—likely enough to make some of them insolvent—if they do not negotiate settlements. Moreover, LIBOR fraud would provide a moral high ground in demanding the renegotiation of bad municipal debt deals. The banks cheated when they rigged the allegedly "free market," so now they owe a fair deal to those that suffered because of it.

Toxic Swap Deals

Big Wall Street banks are profiteering off the bailout by gouging cities and states on interest rate swaps. Interest rate swaps are a type of municipal derivative that banks sold to state and local governments as a way to save money on variable-rate bonds. However, these deals have become a major drain on public budgets since the Federal Reserve slashed interest rates to bail out the banks. LIBOR fraud drove up taxpayer losses on these deals even more. Nationally, taxpayers lost an estimated $48 billion on these toxic deals between 2008 and 2012 (S. Lerner and S. Bhatti, unpublished data). For example, according to the ReFund Transit Coalition's June 2012 report on the impact of toxic swap deals on public transit agencies, the New York City Metropolitan Transportation Authority (MTA) has lost more than $658 million since its swap deals went into effect, and it continues to lose another $114 million a year.

Opposition to toxic swap deals is growing. In July 2012, as a result of a campaign by the Coalition to Stop Goldman Sachs, the Alliance of Californians for Community Empowerment (ACCE), and Local 1021 of the Service Employees International Union (SEIU), the Oakland City Council voted to boycott Goldman Sachs when it refused to let the city out of its toxic swap deal.[1] Several cities, counties, and public agencies have filed lawsuits against

---

1. Oakland City Council Resolution No. 83962 C.M.S. (July 3, 2012).

the banks that manipulated LIBOR, seeking damages for losses on their swaps. The City of Baltimore has become the lead plaintiff in a class action lawsuit against the LIBOR panel banks,[2] and Philadelphia has hired a law firm to explore options for getting out of its swaps (Ransom 2012). Momentum from Oakland's swap campaign and the LIBOR fraud scandal has opened up the opportunity for a national movement to renegotiate swaps.

We need to demand that banks renegotiate their toxic swap deals without enforcing penalties and that they pay back the money they have overcharged since the financial crash. Cities should follow Oakland's lead by refusing to do business with banks unless they renegotiate. We can demand hearings into potential wrongdoing and hold creative actions at bank offices and branches to raise public awareness and put pressure on the banks. We can have an escalation action plan in each city and coordinate it nationally to bring the crisis to the banks' doorsteps.

Letters of Credit

A letter of credit (LOC) is a type of bond insurance policy that banks sell to public entities, and without which cities and states can be forced to pay back thirty-year bonds immediately, making them scramble to find money they do not have. While bonds typically have thirty-year terms, banks sold LOCs with two-to-three year terms with the promise that they would be easy to renew. But when these deals come up for renewal, banks tend to either hike up fees or refuse to renew them altogether, putting governments in a bind.

More than $200 billion of LOCs came up for renewal in 2010 and 2011 (Seymour 2010). Banks typically overcharged municipalities by more than 1 percent in fees (Mollenkamp and Corkery 2011), gouging taxpayers for an estimated $2 billion. Wall Street is holding state and local governments hostage, since, unless they choose to pay higher fees, they will have to pay back entire outstanding bonds on extremely accelerated timelines, which they cannot afford to do. As a result, they are forced to buy overpriced LOCs from the banks.

We need to demand that banks stop overcharging taxpayers on LOCs and that they pay back the money they have overcharged on these renewals since 2010. When JPMorgan Chase refused to renew its LOC with the Asian Art Museum of San Francisco in 2010, SEIU Local 1021, which represents workers at the museum, used the threat of a public campaign to force the bank to restructure the deal. According to a joint press release from the San Francisco

---

2. Mayor and City Council of Baltimore, et al. v. Credit Suisse Group AG, et al., No. 1:11-md-2262-NRB (S.D.N.Y. Filed 2012).

mayor's office and the museum, the new deal saved nearly $40 million (Office of the Mayor of San Francisco 2011). An LOC campaign would be similar to a swaps campaign in that it would put public pressure on the banks through creative actions, city council resolutions, and hearings to force them to come to the table and renegotiate.

Municipal Payday Loans

Because of revenue shortfalls, cities and states often have to take out short-term or bridge financing to cover their costs. When they take out these loans, banks charge them high interest rates of 3 to 5 percent even though the banks are able to borrow short-term money from the Federal Reserve for close to zero percent as a result of ongoing bailout programs. Instead of passing these savings on to taxpayers, the banks profiteer off the bailout, borrowing money for free from the Federal Reserve and lending it to cities and states at much higher interest rates. They are charging taxpayers exorbitant rates to lend us back our own money.

California was forced to borrow $1.5 billion for one month in 2009 to solve a cash-flow crisis (Petruno 2009). JPMorgan Chase lent the state money at 3 percent interest, which meant taxpayers were forced to pay $4 million in interest for just one month, at the same time that the bank was getting free money from the Federal Reserve. Similarly, JPMorgan Chase extended a $275 million short-term loan to Philadelphia in 2009 (DiStefano 2009). Taxpayers there were forced to pay $690,000 a month in interest for the first three months and then $1.8 million a month after that.

When banks provide short-term loans, we need to demand that they charge the same low interest rates they get from the Federal Reserve. In the consumer finance world, there is a term for short-term, high-interest debt: payday loans. We need to brand these deals as payday loans for cities and states and turn them into a public relations nightmare for the banks with creative actions, op-eds, and city council resolutions.

Education Debt

Being able to send your kids to college has always been a key part of the American Dream. We teach our children that a college education is the key to success in life—that it enables us to do whatever we set our minds to. Like homeownership, a college education has long been touted as the key to upward mobility in America.

However, like homeownership, this dream too has turned into a uniquely American Nightmare. As college costs have soared more than 1,000 percent over the past thirty-five years (Jamrisko and Kolet 2012) and states have slashed funding for public universities, American families have been forced to take on debt to pay for college. This is a crisis for the thirty-seven million students, parents, and even grandparents who owe more than $1 trillion in education loans (Johnson, Van Ostern, and White 2012, 10). It is also a crisis for those people who have effectively been priced out of college because they cannot afford to take on thousands in debt, as well as for those who are being robbed by for-profit colleges whose primary mission is to take students' money rather than provide them with an education.

All of this is exacerbated by the lack of job opportunities following the economic crisis for students after they leave college. With chronic unemployment and underemployment, these recent graduates are hard-pressed to find jobs that will pay the rent, let alone their college loans. Never before have so many people carried so much debt with so few opportunities for paying it.

Making Our Crisis Their Crisis: Organizing Thirty-Seven Million Around Debt Relief

Thirty-seven million people either have or are responsible for someone else's education debt. These millions of families that are drowning in debt can be the central organizing engine of a campaign that works to renegotiate this debt, fight for universal access to higher education, and challenge the defunding and privatization of education. A campaign for debt relief naturally leads to an analysis of a broken system that has forced people who just wanted to get a decent education to take on a trillion dollars in debt.

Consumer Debt

Since the 1970s, wages have stagnated even as prices have continued to climb. Working families have clung to the illusion of a middle class by taking on record debt. According to the Federal Reserve's (2013) G.19 report on consumer credit, American families had $2.8 trillion in consumer debt as of November 2012, of which approximately $860 billion was credit card debt. Banks have figured out a million ways to make money off of our personal cash flow problems. This ranges from the obvious—high interest rates on credit cards—to the insidious—reordering debit card transactions to maximize overdraft fees. Furthermore, the big banks are the financial backers of the major payday lenders, providing them with the money they need to sustain their predatory business model, and banks like Wells Fargo and U.S. Bank actually offer payday loans themselves.

Credit Card Interest Rate Caps

Nearly six in ten US households with a credit card carry a balance (Garcia 2007, 5), which means they are forced to pay high interest rates on their purchases. All states used to have caps on credit card interest rates, but in 1978, the US Supreme Court ruled that credit card companies only had to abide by the cap in the state in which they were based (Gilson 2007). As a result, some states eliminated their caps in order to attract business, and credit card companies moved their headquarters to those states, undermining usury laws elsewhere in the country.

Twenty-one states and the District of Columbia still have credit card interest rate caps, but they are unenforceable on banks headquartered outside of the state (Lazarony 2002). In 2010, Massachusetts State Treasurer Timothy Cahill took a bold step to pressure banks to comply with the state's 18 percent interest rate cap. He announced that he would move state investments out of banks that did not comply with the state's interest rate cap. As a result, he divested $243 million of state funds from Bank of America, Citigroup, and Wells Fargo (Mui 2010).

If the other twenty states that have credit card interest rate caps on their books followed Massachusetts's lead, it would be a tremendous blow to the banks. If large states that no longer have caps—like California, New York, Illinois, and Pennsylvania—brought them back and similarly divested from banks that did not abide by them, it would cost those banks billions of dollars in lost revenues. If we organize state and local campaigns to get our cities and states to divest from banks that charge predatory interest rates, we can force banks to start complying with age-old usury laws once again.

Payday Lending

Payday lending is the seedy underbelly of the finance industry in the United States. Payday lenders take advantage of cash-strapped Americans to lock them into a cycle of debt at predatory interest rates. According to a report by National People's Action and the Public Accountability Initiative, annualized interest rates on payday loans average 455 percent (Connor and Skomarovsky 2011, 5). However, even though big banks prefer to distance themselves from payday lenders, in reality, banks like Wells Fargo, Bank of America, JPMorgan

Chase, and U.S. Bank provide the financial infrastructure that keeps the payday lending industry in business by giving payday lenders the money they need to make loans (Connor and Skomarovsky 2011, 3).

Furthermore, at least three major banks—Wells Fargo, U.S. Bank, and Fifth Third Bank—offer direct payday lending products with annualized interest rates of up to 120 percent (Plungis 2010). They have decided to cut out the middlemen and embrace the predatory payday lending business model themselves.

A campaign to highlight Wall Street's role in the payday lending industry would seriously damage the big banks' image. Exposing how big banks support payday lenders and make predatory payday loans themselves would also serve as the basis for cities, states, and religious organizations to divest from those banks.

Whistleblower Campaign

Some of the banking industry's worst abuses of the 2000s would have been prevented if workers had been able to speak out without fear of reprisals when they saw those abuses taking place. Since the financial crash of 2008, bank workers have come out of the woodwork, saying they were forced to sell overpriced subprime mortgages to prime borrowers, offer higher credit card interest rates to Spanish speakers, resort to unethical and sometimes unlawful debt collection methods, take advantage of active military service members and their families, and sign fraudulent paperwork to illegally foreclose on homes. We have seen that every area of banking was laced with fraud and corruption.

In other countries, unionized bank workers are empowered to protect consumers from industry abuses and can play a key role in policing the industry because of the added workplace protections their union contracts afford them. We need to organize bank workers in the United States as well. A bank whistleblower campaign in the US would demonstrate how workplace protections for frontline bank workers would benefit the broader American public. Whistleblowers who come forward would make a compelling case for why bank worker unionization is in the public interest and why ordinary Americans should support collective bargaining rights for bank workers.

In turn, bank worker unionization would play three very important roles in advancing the fight against predatory consumer debt. First, unionized bank whistleblowers could help make the case for real reform by exposing the culture of recklessness and unlawfulness from within. Banks often dismiss stories of fraud and deception as isolated incidents perpetrated by rogue employees.

Whistleblowers could expose the pervasiveness of these problems and lay bare the systemic corruption at these institutions. Second, bank workers understand better than all of us exactly how banks take advantage of consumers, which laws they skirt, and what morally objectionable practices they engage in. Unionized bank whistleblowers could help identify the real problems that need to be fixed and could offer real solutions.

Finally, a workforce that was well educated about its whistleblower rights would serve as a regulatory force within a bank. We could "deputize" frontline bank workers as industry watchdogs to regulate banks from below without fear of retaliation. This would create a culture of vigilance at the banks and put them on notice that their every action is being closely scrutinized.

Size Matters

Rolling Stone's Matt Taibbi (2009) once called Goldman Sachs a "great vampire squid wrapped around the face of humanity, relentlessly jamming its blood funnel into anything that smells like money." This is emblematic of the big banks' business model. Their power derives in large part from their ubiquity. They are so big they really are everywhere, and they have found ways to make money off of everything. In the early 2000s, prior to the financial crash nearly 40 percent of all profits in America's national economy came from the financial sector, more than double the figure from thirty years prior (see Figure 2).

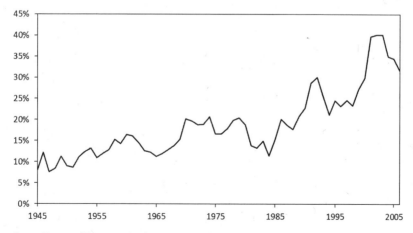

Source: Bureau of Economic Analysis 2009.

Figure 2. Financial industry's share of total corporate profits, 1945–2006.

Corporate Web

Whether it is through their private equity holdings, the corporate and civic boards their executives sit on, their financing relationships, or their political contributions, Wall Street banks have cemented their control over both the US economy and democracy. The top banks are not just too big to fail, they are too big to fathom. Figure 3 shows the economic and political reach of Wells Fargo & Company. The bank is a key financial backer of payday lenders like Advance America and Cash America and private prisons contractor Corrections Corporation of America (CCA). It gives money to right-wing organizations like the American Legislative Exchange Council (ALEC), which supports voter suppression laws; the US Chamber of Commerce, which pushes an anti-worker agenda; and the American Bankers Association and Financial Services Roundtable, both of which are key obstacles to meaningful financial reform. Furthermore, Wells Fargo CEO John Stumpf also sits on the boards of both Chevron and Target. The actions of Wells Fargo and the companies and organizations it is connected to impact millions of Americans.

A similar chart to Figure 3 can be created for any of the big banks. Bank of America board member Monica Lozano is a regent of the University of California system, where she has voted to raise tuition on students as a result of revenue shortfalls, even though the foreclosure crisis caused by her bank is the reason why those shortfalls exist. Goldman Sachs CEO Lloyd Blankfein is a director of the Partnership for New York City, a pro-austerity organization that prefers to slash Medicaid funding and cut mental health programs in order to cut New York City's deficit rather than taxing the millionaires on Wall Street (Partnership for New York City 2011, 4). The private equity arm of Goldman Sachs used to own Burger King, retailer Dollar General, and cell phone carrier Alltel Wireless. JPMorgan Chase CEO Jamie Dimon is a trustee of the University of Chicago and a director of the Federal Reserve Bank of New York (Bloomberg BusinessWeek 2013a). JPMorgan Chase board members are executives at Comcast, Honeywell, ExxonMobil, and Siemens (Bloomberg BusinessWeek 2013b).

However, the banks' ubiquity is also their weakness. Figure 3 shows that a comprehensive campaign focused on forcing Wells Fargo to renegotiate its relationship with the rest of the country can involve a wide swath of the American population. Immigration reform activists who are working to fix America's broken immigration system have a bone to pick with Wells Fargo, which provides critical financing to CCA—a company that lobbies against comprehensive immigration reform in order to keep its immigrant detention centers filled. The low-wage workers who work at Target can ask Wells

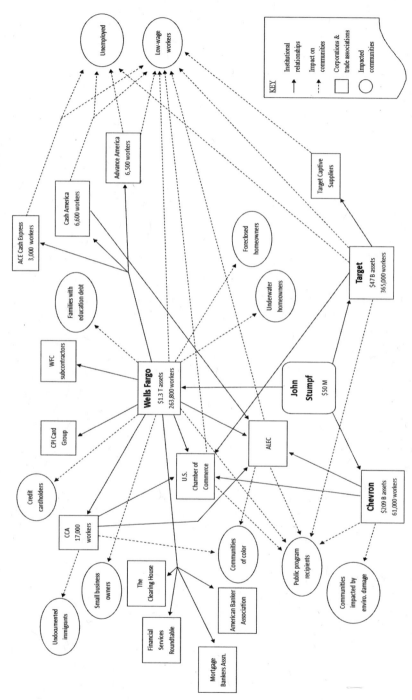

KEY

→ Institutional relationships

⇢ Impact on communities

☐ Corporations & trade associations

◯ Impacted communities

Credit: Lerner and Bhatti.

Figure 3. John Stumpf's America.

Fargo's Stumpf why he approves multimillion-dollar wages for Target CEO Gregg Steinhafel while they scrape by with poverty-level wages. The fact that big banks have their tentacles in every part of the American economic and political system means that their actions impact Americans from all walks of life. A campaign that unites those disparate constituencies could shake Wall Street to its core.

Too Big to. . .

In the ultimate irony, the 2008 financial crisis—that was caused by the failure and near failure of banks considered "too big to fail"—actually saw those same banks grow even bigger (see Figure 4). Furthermore, because of their size and reach, big Wall Street banks have convinced politicians that they are so big that America cannot succeed without them. They claim that any disruption to their business model would deal a fatal blow to the national economy. They effectively use their size to hold the US hostage. The paradox is that we cannot ultimately limit the power of banks unless we break them up, but they are so big and powerful that the government refuses to do this, no matter how unseemly the alternative. The banks treat their designation as "too big to fail" as license to do whatever they please, with impunity. However, their size has made the banks arrogant, and, ultimately, that can be their undoing.

In 2012, a single trader at JPMorgan Chase, dubbed the "London Whale," cost the bank $5.8 billion by making risky bets that backfired (Fitzpatrick and Zuckerman 2012). These losses sent tremors throughout the global economy and showed us just how vulnerable the financial system remains. America's biggest banks are still in dire straits, and they would be bankrupt if it were not for repeated backdoor bailouts, whether they come in the form of free money from the Federal Reserve or legal settlements for pennies on the dollar. A fair resolution to the robo-signing scandal, which saw banks fraudulently foreclosing on thousands of homeowners, would have given struggling home-owners real relief, but could have bankrupted the big banks. It was settled for pennies on the dollar to protect the banks, at homeowners' expense. Banks like JPMorgan Chase and Bank of America were also allowed to settle municipal derivatives bid-rigging lawsuits on the cheap, at taxpayers' expense. The same will likely be true of the LIBOR fraud scandal unless we organize to make sure we get back every penny the banks stole.

The big banks are so financially unstable that the legal and financial fallout from any one of their illegal or unethical business practices could cause them to collapse. That is why the federal government continues to bail them out by pushing cheap legal settlements and through access to secretive emergency

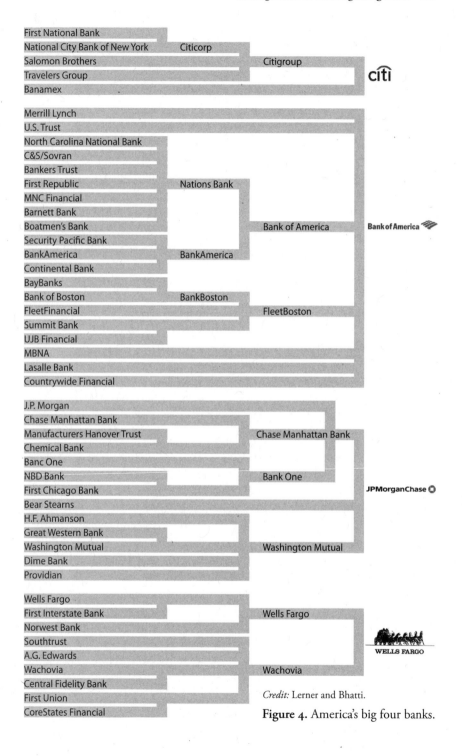

Credit: Lerner and Bhatti.

Figure 4. America's big four banks.

lending programs with interest rates as low as 0.01 percent (Ivry 2011). But these ongoing backdoor bailouts give us a tremendous organizing opportunity because each of these bailouts only reinforces the notion that Wall Street and the richest 1 percent play by a different set of rules than the rest of us, and that breeds widespread resentment.

If we tap into the anger over bailouts and people's innate sense of fairness, we can organize and turn the banks' unmanageable size into a key piece of leverage in a campaign to renegotiate their relationship with our communities. That, in turn, will provide the impetus for breaking up the big banks. The fact is that any campaign to force the banks to the bargaining table will have to cost them a lot of money. Given how fragile the banks are, any kind of formidable pressure would expose how, without their illegal and unethical schemes and government subsidies, they are not financially stable. If they are not financially stable, the only solution is to break them up.

Matching Bold Strategies with Creative Tactics

In order to be successful in forcing banks to the bargaining table, we have to capture the public imagination and build a movement that engages the millions of people impacted by Wall Street's predatory practices. To do that, we need to plan creative actions that rise to the urgency of the crisis in impacted communities and that empower ordinary people to do extraordinary things. Organizers who have been campaigning against banks around the US have already developed a wide array of tactics. The best ones accomplish multiple goals at the same time. They engage new people and help build bigger organizations, they put direct pressure on the bank, and they draw media coverage and help educate the broader public by dramatically illustrating the ways in which Wall Street continues to rip us off. The lesson we have learned again and again is that focusing all of the energy on one big march or rally is draining and can be a distraction. However, through creative, militant, and relentless actions—both big and small—we can start to win real victories and challenge Wall Street domination.

Stopping Foreclosures

Some of the most militant and creative tactics in the Wall Street accountability movement have been used to physically stop foreclosures and evictions. Occupy Our Homes (2013) has even developed a home defense manual called *How to Defend Your Home* that describes some of these tactics:

Figure 5. Activists from Occupy Our Homes gather for an
eviction blockade outside a home slated for
foreclosure in Minneapolis.
Photo credit: Occupy Our Homes Minnesota.

- **Blockades**: During an eviction blockade, people sit in the doorway
  of a home at the moment of eviction and refuse to leave, risking arrest
  (Figure 5). According to the Occupy Our Homes (2013) home defense
  manual, there were twenty-eight blockades nationally between 2008
  and 2012, and three of them resulted in arrests.

- **Camp-outs**: In Minneapolis and Atlanta, Occupy Our Homes and
  Neighborhoods Organizing for Change (NOC) set up encampments
  around homes threatened with eviction by using nonviolent civil disobedience to physically interfere with foreclosure.

- **Sing-ins**: In New York City, people have used their voices to disrupt
  foreclosure auctions by singing over the auctioneer.

Taking the Fight Directly to the Banks

As noted in the introductory chapter of this book, organizers across the United
States have developed tactics that force banks to directly confront the impact
of their policies on the broader community. Additional actions include the
following:

- **Trash-ins**: Vacant, foreclosed homes often become blighted, over-
  run with garbage, and magnets for crime. Neighbors living in nearby
  homes are forced to suffer the consequences, and local governments
  are forced to spend taxpayer dollars to prevent further deterioration.

Communities are fighting back by collecting trash from these homes and "depositing" it in the lobbies of foreclosing banks. Members from Action Now in Chicago, Communities United for Action in Cincinnati, ACCE in California, ıMiami, and Occupy St. Louis are among the thousands of community members who have used this tactic to force banks to deal with the neighborhood impacts of foreclosure.

- **Move-ins:** In Los Angeles, ACCE moved a family's furniture into the downtown offices of a bank to protest unfair foreclosures, shutting down the office and forcing the bank to confront the human impacts of foreclosure on individual families (see Figure 6).

- **Delivering the bill:** Groups across the US have performed actions where they deliver giant bills at bank offices and branches, demanding that the banks pay back the money they stole from the community through illegal or unethical business practices. Sometimes the bill is paired with a giant check from the bank to the taxpayers that community members ask the bank manager to sign.

- **Foreclosing on the bank:** Another tactic that forces banks to directly confront the crisis they caused is foreclosing on the bank itself. A variation on this is wrapping the outside of the bank with crime scene tape. Community members in Portland, Los Angeles, and Chicago have all used variations of this tactic.

Figure 6. Leaders from ACCE and SEIU moved a family facing foreclosure into the plaza outside of the JPMorgan Chase offices in Los Angeles.

Photo credit: Slobodan Dimitrov.

- **Crashing industry events:** In addition to bank branches, any of the above tactics can also be carried out at industry gatherings and events. For example, Chicago's Southsiders Organized for Unity and Liberation (SOUL) did an inside/outside action at the Mortgage Bankers Association convention in 2011. Sixteen SOUL members were arrested after setting up a living room inside the hotel where the convention was being held and refusing to leave, while hundreds rallied outside in the street and cheered them on. American Bankers Association conventions in Chicago and Boston have also been met with similar inside/outside actions marked with dramatic props like oversized puppets of bank executives. Industry events provide a natural news hook, an opportunity to reach a broader audience, and a chance to change the broader narrative about the industry.

Educating the Public

One of the biggest challenges in mobilizing populist anger against Wall Street is that most people do not understand the inner workings of high finance. That is why it is important to develop tactics to make the critiques accessible and educate the public about the ways in which banks work to rip us off.

- **Grade-ins:** As teachers were being publicly scapegoated for public school budget deficits in Chicago, the Chicago Teachers Union organized "grade-ins" at bank branches to educate parents about how banks were gouging the school district through toxic swap deals. Teachers graded homework in the lobbies of bank branches with signs encouraging customers to talk to them about how their bank was harming students. They passed out leaflets directly linking the banks' swap profits to increased class sizes and program cuts at neighborhood schools and asked parents to call bank executives and demand that they renegotiate their toxic deals with the school district.

- **Bus teach-ins:** In Oakland, members of ACCE Riders for Justice regularly hold teach-ins on buses to educate riders about how banks are squeezing the transit agency for millions. They board public buses, give a short talk about how bad bank deals have led to service reductions and cuts in public transit, and then ask the riders to pick up their cell phones and call the bank to demand a better deal. ACCE's bus teach-ins were the inspiration for the ReFund Transit Coalition's national day of action in June 2012, when bus and subway teach-ins were held coast to coast.

Winning

The United States economy has been transformed since the 1970s into a system that allows for unprecedented amounts of wealth and power to be concentrated in the hands of Wall Street's top bankers. The housing justice movement must transform as well to be able to win in this new world order. We cannot solve the housing crisis by focusing on housing issues alone. The struggle for fair housing needs to be a central part of a larger battle to rein in the power of big Wall Street banks and, in doing so, to reclaim democracy and build an economy that creates real opportunities for working people in America.

The banks' size may be their greatest asset, but it is also their greatest liability. The financial crash demonstrated definitively that the debtor class has the financial leverage to break the power of the big banks. We need to use that leverage as part of a strategic campaign to force banks to renegotiate their relationship with our communities and to pay back the trillions that they stole from us through toxic and predatory deals and outright fraud. We need to put enough economic, political, and legal pressure on them to force them to do right by homeowners and communities more broadly. If this campaign to force the banks to the bargaining table is successful, then we will be sitting across from smaller banks because it means we will have successfully broken up the titans of Wall Street.

References

Allegretto, Sylvia A. 2011. *The State of Working America's Wealth, 2011*. Economic Policy Institute Briefing Paper 23, March 23. http://www.irle.berkeley.edu/cwed/wp/wealth _in_the_us.pdf.

American Bankruptcy Institute. 2013. "U.S. Bankruptcy Filings 1980-2011 (Business, Non-Business, Total)." American Bankruptcy Institute. Accessed February 10. http:// www.abiworld.org/AM/AMTemplate.cfm?Section=Home&TEMPLATE=/CM /ContentDisplay.cfm&CONTENTID=65139.

Bloomberg BusinessWeek. 2013a. "Executive Profile: Jamie Dimon." Bloomberg Business-Week. Accessed February 10. http://investing.businessweek.com/research/stocks /people/person.asp?personId=170444&ticker=JPM.

———. 2013b. "JPMorgan Chase & Co. Profile." Bloomberg BusinessWeek. Accessed February 10. http://investing.businessweek.com/research/stocks/people/board.asp?ticker=JPM.

Bureau of Economic Analysis. 2009. "Table 6.16D. Corporate Profits by Industry." Bureau of Economic Analysis. Accessed November 24.

Connor, Kevin, and Matthew Skomarovsky. 2011. *The Predators' Creditors: How the Biggest Banks Are Bankrolling the Payday Loan Industry*. National People's Action and Public Accountability Initiative. http://public-accountability.org/wp-content/uploads/2011/09 /payday-final-091410.pdf.

Cooper, Michael, and Mary Williams Walsh. 2012. "Unions Fight Scranton Mayor After He Cuts Pay to Minimum Wage." *New York Times*, July 10. http://www.nytimes.com /2012/07/11/us/unions-fight-scranton-mayor-after-he-cuts-pay-to-minimum-wage.html.

Defend Our Homes PAC Memorandum. 2012. "Re: Defend Our Homes Underwater Test." *Defend Our Homes*, September 10.

DiStefano, Joseph N. 2009. "JPMorgan Offers Philly Emergency Cash—at a Price." *Philadelphia Inquirer*, September 1. http://www.philly.com/philly/blogs/inq-phillydeals /JPMorgan_offers_Philly_emergency_cash_-_at_a_price.html.

Erickson, Jennifer, Tamara Fucile, and David Lutton. 2012. "Dodd-Frank Financial Reform After 2 Years: 5 Successes and 5 Things That Will Make Our Markets Stronger." *Center for American Progress*, July 20. http://www.americanprogress.org/issues/regulation /report/2012/07/20/11910/dodd-frank-financial-reform-after-2-years.

Federal Reserve. 2013. "G.19 Release on Consumer Credit for November 2012." *Board of Governors of the Federal Reserve System*, January 8. http://www.federalreserve.gov/ releases/g19/20130108.

Fitzpatrick, Dan, and Gregory Zuckerman. 2012. "J.P. Morgan 'Whale' Report Signals Deeper Problem." *Wall Street Journal*, July 14. http://online.wsj.com/article/SB1000 1424052702303740704577524451161966894.html.

Garcia, José A. 2007. *Borrowing to Make Ends Meet: The Rapid Growth of Credit Card Debt in America*. New York: Demos. http://www.demos.org/sites/default/files/publications /Demos_BorrowingEndsMeet.pdf.

Gilson, Dave. 2007. "House of Cards." *Mother Jones*, September/October. http://www .motherjones.com/politics/2007/09/house-cards.

Ivry, Bob. 2011. "Fed Gave Banks Crisis Gains on $80 Billion Secretive Loans as Low as 0.01%." *Bloomberg*, May 26. http://www.bloomberg.com/news/2011-05-26/fed-gave -banks-crisis-gains-on-secretive-loans-as-low-as-0-01-.html.

Jamrisko, Michelle, and Ilan Kolet. 2012. "Cost of College Degree in U.S. Soars 12 Fold: Chart of the Day." *Bloomberg*, August 15. http://www.bloomberg.com/news/2012-08 -15/cost-of-college-degree-in-u-s-soars-12-fold-chart-of-the-day.html.

Johnson, Anne, Tobin Van Ostern, and Abraham White. 2012. *The Student Debt Crisis*. Washington, DC: Center for American Progress. http://www.americanprogress.org /wp-content/uploads/2012/10/WhiteStudentDebt-3.pdf.

Kochhar, Rakesh, Richard Fry, and Paul Taylor. 2011. *Wealth Gaps Rise to Record Highs between Whites, Blacks and Hispanics*. Washington, DC: Pew Research Center. http://www.pewsocialtrends.org/files/2011/07/SDT-Wealth-Report_7-26-11_FINAL .pdf.

Lazarony, Lucy. 2002. "States with Credit Card Caps." *Bankrate.com*, March 20. http:// www.bankrate.com/brm/news/cc/20020320b.asp.

Lazo, Alejandro. 2012. "San Bernardino Eminent Domain Plan Draws Wall Street Criticism." *Los Angeles Times*, August 16. http://articles.latimes.com/2012/aug/16/business /la-fi-mo-eminent-domain-20120816.

Levy, Dan. 2009. "Morgan Stanley to Give Up 5 San Francisco Towers Bought at Peak." *Bloomberg*, December 17. http://www.bloomberg.com/apps/news?pid=newsarchive& sid=aLYZhnfoXOSk.

Luhby, Tami. 2012. "California Bankruptcies Are Only the Beginning." *CNNMoney*, July 12. http://money.cnn.com/2012/07/12/news/economy/california-bankruptcies/index.htm.

Mollenkamp, Carrick, and Michael Corkery. 2011. "Banks Get Tough with Municipalities." *Wall Street Journal,* January 27. http://online.wsj.com/article/SB1000142405274870406 260457610628251268331.html.

Mui, Ylan Q. 2010. "Massachusetts Moving Money Out of 3 Big Banks to Protest Credit Card Rates." *Washington Post,* April 15. http://www.washingtonpost.com/wp-dyn /content/article/2010/04/14/AR2010041404863.html.

National Information Center. 2012. "Top 50 Bank Holding Companies." Board of Governors of the Federal Reserve System, December 31. http://www.ffiec.gov/nicpubweb /nicweb/Top50Form.aspx.

New Bottom Line. 2011. *The Win/Win Solution: How Fixing the Housing Crisis Will Create One Million Jobs.* New Bottom Line. http://www.newbottomline.com/download _report_the_win_win_solution.

———. 2012. *Pulling Back the Curtain: The 1% behind the 2011 Big Bank Bonuses.* New Bottom Line. http://d3n8a8pro7vhmx.cloudfront.net/bac/pages/456/attachments/original /PullingBacktheCurtainReport.pdf?1327276996.

Occupy Our Homes. 2013. *How to Defend Your Home.* Occupy Our Homes. Accessed February 10. http://occupyourhomes.org/resources.

Office of the Mayor of San Francisco. 2011. "Mayor Newsom, City Attorney Herrera, City Controller Ben Rosenfield, President Chiu and Asian Art Museum Foundation Announce Proposal to Restructure Foundation's Debt." Press release, January 6.

Oliff, Phil, Chris Mai, and Vincent Palacios. 2012. *States Continue to Feel Recession's Impact.* Updated June 27. Washington, DC: Center on Budget and Policy Priorities. http:// www.cbpp.org/files/2-8-08sfp.pdf.

Partnership for New York City. 2011. *2011 Public Policy Priorities: Focusing on Economic Growth and Job Creation in New York.* New York: Partnership for New York City. http://www.pfnyc.org/reports/Priorities%202011.pdf.

Petruno, Tom. 2009. "California to Get $1.5-Billion Loan from JPMorgan Chase." *Los Angeles Times,* August 19. http://articles.latimes.com/2009/aug/19/business/fi-state -loan19.

Plungis, Jeff. 2010. "Banks May Use Payday-Style Loans to Replace Lost Overdraft Fees." *Bloomberg,* February 23. http://www.bloomberg.com/apps/news?pid=newsarchive&sid =a25EweZDVeAU.

Popper, Nathaniel. 2012. "Rate Scandal Stirs Scramble for Damages." *New York Times,* July 10. http://dealbook.nytimes.com/2012/07/10/libor-rate-rigging-scandal-sets-off -legal-fights-for-restitution.

Ransom, Jan. 2012. "City Aims to Get Money from Banks." *Philadelphia Inquirer,* June 28. http://articles.philly.com/2012-06-28/news/32442068_1_swap-deals-royal-bank -interest-rates.

RealtyTrac Staff. 2013. "1.8 Million U.S. Properties with Foreclosure Filings in 2012." *Realty-Trac.com,* January 14. http://www.realtytrac.com/content/foreclosure-market-report /2012-year-end-foreclosure-market-report-7547.

ReFund Transit Coalition. 2012. *Riding the Gravy Train: How Wall Street Is Bankrupting Our Public Transit Agencies by Profiteering off of Toxic Swap Deals.* June. ReFund Transit Coalition. http://refundtransit.org/wp-content/uploads/2012/06/STRAT_Transit SWAPS.pdf.

Rickards, James. 2012. "LIBOR Fraud May Be the Mother of All Bank Scandals." *US News & World Report*, July 23. http://www.usnews.com/opinion/blogs/economic-intelligence/2012/07/23/libor-fraud-may-be-the-mother-of-all-bank-scandals.

Ross, Andrew S. 2012. "Eminent Domain Plan Gaining Support." *San Francisco Chronicle*, July 31. http://www.sfgate.com/business/bottomline/article/Eminent-domain-plan-gaining-support-3751091.php.

Securities Industry and Financial Markets Association. 2013. *Outstanding U.S. Bond Market Debt*. Washington, DC: Securities Industry and Financial Markets Association. Accessed February 10. http://www.sifma.org/uploadedfiles/research/statistics/statistics files/cm-us-bond-market-outstanding-sifma.xls.

Seymour, Dan. 2010. "Floating-Rate Debt Faces a Liquidity Issue." *Bond Buyer*, May 20. http://www.bondbuyer.com/issues/119_346/floating_rate_debt-1012407-1.html.

Taibbi, Matt. 2009. "The Great American Bubble Machine." *Rolling Stone*, July 9. http://www.rollingstone.com/politics/news/the-great-american-bubble-machine-20100405.

USDA (United States Department of Agriculture). 2012. *Program Information Report*. Washington, DC: US Department of Agriculture. http://www.fns.usda.gov/sites/default/files/datastatistics/october-2012.pdf.

US Senate Lobbying Disclosure Act Database. 2013. "Query the Lobbying Disclosure Act Database." United States Senate. Accessed February10. http://soprweb.senate.gov/index.cfm?event=selectfields.

Walker, Tom. 2005. "Bankruptcy Law Gift to Credit-Card Firms." *Providence Journal*, July 6.

Zillow. 2012. "Despite Home Value Gains, Underwater Homeowners Owe $1.2 Trillion More than Homes' Worth." *Zillow.com*, May 24. http://investors.zillow.com/release detail.cfm?releaseid=676600.

10

Housing as a Human Right
Where Do Immigrants Stand?

Janis Bowdler, Donald L. Kahl, and José A. Garcia

S INCE THE 1980S, the United States has been experiencing a significant shift in its demographic makeup. The faces that have come to dominate and represent the American landscape can no longer be defined solely in
terms of black or white. While heralded in newspapers across the country as
"the next wave," the incendiary anti-immigrant and discriminatory rhetoric
that ethnic minorities encounter on a daily basis threatens the future cohesion of this country. Nowhere is this more prevalent than in housing systems
and policies. Whether trying to rent, buy, lease, sell, or finance, Latinos and
other ethnic groups often face obstacles and roadblocks to equal housing
opportunities.

At the federal level, the Fair Housing Act[1] prohibits discrimination based
on race, color, religion, national origin, sex, family status, or disability, and
those statutory rights are available to all regardless of citizenship status (American Immigration Lawyers Association 2009). Yet, these housing rights have
come under serious attack as vitriolic anti-immigrant sentiments and economic pressures have led to the scapegoating of immigrants. Federal governmental institutions, fair housing allies, and housing industry stakeholders must
readjust their approach to address the more varied mix of realities and challenges facing today's American housing situation. Furthermore, housing and
immigration stakeholders must work more closely to address concerns that cut
across both fields. Movement building is underway within both stakeholder

---

1. Title VII of the Civil Rights Act of 1968, 42 U.S.C. §§ 3601–31.

groups, but intentional collaboration is required to ensure the interests of vulnerable families will not continue to go unaddressed.

Latinos Are Changing the Face of the Nation

There are over fifty million Latinos living in the United States—accounting for roughly one in six Americans.[2] This growth has been driven by a population increase of 15.5 million among Hispanics between 2000 and 2010 (see Figure 1) and accounts for more than half of the total US population increase during that time.

High birth rates are driving the growth among communities of color. Non-Hispanic whites accounted for less than half (49.6 percent) of newborn children in the twelve-month period that ended July 2011, while Latinos, African Americans, Asians, and those of mixed race accounted for 50.4 percent of newborns during the same period—an important demographic shift (US Census Bureau 2012). This trend is only reinforced by the fact that minority women in the US, on average, are younger than their non-Hispanic white counterparts and still in their childbearing years.

The reason for the rapid growth of Hispanics[3]—that it is driven primarily by native births—has been overshadowed by a persistent myth that most Hispanics are foreign-born. On the contrary, only a third of Latinos in the US are foreign-born (US Census Bureau 2010), and even among foreign-born Latinos, one in four is a naturalized citizen (Immigration Policy Center 2012a). Moreover, the number of new Mexican immigrant arrivals from 2006 to 2010 fell by 60 percent, from more than 1 million in 2006 to 404,000 in 2010 (Pew Hispanic Center 2011).

The growth in population and the relatively young age of the community make Latinos a driving force in the housing, consumer, and labor markets. Estimates put the purchasing power of Latinos at approximately $1 trillion annually, and this is only expected to grow, given that Latinos are relatively young compared to the total population (Immigration Policy Center 2012b). Experts predict that by 2020, nearly half of first-time home buyers will be Latino (Masnick and Belsky 2009). If projections hold true, Latinos will

---

2. Nationally, according to the 2010 Census, non-Hispanic whites account for 63.7 percent of the total population, while Latinos, African Americans, and Asians make up 16.3 percent, 12.3 percent, and 5 percent of the total population, respectively (US Census Bureau 2011).

3. The terms "Hispanic" and "Latino" are used interchangeably by the US Census Bureau and throughout this chapter to refer to persons of Mexican, Puerto Rican, Cuban, Central and South American, Dominican, Spanish, and other Hispanic descent; they may be of any race.

	2010 population	2000 population	Change, 2000-2010	Percent change, 2000-2010	Share of total change (%)
Hispanic	50,729,570	35,204,480	15,525,090	44.1	55.6
*Native born**	31,912,465	21,072,230	10,840,235	51.4	38.8
*Foreign born**	18,817,105	14,132,250	4,684,855	33.2	16.8
White alone, not Hispanic	196,931,448	194,527,123	2,404,325	1.2	8.6
Black alone, not Hispanic	37,936,978	33,706,554	4,230,424	12.6	15.1
Asian alone, not Hispanic	14,558,242	10,088,521	4,469,721	44.3	16.0
Other, not Hispanic	9,193,451	7,895,228	1,298,223	16.4	4.6
Total	309,349,689	281,421,906	27,927,783	9.9	100.0

Note: "Other, not Hispanic" includes persons reporting single races not listed separately and persons reporting more than one race.

* Native and Foreign born figures are subsets of the Hispanic figures.

Source: Pew Hispanic Center tabulations of 2000 US Census and the US Census Bureau 2010.

Figure 1. Population change by race and ethnicity, 2000 and 2010.

account for three out of every four new workers joining the labor force by 2020 (Department of Labor 2012).

The steady growth of Latinos and other racial and ethnic minorities and their increasingly important role in the economic dynamics of this country requires practices and policies that foster integration into the economic and social fabric. Addressing the housing needs of Latinos will require attention to demographics and the impact of discrimination on their housing choices or lack of choices. When Latinos have fair and equitable access to housing choices, they are able to create wealth and give back to the communities they live in. This does not benefit Latinos alone, it benefits us all.

Social and Economic Shifts Lead to the Targeting of Immigrants

At the turn of the twenty-first century, many US policymakers and advocates believed that an overhaul of the broken immigration system was around the corner. Comprehensive immigration reform would have provided a path to citizenship for millions, reunited families, and brought undocumented workers out of the shadows (Immigration Policy Center 2009). Instead, the 2000s have unfolded very differently. A confluence of social and economic shifts has changed the arc of public discourse, the path of immigration reform, and, unfortunately, the way immigrants are portrayed and perceived. In the last decade, Hispanic families have moved away from traditional "gateway" regions such as San Francisco, New York, and Chicago (Singer 2004). The tragedies of September 11, 2001 and an economic recession in the latter part of the decade have put Hispanic and other immigrant workers on the defensive. These issues, and a growing generational gap, shape the conversation on the investment in public resources for the next generation. Consequentially, immigrants are under frequent attack and have unfairly become scapegoats for a wide range of social ills. The predictable result has been a new tidal wave of hostility, harassment, and discrimination against anyone perceived as foreign-born—regardless of actual citizenship or immigration status.

Terrorism, New Frontiers, the Generation Gap, and a Recession

The terrorist attacks of September 11, 2001 fundamentally changed the way immigrants are perceived and portrayed in the United States. The national discourse shifted away from a discussion on fixing a broken immigration system for the sake of labor markets and family reunification to one centered on enforcement. The effect has been dramatic: from 2002 to 2010, deportations in the United States increased 134 percent, with over one million individuals being deported between 2008 and 2011 alone (see Figure 2).

The so-called enforcement-first policy was purportedly aimed at the worst criminals, but many hardworking families were torn apart by workplace raids (Capps et al. 2007), fostering a hostile atmosphere for Latinos. The Pew Hispanic Center reports that three out of five Latinos believes discrimination is a "major problem," up from 54 percent who said the same in 2007, and more than a third attributed this discrimination to immigration issues (Lopez, Morin, and Taylor 2010). Research by the National Council of La Raza (NCLR) also found that many Latino youth feel they are regularly being negatively stereotyped by institutional actors as varied as teachers, employers, and police officers (Foxen 2010).

The change in political tone on the issue of immigration has intensified as Hispanics and other immigrant populations move beyond traditional gateway cities like New York City, Chicago, and Los Angeles. Demographic data from 2011 show that the greatest growth in recent years has been in the South and Midwest, which experienced growth of 57 percent and 49 percent, respectively, in its Latino population (US Census Bureau 2011). It is no surprise that several of the states with the fastest and most recent growth have pursued the harshest anti-immigrant laws, such as South Carolina, Georgia, and Alabama.

The age gap between a relatively young Hispanic population and an aging white population has further complicated the perceptions of Latinos and other immigrants. Research conducted by the University of Southern California and PolicyLink found that states with a wide gap between the number of

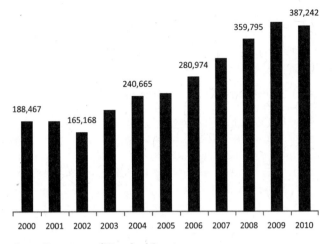

Source: Department of Homeland Security 2010, 2011.

Figure 2. Deportations, 2000–2010.

whites under eighteen years old and those sixty-five years old and older have the lowest spending on infrastructure for the future and also spend less on education (Treuhaft, Blackwell, and Pastor 2011). For the older, established community, tension arises when they believe their tax dollars are being used only to subsidize a younger generation of "others." These perceptions appear to be particularly negative when it is believed that those being helped are from minority groups. For example, in Arizona, where 82 percent of those sixty-five years old and older are non-Hispanic whites and youth of color represent 58 percent of the state's young, the state ranks among the lowest in public expenditure per pupil (Pastor and Carter 2012).

Finally, the still-recent collapse of the housing market helped usher in the nation's most profound recession since the Great Depression. Since the start of the recession, one out of six job seekers cannot secure full-time employment and eight million families have been forced to leave their home. The situation is even more desperate among communities of color, where double-digit unemployment has been the norm since 2008 and nearly a quarter of Latino families that took out mortgages between 2004 and 2008 were at risk of foreclosure. Meanwhile, income and assets have increased for the top 1 percent. In 2007, the top 0.1 percent of American households had an income that was 220 times larger than the average of the bottom 90 percent, and they own more than a third of the nation's wealth (Mishel and Sabadish 2012). While Latinos did not create this economic disparity, they have become a favorite target for those playing the blame game. Hispanic workers have been frequently accused of taking jobs that should go to American (meaning non-Hispanic) workers (Hopkins 2007), and conservative pundits have claimed, falsely, that lending to borrowers of color underpins the mortgage crisis.

From Shifting Dynamics to Discrimination

Taken together, the toxic political landscape that willfully scapegoats immigrants, the widespread foreclosures, and the stubborn unemployment rates have left Hispanic families reeling. However, it is difficult to assess the number of times the housing rights of foreign-born individuals are violated. According to the US Department of Housing and Urban Development (HUD), an estimated one in four Hispanic renters, and one in five Hispanic home buyers, are likely to face some type of discrimination in their home search (HUD 2005). While these statistics are reason enough for concern, the social environment impacting home searches has changed dramatically since these data were collected in 2001. There exists ample and tangible evidence that speaks to the discrimination and hostility aimed at immigrants that shape their housing experiences.

Hate speech and hate crimes against Hispanic Americans have escalated dramatically over the last decade. Particularly disturbing, national organizations such as NCLR, Mexican American Legal Defense and Education Fund, and the Southern Poverty Law Center have documented the use of hate speech by public figures in the media. Lou Dobbs, a former correspondent for CNN, exemplified this activity in his nightly segment titled *Broken Borders*, where he regularly characterized Hispanic immigrants as "invaders" and as posing a major health risk to Americans. Another CNN commentator, Glenn Beck, jokingly read a "fake" advertisement on his national radio program for a "giant refinery" that produced "Mexinol," a fuel made from the bodies of illegal immigrants coming here from Mexico, as a solution to both the immigration and energy crises (Murguía 2008).

While those employing anti-immigrant rhetoric claim legal immigrants or native-born Hispanics are not the primary targets, the impact of hate speech makes no such distinction. As explained by Jack Levin, a hate crime expert at Northeastern University, such dehumanizing speech often leads to hate crimes (Southern Poverty Law Center 2012). According to the Federal Bureau of Investigation (FBI), 795 people were victims of anti-Hispanic hate crimes in 2010, the most recent figure available, which is up from 595 in 2003 (FBI 2011). One of the most egregious examples is the tragic shooting death of Juan Varela—a fifth generation American of Mexican descent. Varela was targeted and shot in his front yard in Phoenix, Arizona, in May 2011 by his neighbor, who yelled, "Go back to Mexico or die!" (Costantini 2011).

The acrimony has spilled over into the political sphere as well. In 2006, Hazelton, Pennsylvania, passed the Illegal Immigration Relief Act Ordinance (IIRA), requiring landlords to verify immigration status and impose a fine of $1,000 for each undocumented tenant. Within five years, more than one hundred similar local ordinances were under consideration or had passed at the local level (American Immigration Lawyers Association 2009). Since many landlords are ill equipped to determine the immigration status of their tenants, they are likely to simply turn away minority individuals—virtually guaranteeing wholesale discrimination based on national origin.

A different approach to reducing its Hispanic population was attempted by the City of Manassas, Virginia. The City responded to resident complaints about immigrants by establishing a hotline to lodge anonymous complaints about overcrowded housing conditions. In the first month of the program, 99 percent of inspections were of Hispanic households, and few, if any, violations were discovered (City of Manassas 2004a). Undeterred, the City obtained information regarding household residents and their relation to one another from the Manassas City Public Schools. The data were shared with local city officials despite prohibitions against the sharing of such personal information. In a final effort to intimidate Hispanic families, the Manassas City Council amended the City Code to define "family" as only the nuclear family and one extended family member, therefore limiting a common scenario for Hispanic families of including extended relatives such as cousins, uncles, aunts, nieces, and nephews in their homes—even if the total was below the legal occupancy limit. Although litigation ultimately caused the repeal of the zoning amendment, inspections of Hispanic households continued for some time on the basis of anonymous complaints received through the hotline. This program was ultimately shut down. Unfortunately, during the time of Manassas's anti-Hispanic efforts, approximately 80 percent of all homes investigated for overcrowding were owned by Hispanic families, and, faced with such harassment, intimidation, and hostility, hundreds of Hispanic residents left Manassas and Prince William County (City of Manassas 2004b).

Such local ordinances foreshadowed more egregious efforts at the state level to intimidate immigrants. Arizona signed into law in 2010 a sweeping immigration bill that aimed to identify, prosecute, and deport undocumented persons in the state. Sections of the law were eventually struck down by the Supreme Court in *Arizona v. United States*, but the provision requiring immigration status checks during law enforcement stops was upheld. Arizona-like bills have been introduced in dozens of states since 2010, many of which have been experiencing a growth in their Latino population. Alabama, which saw a 145 percent increase in its Hispanic population from 2000 to 2010 (US Census Bureau 2011), passed the most draconian of the anti-immigrant state laws. The law authorizes local law enforcement officers to arrest and detain anyone suspected of being in the country illegally, penalizes people who knowingly transport, harbor, or rent property to illegal immigrants, requires public schools to confirm students' legal status through birth certificates or sworn affidavits, and makes it a felony to present false documents or information when applying for a job (NCLR 2011).

Discrimination does not always present itself so maliciously or obviously as it does in the case of restrictive ordinances and state laws. Throughout the 2000s, Hispanic and immigrant families have been subjected to unfair price discrimination and deception in the home buying market. It has been well documented that, even after controlling for key risk characteristics, black and Hispanic families have been at least twice as likely as their white peers to be steered toward more costly and higher-risk subprime loans throughout much of the last decade (Apgar, Herbert, and Mathur 2011; Bocian, Ernst, and Li 2006). Rather than providing creditworthy borrowers with prime mortgages for which they qualified, misaligned incentives in the retail market have led to many being placed in subprime loans with troubling features such as restrictive prepayment penalties, "interest only," plus negative amortization, or interest rates that are adjustable in double digit increments (Bowdler 2005). It is no surprise then that foreclosures have had a disproportionate effect on Hispanic homeowners. According to the Center for Responsible Lending, 17 percent of Hispanic homeowners in 2010 have lost their home or are at risk of experiencing foreclosure in the near future (Bocian, Li, and Ernst 2010).

Moreover, the concentration of foreclosures in certain neighborhoods has ensured that the repercussions of predatory lending are felt well beyond the homeowner. Foreclosures deflate surrounding property values and reduce the tax base for local municipalities (Center for Responsible Lending 2009; Immergluck and Smith 2005). An investigation by the National Fair Housing Alliance (NFHA) found major differences in the maintenance and upkeep of foreclosed properties owned by banks, known as real estate owned (REO) properties, in Hispanic neighborhoods as compared to predominantly white neighborhoods (NFHA 2012b). For example, in Phoenix, Arizona, 73 percent of REOs in Hispanic neighborhoods had more than five maintenance problems compared to only 25 percent of homes in white neighborhoods. Notably, 73 percent of REO properties evaluated in Latino neighborhoods were missing a "For Sale" sign. The combined result of these problems is frightening—

foreclosures and the depression of home prices have eroded 66 percent of the wealth held by Latino households (Kochhar, Fry, and Taylor 2011).

Ultimately, the tumultuous homeownership market and heightened anti-immigrant sentiments have led to destructive trends in the rental housing market as well. In a report released in 2010, the Equal Rights Center (ERC) found that 79 percent of Latinos in Frederick, Maryland, experience some type of disparate, adverse treatment when they sought rental housing. The ERC (2010) began its investigation after Hispanic residents reported racial profiling by local law enforcement and others in the community. These results are not isolated. In a survey of Hispanic families living in the South, 60 percent in Tennessee reported experiencing racism while looking for a home to rent. The Southern Poverty Law Center (2009), author of the report, raised concerns that weak enforcement of the Fair Housing Act throughout the South is leaving immigrants vulnerable to violations of their housing rights.

Where Is the Justice?

Despite clear and compelling evidence that immigrant and Hispanic families face intense challenges to their right to live in the neighborhood of their choosing, there has not been a coordinated fair housing response to the attack on immigrants—and, by extension, on Hispanic households. Certainly, there are notable, high-profile cases brought in defense of Hispanic families for which much credit is deserved. In 2012, the US Department of Justice (DOJ) settled the two largest fair lending cases in its history. Its investigations into the mortgage lending practices of Countrywide and Wells Fargo revealed unfair price discrimination and steering—the practice of pushing borrowers into subprime loans despite their ability to qualify for prime loans. The Central Alabama Fair Housing Center, the Fair Housing Center of Northern Alabama, and the Center for Fair Housing, Inc., along with two residents on behalf of a large class of borrowers, filed a lawsuit under the federal Fair Housing Act and asserted violations of the Supremacy and Due Process Clauses of the United States Constitution.[4]

As important as these fair lending cases are, it is disappointing that, given the sustained campaign against immigrants and the ripple effect on members of the national origin protected class, there has not been a more significant, coordinated response from the fair housing community. In 2007, Charles

---

4. See United States of America v. State of Alabama, Governor of Alabama, and National Fair Housing Alliance, Inc., No. 11-14532 (D.C. Doc. No. 2:11-cv-02746-SLB, filed August 20, 2012) (11th Cir.).

Basis	FY 2007		FY 2008		FY 2009		FY 2010	
	Number of Complaints	% of Total	Number of Complaints	% of Total	Number of Complaints	% of Total	Number of Complaints	% of Total
Disability	4,410	43%	4,675	44%	4,458	44%	4,839	48%
Race	3,750	37%	3,669	35%	3,203	31%	3,483	34%
Familial Status	1,441	14%	1,690	16%	2,017	20%	1,560	15%
National Origin	1,299	13%	1,364	13%	1,313	13%	1,177	12%
National Origin - Hispanic or Latino	784	80%	848	8%	837	8%	722	7%
Sex	1,008	10%	1,133	11%	1,075	10%	1,139	11%
Religion	266	30%	339	3%	302	3%	287	3%
Color	173	20%	262	2%	251	2%	219	2%
Retaliation	588	60%	575	5%	654	6%	707	7%
Number of Complaints Filed	10,154		10,552		10,242		10,155	

Percentages do not total 100 percent because complaints may contain multiple bases
Percentages are rounded to the nearest whole number

Source: HUD 2010.

Figure 3. Bases of HUD and FHAP complaints, FY 2007–FY 2010.

Kamasaki and Janis Bowdler argued that the fair housing system underserved Hispanic families. Little has changed in the fair housing world in the years that have followed, while the situation facing immigrants has become substantially worse. Complaints based on national origin remain low, as does the level of government and private grants to private and public fair housing groups focused on the Latino community. In 2010, HUD received 10,155 reported housing discrimination grievances, the fifth consecutive year that housing discrimination grievances exceeded ten thousand. However, Figure 3 shows that the number of complaints based on national origin have remained flat since 2007 despite two of the worst anti-immigrant state laws and countless restrictive local ordinances having been enacted during that time. Nearly 82 percent of all HUD fair housing complaints were related to disabilities and race, while only 12 percent were attributed to national origin concerns—more than half of which were against those with Hispanic backgrounds (NFHA 2012a).

Without question, millions of incidences of discrimination go unreported every year (conservative estimates put the number of violations of fair housing laws at four million annually), but participation is disconcertingly low among Latinos. Nearly 83 percent of people who believe they have experienced housing discrimination do not report it (see Figure 4). Many people either do not know their rights under the Fair Housing Act and local antidiscrimination laws or cannot detect the differential adverse treatment that they receive.

Still, others do not believe anything will come of their complaints. But a key concern in anti-immigrant hot spots is the fear of retribution for filing a complaint. This concern is not a baseless one. While HUD claims not to share information about complainants with the Immigration and Customs Enforcement (ICE), that policy is not in writing.

HUD's (2013) mission is "to create strong, sustainable, inclusive communities and quality affordable homes for all" and can be traced to the work of civil rights activists and leaders who worked tirelessly for the creation of a federal agency that protected minorities from housing discrimination. The nation's changing demographics pose new challenges that will require HUD to adapt its fair housing outreach and enforcement models. Workforce diversity is an important place to start. An analysis of HUD employment data shows that 38 percent of all employees at HUD are black, 49 percent are white, and 7 percent are Hispanic (NCLR, unpublished data). Greater representation of the communities it seeks to serve would improve HUD's reach and impact.

Another important step for HUD would be to adjust its grant-making approach to be more inclusive. NCLR's review of fair housing grants made between 2006 and 2010 shows a meaningful shift to include more Latino-focused organizations in enforcement activity, as shown in Figure 5. However, funding directed at Hispanic-serving organizations remains proportionately small. Most funding earmarked for Latinos goes toward outreach and education (see Figure 5). Fostering a well-informed community is a critical aspect of

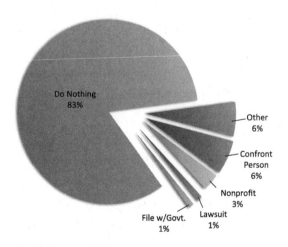

Source: Abravanel and Cunningham 2002.

Figure 4. Action taken by people who believe
they have experienced discrimination.

Year	2006		2007		2008		2009		2010	
Awrd Type	Latino-Focused	Total Awarded	Latino-Focused	Total Awarded	Latino Focused	Total Awarded	Latino-Focused	Total Awarded	Latino-Focused	Total Awarded
Private Enforcement Initiative	8	56	9	55	20	78	12	81	12	95
Education and Outreach Initiative	11	46	7	32	4	16	6	17	9	32
Fair Housing Organization Initiative	0	0	0	0	0	0	0	0	3	11
Total	19	102	17	87	24	94	18	98	24	148

Source: NCLR calculations of HUD fair housing grants made from 2006 to 2010.

Figure 5. HUD fair housing grants by type and focus, 2006–2010.

the broader strategy to defend housing rights. That being said, enforcement of fair housing laws has a measurable impact in deterring discriminatory practices. Based on NCLR's analysis of fair housing grants made between 2006 and 2010, only 13 percent of HUD's enforcement budget is disbursed to organizations that clearly state Latinos or immigrants are a target audience under their grant (NCLR, unpublished data). This issue could be addressed by breaking down the silos that prevent community service nonprofits from receiving funding to conduct fair housing enforcement. These institutions are often closest to the community and have the cultural competency necessary to move swiftly in their defense.

While the fair housing system has not done as much as it could to address the needs of immigrants, immigration advocates have been slow to incorporate fair housing into their tool belt to fight back against the anti-immigrant movement. Anti-immigrant laws have been challenged based on constitutional grounds related to immigration law, and while this approach has had some success in muting or repealing some aspects of these laws, it does little to address the lingering hostility and harassment immigrant families endure. A truly coordinated initiative that joins fair housing and immigrants' rights advocates is essential to addressing and redressing national origin discrimination.

Incorporating Immigrant Rights into the Housing Justice Movement

Addressing discrimination effectively requires a multifaceted approach that engages all relevant stakeholders, including victims of discrimination, violators of civil rights laws, advocates, and the community at large. This is particularly true in dealing with discrimination against members of immigrant communities, where cultural, societal, language, and legal status issues create their own additional complexities. Many in immigrant communities face isolation once relocated to the US, come from countries without a history of individual protectionism, may harbor serious suspicions about dealing with government agencies or officials, and, in the face of the vitriolic debate in America over immigration reform, may fear that any complaint or objection will result in their expulsion from the country. In this next section, we will review a model for bringing housing and immigrant justice together under one roof.

A Model for Success: The Equal Rights Center

Founded as a fair housing organization in 1983, the Equal Rights Center (ERC) in Washington, DC, is a national civil rights organization dedicated to promoting equal opportunity in housing, employment, and access to public accommodations and government services. The ERC has more than six thousand individual members across the United States who act as the eyes and ears of the organization, identifying and reporting emerging issues of discrimination at the earliest possible times.

As a general framework, the ERC has programs in six substantive areas: Fair Housing, Fair Employment, Disability Rights, Immigrant Rights, LGBT Rights, and Corporate Partnerships & Training. Four additional groups, Communication & Outreach, Testing & Special Projects, Administration, and Development, provide further support and specialized expertise. This variety of programmatic areas, and extensive collaboration among the various programs, ensures a comprehensive response to any type of discrimination.

The ERC model's approach to addressing discrimination incorporates five separate, but interrelated, areas of activity: (1) Education and Outreach, (2) Public and Private Collaborations, (3) Victim Intake and Advocacy, (4) Civil Rights Testing, and (5) Targeted Outreach and Enforcement. Through its Immigrant Rights Program, the ERC demonstrates that this model is successful, and replicable, for battling discrimination that targets immigrant communities.

Education and Outreach. On the theory that an educated community is the best guardian of its own civil rights, the ERC provides information in a variety of languages and formats to reach the largest number of individuals in immigrant communities. Alone, and in collaboration with community partners, the ERC conducts scores of "Know Your Rights" workshops, presentations, and trainings, relying on bilingual staff or translators to convey information in the primary languages of the participants. In addition to directly educating attendees at these events, printed materials are distributed to reach the families and friends of workshop participants, as well as other individuals who may not be aware of civil rights protections. To expand its education reach, the ERC distributes tens of thousands of brochures, self-advocacy toolkits, reports, and newsletters each year. This direct community contact results in a flow of information to the ERC about individual instances of discrimination, as well as systemic issues impacting immigrant communities.

Public and Private Collaborations. To leverage its own resources and expand its reach and effectiveness, the ERC regularly partners with federal and local government agencies, allied organizations, for-profit businesses, and others to address established and emerging civil rights issues. In particular, the ERC has collaborated with the Fair Housing and Equal Opportunity Office of HUD, local offices of human rights, and national organizations, such as NCLR, to respond to new issues affecting immigrant communities, such as the emergence of local "anti-immigrant" ordinances and "English only" rules, as well as to document and address trends in discrimination. The ERC also looks for opportunities to bring together diverse partners to address common concerns—such as the intersections of disability rights, LGBT rights, and fair housing advocacy, as they impact immigrant communities. Finally, in a unique program designed to stop discrimination before it occurs, the ERC also works directly with for-profit housing providers and other businesses to make sensitivity to civil rights and diversity part of their corporate culture.

Victim Intake and Advocacy. Receiving and responding to complaints from individuals who experience discrimination is pivotal to promoting equal opportunity. Intakes not only document individual incidents of discrimination but also provide information about patterns of more widespread, systemic discrimination and inform the ERC's policy advocacy. The ERC conducts intakes in the language preferred by the victim, using bilingual staff members or with the assistance of translation services. The ERC model not only advises individuals on their rights and the remedies available to them but also, where appropriate, assists in resolving the problem. ERC staff members regularly investigate intake complaints, communicate with the discriminating party on the individual's behalf, and assist with administrative complaint filings. In some instances, individuals who may not be comfortable lodging a complaint in their own name (e.g., because of their immigration status or a distrust of the government) can rely on the ERC to take action.

Civil Rights Testing. At the core of the ERC's model for promoting civil rights is the extensive use of civil rights testing. Testing is a proven best practice in civil rights investigations because it is designed to identify differences in treatment accorded to individuals who are similar in every significant respect except the variable being tested—such as race, national origin, or language proficiency. With hundreds of on-call trained testers, the ERC uses a variety of innovative testing techniques (matched-pair and individual testers, and in-person, telephone, Internet, and mail testing) to identify and document differences in the quality, quantity, and content of the treatment provided to individuals based on their individual characteristics. Through testing, the nature and extent of illegal discrimination can be exposed and then addressed.

Targeted Outreach and Enforcement. Once discrimination is identified, whether through an individual intake or a systemic testing investigation, the ERC works to ensure that the offender changes their policies and practices and that the victims obtain relief. The ERC regularly contacts housing providers, and others, to inform them of discriminatory conduct at their establishments, to start a dialogue of how to address the discrimination, and to ensure that the discriminatory conduct does not continue. These efforts do not always result in a satisfactory resolution, and the ERC model recognizes that some civil rights violations can only be effectively redressed through enforcement actions. To address such difficult situations, the ERC relies on a long-standing collaboration with the Washington Lawyers' Committee for Civil Rights and Urban Affairs to secure legal representation to address discrimination before administrative agencies and the courts.

The success of the multifaceted approach of the ERC model can be demonstrated by several metrics. Through its efforts, the ERC has:

- Reached thousands of immigrants and their families every year, and educated them on their civil rights;
- Assisted hundreds of individuals faced with discrimination based on their national origin or other protected characteristic;
- Collaborated with HUD and community-based organizations to bring civil rights education to immigrant communities in seven languages;
- Worked with the District of Columbia government to ensure that government services are available in the most common languages found in the immigrant communities of the nation's capital;
- Published reports exposing national origin and language-based discrimination targeting immigrant communities;
- Caused the City of Manassas, Virginia, to repeal its draconian "overcrowding ordinance" that was being used to target Latino families and drive them from the city; and
- Negotiated nondiscrimination agreements with landlords to make more than fifteen thousand apartment units available to families using Housing Choice Vouchers—the majority of whom are racial and ethnic minorities and single mothers with children.

Building a Movement

Movement building has been the linchpin of the civil rights strategy to defend the rights of immigrants. Attacks on immigrants have been laden with racial overtones and with consequences felt well beyond those who are foreign-born. Civil rights organizations recognize the inherent threat and have banded together to fight back against egregious anti-immigrant laws in Arizona and Alabama and protect vulnerable immigrant workers. Civil rights and labor unions stood in solidarity with immigrants in Alabama as they reenacted the march from Selma to Montgomery. DREAM Act students have been the inspiration of the movement, staging marches, protests, and campaigns across the country (Ross 2012). The unity of the civil rights field has produced results. Many of the worst provisions of the Arizona and Alabama laws have been struck down (although the "papers please" provision survived in Arizona). In June 2012, the Obama administration announced a new policy known as Deferred Action that would allow certain immigrants under the age of thirty who were brought to the country as children to apply for temporary status.

Unfortunately, the housing and immigrant rights movements have existed in silos. In fact, the Occupy Wall Street movement did little to incorporate the issue of immigration and the concerns of immigrant families and workers into their platform from the outset. There are a number of reasons why the Occupy movement did not immediately embrace immigration reform or tackle immigrant housing rights. As the editors noted in the Introduction, racial divides are commonplace in American life, and it should come as no surprise that they exist within the Occupy movement. We also acknowledge that it is unfair to characterize the Occupy movement as monolithic. Demonstrators in various cities elevated the issues that hit close to home. But certainly, immigrant workers and families fall squarely within the "99%." Many immigrant advocates reported feeling disappointed that they did not find a welcome home for their cause in the Occupy Wall Street movement from the beginning (Puente 2011; Nittle 2011; Speri 2011; Zerkel 2011; Kennedy 2012; Ramirez de Arellano 2011).

This book focuses on the power of organizing to catapult a movement for a more just housing system that acknowledges and supports an individual's right to live where they choose, obtain mortgages for which they qualify, and access decent and safe shelter. Furthermore, the system must effectively enforce law on behalf of victims when it is broken. In this regard, it is the DOJ that has provided the strongest example of what is possible when we break down our silos. The murder of Mexican immigrant Luis Ramirez in Shenandoah, Pennsylvania, sparked outrage from civil rights and immigration advocates across the country. With racial tensions running high in the community, an all-white jury acquitted the two white teenagers involved of the most serious charges (Rubinkam 2009). The DOJ pursued a different strategy and reopened the case. Ultimately, the attackers were found in violation of the Fair Housing Act because their actions were motivated by a desire to keep Latinos from living in their town. They were sentenced in 2011 to nine years in prison (DOJ 2011).

With the democratic spirit brimming across the country, it is the right time for a paradigm shift for both housing and immigration advocates. The all too frequent attacks on immigrants should serve as a warning call to those marching for justice and equality that our opponents are prepared to fight. Only by joining forces will we overcome such a challenge. In fact, if our own movement cannot learn to be inclusive, it is unreasonable to assume that the broader society will figure it out on its own.

References

Abravanel, Martin D., and Mary K. Cunningham. 2002. *How Much Do We Know?* Washington, DC: Urban Institute.

American Immigration Lawyers Association. 2009. *Navigating the Immigration Debate: A Guide for State and Local Policymakers and Advocates.* Washington, DC: American Immigration Lawyers Association.

Apgar, William Jr., Christopher Herbert, and Priti Mathur. 2011. *Risk or Race: An Assessment of Subprime Lending Patterns in Nine Metropolitan Areas.* Washington, DC: US Department of Housing and Urban Development. http://www.huduser.org/portal/publications/hsgfin/risk_race_11.html.

Bocian, Debbie Gruenstein, Keith S. Ernst, and Wei Li. 2006. *Unfair Lending: The Effect of Race and Ethnicity on the Price of Subprime Mortgages.* Durham, NC: Center for Responsible Lending.

Bocian, Debbie Gruenstein, Wei Li, and Keith S. Ernst. 2010. *Foreclosures by Race and Ethnicity: The Demographics of a Crisis: CRL Research Report.* Durham, NC: Center for Responsible Lending.

Bowdler, Janis. 2005. *Jeopardizing Hispanic Homeownership: Predatory Practices in the Home-buying Market.* Washington, DC: National Council of La Raza.

Bowdler, Janis, and Charles Kamasaki. 2007. "Creating a Fair Housing System that Works for Latinos." In *Fragile Rights within Cities: Government, Housing, and Fairness*, edited by John Goering, 229–51. Lanham, MD: Rowman & Littlefield.

Capps, Randy, Rosa Maria Castañeda, Ajay Chaudry, and Robert Santos. 2007. *Paying the Price: The Impact of Immigration Raids on America's Children.* Washington, DC: The Urban Institute. http://www.urban.org/UploadedPDF/411566_immigration_raids.pdf.

Center for Responsible Lending. 2009. "Soaring Spillover: Accelerating Foreclosures to Cost Neighbors $502 Billion in 2009 Alone; 69.5 Million Homes Lose $7,200 on Average Over Next Four Years, 91.5 Million Families to Lose $1.9 Trillion in Home Value; $20,300 on Average." *Center for Responsible Lending Report*, May. http://www.responsiblelending.org/mortgage-lending/research-analysis/soaring-spillover-3-09.pdf.

City of Manassas. 2004a. Residential Overcrowding Code Enforcement Task Force, meeting minutes for June 24.

———. 2004b. Department of Public Works Report to the Manassas City Council on proactive enforcement, December 13.

Costantini, Cristina. 2011. "Anti-Latino Hate Crimes Rise as Immigration Debate Intensifies." *The Huffington Post Latino Voices*, October 19. http://www.huffingtonpost.com /2011/10/17/anti-latino-hate-crimes-rise-immigration_n_1015668.html/.

Department of Homeland Security. 2010. "Enforcement Integrated Database (EID)." US Department of Homeland Security, December.

———. 2011. "ENFORCE Alien Removal Module (EARM)." US Department of Homeland Security, January.

Department of Labor. 2012. *The Latino Labor Force at a Glance*. Washington, DC: US Department of Labor. https://www.dol.gov/_sec/media/reports/HispanicLabor Force/HispanicLaborForce.pdf.

DOJ (Department of Justice). 2011. "Two Shenandoah, Pa., Men Sentenced for the Fatal Beating of Luis Ramirez." US Department of Justice Office of Public Affairs news release, February 23. http://www.justice.gov/opa/pr/2011/February/11-crt-229.html/.

ERC (Equal Rights Center). 2010. *Fair Housing for All: The Disparate Response to Latino Housing Needs in Frederick County, MD*. Washington, DC: Equal Rights Center.

FBI (Department of Justice Federal Bureau of Investigation). 2011. "FBI Crimes Remain Steady: 2010 FBI Report Released." *FBI Stories*, November 14. http://www.fbi.gov /news/stories/2011/november/hatecrimes_111411/.

Foxen, Patricia. 2010. *Speaking Out: Latino Youth on Discrimination in the United States*. Washington, DC: National Council of La Raza. http://www.nclr.org/images/uploads /publications/youth_focus_group_report.pdf.

Hopkins, Andrea. 2007. "Hispanics Do Jobs Others in U.S. Won't Stand For." *Reuters*, February 25. http://www.reuters.com/article/2007/02/26/us-usa-immigration -hispanics-general-fea-idUSN1649636320070226/.

HUD (Department of Housing and Urban Development). 2005. *Discrimination in Metropolitan Housing Markets: National Results from Phase 1, Phase 2, and Phase 3 of the Housing Discrimination Study (HDS)*. Washington, DC: US Department of Housing and Urban Development. http://www.huduser.org/portal/publications/hsgfin/hds.html.

———. 2010. *Live Free: Annual Report on Fair Housing FY 2010*. Washington, DC: US Department of Housing and Urban Development. http://portal.hud.gov/hudportal /documents/huddoc?id=ANNUALREPORT2010.PDF.

———. 2013. "Mission." US Department of Housing and Urban Development. Accessed May 17. http://portal.hud.gov/hudportal/HUD?src=/about/mission.

Immergluck, Dan, and Geoff Smith. 2005. *There Goes the Neighborhood: The Effect of Single-Family Mortgage Foreclosures on Property Values*. Chicago: Woodstock Institute.

Immigration Policy Center. 2009. *Summary of the Comprehensive Immigration Reform for America's Security and Prosperity Act (CIR ASAP) of 2009*. Washington, DC: Immigration Policy Center. http://www.immigrationpolicy.org/just-facts/summary -comprehensive-immigration-reform-americas-security-and-prosperity-act-2009/.

———. 2012a. *Latinos in America: A Demographic Overview*. Washington, DC: Immigration Policy Center. http://www.immigrationpolicy.org/just-facts/latinos-america -demographic-overview/.

——. 2012b. *Strength in Diversity: The Economic and Political Power of Immigrants, Latinos and Asians*. Washington, DC: Immigration Policy Center. http://www.immigration policy.org/just-facts/strength-diversity-economic-and-political-power-immigrants -latinos-and-asians/.

Kennedy, Julia Taylor. 2012. "The Evolution of Occupy Wall Street." *Policy Innovations*, May 18. http://www.policyinnovations.org/ideas/audio/data/000635.

Kochhar, Rakesh, Richard Fry, and Paul Taylor. 2011. *Wealth Gaps Rise to Record Highs between Whites, Blacks and Hispanics*. Washington, DC: Pew Research Center. http:// www.pewsocialtrends.org/files/2011/07/SDT-Wealth-Report_7-26-11_FINAL.pdf.

Lopez, Mark Hugo, Rich Morin, and Paul Taylor. 2010. *Illegal Immigration Backlash Worries, Divides Latinos*. Washington: Pew Hispanic Center. http://pewhispanic.org /files/reports/128.pdf.

Masnick, George S., and Eric S. Belsky. 2009. *Household Projections in Retrospect and Prospect: Lessons Learned and Applied to New 2005-2025 Projections*. Cambridge, MA: Harvard University Press.

Mishel, Lawrence, and Natalie Sabadish. 2012. "CEO Pay and the Top One Percent: How Executive Compensation and Financial-Sector Pay Have Fueled Income Inequality." Economic Policy Institute, Issue Brief #331, May 2. http://www.epi.org/publication /ib331-ceo-pay-top-1-percent/.

Murguía, Janet. 2008. "Remarks at the Wave of Hope Press Briefing." *Líderes*, May 7. http://lideres.nclr.org/content/article/detail/3502/.

NCLR (National Council of La Raza). 2011. *Alabama's HB 56*. Washington, DC: National Council of La Raza. http://www.nclr.org/index.php/issues_and_programs/immigration /state_local_immigration_initiatives/alabamas_hb_56.

NFHA (National Fair Housing Alliance). 2012a. *Fair Housing in a Changing Nation: 2012 Fair Housing Trends Report*. Washington, DC: National Fair Housing Alliance. http:// www.nationalfairhousing.org/Portals/33/Fair%20Housing%20Trends%20Report% 202012%20with%20date.pdf.

——. 2012b. *The Banks Are Back—Our Neighborhoods Are Not: Discrimination in the Maintenance and Marketing of REO Properties*. Washington, DC: National Fair Housing Alliance. http://www.nationalfairhousing.org/Portals/33/the_banks_are_back_web.pdf.

Nittle, Nadra Kareem. 2011. "Media Coverage of Racial Participation in Occupy Wall Street." *Maynard Media Center on Structural Inequity*, November 8. http://mije.org /mmcsi/business/media-coverage-racial-participation-occupy-wall-street.

Pastor, Manuel, and Vanessa Carter. 2012. "Reshaping the Social Contract: Demographic Distance and Our Fiscal Future." *Poverty & Race* 1 (21): 5–6. http://www.prrac.org /pdf/JanFeb2012PRRACPastor_Carter.pdf.

Pew Hispanic Center. 2011. *The Mexican-American Boom: Births Overtake Immigration*. Washington, DC: Pew Hispanic Center. http://www.pewhispanic.org/2011/07/14/the -mexican-american-boom-brbirths-overtake-immigration/.

Puente, Teresa. 2011. "Will Latino Groups Choose to Occupy?" *In These Times*, December 13. http://inthesetimes.com/main/article/12405.

Ramirez de Arellano, Susanne. 2011. "Linking Immigration to Occupy Wall Street: A Reporter's Notebook." *Fox News Latino*, November 9. http://latino.foxnews.com/latino /news/2011/11/09/occupy-wall-street-reporters-notebook-reveals-ties-between-percent -movement-and/#ixzz2PtboNdHf.

Ross, Janell. 2012. "DREAM Act Activists Push Into Mainstream With American Protest Movement Tactics." *Huffington Post: Latino Voices,* August 21. http://www.huffington post.com/2012/08/21/dream-act-activists-protest-tactics_n_1813273.html/.

Rubinkam, Michael. 2009. "Luis Ramirez Killers Found Not Guilty After Beating Mexican Immigrant to Death." *Huffington Post,* May 2. http://www.huffingtonpost.com/2009 /05/04/luis-ramirez-killers- foun_n_195535.html.

Singer, Audrey. 2004. *The Rise of New Immigrant Gateways.* Washington, DC: The Brookings Institution Center on Urban and Metropolitan Policy.

Southern Poverty Law Center. 2009. *Under Siege: Life for Low-Income Latinos in the South.* Montgomery, AL: Southern Poverty Law Center. http://cdna.splcenter.org/sites /default/files/downloads/UnderSiege.pdf.

———. 2012. "Anti-Immigrant Hate Crimes." *The Intelligence Report.* Accessed August 7. http://www.splcenter.org/intelligence-report/-year-hate/anti-immigrant-hate-crimes.

Speri, Alice. 2011. "Occupy Wall Street Struggles to Make 'the 99%' Look Like Everybody." *New York Times,* October 28. http://cityroom.blogs.nytimes.com/2011/10/28/occupy -wall-street-struggles-to-make-the-99-look-like-everybody/.

Treuhaft, Sarah, Angela Glover Blackwell, and Manuel Pastor. 2011. *America's Tomorrow: Equity is the Superior Growth Model.* Los Angeles: PolicyLink. http://www.policylink .org/atf/cf/%7B97c6d565-bb43-406d-a6d5-eca3bbf35af0%7D/SUMMIT_FRAMING _WEB.PDF.

US Census Bureau. 2010. "Sex by Age by Citizenship Status (Hispanic or Latino), Table B050031." *American Community Survey.*

———. 2011. "Overview of Race and Hispanic Origin: 2010." *2010 Census Briefs,* March.

———. 2012. "Most Children Younger than Age 1 Are Minorities, Census Bureau Reports." *News Release,* May 17. http://www.census.gov/newsroom/releases/archives/population /cb12-90.htm.

Zerkel, Eric. 2011. "Occupy Wall Street Tackles Immigrant Worker Issues." *Pavement Pieces,* December 15. http://pavementpieces.com/occupy-wall-street-tackles-immigrant -worker-issues/.

The Scholars

11

The Limits of Litigation in Fulfilling the Fair Housing Act's Promise of Nondiscriminatory Home Loans

Robert G. Schwemm

Part I. Introduction and Overview

T HIS BOOK INCLUDES a number of reports from private groups and government agencies about their litigation efforts under the federal Fair Housing Act (FHA) and the other laws that prohibit race-based mortgage discrimination. Many of these efforts have been groundbreaking, and I commend them. Nevertheless, this chapter's theme is that such litigation has generally not served, and probably cannot serve in the future, either to effectively deter wrongdoers or to fairly compensate victims of home loan discrimination.

In support of this view, I first examine general tort principles that apply to FHA cases (Part II) and then survey the history of mortgage discrimination litigation over the past four decades (Part III). This history shows that government enforcement of the FHA's fair lending mandate has been erratic and that private litigation in this area has proved inherently difficult to win. The discussion of contemporary lending discrimination issues that begins in the last section of Part III is continued in Part IV, which looks at FHA-based mortgage litigation in the hard times that have characterized America's housing markets since 2007.

My ultimate conclusion is that litigation, though of some value, must be supplemented by other strategies if the goal of a nondiscriminatory mortgage market is to be achieved. Happily, other parts of this book offer some examples of potentially helpful nonlitigation strategies, such as those of community organizations and the Occupy Wall Street protests, and I offer some of my own in Part V.

Part II. Modern Tort Theory and the Goals of FHA Litigation

Throughout the FHA's history, violations of this law have been treated as torts (Schwemm 2012, § 25:4 note 5). During this same time, tort-based challenges have been mounted against harmful products in a variety of industries, including tobacco, asbestos, automobiles, pharmaceutical drugs, and medical devices. Academic analyses of these cases have studied the values and shortcomings of tort litigation as a way of achieving positive social change and other goals.

Two primary goals underlie FHA-based mortgage discrimination litigation: (1) compensation of injured parties and (2) deterrence of wrongdoers designed to achieve compliance with the law. Compensation and deterrence are also the two basic rationales for most other civil rights litigation[1] and even the entire modern tort system (Goldberg 2003, 522–29). The goals of compensation and deterrence complement one another; affording compensation gives an injured party "an incentive to bring the suit that serves the purpose of deterring injurers," and deterring harmful conduct serves to protect persons from being injured in the first place (Schwartz 1997, 1817–18, 1831–33).

The problem with compensation as a justification for most tort litigation is that it is so haphazard, with a few victims being compensated through lawsuits while the vast majority of injured parties do not litigate and receive nothing (Schuck 1995, 942). Tort law can only compensate "those victims who are able to find a competent lawyer, willing to endure a lawsuit, potentially capable of proving their cases to the satisfaction of judge and jury, and lucky enough to have been victimized by a solvent defendant" (Goldberg 2003, 537). As Sugarman (2000, 2430) summarizes, "for some victims the system works fine, but for most it does not."

As a result, most scholars view deterrence as the primary rationale for modern tort rules (Schwartz 1994, 441–42). Whether this works in actual practice, however, is a source of lively debate among torts scholars.

In 1994, Professor Schwartz examined a number of empirical studies dealing with the deterrence value of negligence lawsuits involving auto accidents, medical malpractice, and products liability; while noting that extensive tort

---

1. See US House of Representatives (1991) at 46–47.

litigation had not prevented continuing high levels of poor conduct in these areas (Schwartz 1994, 393, 399, 407), he concluded that tort rules did provide some, though not strong, deterrence against negligently inflicted injuries (Schwartz 1994, 423). For example, Schwartz estimated that the tort system's impact on auto safety "succeeds in reducing the accident and fatality rates by only ten percent" (Schwartz 1994, 425). On the other hand, Professor Sugarman found these studies unconvincing and concluded in 2000 that "a fair appraisal as we start the twenty-first century is that the jury is still out on [the deterrence value of tort law]" (Sugarman 2000, 2431–32).

I have argued with respect to rental discrimination that, until more is known about what actually motivates landlords to obey or disobey the FHA, the deterrence/compliance rationale for FHA suits is little more than wishful thinking (Schwemm 2007, 484; see also Berrey, Hoffman, and Nielsen 2012 for similar doubts about the ability of employment discrimination litigation to eliminate workplace inequality). There are, of course, significant differences between the rental and home-finance markets, most notably the key role played in the latter by large national institutions, which suggests that the deterrent effect might be less dispersed in lending litigation.

Even if a few big firms dominated the home mortgage business, the deterrence value of large settlements could be questioned simply because of the defendants' massive financial resources. In late 2012, it was reported that the seven largest US banks had, presumably without impairing their financial strength or political influence, "spent more than $76 billion on mortgage-related costs and litigation since 2008" (Zibel and Randall 2012; see also Lattman 2012b for a description of recent settlements by mortgage lenders accused of defrauding the government of $1 billion against Bank of America (Countrywide), $200 million against Deutsche Bank, and $158 million against Citigroup Inc., and a report of the filing of a similar suit against Wells Fargo). As Judge Rakoff remarked in rejecting a proposed securities fraud settlement of $285 million against Citigroup in 2011, such "modest penalties [are] frequently viewed, particularly in the business community, as a cost of doing business"[2] (see also Lattman 2012a that quotes a prominent plaintiffs' lawyer who had just negotiated a $2.43 billion securities-fraud settlement against Bank of America as saying, "no matter how good a job we do of getting results and inflicting pain, the government doesn't seem to follow suit, and nobody learns, and it's business as usual").

In short, as Professor Goldberg (2003, 578) argues: "We will never get anywhere until we have more facts about how tort law actually works in practice."

---

2. See U.S. S.E.C. v. Citigroup Global Markets Inc., 673 F.3d 158, at 162–63 (2d Cir. 2012).

Thus, learning how particular businesses respond to litigation sanctions is a prerequisite of knowing "what tort law . . . would have to look like to achieve goals such as deterrence" (Goldberg 2003, 579).

A third rationale for the modern tort system has been identified by some scholars—that of educating the public about the risks associated with certain dangerous products and, through court verdicts, expressing "disapproval of business practices that violated minimum standards of decency" (Ausness 2002, 954–55). A related notion is that lawsuits may provide the stories that are needed to push public attitudes toward more universal acceptance of the justice of certain legal principles. Thus, Sugarman (2000, 2432) points out that the "social benefits that may be achieved by tort law [include satisfying] our collective need to identify and assign blame for wrongdoing when fellow members of society are hurt by that misconduct."

Certain other noteworthy themes have emerged from modern mass-tort litigation that also seem applicable to FHA mortgage cases. One is that litigation brought by private suitors often leads the way, with government enforcement following and then sometimes taking over (Schuck 1995, 951–52, 955–56). Another is that, when such litigation does result in changes in an industry, those changes do not always take the form that the original plaintiffs anticipated or wanted (Ford 2011). Finally, the value of litigation as a method for industry change is related to how much information obtained in discovery is shared with other interested parties and the public as opposed to being kept confidential after the individual lawsuits are settled (Schuck 1995, 956).

To summarize, various facets of the modern tort system do not lend themselves to efficiently achieving either compensation or deterrence. This is troubling. Litigation should not consist simply of a series of random results, but rather society has a right to "expect that the law aspire to coherence—a demand rooted in elemental notions of fairness, predictability, and efficacy" (Goldberg 2003, 580). Still, no one suggests that tort litigation cease. Those advocating improvements and alternative strategies simply recognize that "the tort system is no more than a second-best (if not third- or fourth-best) mechanism for achieving these goals" (Goldberg 2003, 581).

Part III. FHA Litigation Involving Discriminatory Home Loans

Part III provides a chronological survey and some analysis of FHA-based mortgage discrimination cases for three periods: (A) the passage of the 1968

FHA through 1988; (B) the passage of the FHA's 1988 amendments through the end of the 1990s; and (C) the twenty-first century.

A. *The Original FHA and 1968–1988 Cases*

The 1968 FHA's key provision directed against home loan discrimination is § 3605, but the legislative history of this provision is sparse. One of the few references to this topic was a brief letter by the American Bankers Association expressing concern that the law might cause an "undue burden" for lenders by exposing them to "costly" litigation even if their actions were based on "the application of prudent lending practice and not because of [prohibited factors]" (US Senate 1967, 484). Suggesting that "no two real estate loans have the same terms and conditions," this letter opined that Congress could not intend to make "every loan decision made by any lender . . . subject to possible legal action" (US Senate 1967, 484).

The prospect of undue mortgage discrimination litigation was not realized in the FHA's first two decades. During this period, only about a dozen such cases were reported, most of which were pretrial decisions by district judges in cases brought by private complainants. Only one of these cases resulted in a plaintiff's victory on the merits—an Ohio case where a loan officer made numerous explicitly racial statements in the course of demanding blatantly egregious terms from the plaintiff, e.g., a 40- to 50-percent down payment.[3]

A few of these early trial court decisions did establish some useful precedents. The most important of these was that the FHA's ban on race-based mortgage discrimination outlawed not only claims by individual minorities who had been discriminated against but also, as first held by an Ohio federal judge in 1976, "redlining," that is, discrimination based on the racial makeup of the complainant's neighborhood.[4]

Federal courts also assumed that the FHA would be violated if racially influenced low appraisals of homes sought by minorities or in heavily minority areas were used by lenders to deny mortgages.[5] Indeed, the appraisal industry's long-standing reliance on racial demographics in valuing houses

---

3. See Harrison v. Otto G. Heinzeroth Mortg. Co., 430 F. Supp. 893 (N.D. Ohio 1977).

4. Laufman v. Oakley Bldg. & Loan Co., 408 F. Supp. 489 (S.D. Ohio 1976); see also Laufman v. Oakley Bldg. & Loan Co., 72 F.R.D. 116 (S.D. Ohio 1976).

5. See Hanson v. Veterans Administration, 800 F.2d 1381 (5th Cir. 1986); and Thomas v. First Federal Sav. Bank of Indiana, 653 F. Supp. 1330 (N.D. Ind. 1987).

was the target of the Department of Justice's (DOJ) only reported § 3605 case during the 1968 to 1988 period.[6]

Decisions beginning in the mid-1970s also recognized that applying stricter collection and foreclosure standards for minorities than whites could violate § 3605,[7] although the only one of these cases to go to trial—*Harper v. Union Sav. Ass'n*—resulted in a defendant's verdict because the plaintiff failed to prove that the lender had in fact engaged in such discrimination.

The *Harper* case was representative of the fact that proving illegal mortgage discrimination turned out to be extremely difficult. Then, as now, plaintiffs could prevail only by showing that similarly situated nonminorities were treated better by the defendant-lender.[8] The key source of such proof would generally be the defendant's own loan files, which were not available to a complainant until post-complaint discovery and even then often required a court order (*Laufman v. Oakley Bldg. & Loan Co.*; *Harper*). Furthermore, unlike other types of FHA cases where testers could be used to demonstrate discriminatory behavior, testing in lending cases was limited by the fact that federal law prohibits misrepresenting information on a mortgage application (Schwemm and Taren 2010, 386). As noted earlier, only one reported case in the 1968–1988 period succeeded in proving illegal discrimination, and many others failed.[9]

B. The 1988 Amendments and Cases in the 1990s

In 1988, Congress passed a major set of amendments to the FHA known as the Fair Housing Amendments Act (FHAA). In addition to strengthening all of the FHA's enforcement mechanisms and adding "familial status" and "handicap" as forbidden bases of discrimination in the statute's substantive provisions (Schwemm 2012, § 5:3), the FHAA rewrote § 3605, primarily to make clear, as a House report stated, that "the provisions of the Act extend to the secondary mortgage market" (US House of Representatives 1988, 30). Ironically, despite this particular focus of the 1988 amendments, few § 3605 cases challenging discrimination in the secondary market have been filed

---

6. See U.S. v. American Institute of Real Estate Appraisers of Nat. Ass'n of Realtors, 442 F. Supp. 1072 (N.D. Ill. 1977), *appeal dismissed*, 590 F.2d 242 (7th Cir. 1978).

7. See Lindsay v. Modern American Mortgage Corp., 383 F. Supp. 293 (N.D. Tex. 1974); and Harper v. Union Sav. Ass'n, 429 F. Supp. 1254 (N.D. Ohio 1977).

8. See Watson v. Pathway Financial, 702 F. Supp. 186 (N.D. Ill. 1988).

9. See *Harper; Hanson; Thomas;* and Shipley v. First Federal Sav. & Loan Ass'n of Delaware, 703 F. Supp. 1122 (D. Del. 1988), *aff'd*, 877 F.2d 57 (3d Cir. 1989).

(for a rare example, see Silver-Greenberg 2012), and none has resulted in a reported judicial decision.

The pace of mortgage discrimination litigation accelerated in the 1990s. This was prompted in part by passage of the 1989 amendments to the Home Mortgage Disclosure Act (HMDA) that required most financial institutions to make yearly reports on their mortgage activities according to race and census tracts (Schwemm and Taren 2010, 388, 399). The DOJ brought sixteen "pattern or practice" cases involving race or national origin discrimination against home lenders in this decade (DOJ 2001, 2). Most of these cases followed the lead of earlier private litigation by accusing lenders either of denying loans to minorities by applying their underwriting standards more stringently than to comparable whites or by refusing to make loans in minority areas that were comparable to white areas where they did business (DOJ 2001, 2–5). A third type of case also emerged: pricing discrimination, where a lender was accused of allowing its loan officers and brokers to charge higher rates and fees to minorities than similarly creditworthy whites (DOJ 2001, 5–6). All of these DOJ cases were resolved through settlements and consent decrees (DOJ 2001, 5–6).

Privately initiated mortgage litigation also accelerated during the 1990s, but its results were less fruitful. As noted earlier, minority plaintiffs could only prevail by showing that a lender accorded them worse treatment than comparable whites, a daunting task even with the availability of HMDA data. A classic example was a Fifth Circuit decision that a rejected mortgage applicant's proof failed to show intentional discrimination because, although the defendant's treatment of the plaintiff was "arbitrary and unreasonable," there was no "evidence that similar 'non-protected' applications have received dissimilar treatment."[10] In other words, a lending institution's bad treatment of racial minorities or their neighborhoods could not be successfully challenged under the FHA without proof that this lender also treated similarly situated whites or white areas more favorably. No reported case in the 1990s produced such proof.

The 1990s also saw the beginnings of what would prove to be radical changes in the home loan industry. These included the growing use of automated credit scoring systems to evaluate would-be borrowers and the resulting rise of "risk-based pricing" in which lenders would vary rates and fees for loans based on the particular risks that an individual borrower presented (Schwemm and Taren 2010, 390–91). As a result, borrowers whose credit flaws

---

10. Simms v. First Gibralter Bank, 83 F.3d 1546, at 1558–59 (5th Cir. 1996).

might have disqualified them under traditional underwriting standards often obtained mortgages, albeit at worse-than-prime rates that were available to borrowers with better credit scores (DOJ 2001, 4). The growth of subprime loans was also fueled by "securitization," the process by which housing lenders sold their loans to government-backed or private financial institutions in the secondary market (Schwemm and Taren 2010, 379–80). These institutions then pooled these loans in large bundles for ultimate resale to investors as residential mortgage-backed securities. Through this process, virtually any mortgage could be sold by the originating lender, thereby passing on to others the risk of nonpayment by borrowers and freeing up funds for ever more new mortgages (Engel and McCoy 2007).

These changes ultimately shifted the focus of mortgage discrimination problems from the denial of credit to minorities and their communities to the higher prices and worse terms that minorities paid. But litigation in response to these new forms of "terms-and-conditions" discrimination was generally slow to respond and did not become widespread until some years later, as described in the next section.

C. Twenty-First Century Cases

1. Traditional Private Cases. The number of FHA claims by private individuals alleging that they were turned down or given inferior terms by mortgage lenders has grown throughout the new century. By 2010, over five hundred complaints of § 3605 violations were filed with the Department of Housing and Urban Development (HUD) and state and local fair housing agencies (HUD 2011, 24), and well over a thousand mortgage discrimination complaints were made to private fair housing groups in both 2010 and 2011 (NFHA 2012b, 9). Such complaints, however, continued to be extraordinarily difficult to win.

One of the few such cases in the past decade to result in a victory for a minority plaintiff was *Paschal v. Flagstar Bank*, but even this case demonstrates how difficult obtaining such a result can be. In *Paschal*, eight sets of African American plaintiffs in the Detroit area, represented by a distinguished FHA lawyer and supported by an experienced local fair housing organization, claimed that Flagstar Bank racially discriminated against them in handling their mortgage applications. The claims of three of these plaintiffs were dismissed prior to trial as being outside the applicable statute of limitations. After a lengthy trial that included substantial preapplication testing evidence by the organization and two expert witnesses for the plaintiffs, the jury ruled against three of the remaining plaintiffs and in favor of the other two. The bank's appeal succeeded in reversing one of two plaintiffs' wins on statute-of-limitations grounds, but the appellate court did affirm the other plaintiff-couple's victory and their jury award of $125,000 in compensatory damages.[11] Thus far, however, no other privately initiated mortgage case has been reported in this century in which a plaintiff has won a trial verdict.

2. Procedural Problems and Heightened Pleading Standards. As the *Paschal* case illustrates, private mortgage discrimination claims may encounter statute-of-limitations problems (see also Part IV.A). Another procedural problem may be posed by Supreme Court decisions holding that a mandatory-arbitration clause in commercial contracts should generally be enforced in derogation of the parties' right to pursue court litigation.[12]

Perhaps the most daunting problem for mortgage discrimination litigation will be the Supreme Court's recent decisions to raise the pleading standards for federal court suits,[13] which make it more difficult for complaints to survive a motion to dismiss and thus proceed to the discovery stage of litigation. Under the new tougher standards, a complaint is no longer sufficient if it sets forth only conclusory allegations reciting the elements of the claim. Thus, for example, a minority homeseeker rejected for a loan cannot merely allege that the bank's refusal was racially discriminatory. Instead, this conclusion must be supported by factual allegations that are sufficiently detailed to "plausibly give rise to an entitlement to relief."[14] This "plausibility" standard also means that a complaint may fail if it suggests an "obvious alternative explanation,"[15] such as that the plaintiff has a poor credit score.

Some appellate courts have already relied on these tougher pleading standards to rule against plaintiffs' FHA-based mortgage discrimination complaints.[16] These decisions generally hold that a mortgage discrimination complaint must now identify similarly situated nonminorities who have received better treatment from the defendant than the plaintiff. In basic mortgage discrimination cases, therefore, the new pleading standards have essentially moved the requirement of identifying better-treated white comparables

---

11. Paschal v. Flagstar Bank, 295 F.3d 565 (6th Cir. 2002).

12. See American Express Co. v. Italian Colors Restaurant, 133 S.Ct. 2304 (2013); and AT&T Mobility LLC v. Concepcion, 131 S.Ct. 1740 (2011).

13. See Ashcroft v. Iqbal, 556 U.S. 662 (2009); and Bell Atlantic Corp. v. Twombly, 550 U.S. 544 (2007).

14. *Iqbal* at 679.

15. *Iqbal* at 682.

16. See Henderson v. JPMorgan Chase Bank, N.A., 436 Fed. Appx. 935 (11th Cir. 2011); and Gorham-DiMaggio v. Countrywide Home Loans, 421 Fed. Appx. 97 (2d Cir. 2011).

from the post-discovery summary judgment stage to the pre-discovery pleading stage. A private complainant's ability to satisfy this requirement without
having access to a lender's loan files through discovery is virtually impossible.

Even the one positive appellate pleading decision—*Swanson v. Citibank*,
where the Seventh Circuit by a 2-1 vote upheld a black plaintiff's complaint
that defendants' low appraisal of her home and resulting loan denial were
racially discriminatory because she was able to cite a third party's higher appraisal—includes some ominous signals. *Swanson* produced a vigorous dissent
by Judge Posner, who argued that innocent errors in home appraisals are so
common that the plaintiff's "alternative hypothesis of racial discrimination . . .
is implausible" and thus should fail under the new pleading standards.[17] Even
the *Swanson* majority, while upholding the plaintiff's "straightforward" FHA
claim, recognized that a "more complex case . . . will require more detail."[18]
As shown in the next sections, these more complex cases have become increasingly important in mortgage discrimination litigation, where the tougher
pleading standards are likely to cause serious problems in private litigation.

3. Reverse Redlining. One type of claim produced by the proliferation
of subprime loans in the recent housing boom accused lenders of targeting
minorities and minority neighborhoods for particularly unfavorable mortgages—a practice that came to be known as "reverse redlining." In 2000, two
trial court decisions upheld claims by minority plaintiffs that this practice
violated the FHA,[19] a conclusion that the DOJ supported with an *amicus* brief
in *Hargraves v. Capital City Mortgage Corp.* and that was later endorsed by a
number of other trial judges around the country (Schwemm 2012, § 18:3 note
13). These cases established an important legal principle, but, like the original
redlining cases brought in the 1970s (see Part III.A), the reverse redlining
cases rarely resulted in the plaintiffs actually obtaining any relief. Indeed,
a typical result was that the defendant—often a small local operator, as in
Hargraves—would go out of business before the case reached trial. (In more
recent times, reverse redlining claims have been asserted by some minority
homeowners seeking to rescind or avoid foreclosure on their mortgages, but
these claims have invariably failed, usually for lack of proof that the lender
involved actually targeted minorities for its worst loans (see Part IV.A).)

---

17. Swanson v. Citibank, N.A., 614 F.3d 400, at 411 (7th Cir. 2010).

18. *Swanson* at 405.

19. See Hargraves v. Capital City Mortgage Corp., 140 F. Supp. 2d 7 (D. D.C. 2000),
reconsideration granted in part and denied in part, 147 F. Supp. 2d 1 (D. D.C. 2001); and
Honorable v. Easy Life Real Estate System, 100 F. Supp. 2d 885 (N.D. Ill. 2000).

As the housing boom turned to bust and foreclosure rates began to sky-rocket, a variation on the original reverse redlining cases appeared in the form of suits brought by cities claiming that they suffered a variety of negative effects as a result of lenders having focused their predatory loans in the plaintiffs' minority neighborhoods. The leading example was a FHA-based suit brought by Baltimore against Wells Fargo, with Memphis later making a similar claim against the same lender. After Baltimore pared down its complaint in response to a negative ruling in 2009 based on the tougher pleading standards discussed in the previous section, the trial court upheld the plaintiffs' standing to make such a claim in 2011.[20] The trial judge in the Memphis case made a similar positive ruling.[21] Meanwhile, Cleveland asserted similar allegations against numerous large lenders in a suit based not on the FHA but on state nuisance law, but this suit ultimately failed.[22]

4. Impact-Based Class Actions Challenging Discretionary Pricing. Another innovative private litigation effort begun around 2007 was a series of class actions brought against large lenders on behalf of tens of thousands of minority homeowners who alleged that the defendants' discretionary pricing policies had resulted in their paying substantially more for mortgages than credit-comparable whites (Schwemm and Taren 2010, 404). The basic complaint in each of these cases was the same—that loan officers and mortgage brokers of the named defendant had exercised the discretion given them in setting rates and fees in a way that negatively impacted minorities. Individual suits were brought against Countrywide, Wells Fargo & Company, and at least six other major subprime lenders (Schwemm and Taren 2010, 404–05). Most of the defendants responded by filing motions to dismiss that challenged the plaintiffs' impact theory, but the various trial courts generally denied these motions (Schwemm and Taren 2010, 405–06), thereby producing the first significant set of judicial endorsements of the impact theory in FHA-lending cases and allowing the cases to proceed to the discovery stage.

Thereafter, one of these cases settled. While the others were pending, however, the Supreme Court ruled in *Wal-Mart Stores, Inc. v. Dukes* that a nationwide class action could not be used to challenge an employer's policy of giving its local managers discretion over promotion and salary decisions

---

20. Mayor and City Council of Baltimore v. Wells Fargo Bank, 631 F. Supp. 2d 702 (D. Md. 2009), and 2011 WL 1557759 (D. Md. 2011).

21. City of Memphis v. Wells Fargo, 2011 WL 1706756 (W.D. Tenn. 2011).

22. City of Cleveland v. Ameriquest Mortgage Securities, 615 F.3d 496 (6th Cir. 2010), *cert. denied*, 131 S.Ct. 1685 (2011).

that allegedly resulted in women receiving worse treatment than men.[23] The *Wal-Mart* decision held that, in order for a class action to challenge such "subjective decision making," the plaintiffs would have to "identif[y] a common mode of exercising discretion that pervades the entire company."[24] The Supreme Court discounted the plaintiffs' evidence showing "statistically significant disparities between men and women at Wal-Mart," holding that "merely proving that the discretionary system has produced a racial or sexual disparity *is not enough*."[25]

Wal-Mart dealt a devastating blow to the discretionary pricing mortgage cases. Prior to the Supreme Court's decision, at least one court had certified a class action in these cases, but it reversed itself after *Wal-Mart*,[26] and other courts also held that these cases could not proceed as class actions. Thus far, plaintiffs' appeals of these negative decisions have failed.[27] If class actions cannot be used in these cases, they will be economically impossible for private litigants to pursue, both in terms of attracting the lawyers and other litigation resources needed to compete with the huge national lender-defendants and as the only cost-effective way of prosecuting the plaintiff-class's tens of thousands of claims.

5. Government Cases. Some of the liability theories put forth in the class action cases discussed in the previous section were eventually also pursued by federal agencies. The DOJ, which filed only a few mortgage discrimination cases during the eight years of the Bush administration (Schwemm 2012, § 18:2), created a special fair lending task force early in the Obama administration to prosecute these cases, and that unit brought and settled some sixteen lending cases in its first two years (DOJ 2012a, 1). (Settlement, rather than trial, continues to be the only way that all government-prosecuted FHA-based lending cases have been resolved.) These DOJ cases included at least five based on discretionary pricing, the two most prominent of which involved Countrywide (actually brought against that lender's new owner, Bank of America, and settled for $335 million in December 2011) and Wells

---

23. Wal-Mart Stores, Inc. v. Dukes, 131 S.Ct. 2541 (2011).

24. *Wal-Mart* at 2554–55.

25. *Wal-Mart* at 2555.

26. Barrett v. H & R Block, 2011 WL 1100105 (D. Mass. 2011), and 2012 WL 4076465 (D. Mass. 2012).

27. See In re Countrywide Financial Corp. Mortgage Lending Practices Litigation, 708 F.3d 704 (6th Cir. 2013). Plaintiffs' appeal from a similar negative decision in Rodriguez v. National City Bank, 277 F.R.D. 148 (E.D. Pa. 2011) is currently pending.

Fargo (settled for $125 million in July 2012) (DOJ 2012b, 1–2; DOJ 2012c). All of these pricing cases were based on the government's review of a large number of loans (some 2.5 million in the Countrywide case) and its conclusion that thousands of minorities (200,000 in the Countrywide case; 34,000 in the Wells Fargo case) had been overcharged vis-à-vis similarly creditworthy whites during the periods examined (2004 to 2008 for Countrywide; 2004 to 2009 for Wells Fargo). The $335 million recovered from Countrywide (Bank of America) and the $125 million from Wells Fargo are the biggest settlements in FHA-based lending discrimination cases in history (DOJ 2012a, 1).

HUD and other federal agencies also referred some fifty-five lending cases involving race and national origin discrimination to the DOJ in the 2009 to 2011 period, far more than the total of thirty during the entire eight years of the prior Bush administration (DOJ 2012a, 1). Also, HUD on its own prosecuted and settled a number of such cases (HUD 2011, 39–40).

As impressive as these settlements appear, they do not undercut the sense that FHA litigation is not a fair way of compensating victims of this type of mortgage discrimination. Most of the lenders in the private discretionary pricing class actions were not sued by the DOJ, which means that their borrowers will collect nothing. Even when a lender like Countrywide or Wells Fargo is the target of both private and DOJ suits, the borrowers actually compensated may be quite different in the two cases. The Wells Fargo settlement did include funds to settle the private suits brought by Baltimore and Memphis (see Part III.C.3), but the only distinction between the minority neighborhoods in those cities that will benefit and similar neighborhoods in Cleveland and other cities, which will not, is that the former cities pursued a more clever litigation strategy. Finally, even if all minority borrowers harmed by the discriminatory effect of discretionary pricing could share in the DOJ settlements, the average recovery is less than $1,700, a small fraction of the actual damages that were likely suffered.

As for deterrence, it is discounted for a number of reasons. First, the amounts assessed, though impressive by FHA standards, are modest given the size of the defendants and their demonstrated ability to absorb huge settlements in other types of litigation without serious consequences. Second, the sanctions called for in the government's FHA settlements occurred years after the alleged wrongdoing (e.g., 2004 to 2008 in the Countrywide case); indeed, in the Countrywide case, the DOJ's suit and settlement took place well after that lender had gone bankrupt and been taken over by Bank of America with, it might be noted, substantial federal funds to smooth the deal. Further, one of the key techniques alleged to have caused the discrimination—allowing mortgage brokers and loan officers wide discretion to set prices and terms—had already been abandoned by most lenders by the time the DOJ acted and was virtually ended for the entire industry as a result of a regulation adopted by the Federal Reserve Board in 2010.[28]

Finally, the DOJ's willingness to use the impact theory of discrimination to pursue some of these cases, while noteworthy, was late in coming. The DOJ, along with HUD and other regulatory agencies, had recognized in 1994 that the FHA outlawed lending practices that disproportionately harmed minorities (HUD et al. 1994), but the DOJ did not assert this theory in any mortgage case until 2010. Now that lenders have changed how they do business and have generally reverted to imposing strict, nondiscretionary underwriting rules, the particular problems addressed by these impact-based discretionary pricing cases are largely gone, and the impact theory's applicability to today's problems is less certain.

Part IV. Modern Discrimination Claims in an Era of Hard Times

A. Foreclosure-Avoidance Cases

Ever since the housing boom went bust in 2007, homeowners seeking to avoid foreclosure or rescind their mortgages have often alleged that the underlying loan or how it was processed violates one or more federal or state laws. In such a case, a minority borrower may add a mortgage discrimination claim (e.g., a reverse redlining claim; see Part III.C.3), with this FHA claim being just part of a scatter-shot set of legal defenses to the foreclosure; however, the FHA is often harder to support than the borrower's other claims because it requires plausible allegations of race-based or other FHA-condemned discrimination.

The typical result in these foreclosure-avoidance cases is that the FHA claim is defeated at an early stage[29] even if some of the plaintiff's other claims survive. The claimant rarely has the type of "white comparables" evidence of the lender's discrimination that the courts require, now at the pleading stage (see Part III.C.2). FHA-based claims in this situation are also often dismissed

---

28. 24 C.F.R. § 226.36(d), adopted 75 *Fed. Reg.* 58533 (Sept. 24, 2010).

29. See Bowden v. American Home Mortg. Servicing, Inc., 2012 WL 628543 (E.D. Mich. Feb. 27, 2012).

for being untimely; typically, the borrower is complaining about the payments or foreclosure techniques of a loan obtained years earlier, and courts tend to hold that the date of the original loan, rather than its ongoing payments or other negative effects, begins the FHA's two-year limitations period.[30]

Thus, FHA-based claims are rarely helpful in defeating a foreclosure, except in the sense that the delay caused while a court considers such a claim may allow the borrower to stay in his home pending the court's ruling. Indeed, as a general matter, borrowers facing foreclosure generally lack the resources to litigate effectively against their lenders; "the major risk to lenders from lawsuits by [such] borrowers is class actions, and since ability-to-repay cases are focused on individual circumstances, class actions would not be available" (Center for Responsible Lending et al. 2012, 26).

B. Déjà Vu: A Return to Traditional Underwriting Standards

The modern mortgage market—while more complicated than it was in the early decades of the FHA due, inter alia, to new requirements generated by the Dodd-Frank Act and the Consumer Financial Protection Bureau—is clearly similar in its embrace of older, stringent underwriting standards. These standards, which seemed all but to have disappeared in the boom years of a decade ago, now may require mortgage applicants to make a substantial down payment or have a strong credit score. Such standards are facially non-discriminatory and, absent proof that they are being applied more harshly to minorities, would presumably withstand an intent-based FHA challenge. Underwriting standards based on a maximum loan-to-value or loan-to-income ratio or a minimum credit score may well have a harsher impact on minorities as a group than whites (Center for Responsible Lending 2012, 10–11), and thus could theoretically be subject to an impact-based FHA challenge. But, to date, no litigation based on this theory has been brought to attack such old-fashioned underwriting requirements.

C. Refinance Cases: Refusals and Scams

Few, if any, modern cases have asserted a FHA-based claim in the context of refinancing. To the extent that a lender rejects a minority's application to

---

30. See Silvas v. G.E. Money Bank, 449 F. Appx. 641, at 644 (9th Cir. 2011); Grimes v. Fremont General Corp., 785 F. Supp.2d 269, at 290–92 (S.D. N.Y. 2011); and Battah v. Resmae Mortgage Corp., 746 F. Supp.2d 869, at 876–77 (E.D. Mich. 2010).

refinance a home loan based on its underwriting standards, the issues dealt with in the previous section would control. To the extent that the complaint alleges a fraudulent refinance scam, the issues dealt with in Section A would seem to arise—that is, various state and federal laws may be claimed to be violated by the scam, but for a discrimination claim to prevail, the plaintiff would have to produce evidence that the defendant targeted minorities for its fraudulent activities.

D. REO Cases

In separate reports in 2011 and 2012, the National Fair Housing Alliance (NFHA) documented the fact that, in certain communities, banks that foreclosed on mortgaged houses have often done a worse job of maintaining those real estate owned (REO) properties in minority neighborhoods than in white areas (NFHA 2011; NFHA 2012a). Believing this practice to violate the FHA, the NFHA and certain local fair housing organizations filed two HUD complaints in April 2012, one against Wells Fargo based on its discriminatory treatment of REO properties in eight metropolitan areas and one against U.S. Bancorp for similar practices in seven metropolitan areas (both cases involve Atlanta, Baltimore, Dayton, Miami/Ft. Lauderdale, Oakland, and Washington, DC; only Dallas and Philadelphia are part of the Wells Fargo case, and only Chicago is part of the U.S. Bancorp case). Later in 2012, the NFHA brought a similar case against Bank of America based on its REO operations in thirteen metropolitan areas. These cases reflect a new type of problem symptomatic of today's high foreclosure rates and a new theory of FHA liability for mortgage lenders. The cases are at an early stage, and no decision has yet been rendered in them. Nor is it clear whether, even if NFHA's theory and proof do succeed in these cases, they can be translated to other lenders and other parts of the country.

E. The New Consumer Financial Protection Bureau

The Consumer Financial Protection Bureau (CFPB) became operative in 2011 and a year later began to issue regulations, including some significant ones dealing with mortgages. The CFPB also has the authority to file lawsuits independent of the DOJ, and it has a section devoted entirely to discrimination cases. Thus, the CFPB has the potential to add to the government's enforcement of fair lending, but it is too early to know how this potential will develop.

Part V. Conclusions

This chapter's survey of FHA-based mortgage discrimination litigation reveals a number of themes. Such litigation, consistent with tort litigation generally, focuses on past problems. It has been a haphazard way of compensating victims of FHA lending violations, although, again like most tort litigation, the compensation record of fair lending cases is probably no worse than, say, that of the tobacco cases or other product-liability litigation.

A positive note is that private FHA lending lawsuits have often established useful precedents and have regularly shown the way for later government enforcement. The DOJ, while slow to bring FHA lending cases in the statute's first two decades, has since produced some periods of significant activity, particularly in Democrat-led administrations.

During the FHA's history, the home mortgage industry has undergone major changes. At the same time, America's acceptance of the goal of non-discrimination in all housing-related activities has grown. As a result, today's mortgage industry would never advocate making decisions based on race or national origin, as was regularly done in the 1970s by loan officers and appraisers. The stories told by some of the early FHA cases involving redlining and discriminatory appraisals helped make unacceptable—in the nation and, therefore, the industry—explicit racial discrimination in home lending.

However, the deterrence value of FHA lending cases is far from clear. The process of sanctioning wrongdoers has been too delayed and uncertain to provide much deterrence. Furthermore, the ever-changing techniques by which lending discrimination manifests itself mean that even substantial settlements for past unlawful behavior may have only a modest effect in deterring future types of discrimination.

Fair lending litigation has done a good job in identifying, albeit somewhat tardily, emerging practices that need to be addressed to end discrimination. Here again, private claims, despite rarely achieving ultimate success on the merits, have shown the government where to focus its enforcement energies. This theme seems likely to recur in the future, as private advocates consider how to address lenders' discriminatory maintenance of their REO properties and the discriminatory impact of their current underwriting standards.

Indeed, impact-based cases seem to be where future productive litigation must be focused. Individual intent-based claims, always difficult to win, have been made nearly impossible by the Supreme Court's new pleading rules. Further, whatever deterrence and precedent-setting values are available most likely would involve big banks whose practices affect tens of thousands of people and whose growing role in the mortgage market make them more likely to attract the attention of enforcement agencies. These large lenders also have the resources to regularly evaluate the impact of their underwriting practices on minorities and the knowledge that, if they do select the more discriminatory among various alternative practices that would equally serve their business interests, they are likely to be in violation of the FHA as currently administered.

While many values are served by vigorously pursuing FHA-based lending litigation, it needs to be recognized that litigation is only one, and perhaps not even the best, tool in the equal-opportunity toolbox. Other strategies and approaches are needed as well.

A first step in all efforts to help realize the law's promise of a nondiscriminatory mortgage market is gaining knowledge—about what lenders are doing and how their current practices are impacting different groups of people and geographic locations. Knowledge requires basic research of the kind done by the Woodstock Institute, the National Community Reinvestment Coalition, and the Center for Responsible Lending.

But more is needed in terms of understanding the inside facts about lenders and their policies and corporate cultures. Much of what banks currently hide as proprietary information can and should be made more transparent. At the very least, Fannie Mae, Freddie Mac, and other government-supported lenders should be made to share more information about the underlying justifications for their underwriting standards with the public. Another knowledge-generating possibility is to have a civil rights organization form a partnership with a bank to see if a lender dedicated to nondiscriminatory principles can succeed and, in the process, identify the special challenges that face such an entity and whatever effective strategies may exist for dealing with these challenges.

Knowledge then needs to be translated into action. The ultimate goal here is a national set of best practices, which would probably require the backing of federal regulations. The process of producing such regulations can be long and tortious, as demonstrated by the 2011–2013 battle over HUD's FHA-impact regulation, though history shows that litigation can provide a useful role in this process by producing individual case stories that show the need for national action.

Finally, since so much depends on governmental action, the key role that politics plays must be recognized. Litigation can identify problems and point the way to needed reforms, but the government must have the will to follow through with effective policies. This, in turn, requires strong political action at both the grassroots and national levels in order to counter the daunting powers of resistance. Given the lending community's awesome financial and political resources, it is little wonder that the government's record of pushing the FHA's nondiscrimination goals has been erratic and often timid. Movements like Occupy Wall Street have helped heighten awareness of the economic inequalities in the United States and of the need for curbing the power of giant financial institutions, but whether such movements can also succeed in encouraging policymakers to pursue effective measures to protect minorities and minority communities seeking nondiscriminatory home loans remains to be seen.

References

Ausness, Richard C. 2002. "Tort Liability for the Sale of Defective Products: An Analysis and Critique of the Concept of Negligent Marketing." *South Carolina L. Rev.* 53: 907–66.

Berrey, Ellen, Steve G. Hoffman, and Laura Beth Nielsen. 2012. "Situated Justice: A Contextual Analysis of Fairness and Inequality in Employment Discrimination Litigation." *Law & Society Review* 46: 1–36.

Center for Responsible Lending. 2012. *Balancing Risk and Access: Underwriting Standards for Qualified Residential Mortgages.* Durham, NC: Center for Responsible Lending.

Center for Responsible Lending, Consumer Federation of America, and the Leadership Conference on Civil and Human Rights. 2012. *Comments to the Consumer Financial Protection Bureau, Docket No. CFPB-2012-0022, RIN 3170-AA17: Request for Comment on Qualified Mortgage,* July 9.

DOJ (Department of Justice). 2001 [revised 2008]. *Fair Lending Enforcement Program.* Washington, DC: US Department of Justice.

———. 2012a. *Assistant Attorney General Thomas E. Perez Testifies Before the Senate Judiciary Committee at Hearing on Fair Lending.* Washington, DC: US Department of Justice.

———. 2012b. *Recent Accomplishments of the Housing and Civil Enforcement Section.* Washington, DC: US Department of Justice.

———. 2012c. *Justice Department Reaches Settlement with Wells Fargo Resulting in More Than $175 Million in Relief for Homeowners to Resolve Fair Lending Claims.* Washington, DC: US Department of Justice.

Engel, Kathleen C., and Patricia A. McCoy. 2007. "Turning a Blind Eye: Wall Street Finance of Predatory Lending." *Fordham L. Rev.* 75: 2039–103.

Ford, Richard Thompson. 2011. "Moving Beyond Civil Rights" *New York Times,* October 28.

Goldberg, John C. P. 2003. "Twentieth Century Tort Theory." *Georgetown. L. J.* 91: 513–83.

HUD (Department of Housing and Urban Development). 2011. *Live Free: Annual Report on Fair Housing FY 2010.* Washington, DC: US Department of Housing and Urban Development.

HUD (Department of Housing and Urban Development), Office of Federal Housing Enterprise Oversight, Department of Justice, Office of the Comptroller of the Currency, Office of Thrift Supervision, Board of Governors of the Federal Reserve System,

Federal Deposit Insurance Corporation, Federal Housing Finance Board, Federal Trade Commission, and National Credit Union Administration. 1994. "Interagency Policy Statement on Discrimination in Lending." *Federal Register* 59 (73): 18266–74.

Lattman, Peter. 2012a. "Investors' Billion-Dollar Fraud Fighter." *New York Times*, October 9.

____.2012b. "U.S. Accuses Wells Fargo Of Lying About Mortgages." *New York Times*, October 10.

NFHA (National Fair Housing Alliance). 2011. *Here Comes the Bank—There Goes the Neighborhood*. Washington, DC: National Fair Housing Alliance.

____. 2012a. *The Banks Are Back—Our Neighborhoods Are Not: Discrimination in the Maintenance and Marketing of REO Properties*. Washington, DC: National Fair Housing Alliance.

____. 2012b. *Fair Housing in a Changing Nation: 2012 Fair Housing Trends Report*. Washington, DC: National Fair Housing Alliance.

Schuck, Peter H. 1995. "Mass Torts: An Institutional Evolutionist Perspective." *Cornell L. Rev.* 80: 941–89.

Schwartz, Gary T. 1994. "Reality in the Economic Analysis of Tort Law: Does Tort Law Really Deter?" *U.C.L.A. L. Rev.* 42: 377–444.

____. 1997. "Mixed Theories of Tort Law: Affirming Both Deterrence and Corrective Justice." *Texas L. Rev.* 75: 1801–34.

Schwemm, Robert G. 2007. "Why Do Landlords Still Discriminate (and What Can be Done About It)?" *John Marshall L. Rev.* 40: 455–511.

____. 2012. *Housing Discrimination: Law and Litigation*. St. Paul, MN: Thomson Reuters/West.

Schwemm, Robert G., and Jeffrey L. Taren. 2010. "Discretionary Pricing, Mortgage Discrimination, and the Fair Housing Act." *Harvard Civil Rights–Civil Liberties L. Rev.* 45: 375–433.

Silver-Greenberg, Jessica. 2012. "ACLU Filing Suit Over Loans." *New York Times*, October 15.

Sugarman, Stephen D. 2000. "A Century of Change in Personal Injury Law." *California L. Rev.* 88: 2403–36.

US House of Representatives. 1988. *Report 100-711: the Fair Housing Amendments Act of 1988*. Washington, DC: US Government Printing Office.

____. 1991. *H.R. Rep. No. 102-40(I)*. Washington, DC: US Government Printing Office.

US Senate. 1967. *Hearings on the Fair Housing Act of 1967 before the Subcommittee on Housing and Urban Affairs of the Senate Committee on Banking and Currency on S. 1358, S. 2114, and S. 2280 Relating to Civil Rights and Housing*. Washington, DC: US Government Printing Office.

Zibel, Alan, and Maya Jackson Randall. 2012. "Home Loans May Get Shield." *Wall Street Journal*, October 16.

12

Housing, Race, and Opportunity

john a. powell

H OUSING JUSTICE AND racial justice are profoundly linked in this country because one of the primary ways we have created racial dispar-ities in this county is through spatial segregation. Over my past forty years of working on racial justice issues, from both legal advocacy and research standpoints, I have argued both for the centrality of housing policy and for linking housing policy to other social policies. I have asked that we con-sider how housing fits into an overall landscape of structures that reproduce racial hierarchy and entrenched inequality. In this chapter, I want to look at both how my understanding of these things has changed over the past four decades and about how the discourses around fair housing have been shaped by activists, landmark legal cases, increasingly sophisticated research, and changing racial narratives within the United States.[1]

During my lifetime, we have seen considerable evolution in our under-standing of race, of racialization and racial disparities, and about what socially just housing means. We have been somewhat successful in removing the racist actor from arguments about racially disparate impacts of poor housing policy

---

1. There are many people who have dedicated their lives to housing justice in this country. My work has always been a bit broader and less sharply defined, dedicated to social justice in general and racial justice in particular. So in this work, I stand on the shoulders of giants, on activists who have done tremendous amounts of good work around housing, and academics who haven't lost touch with their roots in organizing and advocacy. I dedicate this piece to them. Thanks to Stephen Menendian and Eric Stiens for assistance with this chapter.

(see later section on *Thompson v. HUD*[2]). We have slowly moved from in-place strategies of development to race-neutral dispersal strategies (such as Moving to Opportunity for Fair Housing) to a more nuanced understanding of how opportunity plays out across a region in dynamic and racially specific ways. And, just this past decade, we saw the unexpected and catastrophic effects of bundling subprime loans into highly leveraged "financial weapons of mass destruction" ("Buffett Warns on Investment 'Time Bomb'" 2003) and are still coming to terms with what happened. Lastly, as cognitive science and social theory advance, we are also beginning to understand housing not only as a distributor of material opportunities but also as a key way in which we define our selves and our communities. We have long known that housing was a key intervention point for asset building, but what has not been so clear is that housing is also a key way in which we construct identities—self-identities, group-identities, and our ideas of community.

A Brief Story

I would like to start this chapter with a story that represents the first time I saw something shift in housing justice work; when recognition emerged that housing work went beyond what we were doing and that other strategies for addressing housing issues were possible. This was the first glimmer of the work many of us would continue doing. We began to think about housing not as just a single issue, but as an issue with a complex set of benefits and one of the key sites of intervention that could affect access to opportunity in a wide variety of areas.

I first started working on landlord-tenant issues and eviction as a young attorney at Evergreen Legal Services in Seattle in the early 1970s. It struck me then that we were working on symptoms and not core issues. We were essentially attacking a systemic problem one tenant at a time. First, the client had to find us and get through the screening process. Then, there had to be a legal claim or defense based on the law. Then, we might prevail. And sometimes when we prevailed, we still were facing the same landlords over and over again. Even in a limited view of victory as being able to get single landlords to change their practices, we were not always successful.

This is not to suggest that the work did not have value. It did. We helped many people get into or stay in their homes. But, as with all symptomatic

---

2. Thompson v. HUD, 348 F. Supp. 2d 398, 406, 467 (D. Md. 2005).

work, the impact of it was limited. We were the proverbial "baby catchers," pulling individual babies out of the water without ever getting to look upstream.

We were not naïve. We did annual need assessments. We talked with our clients. We knew one of the main problems was an overall lack of affordable housing in the community. However, we believed that this was the province of policymakers and not Legal Services attorneys. After all, what could we possibly do about the supply of housing?

Eventually, a small group of us started to explore and push the idea that we *could* do something about the overall supply of affordable housing. We had some support from the leadership of the office, but, of course, there was pushback. We were taking resources away from the things we could do to focus on the things we could not do. In part, our critics were right. We did not have the technical skills for building the supply of affordable housing. However, we could work with law firms that did, and we did this. So, we began to work with tax attorneys to figure out better ways of subsidizing and incentivizing the development of affordable housing.

At one point during this process, Sean Bleck, an attorney in the office, decided that we should develop some of the needed specialized skills internally. He decided that he would go back to New York University (NYU) to get a master of laws degree in tax law with a focus on housing syndications. The howls of disbelief followed: an NYU tax attorney working for Legal Services! Many thought that if he left, he would not come back. They were wrong. He earned his degree, came back, and was an incredible asset for the work that would follow.

The work that was done out of that office in Seattle in the 1970s and 1980s has many lessons, and many valuable friendships were forged that endure today, almost forty years later. It shaped my view that our work, no matter how we pursue it, is about social justice. Sometimes the law is a useful instrument for that work, and sometimes it is not. As an aside, the supervising attorney at that office, Steve Frederickson, is still doing innovative work for social justice (and we are still friends!).

I opened the chapter with this story because I think it might be useful. It might help others to dream. Rather than focusing on what we think we can or cannot do, it is useful to focus on the nature of the problem and then explore how that could be shifted. If we can do this, new ways to apply our skills open up, or we have the impetus to learn new skills. We need not be constrained by what we think is possible because we surely do not know what is possible until we have a better understanding of the problems facing us.

Evolution of a Problem Statement

Over the past forty years, I have watched my own understandings of what exactly the "housing problem" is change, as well as the field's. Sometimes this has been in tandem, and at other times, I have been at odds with many other advocates in what I was arguing. Many times, I have been told, just as we were told in Seattle, that I was sacrificing what could be done by arguing for something that could not be done.

In the 1970s and early 1980s, most legal service offices doing housing work were focused strictly around the parameters of the landlord-tenant contractual relationship: unpaid rent, health and safety violations, broken promises, etc. In Seattle, nearly all of our clients were low-income households. This makes sense because we were antipoverty lawyers and we all took our jobs with the knowledge that part of our mission was to make sure that even the poorest among us could have a fair date in court. (That these court dates were rarely "fair" is another thing entirely.) However, it was apparent that most of our clients were not just low-income individuals, but that they were also people of color. Even in Seattle in the 1970s, not the most diverse place on Earth, there were times when the majority of our clients were nonwhite.

So, does it matter that many of our clients were not white, and why? What would it mean to suggest that our work was deeply racialized? The easy answer is simple statistics: people of color were disproportionately likely to be poor, and because we represented poor people, we were more likely to represent people of color. (In other words, we did not need to have a racial analysis that went beyond understanding that nonwhite people, through some set of mechanisms, were more likely to be poor.) While this may be descriptively correct, it is analytically vacuous. It offers us no insight, much less tools, to address the differences between black poverty and white poverty, between concentrated poverty and dispersed poverty, and between being low-income and being poor.

It was during this time that some of us, including myself, began to push for a more explicit racial analysis in both housing debates and larger debates around equity, poverty, and fairness. Many advocates and policy workers began to articulate what Gunnar Myrdal had observed in the 1940s: that the condition of poor blacks and poor whites in the US had never been symmetrical (Myrdal, Rose, and Sterner 1944). We argued that to understand the particular challenges of addressing black poverty in the United States, people needed to understand more deeply the way that racial hierarchy functioned in the US. I believe that this view has been advanced quite a bit over the past forty years, and is now a prominent view of many organizations working on poverty issues. At least among advocates and activists, the early "color-blind" paradigm of justice has mostly disappeared.

However—and I will come back to this point at the end of the chapter—I believe there is a parallel assertion that can be made that has not been advanced nearly as far. Lani Guinier and Gerarld Torres (2002) made it eloquently in *The Miner's Canary*, and it is this: The structural forces affecting marginalized people of color in the US also threaten white people because they are signs of a malfunctioning democracy, of mechanisms that are reproducing inequality, and of a prison-industrial system run amuck. One cannot understand the poverty that the white community faces without understanding racial dynamics in the US. Moreover, segregation and structural racism harm white people—most especially (and materially) low-income white people, but also, on a more existential level, all of us (powell 2012a).

In much of my earlier writing and thinking, I have asserted that in the US and other mature democracies with relatively strong economies, poverty is more about status than objective conditions of deprivation. To be sure, being low-income matters, but what poverty connotes in our society is a lack of basic membership (powell 2012b). Here, I draw on the work of Amartya Sen and others in talking about opportunity deprivation. Sen would argue that a famine is not truly possible in a democracy (Sen 1983). I would argue the same about racialized inequalities and segregation. Segregation is not possible in a true democracy, and neither are intractable disparities. If we see these disparities, it must be because people have unequal access to decision power—to the power to shape their lives.

Charles Tilly (1998) talks about "durable inequality"—the inequalities that are reproduced across time and generations, especially those that are group-based. I tend to use the phrase "structural racialization" to make the point that there are processes at work that promote racially unequal outcomes. These need not be racist processes—which is one thing that the courts have had trouble grappling with in regard to fair housing law. These unequal groups need not even cleave along racial lines. We could expect any society that has uneven access to opportunity structures to reproduce inequality (and probably widening inequality because wealth tends to multiply exponentially and access to opportunity tends to increase access to further opportunity). However, in the US, many of these structures emerged at a time when racial hierarchy was quite explicit. Thus, even though the overtness of that hierarchy has diminished, the structures continue doing the work of racialization, and, in many ways, the hierarchy has become more entrenched.

So much of the work I and others have done—in the arena of housing, but also in other arenas over the past forty years—is both widening and sharpening our problem statement so that new solutions emerge. Over the past two decades especially, I have argued not only that is it impossible to talk about poverty without talking about race (powell 1996) but also that it is impossible to talk about concentrated poverty without talking about concentrated wealth; that it is useless to talk about the ghetto without talking about the exurbs; and that, perhaps most importantly, it brings us no closer to wholeness to talk about how well or poorly white America is doing without also asking the same of brown, black, and Native America.

We do ourselves no favors if we trap ourselves in limited and false dichotomies. Thirty years ago, I rejected the assertion that we could either have affordable housing or integrated housing, but not both. Today, I reject the paradoxical assertion (that the Obama administration has used many times) that we can be more effective in addressing racial disparities if we do not talk about race and focus our interventions on poverty in general. I do not believe that suburbs and cities are in a zero-sum resource game—regions thrive as a whole. I do not think we can talk about education policy without talking about housing and taxation policy. I do not think we can fix things simply by pouring more resources onto a stacked playing field.

In some very important ways—both in our discourse and in the legal remedies and arguments available to us (which I will track in the rest of this chapter)—we are able to address segregation and racial hierarchy in more sophisticated and explicit ways than we were able two, three, or four decades ago. However, in some equally important ways, we are still not adequately addressing the structural factors that reproduce racial inequality—where housing is key.

Key Housing Developments: A Shifting Legal Landscape and Imperfect Remedies

Prior to the Fair Housing Act of 1968, there was almost no large-scale housing desegregation success. Restrictive covenants, segregation, and racial steering were the norm. In 1948, *Shelly v. Kraemer*[3] held that restrictive covenants were judicially unenforceable (although not necessarily illegal or unconstitutional), and in the 1950s, the National Association for the Advancement of Colored People (NAACP) won two legal victories[4] that banned segregation in public

---

3. Shelley v. Kraemer, 334 U.S. 1 (1948).
4. Banks v. Housing Authority of City and County of San Francisco, 120 Cal. App. 2d 1, 260 P.2d 668 (1953) and Detroit Housing Commission v. Lewis, 226 F. 2d 180 (1955).

housing. However, despite these victories and the enactment of the 1964 Civil Rights Act, federal housing programs remained largely segregated. (Indeed, as Florence Roisman (2007) points out, the Supreme Court's desegregation mandate in *Brown v. Board of Education*[5] may have intensified housing segregation to avoid school integration.)

Gautreaux

Another major court case that dealt with race and housing is *Gautreaux v. Chicago Housing Authority*[6]—a huge breakthrough in housing desegregation. In 1966, the American Civil Liberties Union (ACLU) filed a lawsuit against the Chicago Housing Authority (CHA) and the Department of Housing and Urban Development (HUD) on civil rights grounds (for a history of the litigation, see Polkoff 2005). In it, black plaintiffs argued that the CHA had deliberately selected public housing sites in the "black ghetto" to avoid placing black families in white neighborhoods and that HUD had assisted in this practice with financing and other support. The plaintiffs won.

The significance of the *Gautreaux* case was not only the declaration that the defendants had segregated public housing but also finding an expansive remedy for the issue. The district court ordered HUD to initiate interdistrict, metropolitan-wide relief, and the Supreme Court affirmed. The district court also ordered the CHA to develop the next seven hundred units in predominantly white sections of Chicago and for 75 percent of all public housing to be located in predominantly white areas of Chicago or Cook County.

In a pattern we have seen repeated in other desegregation cases (both school and housing), multiple delays and refusals to cooperate marked the litigation, which led to a 1972 order joining the City of Chicago as defendants and invalidating a state law that required approval before construction could begin. The Supreme Court's affirmance of the remedy in 1976—bolstered by the intervening passage of the Fair Housing Act of 1968—initiated one of the largest public housing mobility efforts up to that time.

Perhaps the most important legacy of the *Gautreaux* case is the sociological data on the effects of the move on the 7,100 African American families that relocated to less racially and economically segregated neighborhoods. These families were studied for decades, and the relationship between race and place became more central in not only our jurisprudence but also our social science research and national conversation (Rosenbaum and DeLuca

---

5. Brown v. Board of Education, 347 U.S. 483 (1954).
6. Gautreaux v. Chicago Housing Authority, 296 F.Supp. 907.

2008; Rosenbaum and Rubinowitz 2000; DeLuca and Rosenbaum 2009; Rosenbaum and Zuberi 2010; Rosenbaum, Kulieke, and Rubinowitz 1988). The *Gautreaux* studies demonstrated marked benefits that accrued through adulthood of those who moved under the program. They would set the stage for the ambitious Moving to Opportunity experiments that would take place a few decades later.

Fair Housing Act

Against the backdrop of the *Gautreaux* case was the passage of the Fair Housing Act. In 1968, the Kerner Commission issued its remarkable inquiry into the various causes of civil disorder in the major metropolitan areas in the United States. The report opened with a warning that the nation was "moving toward two societies, one Black, one white—separate and unequal" and warned that the failure to address this schism threatened the fabric of the nation (Kerner Commission 1968, 1–2). Despite this impetus, both Congress and President Johnson refused to pass a fair housing act. It was not until the assassination of Dr. Martin Luther King, Jr., which threatened further unrest, that the Fair Housing Act became law. The Fair Housing Act is not simply an antidiscrimination measure; it also requires HUD to affirmatively further fair housing, a legal requirement that has been expanded over the years to cover any urban redevelopment activity receiving HUD funds.[7] Unfortunately for advocates, this responsibility has never been specifically defined. The overall orientation of the Fair Housing Act was individualistic, and the various exceptions and exemptions meant that patterns of segregation would largely be unaltered.

I have written elsewhere about the problems with the antidiscrimination and tort approach for remedies and why the Fair Housing Act may actually undermine its own stated purposes (powell 2008). Just as Southern-sponsored "freedom of choice" school options following the *Brown* case left patterns of segregation intact, provisions designed to increase freedom of choice for home buyers have done surprisingly little to address entrenched patterns of racial residential segregation.

---

7. See 42 U.S.C. § 3608(d) ("all executive departments and agencies shall administer their programs and activities relating to housing and urban development . . . in a manner affirmatively to further the purposes of this title and shall cooperate with the Secretary [of Housing] to further such purposes").

Mt. Laurel as a Response to National Decisions

The same year as the Fair Housing Act, the Supreme Court upheld litigation under the Civil Rights Act of 1866 in the surprising landmark decision of *Jones v. Alfred Mayer Co.*[8] on the grounds that the Civil Rights Act of 1866 was passed under the Thirteenth Amendment and could therefore regulate private behavior without state action. However, broader efforts at structural reform were stymied in the 1970s by both the *Arlington Heights v. Metropolitan Housing Corp.*[9] and *Washington v. Davis*[10] cases. The *Arlington Heights* case involved a zoning request to rezone a parcel from single-family units to multifamily to accommodate a plan to build units for low- and middle-income families. The refusal to grant the rezoning request was justified on the grounds of lowering property values, but had a clear racial impact.

The Supreme Court's refusal to overturn the *Arlington Heights* case and the zoning refusal essentially sanctioned zoning efforts that insulated white privilege and residential segregation. Exclusionary zoning became one of the principal means of maintaining residential segregation patterns. The Supreme Court held here and in the *Washington v. Davis* case that plaintiffs had to establish invidious intent and not just rely on a discriminatory impact. This focus on the need for a racist actor, with racist intent, has haunted the movement for racial justice ever since (see powell 1996).

So instead, advocates turned to state courts, and in the mid-1970s, the New Jersey Supreme Court overturned exclusionary zoning ordinances in the *Southern Burlington County N.A.A.C.P. v. Mount Laurel Township*[11] decision. Like the *Gautreaux* case, this case also focused on geography, but unlike *Gautreaux*, race got deliberately lost. Race issues were in the early pleading but were not in the decision. During this period, advocates were increasingly aware of race, but there was ambivalence to addressing it head-on. Advocates thought that possibly the race issues could be solved by just using a poverty lens—or worse, that using racially explicit arguments and frameworks for decision making would impede the progress that could be made in more racially neutral ways. I have always thought this attitude was wrong. We have seen many times that the more narrowly focused an intervention, the more likely it

---

8. Jones v. Alfred H. Mayer Co., 392 U.S. 409 (1968).

9. Village of Arlington Heights v. Metropolitan Housing Development Corp, 429 U.S. 252 (1977).

10. Washington v. Davis, 426 U.S. 229 (1976).

11. Southern Burlington County N.A.A.C.P. v. Township of Mount Laurel, 67 N.J. 151 (1975).

is to be undermined by forces that lay outside of its definition of the problem. This brings us to the Moving to Opportunity experiment.

Moving to Opportunity

Both the strengthening of the Fair Housing Act in 1988 and the relative success of the *Gautreaux* remedy helped spur the Moving to Opportunity (MTO) experiment in five cities across the US. With a robust experimental design, MTO set out to test the effects of moving families into low-poverty neighborhoods. It was thought of as a sort of *Gautreaux*-plus, hopefully making the case for mobility and poverty deconcentration strategies. It was exciting. It was big. It was regional in scope. It was explicit about fairly siting low-income housing around the region and the reasons to do so. Yet, its successes were underwhelming.

The project did succeed in moving families to safer neighborhoods. It showed both physical and psychological benefits, especially for children and women. Obesity and diabetes, for example, were significantly affected even without any sort of health supports built into the experiment (Acevedo-Garcia et al. 2008). However, it failed to achieve any measureable employment benefits or much of an educational benefit. I argued in my expert report for *Thompson v. HUD* that MTO was significantly flawed because it used a single indicator approach—neighborhood poverty rates—as well as vouchers without identifying and removing other barriers to integration (powell 2005). By doing so, many MTO participants wound up in a different neighborhood within the same school district, in a downwardly transitioning area, or in a lower-poverty neighborhood, but one that lacked access to good jobs (Briggs, Popkin, and Goering 2010; Ferryman et al. 2008; Tegeler 2007).

It was during this time that I really started shifting my analysis from a place-based indicator approach to a multi-indicator framework that ultimately focuses on both regions and people. I envisioned a process of measuring opportunity in a more complex way, and hired staff with geographic information system (GIS) expertise at the Kirwan Institute at Ohio State University to help me accomplish this goal. For the next few years, we developed a model called opportunity-based mapping that could summarize an array of indicators and relevant factors into a clear, spatial representation of the distribution of opportunity (Kirwan Institute 2012). The opportunity-based housing concept was influenced by my earlier work mediating a dispute between advocates of in-place affordable housing strategies and mobility-based affordable housing strategies in the Chicago region.

While MTO was primarily an antipoverty effort with little attention to race, education, or other factors, the opportunity approach is far more robust, relying on a broad array of indicators. Dynamic real estate markets and employment opportunities affected MTO effectiveness over time. An opportunity-based remedy must account for the need to adjust targets for changed circumstances while recognizing that demographic patterns shift and the opportunity structures themselves change over time. As new data become available, particularly the decennial census, there is a need to update and revise remedial processes to achieve target goals.

Thompson v. HUD

It was in this context that I was asked to be a lead expert in the *Thompson v. HUD* case, one of the most significant fair housing cases in recent years. In 1995, a suit was filed by the NAACP and the ACLU on behalf of fifteen thousand public housing residents in Baltimore, Maryland, alleging that HUD had effectively restricted minority families to segregated neighborhoods in the central city. In 2005, Judge Garbis ruled that HUD had violated Title VIII of the Fair Housing Act by failing to affirmatively further fair housing.

In response to this ruling, the Supreme Court asked the parties to brief the court on a potential remedy. In my report, I developed an opportunity index for the Baltimore region made up of over a dozen variables related to opportunity (see, for example, Kirwan Institute 2005). The multifactor analysis was an attempt to move past the simplistic single indicator or binary divides of urban and suburban, black and white, and rich and poor. The emphasis in my report was on affirmatively connecting public housing residents to multiple opportunity structures (education, health, and employment), as well as reducing the concentration of poverty in Baltimore's inner-city neighborhoods (powell 2005).

Most recently, the *Thompson* parties have settled and have explicitly agreed to adopt the opportunity approach. It continues the current and successful poverty deconcentration program, the Baltimore Housing Mobility Program, through 2018. It also requires HUD to conduct a regional opportunity assessment to inform its efforts. Furthermore, HUD will conduct civil rights reviews of housing proposals submitted for approval, paying specific attention to creating strong and inclusive communities.

These recommendations were not only adopted in this case, but by HUD as a part of its five-year plan to reanalyze its public housing programs. In 2011, HUD Secretary Shaun Donovan visited with me at the Kirwan Institute to get a greater understanding of what it means to have an opportunity-based evaluation framework that takes explicit account of racial integration. The NAACP Legal Defense and Education Fund (2012) quotes Donovan: "[when] you don't have mobility, you don't have access to opportunity. That's because when you choose a home, you choose so much more than a home. You also choose access to jobs, to schools for your children, to public safety. You choose a community—and the choices available *in* that community." Donovan further stressed that HUD is "committed to mobility efforts" like the Baltimore Housing Mobility Program, which will be continued by this settlement, because "it represents . . . justice for families who were wronged."

Subprime Crisis

While at the Kirwan Institute, my colleagues and I convened nearly two hundred civil rights, housing, and legal activists and scholars for an in-depth look at the subprime and foreclosure crisis. One of the things we were all in agreement about was that the subprime loan process had deeply disproportionate effects on communities of color.[12] Rugh and Massey (2010) have done an excellent job quantifying this hypothesis. Their model shows that black residential segregation explains significant amounts of the variation of foreclosures in metropolitan areas, and actually exceeds that of other causative factors that have been commonly cited as contributing factors (oversupply, housing price inflation, etc.).

An interesting legal avenue is emerging based on the Fair Housing Amendments Act of 1988, which prohibits discrimination not only in lending but also in the securitization of mortgages. Since disparate impact liability, not just disparate treatment liability, can be established under the Fair Housing Act, all targeting of minority neighborhoods for subprime loans can provide a basis for litigation under the act. Unfortunately, there is almost no case law under these regulations so far. The US Securities and Exchange Commission (SEC) has, for example, targeted Goldman Sachs for fraudulent investment practices, but the case has not been made that these practices were not only fraudulent but also racially discriminatory. However, the ACLU is, as of this writing, about to file a major suit on these grounds.

There is still an urgent need to talk about access to credit and lending practices that could be used to build wealth in communities of color in

---

12. A complete discussion of the securitization process and how it played out in segregated communities is too much for this chapter, but see Kirwan Institute (2008) for a good primer.

sustainable ways. Fair access to credit means little if that credit only allows someone access to a house in an opportunity-poor and segregated area. I and other racial justice advocates have argued that the federal government has an affirmative duty to further fair housing and fair credit—a duty that should be operationalized and monitored, with policy adjustments to meet targets (Rogers et al. 2010). Enforcement has also been extraordinarily lax over the past two decades—partly through rollbacks and partly by regulation schemes that simply have not been able to keep up with the technology of securitization. As the housing market slowly moves towards a new equilibrium, we cannot simply keep focusing on efforts to prevent more foreclosures from taking place. We need to focus on skewed incentives, a monopolistic banking landscape, and large-scale financial reform. On this, the federal government has unfortunately taken its usual strategy of not wanting to explicitly talk about race. For example, as the Kirwan Institute noted, the Financial Crisis Inquiry Commission listed twenty-two areas of interest in investigating the causes of the crisis, and not one of which includes any mention of the history of racial segregation in credit markets, redlining, predatory lending targeted to communities of color, etc. (Rogers et al. 2010).

Principles of Fair Housing for the Twenty-First Century

While I am excited by HUD's movement towards embracing regional and opportunity-based solutions for public housing, it is clear that more needs to be done (and we cannot singularly rely on HUD as our only federal avenue to fair housing and fair credit). While we have made progress in quantifying opportunity, more robust theories and methodologies need to be developed to be able to visualize the dynamic nature of opportunity across a region. This is especially true as the old city-suburb divide is rapidly breaking down. Some of this suburban diversity should be celebrated, but much of it represents old patterns in new spaces. We need more sociologists, geographers, public policymakers, legislators, and others working on models of opportunity that focus on successful, stable, and sustainable communities.

The housing and credit crash, ongoing employment challenges, and the possibility of shrinking exurbs represent both a profound crisis and an opportunity for shaping metropolitan dynamics. On the one hand, we have a shrinking pie, which means that fragmented fiefdoms will potentially fight even harder to hold on to the privileges that they have. On the other hand, we have this moment of great uncertainty and rapid change where anything is possible. Just as urban sprawl (combined with white flight and jurisdictional fragmentation) was one of the key forces maintaining white privilege in the second half of the twentieth century, the reversal of those forces can be used as tools to create more equitable and integrated communities in the twenty-first century. However, it will not happen without foresight, planning, and all the policy tools we have at our disposal.

The opportunity communities model I have helped advance focuses on in-place, mobility, and linkage strategies. Added to the traditional arsenal of neighborhood development and individual approaches that focus on building social capital, these strategies focus on the mobility and degree of access people have to high-opportunity areas and include regional housing, tax-base sharing and school integration, and public transit expansion strategies. Without these linkages, in-place development or personal development is much less effective. An example I often use is of a leaky bucket: we surely need water to fill the bucket, and we may need even more water than we thought because the bucket is leaking, but unless we fix the structural parameters, all the water is going to leak back out again.

Thoughts on Segregation, Integration, and Opportunity

Elsewhere, I have written that "housing lies at the very heart of a system of institutional relations that reproduce inequality" (powell 2008, 606). Thomas Pettigrew (1979, 122) referred to it as the "structural linchpin of American race relations." Massey and Denton (1993) refer to it as an American form of apartheid. It is clear that not only does housing act as a key opportunity structure for access to employment, education, and much more, but the way we think about race is deeply impacted by the presence of white exurbs and racialized concentrated poverty in parts of central cities and inner-ring suburbs.

In her book *The Failures of Integration*, Sheryll Cashin (2004) talks about the cost of the ghetto. What she is talking about here is not only the very real costs (both material and nonmaterial) to having neighborhoods of concentrated black poverty, but the way that the social and cultural norms of such spaces become a part of the meaning of the category of black in this country.

At the beginning of this chapter, I mentioned that the costs to whites had not been grappled with by social justice advocates. Historically, much of the resistance to policies that share both risk and opportunity—metropolitan tax pools, fair housing quotas, universal health insurance, taxation, and social welfare programs in general—has been animated by a strong semiconscious fear of the underserving other. This is true even when those policies would help the very people (poor whites) that are most strongly against them. In *The*

Spirit Level: Why Greater Equality Makes Society Stronger, Richard Wilkinson and Kate Pickett (2010) demonstrate empirically how high levels of inequality weaken the fabric of society and reduce quality of life and health outcomes, increase crime and violence, and lead to a higher level of dissatisfaction for everyone—both the favored populations and the marginalized populations.

I will make three bold statements about the state of housing and racial justice in the United States:

1. We will not achieve racial equality if we cannot achieve residential integration and eliminate concentrated black poverty.

2. We cannot address poverty unless we fundamentally transform exclusive structures into inclusive structures—that is, structures of separation and racialization into structures of concern and shared well-being.

3. This is a spiritual and moral project, as well as a political project.

In other words, when we talk about transforming housing policy, we are moving beyond housing as a right, or even housing connected to opportunity, and talking about housing policy as being a key way in which we create meaningful communities in the US. Racialization has always been about creating an "other"—and in the presence of that other, there is a block, a cognitive and imaginative block, on a shared sense of vulnerability and concern.

Here, I am not even giving a prescriptive policy (or set of policies), but instead animating the idea for a framework for thinking about policy changes. Sen (1999, 283) wrote: "It is not so much a matter of having exact rules about how precisely we ought to behave, as of recognizing the relevance of our shared humanity in making the choices we face." Similarly, another one of my favorite social theorists, Roberto Unger (2007), talks about becoming attached to various institutional forms (and forms of dissent) rather than having political praxis that is guided by a sort of revolutionary pragmatism—the ability to question, reshape, and transform socioeconomic structures so that they can create not only a better society, but better selves.

In fact, it is important that we do not get locked into certain strategies while still continuing to pursue them even as conditions change. This is one of the ways that racial hierarchy has proven to be so durable—by finding new ways to inscribe itself. Fifteen years ago, it made sense to write an article with the title, "What We Need to Do About the 'Burbs?" (Wing 1999). However, today, the city-suburban opportunity divide is not nearly so clear. There are inner-ring suburbs that are diverse, but they are declining rapidly in terms of opportunity and tax base.

We have come a long way from talking about affordable housing through a color-blind and contractual lens. We also understand, at least theoretically, the complex interplay of structures across time and space. Occasionally, as in *Thompson v. HUD*, even our legal institutions get it mostly right (albeit with a two-decade delay).

Final Thoughts

I started this chapter by talking about my early learning; I will end by talking about some of my emerging learning. If I had to sum up this learning with one word, it would be *relationship*. Far too often in the advocacy field we end up focusing so singularly on something—a proposed policy or a particular social problem—and we think that if we can win this battle, we will win the war. But we ignore how this particular problem is created within a web of structures and causal relationships that go in both directions. These directions are no longer just regional, but also global.

Furthermore, we tend to forget that we are also talking about how we are constituted as selves within larger social structures. Segregation has been a key part of creating the modern white identity and the process of racial othering. All of the processes of racialization distribute meaning—categorical meaning and existential meaning, as well as material benefits and burdens. In very important ways, we are not just trying to get *things* right, but trying to get *us* right. New strands of cognitive science and neuroscience are emerging that show that many of the decisions we make are happening below conscious awareness—including many of our racial attitudes. We need to find more ways to shape these deep parts of ourselves in accordance with our higher principles of who we want to be.

We still need to forcefully articulate our vision of social justice and how both our selves and our structures fit within that vision. There is a way of thinking about the individual that is not in opposition to connection, but rather sees the self as both relational and autonomous. This self finds safety in a sense of shared vulnerability. It finds freedom not in independence but in interdependence. What would fair housing look like if we understood that housing is a key way in which we build relationships? What would our strategies for fair housing justice look like if we embraced and created better tools for analyzing the complex web of employment-, educational-, financial- and health-related opportunity structures that it intersects with? What if we brought racial justice to the foreground rather than the background of our fair housing efforts? If we were truly living and working in Dr. King's vision of a "beloved community," a fully integrated society, what would our housing look like?

References

Acevedo-Garcia, Dolores, Theresa L. Osypuk, Nancy McArdle, and David R. Williams. 2008. "Toward a Policy-Relevant Analysis of Geographic and Racial/Ethnic Disparities in Child Health." *Health Affairs* 27 (2): 321–33. doi: 10.1377/hlthaff.27.2.321.

Briggs, Xavier de Souza, Susan J. Popkin, and John M. Goering. 2010. *Moving to Opportunity: The Story of an American Experiment to Fight Ghetto Poverty*. New York: Oxford University Press.

"Buffett Warns on Investment 'Time Bomb.'" 2003. *BBC News*, March 4. http://news.bbc.co.uk/2/hi/2817995.stm.

Cashin, Sheryll. 2004. *The Failures of Integration: How Race and Class Are Undermining the American Dream*. New York: Public Affairs.

DeLuca, Stefanie, and James E. Rosenbaum. 2009. "Residential Mobility, Neighborhoods, and Poverty: Results from the Chicago Gautreaux Program and the Moving To Opportunity Experiment." In *The Integration Debate: Competing Futures for American Cities*, edited by Chester Hartman and Gregory Squires, 185–98. New York: Routledge.

Ferryman, Kadija., Xavier De Souza Briggs, Susan J Popkin, and Maria Rendon. 2008. "Do Better Neighborhoods for MTO Families Mean Better Schools?" Metropolitan Housing and Communities Center, Brief no. 3, March. http://www.urban.org/Uploaded PDF/411639_better_schools.pdf.

Guinier, Lani, and Gerald Torres. 2002. *The Miner's Canary: Enlisting Race, Resisting Power, Transforming Democracy*. Cambridge, MA: Harvard University Press.

Kerner Commission. 1968. *Report of the National Advisory Commission on Civil Disorders*. Washington, DC: US Government Printing Office.

Kirwan Institute. 2005. *Map 12: Comprehensive Opportunity Index for the Baltimore Region*. Columbus, OH: Kirwan Institute for the Study of Race and Ethnicity. http://www.aclu-md.org/uploaded_files/0000/0165/opportunity_map.pdf.

———. 2008. *Subprime Loans, Foreclosure, and the Credit Crisis: What Happened and Why? A Primer*. Columbus, OH: Kirwan Institute for the Study of Race and Ethnicity. http://www.racialequitytools.org/resourcefiles/kirwan3.pdf.

———. 2012. "Understanding Opportunity Mapping." Kirwan Institute for the Study of Race and Ethnicity. http://kirwaninstitute.osu.edu/research/opportunity-communities/mapping/understanding-opportunity-mapping/.

Massey, Douglas S., and Nancy A. Denton. 1993. *American Apartheid: Segregation and the Making of the Underclass*. Cambridge, MA: Harvard University Press.

Myrdal, Gunnar, Arnold Rose, and Richard Sterner. 1944. *An American Dilemma: The Negro Problem and Modern Democracy*. New York: Harper & Brothers.

NAACP Legal Defense and Education Fund. 2012. "Baltimore Public Housing Families Win Settlement in Fair Housing Lawsuit." Press release, August 24. http://www.naacpldf.org/press-release/baltimore-public-housing-families-win-settlement-fair-housing-lawsuit.

Pettigrew, Thomas F. 1979. "Racial Change and Social Policy." *Annals of the American Academy of Political and Social Science* 411: 114–31.

Polikoff, Alexander. 2005. *Waiting for Gautreaux: A Story of Segregation, Housing, and the Black Ghetto*. Evanston, IL: Northwestern University Press.

powell, john a. 1996. "Injecting a Race Component into Mt. Laurel Style Litigation." *Seton Hall Law Review* 2: 1369–85.

———. 2005. *Remedial Phase Expert Report of john powell in Thompson v. HUD, August 19*. Columbus, OH: Kirwan Institute for the Study of Race and Ethnicity. http://kirwan institute.osu.edu/docs/publications/powellremedialreport_submit_3_10_06.pdf.

———. 2008. "Reflections on the Past, Looking to the Future: The Fair Housing Act at 40." *Indiana Law Review* 41: 605–27.

———. 2012a. *Racing to Justice: Transforming Our Conceptions of Self and Other to Build an Inclusive Society*. Bloomington: Indiana University Press.

———. 2012b. "Poverty and Race through a Belongingness Lens." *Policy Matters* 1 (5): 3–27.

Rogers, Christy, Jason Reece, Jillian Olinger, Craig Ratchford, Mark Harris, and Keischa Irons. 2010. *Fair Credit and Fair Housing in the Wake of the Subprime Lending and Foreclosure Crisis*. Columbus, OH: Kirwan Institute for the Study of Race and Ethnicity. http://kirwaninstitute.osu.edu/docs/publications/fair_credit_fair_housing _summary_report.pdf.

Roisman, Florence. 2007. "Affirmatively Furthering Fair Housing in Regional Housing Markets: The Baltimore Public Housing Desegregation Legislation." *Wake Forest Law Review* 42: 333–92.

Rosenbaum, James, and Stefanie DeLuca. 2008. "Does Changing Neighborhoods Change Lives?" In *Social Stratification*, edited by D. Grusky, 393–99. Philadelphia: Westview.

Rosenbaum, James, and Leonard Rubinowitz. 2000. *Crossing the Class and Color Lines: From Public Housing to White Suburbia*. Chicago: University of Chicago Press

Rosenbaum, James E., and Anita Zuberi. 2010. "Comparing Residential Mobility Programs: Design Elements, Neighborhood Placements, and Outcomes in MTO and Gautreaux." *Housing Policy Debate* 20 (1): 27–41.

Rosenbaum, James E., Marilyn J. Kulieke, and Leonard S. Rubinowitz. 1988. "White Suburban Schools' Responses to Low-Income Black Children: Sources of Successes and Problems." *The Urban Review* 20 (1): 28–41.

Rugh, Jacob S., and Douglas S. Massey. 2010. "Racial Segregation and the American Foreclosure Crisis." *American Sociological Review* 75 (5): 629–51. doi:10.1177/0003122410380868.

Sen, Amartya. 1983. *Poverty and Famines: An Essay on Entitlement and Deprivation*. New York: Oxford University Press.

———. 1999. *Development as Freedom*. New York: Knopf.

Tegeler, Philip. 2007. "Connecting Families to Opportunity: The Next Generation of Housing Mobility Policy." In *All Things Being Equal: Instigating Opportunity in an Inequitable Time*, edited by Brian Smedley and Alan Jenkins, 79–95. New York: The New Press.

Tilly, Charles. 1998. *Durable Inequality*. Berkeley: University of California Press.

Unger, Roberto Mangaberia. 2007. *The Self Awakened: Pragmatism Unbound*. Cambridge, MA: Harvard University Press.

Wilkinson, Richard G., and Kate Pickett. 2010. *The Spirit Level: Why Greater Equality Makes Societies Stronger*. New York: Bloomsbury Press.

Wing, Bob. 1999. "What We Need to Do About the 'Burbs." *ColorLines*, September 15.

13

Winning Battles and Losing the War
The Progressive Advocacy World

Mike Miller

I S THERE A new social movement brewing in the United States? A few signs are there, but they are far from certain. Was the initial surge of Occupy Wall Street energy the opening step on the long march it will take to slow, halt, and reverse the power of the plutocracy? For those of us who thirst for a new social movement, we need to be careful that we do not ignore the realities that are on the ground and consider the following questions. If we fail to consider these questions, we will continue to win battles—for example, millions of dollars for this or that program—but we will continue to lose the war—for example, billions of dollars taken from the low-to-middle class people of the country by means of foreclosures, destruction of good jobs, undermining of public education, weakening of Social Security and Medicare, and an increased concentration of wealth and power in the hands of the few.

If there is a new surge of populist spirit and small "d" democratic energy, can it both win concrete victories and alter the relations of power? We have many examples of the former, but few of the latter.

What does it mean to alter the relations of power rather than just win a campaign, or even a series of campaigns? We have paid a steep price for not looking carefully at this question in the past.

If winning campaigns is not sufficient to alter the relations of power, what is missing in the conduct of our side of the war? While our army wins campaign battles, we are marching backward and getting smaller.

For the past fifty years, I have been attentive to these questions and to the question of building people power. Along the way, I have been involved in major and minor campaigns that won major and minor battles and achieved major and minor changes in public, corporate, and nonprofit policy and administration. I have seen people gain self-confidence and civic competence and overcome antagonisms toward the "other." I have watched them shift from feelings of powerlessness to believing in the efficacy of collective action. I have seen other positive results as well.

But the truth of the matter is that as I look back at my history of organizing and campaigns, there was relatively little success at changing the relations of power for more than brief periods of time. Observing the past fifty years of labor and community organizing, issue campaign mobilization, electoral engagement, community development, public policy advocacy, and other approaches aimed at realizing democratic values, I draw the same conclusion: with exceptions deserving serious attention, our side—the side of small "d" democracy and social and economic justice—has been on a steady march backward for—give or take—forty to forty-five years.

For the most part, our victories have changed the composition of the lower levels of a hierarchy of wealth and power that is ever more concentrated at the top, with ever more people suffering from its decisions. I welcome people of color, women, gays, the disabled, and others who were once systematically excluded from these hierarchies. But it is the present hierarchy itself that is the problem, not only who occupies its tiers. We have opened American culture to diversity, which is good. But too often diversity is limited to advertising, one of the marketing tools fostering consumerism. Lest we be too self-congratulatory about even these victories, heed this from Michelle Alexander, author of *The New Jim Crow*: "The mass incarceration of poor people of color, particularly black men, has emerged as a new caste system, one specifically designed to address the social, economic, and political challenges of our time. It is, in my view, the moral equivalent of Jim Crow" (Larkin 2012).

Yet, if you ask just about any organizer or activist about their accomplishments, you will hear a litany of victories. This is cognitive dissonance—where detachment from reality is utilized in order to avoid confronting what I believe is now a bleak picture. Some years ago, I heard Peter Dreier make the observation about us that "the whole is smaller than the sum of its parts." He was right then, and his observation is true today.

To tell the truth, I feel rather peculiar as the bearer of this message of gloom about where we stand in the struggle for democracy and social and economic justice. Usually, I am a hope peddler; all organizers are hope peddlers. We could not do what we do if we did not believe things might get better if people became engaged and organized.

The observations in this chapter are, therefore, a caution, a warning against illusions that might be created by Occupy or any other current expression that looks like a significant social movement. I think we need a sober, realistic appraisal of where we are if we are to begin to get to where we want to be.

The Nature of the Times

Where are we after the first decade of the twenty-first century? Where have we been for the past fifty-or-so years? I would like to begin by looking at those questions.

A main problem is that there is a continuing decline of the voluntary associations that are central to civil society. Ask any organizer who was around in the 1960s and who is still in touch with work on the ground, and he or she will tell you about the decline.

The decline in voluntary associations is both a source and consequence of growing isolation, alienation, loneliness, and powerlessness among the vast majority of Americans that, in turn, is accompanied by the destruction of any meaningful sense of community upon which an understanding of the common good can be built. The new social media consolidate that isolation with the fantasy of huge numbers of "friends." In combination, these factors contribute to xenophobia, a culture of rugged individualism, a "watch-out-for-number-one" mentality, and blind consumerism. Together, they result in the continuing erosion of any meaningful idea of democracy.

Even nominally democratic membership associations are, for the most part, advocates for and service providers to relatively inert members. You pay your dues and collect your benefits. But you are not a cocreator of the life of the organization. This is, unfortunately, the character of most unions and many religious congregations.

Without addressing the problem of civil society, we will be unable to address the other two major problems that I will name in a moment. If we had serious, small "d," democratic people power in this country, the housing, employment, education, food, environmental, and other crises we read about daily would not be taking place. If we had serious democratic people power in this country, Huey Long's economic populism would be common sense. In the early 1930s, Long, then governor of Louisiana and threatening to run for president against Franklin D. Roosevelt, had a soak-the-rich campaign. He said at one point, "We do not propose to say there shall be no rich men.

. . . We only propose that when one man gets more than he and his children and children's children can spend or use in their lifetimes, that then we shall say that such person has his share. That means that a few million dollars is the limit to what any one man can own" (Long 1934). (In the Basque region of Spain, the Mondragon cooperatives go further and say the top-to-bottom income ratio (after taxes) should be roughly 6.5 to 1 (Ormaechea 1991).)

Without the pressure from below of Long's campaign (aborted by his assassination in 1935), the Townsend movement's stirrings among the elderly, Upton Sinclair's near-win gubernatorial campaign in California running on a populist and socialist program, and, of course, the stirrings of the industrial union movement, Franklin D. Roosevelt's leadership for a New Deal would not have been possible. If we had serious democratic people power, there would be no private institutions "too big to fail"; no corporations that could move jobs with impunity; no banks that could foreclose on loans they should not have made in the first place; no destruction of between one-half and two-thirds of the wealth of Latino and African American households; no jobs that did not pay a living wage and offer dignity in the workplace; no closure of a vast array of needed public services; no ownership of our politics by people with vast sums of money—I need not continue the list.

Here is the punch line: *We cannot build democratic people power without renewing civil society. And we cannot renew civil society by a series of small or large victories on issues, no matter how important any one of them may be.* We cannot look at issue campaigns through the single lens of what they might win. We need bifocals so that we can simultaneously look at what we might win and what we are seeking to build.

I will return to the question of what we need to build, but first let me note this important contemporary exception: Evangelical and Pentecostal churches are building community and growing. Historically, these revivals in American Protestantism were central to the abolitionist movement and the Social Gospel's prophetic message for economic justice; today, they are the captives of conservative social, political, and economic ideology. These churches, in combination with a mix of small business, property-owner, homeowner, service, interest, and other face-to-face organizations, are the civil society base for American conservatism. Our side has no serious counterpart to them.

The second macro problem we face is the persistence and growth of poverty, near-poverty, and economic stress in growing numbers of the American people, which is magnified by discrimination based on race, ethnicity, gender, age, place, and other characteristics, as well as various unique or particular injustices that exist and persist because of particular identities—such as those faced by undocumented immigrants.

The scope of economic stress for a majority of Americans is partially hidden by two and even three jobs replacing one—whether performed by a single worker, by a second or even third worker contributing to household income not by choice but by economic necessity, by "doubling-up" in housing, by foregoing health insurance, or by other belt-tightening strategies. It is also hidden by the massive amount of debt now borne by tens of millions of Americans. This debt burden, especially among college graduates, is a glowing timber waiting to burn.

The stress is further hidden by large numbers of people participating in the underground economy, where they have no rights and no benefits. It is finally hidden by the loss of public goods (transportation, schools, parks, and other public services) that are cut back or eliminated as a result of the policies of neoliberalism.

Finally, and a primary source of the first two, is the increasing concentration of social, cultural, economic, and political power in the hands of 1 percent (or less) of the country's population. Their rapacity knows no bounds. Our side seems incapable of reining it in.

But it is neither the evils of the 1, .1, .01, or .001 percent nor the stress upon the majority of Americans that I want to focus on. Rather, I want to look at the opportunity lurking in the context of our times. It is the combination of economic stress, widespread sense of alienation, feeling that the country is going in the wrong direction, and anger at both big business and big government that provides the fertile soil in which base building, of the kind I will soon elaborate, can be cultivated.

Let me be crystal clear: this is a struggle for power. Those now at the pinnacles of institutional power have it, want to keep it, and want more of it. We read endless discussions and arguments about who they are, what they are doing, why they are doing it, the horrendous consequences of their actions, and so forth. But if we do not address the problem of powerlessness, these are irrelevant to the course of history. When we focus there, we are forced to ask the question of how to shift people from their experience of, and resignation about, powerlessness to becoming engaged in civic and political life. That is the central question.

Friends who have read drafts of this chapter tell me, "You are blaming the victim." Let me enlist an impeccable source for support. Albert Einstein said, "The world is a dangerous place, not because of those who do evil, but because of those who look on and do nothing" (Einstein Online 2012). Why are they doing nothing? I don't think it is because they like the status quo. Rather, it is because they do not think they can do anything about it. To put it another way, we cannot successfully address evils if we do not look at what we are building. And let me stress that word: building. That is distinct from, though interdependent with, what we are winning or hoping to win.

Building at the Base: An Example from Brazil

Let me offer a specific meaning for the word "community" and put it together with our common understanding of "organization." By community, I mean a group of people, sharing a common bond, faith, or tradition, who affirm, support, and challenge each other to act powerfully on their values and interests. The values of the community I'm interested in building are freedom—both the absence of external and imposed restraint and the opportunity to realize one's full human potential; equality—no great disparities in wealth, income, or status; democracy—as both means and end, both majority rule and minority rights, and highly participatory in character; justice—fairness, due process, and absence of arbitrary and capricious action by those in authority; solidarity, fraternity, interdependence, or community—the understanding that we are our sister's and brother's keepers. Except for a narrow understanding of freedom, these values are under attack and have been on the defense for some time in the United States and other "advanced" industrial countries. Yet, their power with everyday people manifests itself whenever there is a believable option for specific action to realize them.

In summary, "community" refers to a group of people who understand that their destinies are interdependent and intertwined. Earlier, I noted the steady erosion of civil society—that is another way of saying the erosion of community.

Community is built at the base of society, where people can engage in ongoing face-to-face relationships. Whatever might be said for the Internet, it is not a substitute for community. We are so estranged from a meaningful understanding of community that I want to go more deeply into what it would look like. To do that, I want to use the example of base Christian communities in Brazil when they were at their peak of development in the 1980s and 1990s because nothing we have done in the US quite approximates what they achieved in the period of emancipatory Catholicism that once characterized large parts of Latin America. I have drawn what follows from conversations with Latin American organizers and priests and, in particular, from the work of the Presbyterian Reverend, Dr. Richard Shaull, who taught at Princeton Theological Seminary.

Base Christian communities (BCCs) were face-to-face meetings of a group of lay Catholics who supported and challenged each other to act on their faith.

Typically, they met weekly, and sometimes more often. In a BCC meeting, the agenda had some combination of these elements:

- Stories about life experiences and problems told by attendees. These might be problems regarding a landlord or employer, spousal abuse, drinking, difficulty with a child, or something else on the mind of the participant.

- Stories of resistance to oppression by those present. Someone may have stood up to a landlord, a bureaucrat, an employer, or an abusive husband. A group might have gone to a person in charge of sewage to demand action to install sewer pipes under a street. These were thought of as examples of action in behalf of justice and participation in the transformation of the world.

- Biblical reflection that connected the life stories of the people to passages from the Bible meaningful to them.

- Reports or business items on mutual aid projects (buying clubs, a credit union, small producer coops, etc.).

- Plans for future group action—in the form of mutual aid or efforts to change the system. If the latter, people dealt openly with fear of retribution. Responsibilities were assigned, leadership determined, action plans adopted, etc.

- Prayer and conclusion of the meeting.

BCCs were religious communities, not social action groups. Action came organically out of participant stories and shared values. The "expert" (priest, nun, or deacon) who was present facilitated a discovery process and was a resource, perhaps supplying historical information. The people discovered the meaning of the Bible for themselves. Fundamentally, then, a new community emerged out of the poor people participating in the BCC.

BCCs re-created in the city the community of the old village or rural area that had previously existed for most participants—one based on kinship and extended family structures. The kinship structure was no longer able to function as a source for mutual aid because of changes in the economy and technology. The BCC re-created the extended family in a new form—perhaps building on the old, or perhaps not.

In the BCC, participants discovered themselves as fully human; there was a realization of self-worth. They discovered their talents, their calling; they shifted from a fatalistic view of the world—the passive recipients of whatever was given or done to them—to become people who challenged injustice, whether in the world at large or in their own family, and who sought to bring about change. The process of empowerment that went on was one in which people concluded that society must be restructured from the bottom up. The BCC was the new society in embryo—it was prefigurative.

Lay people became pastoral agents. That is, they became organizers. The laity accepted or adopted a new vocation of training for mutual empowerment. Priests and women religious walked alongside or accompanied the people, sharing experiences with them and offering support and assistance, but they were not hierarchically "over" them. Put another way, this was power with not power over (Miller 1983).

The community of faith as a humanizing experience was an alternative to violence against the oppressor as a liberating experience—a view widely held by revolutionaries throughout the world, particularly in this period. Implicitly, this approach challenged the notion of the vanguard party and a transitional stage in which victims of oppression are freed by a dictatorship of the proletariat. The BCC was a profoundly democratic expression.

Richard Shaull noted three reasons for there being radical political implications or consequences from BCCs:

1. They were a new form of social organization; other forms might be created as a result of the experience of people in the BCC. Among these, for example, are the Workers' Party in São Paulo, from which Luiz Inácio Lula da Silva later emerged to become president of Brazil, and the Landless Workers' Movement, now perhaps the largest social movement in the world with hundreds of thousands of members. While these latter formations are not BCCs, many of their leaders received their most important formative experience in them.

2. Mutual aid, or communal self-reliance, is a powerful tool that emerges from BCCs. People who used this tool would often move into politics and action, in part, because the system—in Brazil, the military dictatorship that preceded democratization—would not even allow for the creation of mutual aid institutions. BCCs supported strikes and other efforts at change.

3. BCCs became politically powerful when people took their reading of the Bible into the world (Miller 1983).

Note that the development of the BCC was a slow process. The early communities were typically formed after a priest or nun lived in a barrio for four-to-six years, developing trusting relationships with the people there. A first "core group" might have been only four people, and it was likely that the group grew very slowly. This group might have involved itself in simple mutual aid and support activity along with Biblical reflection for a couple of years before moving into "direct action" or anything directly challenging dominant political and economic institutions.

In discussing the application of the BCC experience to the United States, it is important to note two things that make Brazil of that period qualitatively different: (1) there were, of course, clear cultural differences and (2) the need to choose sides was more apparent in the Latin American context. The second point is becoming less true, however, as more people in the US are increasingly willing to view America's current system as a plutocracy.

It is not the differences, but the application of BCCs to our context that I want to call forth. For social, political, and economic action to be sustained, it must come out of the vital experiences lived in a community where mutual support, shared history, faith (which, by the way, can be secular as well as religious), a sense of vision, and deep values are shared and championed. As a result of these experiences, a belief in the possibility of a better world—one without exploitation and oppression—can be created.

Looking at the failure to apply BCC principles to the United States might help to explain the inability of a lot of our organizing work to create a counter-dominant culture that is based on solidarity and democracy and goes beyond rugged individualism and consumerism. Without such a culture, we will not successfully slow, halt, and reverse the present concentration of wealth and power in the hands of the few, even though we may win minor and even major campaigns.

This slow, careful, multifaceted way of organization building is quite different from the narrowly issue-driven way in which a lot of community-organizing and advocacy work proceeds in the US. But it is not alien to our experience in this country, as I will soon describe.

Building at the Base in the United States

If we look back on the experiences of organizers and activists in the United States, or on what we've read about the experience of others, we learn of labor union locals where a similar community to the BCC existed. Here, there was a rich fabric of mutual aid, negotiation, and confrontation with employers, coalitions with neighborhood, religious, small business, and other organizations on issues affecting working people where they lived, electoral involvement, member education, and a social life that included dances, dinners, picnics, athletic teams, parades, choruses, and drum brigades. The member education program was organized by full-time labor educators who helped workers, some of whom did not even have a high school degree, explore past struggles for economic justice, and taught them how the power structure worked and how the union was part of the small "d" democratic story of this country. The result was a counter-culture created by a vibrant industrial union movement in the 1930s. Looking even earlier, we can find the same development in parts of the Populist movement of the late nineteenth century.

Look at the experience of current institution- or faith-based community organizations, particularly at some of the congregations or parishes that are their members, to find a similar sense of community. Danny Collum (1996) captures how congregations are being renewed so that they can again be vital communities for their members. Union locals need to be renewed as well. Some of these organizations are now participants at state- and nationwide decision-making tables on such issues as health care, immigration, education and foreclosure reform. They are there because of what they have done over the past thirty-five years in order to build at the base. But it is not their presence at these decision-making tables that requires attention (indeed, it is arguable that they are prematurely there, but that is a diversion from the main point). Rather, it is what they did at the very base of their organizations to get themselves there that is my focus.

The reweaving of the fabric of community is not limited, however, to religious congregations. A look at some of the chapters of the Association of Community Organizations for Reform Now (ACORN) before its demise in 2010, as well as the organizations that have arisen to take its place, will reveal a sense of people united to pursue purposes larger than themselves. In many other community organizing efforts around the country, you will find this deep and rich sense of community as well.

For reasons too complex to elaborate in this chapter, I believe it is the institution- or faith-based community organizing groups that have most effectively addressed the issue of community. Conversely, it is in part because of the continuous emphasis on issue campaigns that much of community organizing in the United States has failed to build deeply at the base.

Reweaving the fabric of community in this country will require a mix of the social gospel of Protestantism, the social encyclicals of Catholicism, Qur'anic justice, and the social justice tradition of Judaism, as well as an exploration of the people's history of the United States; of Thomas Paine and his agenda for the American Revolution; of the Declaration of Independence and Bill of Rights as documents that were better than their slave-owning authors' behavior; of slavery's recognition in the US Constitution; of the abolitionists, suffragettes, Knights of Labor, Populists, and Wobblies; of the Congress of Industrial Organizations (CIO) and the mix of political and religious ideas that were its underpinning; of Saul Alinsky and the various strands of organizing that grew from his work; and of Ella Baker and the Student Nonviolent Coordinating Committee.

If nothing of substance is built at the base, no single campaign victory, or even combination of several issue victories, will address the fundamental inequities that lie below the surface of whatever issue is at stake in that campaign. That is because these victories will not change the relations of power. They will not create competitive capitalism, turn present corporate capitalism into worker, consumer, community, or combined cooperatives, nor expropriate and make public the dominant institutions of financial and corporate power that are at the center of the inequities of the world.

Purposive Organization

By "organization," I mean structured, coordinated, and disciplined activity that seeks to accomplish a purpose in the world. Any organization that is going to act powerfully in the world will have leadership—whether formal or informal, hidden or open—and this leadership will involve either individual leaders or collections of leaders. In large organizations that want to exercise significant power, there will be various groupings of leaders (delegate bodies, steering, coordinating or executive committees, or boards of directors). They may be structured hierarchically or horizontally, but they are structured nonetheless. In a democratic organization, leaders are accountable to levels below them that are, in turn, ultimately accountable to an engaged membership. "Power," as used in this context, can be used for good or evil; it is neutrally defined as the ability to act effectively in the world.

Without community organization (which could be in a workplace—I am using the word "community" here in the narrower sense that I defined earlier), even the victories that are won cannot be enforced. Incumbent power is wily; it knows when to concede; it backs off; it coopts; it lives with regulations while it whittles them away until the regulated regulate the regulators; it engages in, or supports, repression—as in the toll taken in the CIO by the purge of its left unions or the systematic infiltration of the black movement by the Federal Bureau of Investigation (FBI) and local police "Red squads" (including the Black Panthers, the Student Nonviolent Coordinating Committee, and local community organizations such as Chicago's Organization for a

Better Austen); it waits for opportunities to reassert itself—as corporations did in the early 1970s with organized labor whose leaders had the illusion they had become partners with corporate America. Even the basic right to vote for minorities, low-income people, and others is now under assault by the Republican Party, the Tea Party, and their corporate and foundation allies.

Community organizations acting on these understandings of how power structures work can use the power of organized people to influence, hold accountable, transform, and, when appropriate, disband dominant institutions of society that are organized around different values, structures, policies, and practices. But none of this will happen if we cannot reconstitute the civil society base of democratic organizations.

Cautionary Tales

There is now a muddied understanding of community organizing that needs to be clarified. I want to use two examples to try to do that. The first is the Deep South civil rights movement during the 1960s. The second is National People's Action during the 1970s.

From 1963 to the end of 1966, I was a field secretary on the staff of the Student Nonviolent Coordinating Committee, or "Snick" as it was nicknamed. Snick developed a distinction between mobilizing, which is what we thought Martin Luther King, Jr. and the Southern Christian Leadership Conference (SCLC) did, and organizing. The former was episodic, dramatic, shook the country, and won the passage of important new legislation, but—and this was the critical element—it left nothing lasting on the ground. When Martin Luther King and SCLC left Birmingham or Selma, we thought there was no change in the relations of power between African Americans and the white power structure. That, we believed, was the Achilles' heel of mobilization.

Snick, we said, did organizing. It engaged local people to build their own organizations that would serve as voices for the marginalized, be there when the media left town, and engage in disruptive direct action, such as boycotts of local merchants, voting rights protests, or whatever tactic was required to express democratic people power. We imagined ourselves building permanent units of democratic people power that would be around for the long haul and capable of not only winning campaigns but also enforcing the victories.

We built upon and sought to deepen a real sense of community in local organizations in which African American domestics, day laborers, tenant farmers, sharecroppers, independent farmers, and others of the excluded gained their own voice. Snick made music and theater central to participation. There was not a mass meeting without the songs of the movement or skits that acted out the roles of the brutal sheriff, Uncle Tom, civil rights workers, and courageous local citizens. The cultural richness of the Deep South civil rights movement offers important lessons for building community.

I thought we were on the right track. But, truth be told, none of the organizations Snick built in Mississippi, for example, were deeply rooted enough to withstand the onslaught against them that came from the national Democratic Party and the cooptation of the Child Development Group of Mississippi. While extraordinarily important victories were won in public accommodations, voting rights, early childhood education, and other arenas, the broader economic and social justice agenda (let alone the antimilitarism agenda shared by both Snick and SCLC) was not realized. Snick's efforts at economic cooperatives and union organizing did not get far off the ground; its plan to organize the white poor barely left the piece of paper on which it was conceptualized. Snick's efforts to build and sustain a counter-community failed.

Gale Cincotta is properly celebrated as a heroine of the 1970s. Hers was the single most important voice from the grassroots movement attacking redlining, blockbusting, racial steering, and other policies and practices that locked African Americans in ghettos and destroyed hundreds of white work-ing-class communities across the country. Her base was National People's Ac-tion (NPA). NPA ran some of the most militant and imaginative direct action campaigns we have ever seen in this country. With great tactical imagination, they won many important policy victories and even saw the implementation of some of those victories.

But there is a downside to what NPA did. With local exceptions that can be found here and there, it failed to build deeply at the base. If you went to its member organizations, their membership was limited to a relatively small number of activists—passionate about their cause, but lacking a strong base in the constituency for whom they spoke. The kind of organizing that changes the relations of power was missing. The results of that failure were to be seen in hundreds of community development corporations that lacked the resources to make a significant dent in the country's affordable housing problems and are now to be seen in the foreclosures that are robbing millions of their dream of homeownership.

Snick was destroyed partly by itself, and much of what NPA did was coopted. As I noted earlier, this has been the fate of most of our work of the past fifty years. Pay attention to that and do not get swept up in new movement euphoria that confuses mobilizing with organizing and, as a result, leads us to battle for new victories while our army retreats.

We cannot build the community that is required to create an army that can advance if we do not pay attention to cooptation. The 1960s saw the War on Poverty as the major source of cooptation. Saul Alinsky (1965) characterized its citizen participation component and meager funding as "political pornography." In the 1970s, the Model Cities program and the Law Enforcement Assistance Administration were the sources of cooptation. But then, and now, it is the foundation-nonprofit industry complex that requires our greatest attention because it is closest to us. Among its members are people who share our values and whose analysis of what is wrong with American society is often like our own. We have to engage in a conversation with them about the impact of their present funding strategies because if we do not, we will be crippled from the start in our efforts toward social transformation.

Exceptions to the Rule

I noted earlier that there were a few exceptions to our failure to alter the relations of power and that we should look more closely at them. I would like to note two of them: (1) collective bargaining and (2) the elimination of literacy qualification to register to vote in the South.

Because most unions have a very narrow purpose in collective bargaining, and because the law constrains what they can bargain about, there has developed in more radical circles a certain disdain for collective bargaining. I think about it differently. Before collective bargaining, employers could essentially pay and otherwise do what they wanted with their workers. Except in times of labor scarcity, if you did not like working on the employer's terms, you could find another job. If you complained, and especially if you tried to get others to complain with you, you were fired.

With collective bargaining, and its institutionalization in the National Labor Relations Act, workers could democratically decide to be represented by an organization paid for with their dues in which they elected the leaders. That organization could bargain with the employer on wages, hours, benefits, and working conditions. That was, in itself, a qualitative change in the relations of power. Under the rubric of "working conditions," workers were able to stop work if they thought a situation was dangerous or unhealthy. Elected stewards, sometimes given released work-time to perform their union responsibilities, enforced the collectively bargained contract at the work site. Union-run hiring halls sent workers to jobs, substituting fair rotational dispatch for the system of favoritism and kickbacks that preceded them. Seniority protected workers from arbitrary or capricious assignment or firings. "Lead men," who were part of the union bargaining unit rather than in management, did work once reserved for supervisory personnel and, in some cases, they were elected.

Lou Goldblatt, former secretary-treasurer of the International Longshore and Warehouse Union, once told me, "We are in a continuous struggle with the employer over prerogatives." To put it another way, the union was altering the relations of power. In one brief visionary moment, the United Automobile Workers union said it would not agree to wage increases if they were at the cost of increased prices for automobiles. The fact that labor now is primarily interested in a fairly narrow agenda, one typically limited to its own members and its sector of the economy, should not make us lose sight of how important its gains were, and are, for the lives of everyday people.

Today, radicals often view collective bargaining as a means of cooptation. I think that confuses the process with the proposals that unions are willing to put on the table and meaningfully struggle for. When militants replace moderates in the leadership of today's unions, they might get more money or benefits for workers, or they might take up and win more grievances. But the agenda they pursue and the means for its pursuit are, for the most part, militant versions of what they replace. They typically do not alter the insurance company culture of the organization, which remains one in which members pay their premiums (dues) and expect the benefits. Nor do unions engage in issues having to do with the quality, effectiveness, appropriateness, or efficiency of the products or services that are the outcome of their members' work. Nor do they enter into ongoing alliances with community groups. As long as unions retain that organizational culture, they will be limited in what they can contribute.

The other exception I would like to note came out of the voter registration work of the Deep South civil rights movement and is more cultural than structural. Snick was its prime instigator, though it was soon adopted across the entire movement. In the early days of trying to get African Americans the right to vote, the civil rights movement's main thrust was to overcome discriminatory application of voter registration literacy tests. At first, Snick and others offered workshops to people so they could learn to take and pass the test. The objective was to obtain equal application of the law and not to challenge the law itself.

But the very notion of voting qualifications soon became the subject of debate. Snick challenged the notion when it rejected literacy as a voting requirement. In so doing, Snick put meat on the skeletal American idea of equality. No longer was Snick willing to paraphrase Anatole France (1910) and say, "The written voter registration test, in its majesty equality, forbids the illiterate from voting." Snick's view was that the segregated South could not deny blacks adequate education and then use their illiteracy to exclude them from voting. And it argued that formally illiterate African Americans had an experiential wisdom about politics that fully qualified them to vote.

From Snick's conclusion came a wide discussion of class as well as race. Many African Americans who were active in the movement had to think twice before they agreed with this conclusion. Without that discussion, it is unlikely that a sharecropper by the name of Fanny Lou Hamer would have had the courage to challenge the Democratic Party at the 1964 Democratic Convention. Nor would her stirring words, "I'm sick and tired of being sick and tired," be part of our civil rights history (Hamer 1964). Nor would President Lyndon Johnson have given a graduation speech at Howard University that called for an expansive view of equality and not simply equality of opportunity.

There are lesser examples of victories that altered relations of power as well. Tenant unions borrowed from labor and negotiated landlord-tenant agreements. Community organizations negotiated agreements with employers requiring the employer to take qualifiable unemployed persons referred by the organization and train and pay them "on the job" in entry-level positions. Parent organizations demanded and won a say in who would be the principal of their children's school. But these are exceptions that tend to prove the rule. Further, none of them relied on dues, fees, or member activities for their budgets, and thus none of them was independent.

The Foundation-Nonprofit Industry Complex

A hallmark of authentic civil society is the independence of the organizations comprising it. They are either small and totally voluntary or large—whether local, regional, or national—and their leaders and staff are paid with the dues, fees, and activities of their members—for example, conservative building trades unions, are funded by their members' dues. These organizations are often what in normal discourse would be considered nonpartisan. Sometimes, they are relatively moderate in their view of the world. It is upon them that we must build because they are the authentic voices of the constituency whose present powerlessness allows the plutocracy to continue on its rampage. Speaking of the black church, I heard Rev. Amos Brown, pastor of San Francisco's oldest African American congregation, say, "the black church is the only institution we own lock, stock, and barrel."

The engagement of congregations, unions, and neighborhood, small business, merchant, and other existing voluntary associations is one of the prerequisites to reach the scale required for transformative power—that is, the ability to alter the relations of power. Renewal of these organizations to address the internal problems they face and reconnect them with their deepest core values is essential to the task of transformation. Transformative social action can emerge organically from these organizations if we engage respectfully with them on their own terms.

At the same time, we have to create from scratch new organizations at the base that can become the authentic voices of the marginalized and excluded. Building at the base in new organizations is equally of merit if we require that these organizations be paid for with the dues, fees, and activities of their members. That is what Cesar Chavez did at the beginning of his work with farm workers before there was a United Farm Workers of America. When he spoke with farm workers, he told them there had to be substantial dues. The dues then charged were equivalent to roughly $25.00 a month in today's dollars (Miller, unpublished data). In addition to insisting upon dues, Chavez built initially around mutual aid activities and not through confrontations with institutional power. These mutual aid activities included a credit union, a burial society, and a buying club for automobile batteries and tires. He also used individual services, often done as group actions, to help people with corrupt merchants, biased bureaucratic government agencies, and other obstacles to a decent life. Chavez was initially interested in solidly building at the base, and used the network of farm worker "shoestring communities"— low-income, underserved, and often unincorporated neighborhoods—to do so. He met individually in "one-to-ones" with farm workers and their families and used face-to-face house meetings as the building blocks for the National Farm Worker Association (NFWA). (Unfortunately, a discussion of what went wrong must be saved for another occasion.)

The secret of scale, that is reaching the level of membership and participation that is a prerequisite to altering the relations of power and democratizing the society, is to go deeply and broadly into every nook and cranny of the country through either existing or newly created authentic voluntary associations that, in combination, include all the constituencies that together are required for a new majority American politics. Here is what Peter Murray wrote in a June 2012 Internet exchange on *Game Changer*:

> The key here is understanding the absolute necessity of building Popular Social Movements in order to win, and the unfortunate inability of the

non-profit sector to produce them. These have been the missing piece for 30 years and without them, we lose. All the recent gains, from Occupy Wall Street's dramatic shifting the public narrative on the economy, to Obama's "Dream Act" Executive Order, have been won by popular organizing initiated outside the Left's existing professional structures. This is crucial to recognize. It's also just as important to recognize that professionals played an important support role in both of these, which is actually the point. When professionals devote resources and skills to supporting popular movements—*on their own organic terms*—we actually achieve wins. What I am suggesting is that the more we support popular movement-building, then the more wins we will score, then the more influence we will have. (Murray 2012, emphasis added)

(Parenthetically, Murray and many others are looking to the Internet as a tool for building—a direction I do not think they will find fruitful unless their measure of participation is clicking links on Web sites or showing up for an occasional demonstration. And some of the organizations they champion are, for example, direct mail organizations where there is little meaningful engagement of members.)

The failure to be connected with strength at the base is connected with how most of the work we do is funded. In a 2012 article, "Capitalism: A Ghost Story," Indian novelist, essayist, peace prize winner, and nonviolent activist Arundhati Roy wrote:

In the NGO [non-governmental organization] universe, which has evolved a strange anodyne language of its own, everything has become a "subject", a separate, professionalized, special-interest issue. Community development, leadership development, human rights, health, education, reproductive rights, AIDS, orphans with AIDS [as well as housing, employment, environment, and many other categories]—have all been hermetically sealed into their own silos with their own elaborate and precise funding brief. Funding has fragmented solidarity in ways that repression never could.

Roy (2012) continues by writing:

Having worked out how to manage governments, political parties, elections, courts, the media and liberal opinion, there was one more challenge for the neo-liberal establishment: how to deal with growing unrest, the threat of "people's power." How do you domesticate it? How do you turn protesters into pets? How do you vacuum up people's fury and redirect it into blind alleys?

Let me repeat a key point that Roy makes: "Funding has fragmented solidarity [i.e., the extension of community to larger arenas] in ways that repression never could." This fragmentation is a major source for why we win battles but continue to lose the war. If you fragment solidarity and put people in separate silos, broadly based people power cannot be built.

Connecting the Dots

Now, let me connect some dots: I do not believe we can begin to win the war and create a meaningful version of democracy if we simply focus on winning campaigns. Nor can we win this battle if we think that by adding campaigns together into some kind of mother-of-campaigns organization, we will accomplish what is required at the base. If you look at much of today's multi-issue organizing, or if you look at most contemporary labor unions, you will find campaign mobilization organizations that either lack, or are disconnected from, the kind of community that comes from sustained face-to-face relationships at the base of an organization.

Whatever we are doing in the way of waging defensive or even offensive battles, we need to be attending to what will build a community at its base. We also need to be searching for the kind of independent or autonomous, relatively permanent, and self-funded organization that we want to serve as the vehicle through which that community will express itself.

Will we be able to do this before climatic disaster drastically alters the very nature of the earth, before plutocracy so institutionalizes itself that it becomes relatively immune to popular pressure, or before the military-industrial complex leads us on the Roman Empire's road to ruin? If we do not deal with the matters that I have raised in this chapter, it is in those directions that I fear and believe we will continue.

References

Alinsky, Saul D. 1965. "The War on Poverty-Political Pornography." *Journal of Social Issues* 21 (1): 41–47.

Collum, Danny Duncan. 1996. "Reweaving the Fabric: The Democratic Hope of Church-Based Community Organizations." *The Other Side* 32 (5): 12–18.

Einstein Online. 2012. "Albert Einstein Quotes—Humanity." The Albert Einstein Website Online. http://www.alberteinsteinsite.com/quotes/#humanity.

France, Anatole. 1910. *The Red Lily*. Edited by Frederic Chapman and translated by Winifred Stephens. New York: John Lane Company.

Hamer, Fanny Lou. 1964. Testimony before the Credentials Committee, Democratic National Convention, Atlantic City, New Jersey, August 22.

Larkin, Mark. 2012. "Michelle Alexander on the Irrational Race Bias of the Criminal Justice and Prison Systems." *Truthout*, August 1.

Long, Huey. 1934. "Share Our Wealth." National radio address, February 23.

Miller, Mike. 1983. "Base Christian Communities: Notes on and Commentary about a Talk by Richard Shaull." Unpublished, available from ORGANIZE Training Center, San Francisco, California.

Murray, Peter. 2012. "RE: [GameChangerSalon] Pay Scales for Progressive Activists (Branching Off from the Teacher Thread)." *Game Changer*, June 26.

Ormaechea, Jose Maria. 1991. *The Mondragon Cooperative Experience*. Arrasate, Spain: Mondragon Corporation.

Roy, Arundhati. 2012. "Capitalism: A Ghost Story." *Outlookinda.com*, March 26.

14

Building a Movement for Fair Lending, Foreclosure Relief, and Financial Reform

Peter Dreier

LIBERALS AND PROGRESSIVES were ecstatic when Massachusetts voters elected Elizabeth Warren to the US Senate in November 2012. The banking industry and right-wing super PACs had spent a huge war chest to defeat Warren, who had been the industry's most outspoken critic as a Harvard law professor and Congress's official monitor of the federal bank bailout program. She had been the leading champion of the Consumer Financial Protection Bureau (CFPB) that was part of the Dodd-Frank Wall Street Reform and Consumer Protection Act passed in 2010 (but too controversial for President Barack Obama to appoint her to run it). She had been a relentless advocate for even stronger regulations on the financial services industry long before its reckless practices had crashed the economy in 2008. Advocates of bank reform rejoiced again when, a few weeks after the election, Senate Majority Leader Harry Reid appointed Warren to the Senate Banking Committee.

Warren's victory showed that the banking industry was not invincible. But the bank lobby and its allies still had enormous power, not only in terms of its campaign contributions to congressmembers in both parties but also in its sway over President Obama's inner circle of economic advisors (Suskind 2011).

Bank reform activists hoped that Warren would use her position as a bully pulpit to challenge Wall Street, help enact stronger laws to hold the industry accountable, and force it to address the problems of widespread foreclosures, predatory mortgages, and speculative practices. She was willing to play that role, but she also knew that enacting tough laws to challenge Wall Street required more than her voice and those of perhaps another dozen

Senate progressives. It required a powerful grassroots movement that could help push moderate Democrats in the Senate to support bank reform and even put pressure on moderate Republicans in the House (which had a 234-201 majority) as well as moderate Democrats in the same chamber. In January 2013, as Warren was sworn in and Obama took the oath for a second term, it was not clear whether the movement for financial reform had the resources or influence to translate widespread public opinion for bank reform into legislation that would make the banking industry more responsible and accountable.

This concluding chapter examines the potential for building a grassroots movement to push for banking reform. It also explores the role that scholars and researchers can play as part of a movement to achieve significant policy reform to make America's financial institutions more accountable so they serve the credit needs of the entire society rather than a relatively small slice.

The Problem

America's banking system is broken, and there is currently a struggle over how to fix it. Public opinion polls reveal widespread concern about the political influence of the banking industry on excessive executive compensation and bonuses, the impact of banking practices on consumers, and the government bailout of major financial institutions. But public opinion has not translated into strong public policy reform. The Dodd-Frank legislation was an important first step. The financial industry—and its allies in other corporate sectors—opposed it but could not thwart its passage. At the same time, the bank lobby used its substantial political clout to water down many of its strongest components, including the regulation of derivatives (Kopecki, Leising, and Harrington 2009).

During the 2012 election cycle, several progressive groups identified what questions need to be asked to put the housing crisis on the public agenda and make it an election issue (Griffith, Gordon, and Sanchez 2012). But, in fact, the outrageous practices of the banking industry that led to the recession, and proposals for reform, were barely discussed by the presidential candidates during the 2012 campaign. Warren was one of the few candidates for Congress who put the issue front and center.

Wall Street's reckless behavior crashed the economy. Between 2006 and 2012, housing prices nationwide fell by a third. Families lost nearly $7 trillion of home equity (Bocian, Smith, and Li 2012; Federal Reserve Board 2012). About five million homeowners lost their homes. Another 3.5 million homeowners were in the foreclosure process or were so behind in their mortgage payments that they would soon be confronted with losing their homes. About fifteen million homeowners owed $700 billion more on their mortgages than their homes were worth (Schwartz and Dewan 2012). Millions of middle-class families watched their major source of wealth stripped away, their neighborhoods decimated, and their future economic security destroyed. The drop in housing values affected not only families facing foreclosure but also families in the surrounding community because having a few foreclosed homes in a neighborhood brings down the value of other houses in the area. The neighborhood blight created by the housing crisis was much worse in African American and Hispanic areas. African Americans and Hispanics have been almost twice as likely as whites to lose their homes to foreclosures, in large part because they have been victims of well-documented racial discrimination by lenders (Bocian and Quercia 2011).

The financial crisis began with "deregulation" during the Carter years, accelerated during the Reagan-Bush years, and continued during the Clinton and George W. Bush eras. The ticking time bomb was then set to go off toward the end of the second Bush administration. Although the crisis began with the bursting of the housing bubble, it soon got much bigger. The Obama administration inherited a financial system on the brink of collapse, one that threatened the entire economy.

The deregulation of the financial services industry that began in the 1970s, and the recession of the past decade that caused many banks to fail, led to a dramatic concentration of ownership. In 1970, the five largest banks combined had 17 percent of the industry's assets. By 2010, among the nation's almost seven thousand banks, the five largest banks controlled 52 percent of industry assets (Rosenblum 2011). Between 2008 and 2011, four hundred financial institutions collapsed, including Lehman Brothers, one of the largest Wall Street banks. The five biggest banks—JPMorgan Chase & Co., Bank of America Corporation, Citigroup Inc., Wells Fargo & Company, and Goldman Sachs Group, Inc.—held $8.5 trillion in assets at the end of 2011, equal to 56 percent of the US economy (Lynch 2012).

The financial services industry has two sources of political influence. The first is its significant campaign contributions and lobbying efforts, which are coordinated by several trade associations, including the American Bankers Association. Wall Street has been a huge contributor to political campaigns among candidates of both parties. But it is not simply the high-profile Wall Street banks, as well as private equity firms and insurance companies, that wield political clout. There are also small-, medium-, and large-sized banks in every community and the industry has a huge network of local influentials, closely tied to other businesses, that can be mobilized around legislative battles.

The second source is the widely held view that the financial services industry, and its loans, mortgages, and investments, is the lifeblood of the economy, making it possible for businesses to grow and create jobs. Since the 1970s, and accelerating in every decade that has followed, the banking industry has used its political clout to persuade Congress to deregulate the sector, removing the "firewall" between investment banks, commercial banks, and insurance companies. It has also persuaded federal regulators and many politicians not only to allow increasing concentration, but also that many banks were "too big to fail." This guaranteed that most government officials, including Republicans and Democrats, will do whatever is necessary—including providing large-scale bailouts and minimal regulations—to keep them solvent for fear that the entire economic system would collapse if major banks went bankrupt.

The Obama administration's initial response to the bursting of the housing bubble was twofold. The first was to push for stronger regulations on the financial industry, which ultimately led to the Dodd-Frank legislation. The new legislation focused primarily on protecting consumers from abusive practices, but it did little to challenge the concentration of ownership or key aspects of the industry's business practices. The legislation was much weaker than what most advocacy groups had hoped for, especially when it came to regulating derivatives, but its stronger consumer protections were welcome even if advocates were concerned about how strongly they would be enforced.

The second response was to argue that strengthening the overall economy, reducing unemployment, and getting the financial sector back on its feet would address the problem of declining housing prices, the "overhang" of housing supply, and the epidemic of foreclosures. Obama's key economic advisors, particularly Larry Summers and Tim Geithner, did not believe that directly addressing the foreclosure problem by providing financial relief to distressed homeowners was necessary or politically feasible.[1] The *New York Times* reported that while Summers and Geithner believed that directly addressing the financial distress of "underwater" homeowners and those facing foreclosure was bad economic policy, "the decision ultimately was political. Mr. Obama and his advisers were convinced that even in the depths of an unyielding crisis, most Americans did not want their neighbors rescued at public expense. Several cited the response to the Arizona speech—including the televised

---

1. This view is confirmed by both Suskind (2011) and Barofsky (2012).

diatribe by a CNBC personality, Rick Santelli, that helped give rise to the Tea Party—as proof that they were wise not to do more" (Appelbaum 2012).

By early 2012, the Obama administration became increasingly aware that their macroeconomic policies and the bailout of large financial institutions were not improving things on the ground among troubled homeowners. It revised some of its policies to promote more direct help for homeowners, but it required cooperation by banks, and the banks were not enthusiastic participants. The administration also realized that troubled homeowners constituted a significant number of potential voters in key swing states, including Florida and Nevada.

Meanwhile, activist groups began accelerating their protests, demanding more direct intervention at all levels of government. These protests began before the emergence of Occupy Wall Street (OWS) in September 2011, but OWS clearly changed the national mood and strengthened the potential of the community activists and unions pushing for policies to help families facing foreclosure.

In 2010, as the foreclosure epidemic continued, several veteran organizers, including George Goehl, executive director of National People's Action (NPA), and Stephen Lerner, a Service Employees International Union (SEIU) organizer, brought unions, community organizations, and faith groups together to pressure banks and the Obama administration to do more for families losing their homes. As the New Bottom Line coalition, they mounted protests at bank headquarters around the country, generating media attention and helping Attorneys General Eric Schneiderman of New York and Kamala Harris of California push for a stronger national settlement with banks over foreclosure relief.

The emergence of OWS strengthened the coalition's hand, and so the New Bottom Line sought to sustain the momentum. Early in 2012, a coalition of unions, community organizations, faith groups, and some OWS members—now dubbed 99% Power—planned a series of protests focusing on specific targets (banks, corporations, and government entities at all levels) with explicit demands for foreclosure relief, fair taxes, student debt relief, and campaign finance reform. The coalition trained about one hundred thousand recruits in civil disobedience and organized protests at the headquarters and stockholder meetings of Cigna, General Electric, Bank of America, and other corporations. In May 2012, NPA led more than one thousand people in a protest at Geithner's suburban home to demand that he and the Obama administration support a financial speculation tax on banks and require banks to help families with underwater mortgages to refinance their loans.

Under the umbrella of the New Bottom Line coalition, as well as in-dividually, these groups focused on getting local and state governments to enact legislation to protect homeowners, better regulate lenders, and clean up neighborhoods hurt by foreclosures. At the federal level, the New Bottom Line coalition, along with Americans for Financial Reform (a coalition of unions, consumer, and community groups), called for the government to require lenders to renegotiate mortgages for "underwater" homeowners to reflect the new market values of their homes; this was called "principal reduc-tion." If mortgages were reset, this would not only fix the foreclosure crisis but also pump $71 billion into the economy annually and create over one million jobs a year.[2] In several cities with high concentrations of underwater mortgages, grassroots groups worked with local officials to design a plan to take these mortgages by eminent domain and resell them to homeowners at current market values with reduced principal (Shiller 2012; Hockett 2013; Kuttner 2013; Said 2013).

Politics = Ideology + Policy

One of the lessons of the current struggle for financial and fair lending reform is the recognition that winning elections is not enough. Or, put differently, that the influence required for electing a president and a Democratic majority is not sufficient to pass progressive legislation.

A solution to the housing crisis requires building a broad political coa-lition that recognizes the specific hardships facing particular groups while also addressing the wider economic turmoil confronting working- and middle-class families. It requires a grassroots movement that can sustain itself through vic-tories and defeats, and keep people "in motion" at the local, state, and federal levels simultaneously.

Most important is the understanding that the nation's economic crisis is primarily due to inequities of political power—the enormous influence of big business in general and the financial and real estate sectors in particular.

---

2. In a *New York Times* op-ed column, two well-known economists, Stiglitz and Zandi (2012), frustrated that Obama would not carry out the principal reduction policy, argued for direct government subsidies for troubled homeowners. In July 2012, the Obama administration began to support this idea, but said that it was unable to do so because Edward J. DeMarco, the head of the agency that oversees Fannie Mae and Freddie Mac, was against it, arguing that it would encourage homeowners who are paying their mortgage to stop doing so in order to qualify for a principal write-down—an idea often called "moral hazard." Activist groups called on Obama to fire DeMarco; in May 2013, he finally did (Lowrey 2013a, 2013b).

By "political," I do not simply mean an ability to push for favorable legislation and regulations, but also an ability to shape the battle of ideas—the ideological battleground—that influences public opinion and how economic issues are framed, including the appropriate role of government in addressing economic concerns.

In 2008, testifying before the House Committee on Oversight and Government Reform, Alan Greenspan, former chair of the Federal Reserve, admitted: "Those of us who have looked to the self-interest of lending institutions to protect shareholders' equity, myself included, are in a state of shocked disbelief.... This modern [free market] paradigm held sway for decades. The whole intellectual edifice, however, collapsed in the summer of last year" (Andrews 2008).

The Wall Street crash was the culmination of several decades of successful political and ideological battles by business and conservative groups to reshape the public debate. The ascendancy of the radical Right's unquestioning faith in unfettered free markets had a long incubation period. In *Before the Storm*, Perlstein (2001) reveals the roots of the coming conservative movement following the defeat of Barry Goldwater in 1964. Big business and conservatives launched a forty-year project to construct a sophisticated conservative movement and create a new American conservative consensus.

In August 1971, Lewis Powell, a prominent attorney and member of the boards of eleven corporations (who later that year would be appointed to the Supreme Court by Richard Nixon), wrote an influential memo to the US Chamber of Commerce, "Attack on the American Free Enterprise System," calling on the business community to go on the attack against activists. He warned of a growing threat to the business establishment posed by consumer advocates, environmentalists, labor unions, and other voices, and of the declining public support for business, as reflected in opinion surveys. The changing mood, he warned, could ultimately threaten business's ability to operate freely and to generate adequate profits to survive. *Business Week* echoed this view in its October 12, 1974 issue: "It will be a hard pill for many Americans to swallow—the idea of doing with less so that big business can have more. Nothing that this nation, or any other nation, has done in modern economic history compares with the selling job that must be done to make people accept this reality" ("The Debt Economy" 1974).

The Chamber of Commerce and business leaders took this advice to heart and began a "selling job" that changed American politics. They began funding a powerful network of organizations designed to shift public attitudes and beliefs over the course of years and decades. In 1972, the CEOs of General Electric and Alcoa founded the Business Roundtable, a lobby group made up of the heads of the nation's two hundred largest corporations. Inspired by the Powell Memo, Joseph Coors, the conservative head of the Coors Brewing Company, wrote a large check to establish a think tank called the Heritage Foundation to enlist academics and journalists to come up with conservative policy proposals. The memo inspired the creation of other conservative policy and lobby groups such as the American Enterprise Institute, the Manhattan Institute for Policy Research, the Cato Institute, Citizens for a Sound Economy, Accuracy in Academia, and other opinion-shaping institutions. The California Chamber of Commerce launched a conservative nonprofit law firm, the Pacific Legal Foundation, the first of about a dozen conservative litigation groups.

In 1973, a conservative political operative, Paul Weyrich, started the American Legislative Exchange Council (ALEC) to provide a forum for state legislatures to share ideas for laws against abortion and in favor of school prayer. Within a few years, however, big corporations—including Coors, Amway, IBM, Ford, Philip Morris, Exxon, Texaco, and Shell Oil—began donating funds to ALEC, and the group shifted its focus toward promoting state legislation to limit government regulation of business. William Simon, former treasury secretary under Nixon, became head of the John M. Olin Foundation and began providing universities with donations to hire conservative faculty members and to fund conservative student organizations. Other corporate-funded foundations, such as the Scaife, Koch, Smith Richardson, and Bradley Foundations, soon followed Olin's example.

These long-term investments began paying off in the 1980s, laying the groundwork for the election of Ronald Reagan in 1980, who had a "hands-off business" philosophy. "Government is not a solution to our problem," Reagan (1981) said. "Government is the problem." Too many government regulations, too much taxation, and too many government employees stifled personal freedom and economic growth. The attack on "big government" and the notion of "getting the government off our backs," once viewed as extreme conservative ideas, moved from the margins to the mainstream.

During his first campaign for president in 1992, Arkansas Governor Bill Clinton (1991) correctly observed that "the Reagan-Bush years have exalted private gain over public obligation, special interests over the common good, wealth and fame over work and family. The 1980s ushered in a Gilded Age of greed and selfishness, of irresponsibility and excess, and of neglect." Clinton initially had bold plans to expand the New Deal and Great Society legacies. These hopes were quickly dashed. After the November 1994 elections put a Republican majority in Congress, any significant progress on such matters was impossible. After a few years as president, Clinton proclaimed, echoing

Reagan, that "the era of big government is over," which he carried out by slashing welfare benefits for poor children.

The business-sponsored attack on government reached a crescendo during the eight-year administration of George W. Bush, who took office in 2001. The Bush administration looked the other way while banks and government regulators triggered a meltdown of the nation's housing market and financial system, leading to a deep and prolonged recession that persisted after his successor took office in 2009.

During the George W. Bush years, a combination of forces that had begun decades earlier triggered the worst economic crisis since the Great Depression. One force was the gluttony of merger mania and outrageous corporate compensation. Second was business's persistent assault on labor unions, which caused the weakening of America's most effective bastion against economic inequality. Third was a dramatic cut in federal taxes for the wealthy and corporate America (resulting in the lowest tax burden on the rich in American history). Fourth was the political influence of big business, which persuaded Congress to weaken regulations designed to prevent banks from taking on too much risk or engaging in predatory practices. Finally, the conservative movement—led by corporate-backed think tanks, right-wing media such as Fox News, the Republican Party, and the Tea Party—effectively led an all-out attack on government initiatives to address inequality and economic insecurity and to protect consumers, workers, and the environment from abusive businesses.

No corporate sector acted as recklessly and irresponsibly as the financial industry. The newly deregulated banking sector had the freedom to charge usurious interest rates on mortgages and credit cards, to bundle and sell collateralized debt obligations and mortgage-backed securities, to take on astonishing amounts of toxic debt, and to make astounding profits while squeezing consumers. The majority of American families, suffering from decades of declining wages, had to borrow more and more money to pay for their mortgages, college tuition, and other basics. Banks invented new loan products with hidden costs and fees, low or no down payments, and low initial interest rates. They often rejected applications for conventional loans from families that had sufficient income and good credit, pushing them into taking out riskier loans.

Black and Hispanic consumers were much more likely to be victims of such predatory practices than white consumers, including those with comparable incomes and credit worthiness. These risky "subprime" loans made up 8.6 percent of all mortgages in 2001 but had soared to 20.1 percent by 2006. After 2004, more than 90 percent of subprime mortgages came with adjustable rates that had initially low interest rates that exploded after several years. As these interest rates rose, the adjustable rate loans got more expensive and families could not make their mortgage payments. Soon, large financial institutions were holding portfolios of loans that were worthless (Harvard Joint Center for Housing Studies 2007).

Every part of the financial industry—mortgage companies like Countrywide Savings, commercial banks like Wells Fargo and Bank of America, Wall Street investment banks like Morgan Stanley and Goldman Sachs, and ratings agencies like Moody's and Standard & Poor's—played a part in the fiasco. A few of the executives and officers of some of these companies cashed out before the market crashed, most notably Angelo Mozilo, the CEO of Countrywide Financial, the largest subprime lender. Mozilo had made more than $270 million in profits selling stocks and options from 2004 to the beginning of 2007 (Creswell and Bajaj 2007).

But borrowers were not so lucky. When the dust settled, millions of Americans were no longer able to make their monthly mortgage payments. Banks initiated a massive wave of foreclosures that touched low-income urban areas and middle-class suburban neighborhoods alike.

There was a time, not too long ago, when Washington did regulate banks. The Depression triggered the creation of government bank regulations and agencies, such as the Federal Deposit Insurance Corporation (FDIC), the Federal Home Loan Bank System, Homeowners Loan Corporation, Fannie Mae, and the Federal Housing Administration (FHA), to protect consumers and expand homeownership. After World War II and until the late 1970s, the system worked. The savings-and-loan industry was highly regulated by the federal government with a mission to take people's deposits and then provide loans for the sole purpose of helping people buy homes to live in. Washington insured those loans through the FDIC, provided mortgage discounts through FHA and the Veterans Administration, created a secondary mortgage market to guarantee a steady flow of capital, and required saving and loan institutions (S&Ls) to make predictable thirty-year fixed loans. The result was a steady increase in homeownership and few foreclosures.

In the 1970s, when community groups discovered that lenders and the FHA were engaged in systematic racial discrimination against minority consumers and neighborhoods—a practice called redlining—they mobilized and got Congress, led by Wisconsin Senator William Proxmire, to enact the Community Reinvestment Act and the Home Mortgage Disclosure Act, which together have significantly reduced racial disparities in lending.

But by the early 1980s, the lending industry began using its political clout to push back against government regulation. In 1980, Congress adopted the

Depository Institutions Deregulation and Monetary Control Act, which eliminated interest-rate caps and made subprime lending more feasible for lenders. The S&Ls balked at constraints on their ability to compete with conventional banks engaged in commercial lending. They got Congress—Democrats and Republicans alike—to change the rules, allowing S&Ls to begin a decade-long orgy of real estate speculation, mismanagement, and fraud.

The deregulation of banking led to merger mania, with banks and S&Ls gobbling each other up and making loans to finance shopping malls, golf courses, office buildings, and condo projects that had no financial logic other than a quick-buck profit. When the dust settled in the late 1980s, hundreds of S&Ls and banks had gone under, billions of dollars of commercial loans were useless, and the federal government was left to bail out the depositors whose money the speculators had put at risk.

The stable neighborhood S&L soon became a thing of the past. Banks, insurance companies, credit card firms, and other moneylenders were now part of a giant financial services industry, while Washington walked away from its responsibility to protect consumers with rules, regulations, and enforcement. Meanwhile, starting with Reagan, the federal government slashed funding for low-income housing and allowed a decline in the role of the FHA, once a key player in helping working-class families purchase a home.

Into this vacuum stepped banks, mortgage lenders, and scam artists looking for ways to make big profits from consumers desperate for the American Dream of homeownership. They invented new loan products that put borrowers at risk. Thus was born the subprime loan market.

Edward Gramlich (2002), a Federal Reserve Board member, repeatedly warned about subprime mortgages and predatory lending, which he said "jeopardize the twin American dreams of owning a home and building wealth." He tried to get chairman Greenspan to crack down on irrational subprime lending by increasing oversight, but his warnings fell on deaf ears, including those in Congress.

As Rep. Barney Frank (2007) wrote in *The Boston Globe*, the surge of subprime lending was a sort of "natural experiment," testing the theories of those who favor radical deregulation of financial markets. And the lessons, Frank (2007) said, are clear: "To the extent that the system did work, it is because of prudential regulation and oversight. Where it was absent, the result was tragedy."

Those who profited handsomely from the subprime market and predatory lending—the commercial banks, investment banks, rating agencies, private mortgage bankers, and mortgage brokers—used their political clout to protect their profits by lobbying in state capitals and in Washington, DC, to keep government off their backs. The banking industry, of course, repeatedly warned that any restrictions on their behavior would make things worse and close needy people out of the home-buying market. Their lobbyists have long insisted that the banking industry could voluntarily police itself. Government regulation was not necessary.

The Key Components of Successful Movements

What is needed to counter the political influence of business and financial industry is a large grassroots movement of consumers who can combine "outside" protest and "inside" politics.

Building and strengthening a progressive movement requires an investment of money in human capital—in people and organizations that have the capacity to win victories that make a difference in changing public policy and improving people's lives. Progressive social change does not just happen because "the time is ripe." It happens because people and organizations ripen the time. They make strategic choices—about mobilizing people, training leaders, picking issues, identifying political opportunities, conducting research, recruiting allies, utilizing the media, and negotiating with opponents—that help win victories that become stepping stones to further and broader reforms.

The theory behind progressive social change is based on an understanding that it is possible to win over a majority of Americans to progressive ideas even if they do not call themselves "progressives." Public opinion polls, for example, suggest that a significant majority of Americans support activist government even if they identify themselves as moderates (Halpin and Teixeira 2009). They may call themselves "moderates" or be labeled as "swing voters" by pollsters and political operatives, but whatever they are called, they need to be organized into organizations and not simply "marketed" to by public relations specialists at election time as though they were "consumers." Most moderates, including a growing number of immigrants and people of color, live outside central cities in older and newer suburbs and in formerly rural areas that have been gobbled up by suburban sprawl.

A progressive movement that wants to leverage significant social change has to address at least six components.

1. A Federated Movement: A bold movement for social justice has to change federal policy. The problems facing neighborhoods, cities, and metropolitan regions cannot be entirely solved in their own backyards. Cities, counties, and even states lack the resources and authority to significantly address the problems of job creation, pollution and climate change, health care, housing, immigration, and other issues. That does not mean that local, county, and even state governments cannot make a dent in addressing those issues, but they are more likely to be Band-Aids, "pilot projects," and "demonstration programs" rather than significant solutions (Dreier 2009).

However, winning policy change at the federal level does not mean pouring all resources into Washington, DC, lobbying. Too many advocacy groups focus on "inside the Beltway" lobbying without having a grassroots base that provides them with the political leverage they need to influence elected officials. At the same time, America has many locally based advocacy and community organizations that focus almost exclusively on local matters without building bridges with other local groups that, together, could influence state and federal policy. Local groups that are not part of national networks can easily become politically parochial or unable to build on victories because larger victories require policy change at higher levels of government. Local leaders can be trained to expand their political horizons to recognize the necessity of ratcheting up issue campaigns beyond neighborhoods and cities.

A successful progressive movement needs to be both local and national at the same time—what Skocpol (2004) calls a "federated" approach. It needs national organizations with state and local bases. It needs to have a grassroots base that can be mobilized for action, but it also needs to have a national component that can coordinate local actions around a common agenda, strategy, and message because most significant problems cannot be solved at the local, regional, or even state levels. Some federated organizations do exist today, but, in broad strokes, we do not yet have a "federated" progressive movement with the capacity to be effective, flexible, and agile in forging coalitions, prioritizing issues, and winning victories on different issue areas that build on rather than compete with each other for the attention of the public and elected officials. In fact, the competition among progressive issue groups is self-defeating. Progressive organizations at the national, state, and local levels need to find ways to forge a common policy agenda as well as timing over issue priorities. Progressive elected officials often find that, once in office, the progressive groups that helped them win the election each want their separate issues and policies to move to the top of the agenda. Progressives have not yet created the kind of agenda-setting table at which these priorities, and allocation of resources, get discussed over a one-, two-, and four-year cycle. This is the role that Grover Norquist, head of Americans for Tax Reform, has played, quarterbacking strategy among the different wings of the conservative movement, particularly the business groups and the social and religious right wing (Cassidy 2005).

2. A Majoritarian Constituency: Similarly, a successful progressive movement must have a "majoritarian" approach—that is, it must build sufficient support to win a majority of votes in Congress. That means it must be diverse geographically and broad demographically. It must build constituency power outside the core urban areas that constitute the "safe" Democratic seats in Congress where most of the key progressive members are from.

It must also seek to address the concerns of at least the bottom 60 percent or 75 percent of the population rather than focus exclusively on narrow niche constituencies that, on their own, lack the numbers or political influence to win significant change. That does not mean that a progressive movement cannot tackle problems facing the poor (the bottom 15 to 20 percent of the population), welfare recipients, African Americans, Latinos, residents of central cities (about 33 percent the population), or people who lack health insurance (about 15 percent of the population). But unless these concerns can be linked to concerns of a broader constituency, they are unlikely to mobilize sufficient support to win significant reform. As much as possible, a successful movement must avoid issues that can seriously divide its constituency.

3. An Inside/Outside Strategy: A successful progressive movement needs to have both an "outside" and an "inside" strategy. Movements need to change the political climate and public debate so that progressive issues are both on the public agenda and politically viable. It also means giving elected officials room for maneuver. For example, President Franklin Roosevelt recognized that his ability to push New Deal legislation through Congress depended on the pressure generated by protestors and workers, veterans of World War I, the jobless, the homeless, and farmers. In what might be an apocryphal story, he once told a group of activists who sought his support for legislation, "You've convinced me. Now go out and make me do it" (Cohen 2008)

Likewise, the civil rights movement and liberal politicians formed an awkward but effective alliance. In the early 1960s, many Americans, including President Lyndon B. Johnson, viewed Rev. Martin Luther King as a dangerous radical. He was harassed by the FBI and vilified in the media as an agitator. But the willingness of activists to put their bodies on the line against fists and fire hoses tilted public opinion. The movement's civil disobedience, rallies, and voter registration drives pricked the public's conscience and put the issue at the top of the nation's agenda. LBJ recognized that the nation's mood was changing, which transformed him from a reluctant advocate to a powerful ally. At the same time, King and other civil rights leaders recognized that the movement needed elected officials to take up their cause, attract more attention, and close the deal through legislation.

Similarly, the victories of the environmental movement starting in the 1970s—such as creation of the Environmental Protection Agency, the Clean Air Act, the Clean Water Act, and the dismantling of nuclear power plants—required activists who knew that a combination of outside protest and inside lobbying, orchestrated by friendly elected officials, was needed to secure reform.

"You need an outside strategy where you have a way to bang on Congress and the White House when it looks like they might start to sell you out," observed one long-term activist and strategist in an interview with the author about the 2009–2010 campaign for health care reform. "Coalitions are by nature more cautious. There are always some players who don't want to lose their access. It makes it difficult to bang on your friends." This activist added: "That's why it's important for outsiders and insiders to constantly be in contact, to develop trust, [and] to acknowledge their different roles."

Activists need advocates in the White House and Congress to voice their concerns and pass legislation. But even with such allies, activists have to keep the heat on, be visible, and make enough noise so that policymakers and the media cannot ignore them. To advance a progressive agenda, a widespread grassroots movement—which provides ordinary Americans with opportunities to engage in a variety of activities, from emailing their legislators to participating in protests—is essential. They need to believe that supporting an increase in the minimum wage, labor law reform, or health care reform will help, not hurt, their political careers.

As Katrina Vanden Heuvel (2008) wrote a few weeks after Obama's 2008 election:

> We need to be able to play inside and outside politics at the same time. This will be challenging for those of us schooled in the habits of pure opposition and protest. We need to make an effort to engage the new administration and Congress constructively, even as we push without apology for solutions on a scale necessary to deliver.

The inside/outside strategy is essential to success, but not all political activists or advocacy organizations are prepared, or willing, to walk this political tightrope.

4. Strategic and Opportunistic Leaders: A successful progressive movement needs a cadre of staff and leaders who are strategic, opportunistic, and flexible. They need to be able to develop and sustain a long-term strategy that involves marshaling and investing resources, recruiting and mobilizing people, identifying and recruiting allies, conducting research, using the media, and understanding when and how to negotiate and compromise. At the same time, they need to be flexible, able to recognize and seize opportunities as they arise, honestly and objectively calculate their organization's or movement's strengths and weaknesses, and negotiate and compromise when it is appropriate to do so. This is what Ganz (2009) calls "strategic capacity"—a characteristic of leaders—or, more accurately, leadership teams, a core of people who work together well, develop trust, and share a common sense of purpose and strategy. One aspect of being strategic and opportunistic is recognizing where resources should be invested to get the biggest bang for the buck.

5. Election Campaigns and Issue Campaigns: A progressive movement has to be able to help candidates win elections. This task would be easier if progressives did a better job of recruiting and grooming people to run for office and providing research, policy, media, and political support once they are in office.

Political victories are about more than Election Day turnout. Successes on Election Day are a by-product of, not a substitute for, effective grassroots organizing in between elections, when organizations and coalitions mobilize people around issues. People make progress when they join together to struggle for change, make stepping-stone reforms, and persist so that each victory builds on the next. This kind of work is slow and gradual because it involves organizing people to learn the patient skills of leadership and organization building. It requires forging coalitions that can win elections and then promoting politics that keep the coalition alive in order to hold elected officials accountable. Equally important, building strong organizations and coalitions around issues can help build strength at election time and expand the number of allies in elected office. The significant number of House Democrats who voted "no" on health care reform testifies to the importance of both electing allies and being able to put pressure on fence-sitting Democrats from swing districts to vote in favor of progressive legislation.

6. Research and Policy Expertise: Movements need various kinds of research to help them carry out a short-term and long-term campaign plan. Some of this research involves policy analysis and proposals, which is the role that many think tanks play on both the conservative and progressive sides. Progressive and liberal think tanks are not as well-endowed as their conservative counterparts and do not generate as much media attention, but they still have significant resources. One problem is that they rarely coordinate their efforts, although there is some evidence of coordination and collaboration, such as a report released in August 2012, *Prosperity Economics: Building an Economy for All*, cosponsored by a diverse group of think tanks, labor unions, and community groups (Hacker and Loewentheil 2012). The importance of the different kinds of research is highlighted in the next section.

The Role of Research in Advocacy Work and Social Movements

All efforts to change public policy require research. Sometimes the research is part of an explicit research agenda, while other times it is done more informally, as when people involved in advocacy work ask each other, "how big is the problem?" or "what's the solution?" or "who can we get to help us?" Some advocacy organizations and movements have paid staff dedicated to research. Sometimes, they farm out the research tasks to others, including academics or students. Sometimes, they simply borrow or draw on useful research done by others for different purposes. The different kinds of research include the following:

1. Research about the History and Causes of the Problem—Why?
Advocates, activists, and organizers need to know about the history of the problem they are seeking to solve. How long has this problem been around? What were its causes? What institutions and organizations were involved? Have people sought to address this problem in the past? What did they try to do, was it effective, and why or why not? Did government policies—at local, regional, state, or federal levels—improve or worsen the problem? Has the seriousness or the demographics of the problem changed over time?

If certain policies have had a positive impact—for example, food stamps, the Clean Air Act, minimum wage, Social Security, Medicare, the Community Reinvestment Act, the Head Start Program, and the Occupational Safety and Health Act—how can activists build on these successes and show the public that the right government policy can make a difference in improving people's lives?

2. Research about the Magnitude of the Problem— Who, How Many, and Where?
Activists need to know how many people are affected by a problem—how many people have been injured in car accidents, died of smoking or second-hand smoke inhalation, live in poverty, are illiterate or hungry, have been

injured in workplace accidents, are homeless or paying more than one-third of their income for housing, and so on. It is also useful to know the demographic characteristics (income, race, gender, etc.) and geography (residences) of the affected people and, for purposes of mobilization, the political jurisdictions (legislative districts, municipalities, etc.) where people live, whether they are registered to vote, and what organizations (churches, unions, social clubs, and voluntary organizations) they belong to or identify with.

It also is useful to know how seriously people are affected by a problem. Is it temporary or long-term? (If most homeless people are only homeless for a few months or homeless for much longer periods of time, that makes a difference to the homeless people's likelihood of political engagement, to the policy solutions, and to the way the issue is framed for the public and policymakers.)

3. Research about Public Opinion—So What?

Activists and advocates need to know what and how the public thinks about a problem—or whether they think about it at all. Many "problems" are not yet "issues"—they are not on the public agenda, they do not spark controversy or debate, and they are not yet part of the political give-and-take. Some people have "no opinion" about a problem because they don't know it exists or they are too confused about it to "take sides."

One of the first tasks of issue campaigns and social movements is to inject an issue onto the public agenda—in other words, to turn a problem into an issue. This means making people aware that the problem exists and framing it in such a way that the public believes the problem is serious enough that it should be addressed, that it can be solved by government action, and that certain public policies are better than others to address the problem.

One can sometimes tap into what people think about a problem—to "feel the pulse" of a community—through informal conversations and anecdotes. This is why many issue groups engage in one-on-one meetings, door-to-door canvassing, small group discussions and house meetings, and other information-gathering techniques.

More formal public opinion polling and focus groups help issue campaigns and movements see the big picture. What do different segments of the public think about a problem or issue? Who does it impact? Who is at fault? What should be done? Who is helped or hurt by different policy solutions? Polls help us understand variations in public opinion by demographic categories and document how widely and deeply (i.e., "strongly agree," "strongly disagree," or "no opinion") they feel about it. Do they think that society or government should help address the problem? Polls and surveys also show whether public opinion is changing over time, how it is changing, which messages and themes are "getting through," and whether enough people care about a problem or agree on a solution to make it possible to influence policymakers.

4. Research about the Opposition—Know Thine Enemy

The playing field for progressives is rarely even. Yet, as Ganz (2009) has written, David sometimes beats Goliath. Progressive groups can win if they are creative, opportunistic, strategic, and do not make a lot of mistakes. This involves evaluating and mapping one's own assets—numbers of people, money, organizational strength, access to allies, relationship with the media, and other key components. This kind of self-assessment is a form of research—in some ways, it means doing "opposition research" on oneself, as though one were the other side evaluating you.

Advocates and organizers need to have a clear sense of the relative power of contending forces and be hard-nosed about what they can achieve. Such realism does not mean that activists should not reach for ambitious goals, but it does mean that they need to understand what is potentially winnable so that they can align their hopes and their demands and negotiate and compromise in ways that recognize that most change comes about incrementally, through stepping-stone reforms.

All political campaigns—election campaigns and issue campaigns—engage in some form of opposition research—to bring opponents to the negotiating table to forge compromises or to pass or defeat specific pieces of legislation. Opposition research is designed to give activists and advocates an understanding of power—who the opposition is, how they are organized, what resources they have, and where (and how) they are vulnerable to public pressure. If they rely on public visibility and goodwill or depend on the government for funds, regulations, or approvals, they might be vulnerable to public pressure. It is helpful to know what tensions and differences exist among the opposition groups and people, including whether some may be pre-disposed to negotiate and compromise. Opposition research also examines whether they can be influenced by shareholder action, by consumer action, by employee action, or by public embarrassment of corporate practices.

5. Research about Potential Allies

All issue campaigns and social movements have a core group of leaders, activists, and participants. These are typically people who are directly impacted by a problem, but it also includes people who are not directly affected by or care about the problem (and the people directly affected) and perhaps see the importance of the issue as impacting the well-being of society and community. For example, people who do not have children in public schools may get involved in efforts to improve public education because they understand its importance.

Identifying, recruiting, and mobilizing people and organizations outside the core groups—allies—are important for any issue campaign and movement. Allies have resources, connections, and influence that may not be directly available to the core constituency group. They can help with research, media, fundraising, lobbying, direct action, and other key tasks of any campaign. They can help demonstrate that the supporters of the campaign are not limited to those directly affected by a problem. They can widen the sphere of influence—influence opponents and policymakers that the core group cannot reach (or reach as effectively) on its own. They can show opponents, the media, the general public, and even the core constituency that support goes beyond the usual suspects.

Identifying potential allies is a research task. Often, the first effort to identify allies is simply to ask key activists and leaders, "Whom do we know?" But once that list has been identified and exhausted, more information is still needed, including how allies can be mobilized to help us understand and even reach the key decision makers in business, government, and nonprofit organizations.

6. Research about Policy Solutions, the Political Process, and Their Political Implications

Finally, and importantly, progressive issue campaigns and social movements require research to identify solutions often (though not always) in terms of new government policies and programs. They need to know which levels of the government have the authority and capacity to address the problem, which committees and committee members in different legislative bodies have authority to enact the policies, and which elected officials, and which staff persons to elected officials, are sympathetic allies.

They need to know how different policy choices will impact the core constituencies, allies, opponents, and the general public. How much will it cost? What are the trade-offs? How can we "sell" this solution to different target audiences and constituencies? They also need to know how different policy options will impact different constituencies and interest groups. The perfect policy solution might trigger massive opposition, while a less-perfect policy solution might divide the opposition or bring in new allies. In other words, they have to calculate which policy choices are potentially winnable, and which "fallback positions" or compromises would still constitute a significant victory.

Missing Parts of the Fair Lending Movement Research Agenda

During the battle over financial reform that ultimately led to passage of the Dodd-Frank bill in 2010, the major umbrella organization coordinating the reform campaign—Americans for Financial Reform (AFR)—was dramatically under-resourced, with only six full-time staff persons in Washington, DC, and another seven staff persons in the "field" and focused on states represented by key senators on the Senate Banking Committee. The key component groups within that umbrella coalition—fair housing, fair lending, community organizing, and consumer groups—were themselves relatively small when compared with the banking lobby and its allies.

The labor movement—individual unions like SEIU and the United Food and Commercial Workers International Union (UFCW) and two key umbrella groups, the American Federation of Labor and Congress of Industrial Organizations (AFL-CIO) and Change to Win—provided some resources—funding, staff, and research—but focused most of their lobbying and organizing resources primarily on jobs and health care during the 2009–2010 period.

The activist groups had access to data through a politically useful screen, such as looking at foreclosure or lending disparity data by Congressional district. But they lacked the resources to take advantage of the information they found (Jourdain-Earl 2009; National Community Reinvestment Coalition 2009).

AFR and its allies had some access to polling results, but lacked the funding to undertake the kind of public opinion surveys that would help frame their message and provide legislators with information about their constituents' views. The public was (and is) angry at the practices of the major banking institutions—often described as "Wall Street" in the media, but also identified by specific companies like Goldman Sachs or AIG. The public blamed these companies and the industry for the mortgage meltdown and the resulting economic crisis. But the public also opposed the government bailouts for these companies. Polls showed that the public barely understood many of the reform proposals that would strengthen regulations on the financial services industry (Jacobe 2010; McCormick and Vekshin 2010). Before the Occupy Wall Street movement began, advocacy groups were unable to devise a common set of themes, talking points, and images to help the public translate their inchoate anger into support for specific policy ideas.

AFR and its allies had too few staff and resources to conduct the kind of strategic opposition research that is critical. For example, AFR lacked basic information about the financial industry's key corporations—information that its health reform counterpart, Health Care for America Now (HCAN), had about the major insurance companies. This includes information about the campaign contributions and lobbying expenditures of the companies and key lobby groups, the names of former Congress members and staff now working for the financial services industry as lobbyists (the "revolving door"), information about the CEOs and other board members of key financial corporations and industry lobby groups, such as their home addresses, salaries, and bonuses, other corporate board memberships, and affiliations with major civic and philanthropic groups. AFR was unable to expose the financial institutions that received federal bailout funds, gave executives outrageous bonuses, laid off many low- and mid-level employees, engaged in predatory lending and otherwise violated federal fair lending laws, and gave contributions to key political office holders. More than half (55 percent) of the lobbyists registered to lobby for the US Chamber of Commerce on financial regulation were former government officials, including the former chief of staff to a key committee member (Blumenthal 2009).

Because they lacked their own research capacity, the advocacy groups relied mostly on mainstream journalists to expose the financial industry's behavior—such as outrageous executive compensation and bonuses, lobbying and campaign contribution expenditures, the use of "front groups" and business alliances, the revolving door between key members of Congress (and their staffs) and industry lobby groups, and many other topics that could help dramatize the industry's outrageous practices and help shape public opinion.

For example, the Obama administration and reform advocates were pushing for regulation of derivatives—a major cause of the financial meltdown. The derivatives lobby headed by large banks such as JPMorgan Chase, Goldman Sachs, and Credit Suisse heavily lobbied key members of Congress—including Rep. Melissa Bean, a key industry ally on the House Banking Committee—to weaken derivative regulations. Bloomberg and other news media uncovered that the major banks that dominate the derivatives market not only have enormous political clout on their own but also enlist other business lobby groups to broaden their influence, such as the National Association of Manufacturers (NAM), the US Chamber of Commerce, the Business Roundtable, as well as about 171 nonfinancial corporations (such as MillerCoors, IBM, and Deere &

Company) to form the Coalition for Derivatives End-Users (Kopecki, Leising, and Harrington 2009).

These are just some examples of the kind of advocacy research that could have been strategically useful to the advocacy campaign if the AFR and its allies had the resources to employ researchers. In contrast, HCAN had one full-time research director (a former *Washington Post* health care reporter), but he enlisted the help of a network of researchers from various nonprofit think tanks and advocacy groups who were in regular communication, responsibly divided up for different research components, reported their findings to each other on a daily basis, and worked with HCAN's media and organizing teams to utilize the research effectively.

The Changing Playing Field of Financial Reform

In contrast to health care reform, the issue of financial reform was thrust upon the national agenda with hardly any advanced warning. Yes, the Association of Community Organizations for Reform Now (ACORN), the Center for Responsible Lending, and other groups, as well as Federal Reserve member Gramlich, had been warning about the dangerous consequences of predatory lending for many years, but the earthquake of financial disaster happened so quickly that it was difficult to assemble the parts of a reform coalition—and policy agenda—in time to create an advocacy infrastructure. Even the Democratic candidates for president in 2008 could not anticipate how quickly the economy would nosedive as a result of the mortgage meltdown, and their policy prescriptions changed regularly as the crisis deepened. By the time Obama won the election in November 2008, the earthquake had devastated large sectors of the economy, every part of the country (although not everywhere to the same extent), and many political constituencies.

The infrastructure of liberal and progressive groups with expertise and experience with financial reform is much weaker and more fragmented than their health reform counterparts. There were fewer progressive experts who could help devise reforms, and there were fewer grassroots organizations and national public interest groups with experience doing battle over banking reform.

Despite the failures of major financial institutions, the industry never blinked or hesitated when it came to utilizing its political clout to forge a policy agenda and identify political allies in Congress and within the business community. Indeed, many Americans were shocked by the hubris of the banking lobby, such as the American Bankers Association (ABA), that took billions of federal dollars in bailouts but nevertheless utilized its political muscle to thwart reasonable reform regulations. The ABA's ability to defeat the so-called cram-down proposals in April 2009—that would have given bankruptcy judges the authority to modify mortgages for owners facing foreclosure—represented a remarkable accomplishment, as even the conservative *Washington Times* pointed out, "Mortgage banking industry lobbyists, who gave more than $1.8 million in campaign contributions to Senate members in 2008, fought fiercely against the legislation, which was offered as an amendment to a housing bill" (Miller 2009). The defeat of the cram-down legislation served as a wake-up call for reformers that the banking lobby was going to fight every effort to pass regulations that would limit its profits and freedom (Labaton and Dash 2009).

The fair housing and community investment groups that mobilized to win local and national reforms in the 1970s and 1980s focused on an important aspect of bank industry practices—racial discrimination in lending. Enactment of the Fair Housing Act in 1968, the Home Mortgage Disclosure Act (HMDA) in 1975, and the Community Reinvestment Act (CRA) in 1977 were important legislative victories. The creation of an infrastructure of local, state, and national fair housing organizations to engage in testing, litigation, and lobbying helped improve enforcement. But the overall track record of fair housing enforcement and its overall impact on reducing discrimination and, more importantly, racial segregation has been very limited (Sidney 2003).

Advocates of community reinvestment have been more successful, in part because the CRA provides community groups with leverage by requiring public involvement in regulatory decisions and also in part because the HMDA provides advocates with important data to make their case. As result, CRA enforcement from the bottom up has produced important victories in terms of community reinvestment agreements, estimated a decade ago to a total of more than $1 trillion and then reaching $4.5 trillion by 2007 (Harvard Joint Center for Housing Studies 2002; Dreier 2003; National Community Reinvestment Coalition 2007).

The banking industry initially used its political clout to oppose the CRA and its amendments, but it ultimately learned to live with the CRA and, in some cases, even profit from the new markets. Some banks did so more reluctantly than others, but eventually most accepted the CRA as one of the costs of doing business, similar to how employers have learned to live with minimum wage laws even if they wish they did not exist. Hiring more people of color, creating CRA units within their operations, and changing some of their lending practices to provide more loans to qualified minority borrowers were now aspects that banks accepted as part of the new business reality.

The more recent battles for banking reform, however, have been several orders of magnitude more complicated and more difficult than the battles over fair lending that took place in the 1970s, 1980s, and 1990s. The stakes are higher for the financial services industry. Community organizations and coalitions that were created or expanded to do battle over redlining and predatory lending have had to rethink their political strategies and the larger political environment in gearing up for the current battle over banking reform.

Since the early days of the CRA movement, the playing field has changed dramatically in terms of the consolidation and globalization of the financial services industry, the suburbanization of the population, the shift from more overt to more covert forms of racial discrimination, the changing ethnic and racial composition of the population (including the impact of immigration), and the changes in the composition of Congress in terms of the growing number of suburban districts (Dreier 2003). But the industry players who contributed to the recent mortgage meltdown and the resulting economic crisis have made the playing field even more complicated for advocates. The respective roles of Wall Street investment banks, large and small commercial banks, private mortgage finance companies, credit-rating agencies like Standard & Poor's and Moody's, and mortgage brokers are still poorly understood by the public (Atlas and Dreier 2007; Atlas, Dreier, and Squires 2008; Sorkin and Walsh 2013). The consolidation of the industry as a result of federal deregulation—insurance companies, commercial banks, investment banks, and others—has changed the political calculus. The evolution of new products and techniques—such as derivatives, ARMs, subprime loans, mortgage-backed securities, and hedge funds—makes us almost long for the simpler days when people could understand blatant redlining by banks and S&Ls. The fact that groups such as the Business Roundtable, NAM, Chamber of Commerce, and other business lobby groups would help create a front group for a handful of big banks engaged in derivatives reveals how, tactically if not ideologically, big business sometimes operates as a capitalist class rather than as a mosaic of companies, industries, and sectors (Andrews 2009; Immergluck 2009; Sorkin 2009; Cassidy 2009; Stiglitz 2009; Katz 2009; Suskind 2011; Barofsky 2012). There is, as yet, no single narrative or explanation that even liberal and progressive journalists, policy wonks, elected officials, and grassroots advocates agree on beyond the general recognition that major banks were permitted to act irresponsibly as a result of the lack of adequate government regulation and enforcement.

For most of the past decade, the array of local community and consumer groups, along with the coalition of national public interest groups, coalitions, umbrella groups, and think tanks that form the infrastructure of the fair lending movement—the Consumer Federation of America, Consumers Union, National Community Reinvestment Coalition, Center for Community Change, the Center for Responsible Lending, the Greenlining Institute, National People's Action, PICO National Network, and ACORN (which in 2009 and 2010 was already significantly weakened by right-wing attacks and the abandonment of many of its foundation funders and which completely collapsed in April 2010)—represented the David in the battle with big business's Goliath. The combined resources of these consumer and community groups were no match for the lobbying clout of their business opponents. Although public opinion was on their side, and the Obama administration and most liberal Democrats in Congress favored stronger regulations of the financial services industry, their ability to persuade a majority of Congress members in both houses was always in doubt. The compromise—the Dodd-Frank legislation—was surprisingly good given the balance of political forces at the time. The bill included tough, new lending and underwriting standards, limited the fees that credit card companies can charge, increased oversight of financial markets and rating agencies, provided greater protection for investors, and created strict capital requirements on banks to reduce the likelihood that they would collapse and new safeguards from the risky behaviors that led to the bailout of billion-dollar banks. The banking and insurance lobbies carved significant loopholes in the bill, but activists nevertheless welcomed the law, including the new CFPB to regulate the abusive business practices of credit card companies, mortgage lenders, and payday lenders. After Dodd-Frank passed, Americans for Financial Reform and other groups kept up the pressure by monitoring the CFPB and lobbying for strong enforcement of the law's key provisions.

Since the Occupy Wall Street movement emerged in September 2011, the national mood and the national conversation have changed. The growing concentration of wealth and income has shifted attitudes and may have set the stage for a movement of middle-class and poor Americans to find common ground, and perhaps for a movement to emerge to seize the opportunity. Indeed, even many Americans who do not agree with Occupy Wall Street's tactics or rhetoric nevertheless share its indignation at outrageous corporate profits, widening inequality, and excessive executive compensation side-by-side with the epidemic of layoffs and foreclosures.

In a November 2011 poll from the Public Religion Research Institute, 60 percent of participants agreed that "our society would be better off if the distribution of wealth was more equal" (Teixeira 2011). A survey conducted by psychologists at Duke and Harvard found that 92 percent of Americans preferred the wealth distribution of Sweden over that of the United States. In Sweden, the wealthiest fifth of the population have 36 percent all wealth compared to the United States where the wealthiest fifth has 84 percent (Norton and Ariely 2011). A Pew Research Center survey released in December 2011 found that most Americans (77 percent)—including a majority (53 percent) of Republicans—agree that "there is too much power in the hands of a few rich people and corporations." Not surprisingly, 83 percent of eighteen- to twenty-nine-year-olds share that view. Pew also discovered that 61 percent of Americans believe that "the economic system in this country unfairly favors the wealthy." A significant majority (57 percent) think that wealthy people do not pay their fair share of taxes (Pew Research Center 2011).

Thanks in part to the Occupy Wall Street movement, the rhetoric of describing the nation's widening economic divide as a gap between the rich and the poor has been replaced by outrage at the gap between the rich and the rest of us or, more precisely, the richest 1% and the 99%. It could be seen in growing media coverage of economic inequality, hardship, insecurity, and poverty. It could be seen in the Republican primaries, where several candidates attacked Romney for his business practices, outsourcing of jobs, and other aspects that some of his opponents called "crony capitalism." It could also be seen in Obama's occasional efforts to seize the new mood. In a December 2011 speech in Osawatomie, Kansas, for example, Obama sought to channel the growing populist outrage unleashed by the Occupy movement. He criticized the "breathtaking greed" that has led to widening income divide. "This isn't about class warfare," he said. "This is about the nation's welfare." Obama (2011) noted that the average income of the top 1 percent has increased by more than 250 percent, to $1.2 million a year. He returned to these themes in his January 24, 2012 State of the Union address. He called on Congress to raise taxes on millionaires. "Now, you can call this class warfare all you want," he said, adding, "Most Americans would call that common sense" (Obama 2012).

Conclusion

It makes little sense to build a national campaign with the component parts needed for success for one issue—health care reform, banking reform, immigration reform, or climate change—and then dismantle that coalition once the legislative victory has been won. With some exceptions, the groups working on health care reform overlap considerably with the groups concerned about banking reform. The major difference is the level of resources they have assembled for the different issue campaigns. Foundations and constituency groups make strategic choices about investing funds in particular issue campaigns.

So far, they have not invested in the movement for financial reform as they did for health care. Thus, advocates for bank reform have lacked sufficient resources to wage a campaign that can contend for power.

Ideally, although some single-issue organizations may go in and out of these national coalitions, the organizational infrastructure should remain in place to move from issue campaign to issue campaign. Even if some of the organizational affiliates and the name of the coalition on the letterhead changes from issue to issue, the key anchor organizations, and the core leadership team that has developed the trust and strategic capacity, need to continue to work together.

Coalitions for specific issue campaigns—such as bank reform, immigration reform, climate change, health care reform, and labor law reform—are critical. But coalitions around a multi-issue agenda, though harder to begin, will ultimately have a bigger impact. Funders can invest in the core leadership institutions of a multi-issue coalition—the top staff, for example—knowing that the assortment of organizations involved in each issue campaign will vary.

Importantly, the progressive movement needs a table around which to discuss priorities on issues, campaigns, timing, staffing, allocation of resources, and candidate recruitment, training, and support. The current way that progressive issue movements operate—a kind of constantly changing "floating crap game" or "musical chairs" of people and organizations—is costly and inefficient. No person or organization plays the role that Grover Norquist and his Americans for Tax Reform has played for the conservative movement, which can be equally fractious, but has been more disciplined than their progressive counterparts (Cassidy 2005).

National coalitions, organizations, and networks must be able to juggle several issue campaigns at the same time. Over the next five or ten years, a number of key issues—jobs and the economy, health care, climate change and the environment, banking reform and consumer protection laws, immigration reform, labor law reform, gay rights and marriage equality, and education reform and funding—will take center stage, assuming that the Democrats maintain control of the White House and Congress.

Building a national progressive movement cannot be done with a quick fix. There are short-, intermediate-, and long-term strategic considerations. Funders need to invest in organizations and institutions with long-term staying power and with an eye to redistricting in state legislative and Congressional races and races for Senate and governor over the next decade.

A progressive movement primarily needs organizations that can mobilize people in elections and in between elections around issue campaigns. But it also requires organizations that can provide the support services that all successful movements need. These include research, policy analysis, media, legislative drafting, and legal strategy. What is critical is the capacity to share this information and these skills so that local groups and coalitions do not have to reinvent the wheel.

A progressive movement must be national in scope, but it must have the strategic capacity to marshal and mobilize resources locally and regionally. These are federated organizations. To build a progressive movement, we need investments in national organizations with local affiliates. No single organization can do this. Thus, what is needed is a coalition of organizations and networks that can work together on different issues. Funders should be skeptical of supporting local organizations that are not part of larger national networks—that is, national organizations and networks that provide training and ongoing support, and, most important, that can strategize together and coordinate resources, including money and staff. If funders want to invest in local organizations or coalitions, they should insist that they become part of a larger national network.

The local affiliates of national federated organizations will be a diverse group by necessity, many of them working on local issues while also juggling work on statewide and national issues. What national federated organizations can do is to provide staff training, leadership development, strategic coordination, and research for local issue campaigns. There is no simple cookie-cutter method for building local organizations. But experience suggests that building membership simply through door-to-door canvassing is not as effective as more intensive organizing that includes house meetings, one-on-one meetings to identify and recruit leaders, and leadership training.

In recent years, progressive activist groups have been rethinking their approaches to social change in light of the success of conservative forces since the 1970s. The late 1970s saw the beginning of several trends: the rise of neo-conservatism as a political and intellectual force, the dismantling of the social safety net, a dramatic decline in union membership, the chronic fiscal crisis of major cities, and the increase in the political power of big business and its political and intellectual allies. Liberals, progressives, and Democrats found themselves on the defensive, seeking to protect the key components of the New Deal, the Great Society, and subsequent victories from being dismantled by the increasingly powerful right wing—led by the uneasy alliance between big business, the Tea Party, the Religious Right, and the mainstream of the Republican Party.

During the past decade, progressives regrouped and fought back. A number of separate, and sometimes overlapping, issues have catalyzed local and national organizing groups. These include campaigns for environmental justice, living wages and community benefit agreements, immigrant rights, fair trade and opposition to sweatshops, and opposition to the US invasion and occupation of Iraq. All of these campaigns have sought to redistribute wealth and power and to restrain the influence of big business and force corporations to be more socially responsible. They challenge the conservative ideas about the role of government.

Other campaigns—those for gay rights, reproductive freedom, gun control, and civil liberties (for example, opposition to the Patriot Act)—have an uneasy alliance with movements that focus more directly on economic justice. Conservatives were able to use these wedge issues to win electoral victories, but the political trajectory has not been entirely toward the Right, as the results of the November 2012 elections suggest. Growing economic insecurity—what Jacob Hacker (2006) calls a major "risk shift"—created the potential for building political bridges between the poor and the middle class, between residents of cities and those of suburbs, and between people who may otherwise disagree about wedge issues.

The proportion of Americans who define themselves as liberals has been declining for several decades. But this does not mean that Americans do not share most liberal values. For example, fewer women call themselves feminists now than they did twenty years ago, but more women agree with once-controversial feminist ideas like equal pay for equal work or women's right to choose abortion. Likewise, more Americans today than twenty years ago believe that government should protect the environment, consumers, and workers from unhealthy workplaces and other dangers. Most Americans believe the federal government should help guarantee health insurance for everyone. A majority of workers support unions, and most Americans are pro-choice, want stronger environmental and gun control laws, and believe that the minimum wage should be raised and that the nation should do more to combat poverty.

What is needed is a contemporary version of the Progressive and New Deal tradition. This involves regulating capitalism to prevent excessive greed by pushing for housing and banking reforms, workplace safety laws, raising the minimum wage, strengthening the safety net, expanding protections for consumers and the environment, protecting Social Security, and expanding the right of workers to organize and bargain collectively for better wages and working conditions.

Progressive movements succeed when people join together to struggle for change, make stepping-stone reforms, and persist so that each victory builds on the next. Occasionally, there are major breakthroughs—legislation, court decisions, and changes in corporate practices—but these happen because the ground has been laid, captured in the phrase "successful people make their own luck." This kind of work is slow and gradual because it involves organizing people to learn the patient skills of leadership and organization building. It requires forging coalitions that can win elections and then promote politics that keep the coalition alive.

Is the American progressive movement up to the task? All movements for social justice face enormous challenges to success. Disparities in financial resources give big business and its allies disproportionate influence in getting their voices heard and gaining access to political decision makers. This influence does not guarantee that they will get everything they seek, but it does mean that they have an advantage. To be effective, progressive forces must be well organized, strategic, clever, and willing to do battle for the long haul.

Too often, however, the progressive movement has suffered from self-inflicted wounds of fragmentation. Since the 1960s, the progressive movement has been a mosaic of organizations that focus on separate issues and separate constituencies, which has undermined its effectiveness.

All of these organizations do good work, but there is little coordination or strategizing among them and no ongoing mechanism for discussing how to best utilize their substantial resources in the most effective way. If they were to pool their resources and sit around a large table, they might discuss the following issues: How many organizers, researchers, lawyers, public relations, and communications staffers should there be? What kind of single-issue and multi-issue organizations, online groups, and training centers for organizers, volunteers, and candidates are needed? How much money and support should be allocated to unions, community organizing, environmental groups, women's rights groups, civil rights organizations, and gay rights groups? In what parts of the country, including cities, states, and Congressional districts, should organizing work be focused? How many staff members would be based in Washington, DC, and how many in the field? What issues and policy agenda should they focus on?

But, of course, the progressive movement has no coordinating committee to assemble all these resources and make a rational allocation of money based on agreed criteria. It is not really a coherent movement, but rather a mosaic of organizations and interests that share a broad notion of social justice and a general belief in the positive potential of an activist government, which occasionally collaborate on election and issue campaigns.

Although progressive groups share a broad consensus about policy issues (for example, progressive taxation, strong consumer protection laws, supporting reproductive rights, stronger environmental laws, and expanded anti-poverty programs), they rarely join forces to mount sustained organizing campaigns to get policies adopted at the local, state, or federal levels. The one time these groups break out of their separate issue silos and work together is at election time, typically by supporting liberal Democrats through endorsements, voter drives, campaign contributions, policy work, publicity, and other means. These fragile electoral coalitions are typically forged by the candidates, the Democratic Party, or some loose and temporary alliance, and are soon dismantled after each election is over.

Obama's 2008 election, along with a Democratic majority in both houses of Congress, created a major sense of expectation about enacting a progressive agenda. It was clear, however, that winning elections is a necessary but not sufficient condition for winning a progressive legislative agenda. The progressive movement has had some significant victories in the past decade in terms of elections, policies, and issue campaigns (Dreier 2013), but creating real structural reform requires a combination of electoral success and grassroots organizing power (Dreier and Cohen 2012). As Obama began his second term, it appeared that he and his inner circle of advisors may have learned that lesson, too—as evidenced by his second inaugural address, his State of the Union speech, his decision to reenergize his electoral base as Organizing for Action, and his initial second-term initiatives on immigration reform, climate change, gun control, and raising the minimum wage. Whether he is willing to align himself strategically with a progressive movement was still unclear.

Presidents cannot change the course of the country on their own. That is what movements do. Each time there has been a political realignment, it has occurred in ways that even its strongest proponents could not have anticipated. America today is holding its breath, trying to decide what kind of society it wants to be. Liberal and progressive forces are gaining momentum, but they still lack the organizational infrastructure needed to effectively challenge the conservative message and movement.

References

Andrews, Edmund. 2008. "Greenspan Concedes Error on Regulation." *New York Times*, October 23.

——. 2009. *Busted: Life Inside the Great Mortgage Meltdown*. New York: W. W. Norton.

Appelbaum, Binyamin. 2012. "Cautious Moves on Foreclosures Haunting Obama," *New York Times*, August 19.

Atlas, John, and Peter Dreier. 2007. "The Conservative Origins of the Sub-Prime Mortgage Crisis." *American Prospect*, December 18.

Atlas, John, Peter Dreier, and Gregory Squires. 2008. "Foreclosing on the Free Market: How to Remedy the Subprime Catastrophe." *New Labor Forum* 17 (3): 18–30.

Barofsky, Neil. 2012. *Bailout: An Inside Account of How Washington Abandoned Main Street While Rescuing Wall Street.* New York: Free Press.

Blumenthal, Paul. 2009. "Chamber of Commerce Deploys Former Government Officials to Lobby On Financial Regulation." *Sunlight Foundation,* October 15.

Bocian, Debbie Gruenstein, and Roberto G. Quercia. 2011. *Lost Ground, 2011: Disparities in Mortgage Lending and Foreclosures.* Charlotte, NC: Center for Responsible Lending.

Bocian, Debbie Gruenstein, Peter Smith, and Wei Li. 2012. *Collateral Damage: The Spillover Costs of Foreclosures.* Charlotte, NC: Center for Responsible Lending.

Cassidy, John. 2005. "The Ringleader: How Grover Norquist Keeps the Conservative Movement Together." *The New Yorker,* August 1.

———. 2009. *How Markets Fail: The Logic of Economic Calamities.* New York: Farrar, Straus and Giroux.

Clinton, William. 1991. "The New Covenant: Responsibility and the Rebuilding the American Community: Remarks to Students at Georgetown University." Speech, Georgetown University, Washington, DC, October 23. http://clintonpresidentialcenter.org/georgetown/speech_newcovenant1.php.

Cohen, Adam. 2008. *Nothing to Fear.* New York: Penguin Press.

Creswell, Julie, and Vikas Bajaj. 2007. "The Home Mortgage Crisis Spirals, Taking a Toll in the U.S." *New York Times,* March 5.

Dreier, Peter. 2003. "The Future of Community Reinvestment: Challenges and Opportunities in a Changing Environment." *Journal of the American Planning Association* 4 (69): 341–353.

———. 2009. "Good Jobs, Healthy Cities." *American Prospect,* September 20.

———. 2013. "The 25 Best Progressive Victories in 2012." *Huffington Post,* January 8.

Dreier, Peter, and Donald Cohen. 2012. "Obama Won. Now Its Time to Change the System." *The Nation,* November 14.

Federal Reserve Board. 2012. *The U.S. Housing Market: Current Conditions and Policy Considerations.* Washington, DC: Federal Reserve Board. http://federalreserve.gov/publications/other-reports/files/housing-white-paper-20120104.pdf.

Frank, Barney. 2007. "Lessons of the Subprime Crisis." *Boston Globe,* September 14.

Ganz, Marshall. 2009. *Why David Sometimes Wins: Leadership, Organization, and Strategy in the California Farm Worker Movement.* New York: Oxford University Press.

Gramlich, Edward. 2002. *Remarks by Governor Edward M. Gramlich at the Housing Bureau for Seniors Conference.* Ann Arbor, MI: Federal Reserve Board. http://www.federalreserve.gov/boarddocs/speeches/2002/20020118/default.htm.

Griffith, John, Julia Gordon, and David Sanchez. 2012. *It's Time to Talk About Housing: 7 Questions the 2012 Presidential Candidates Need to Answer on the Ongoing Housing Crisis.* Washington, DC: Center for American Progress.

Hacker, Jacob. 2006. *The Great Risk Shift.* New York: Oxford University Press.

Hacker, Jacob, and Nate Loewentheil. 2012. *Prosperity Economics: Building an Economy for All.* Washington, DC: Prosperity for America. http://www.prosperityforamerica.org/read-the-report.

Halpin, John, and Ruy Teixeira. 2009. *Progressivism Goes Mainstream.* Washington, DC: Center for American Progress.

Harvard Joint Center for Housing Studies. 2002. *The 25th Anniversary of the Community Reinvestment Act: Access to Capital in an Evolving Financial Services System.* Cambridge, MA: Harvard Joint Center for Housing Studies.

_____. 2007. *The State of the Nation's Housing 2007*. Cambridge, MA: Harvard Joint Center for Housing Studies.

Hockett, Robert. 2013. "Paying Paul and Robbing No One: An Eminent Domain Solution for Underwater Mortgage Debt." *Federal Reserve Bank Current Issues in Economics and Finance* 19 (5): 1–9. http://www.newyorkfed.org/research/current_issues/ci19-5.pdf.

Immergluck, Dan. 2009. *Foreclosed: High-Risk Lending, Deregulation, and the Undermining of America's Mortgage Market*. Ithaca, NY: Cornell University Press.

Jacobe, Dennis. 2010. "Americans Confidence in Banks Remains at Historic Low." *Gallup Economy*. April 6.

Jourdain-Earl, Maurice. 2009. *Politics and the Subprime Mortgage Meltdown: An Examination of Disparities by Congressional District, Political Party, Caucus Affiliation, and Race*. Arlington, VA: ComplianceTech.

Katz, Alyssa. 2009. *Our Lot: How Real Estate Came to Own Us*. New York: Bloomsburg.

Kopecki, Dawn, Matthew Leising, and Shannon D. Harrington. 2009. "Derivatives Lobby Links With New Democrats to Blunt Obama Plan." *Bloomberg*, October 9.

Kuttner, Robert. 2013. "Seize the Mortgages, Save the Neighborhood." *Los Angeles Times*, June 29.

Labaton, Stephen, and Eric Dash. 2009. "Banks Sway Bills to Aid Consumers." *New York Times*, April 21.

Lowrey, Annie. 2013a. "White House Urged to Fire a Housing Regulator." *New York Times*, March 17.

_____. 2013b. "Obama Nominates Congressman to Lead Mortgage Agency." *New York Times*, May 1.

Lynch, David. 2012. "Banks Seen Dangerous Defying Obama's Too-Big-to-Fail Move." *Bloomberg*, April 16.

McCormick, John, and Alison Vekshin. 2010. "Wall Street Despised in Poll Showing Most Want Regulation." *Bloomberg*, March 24.

Miller, Steven A. 2009. "Obama Loses Against Banks in Congress." *Washington Times*, May 1.

National Community Reinvestment Coalition. 2007. *CRA Commitments*. Washington, DC: National Community Reinvestment Coalition.

_____. 2009. *Black 2006 Subprime Disparity Index by Congressional District*. Washington, DC: National Community Reinvestment Coalition.

Norton, Michael I., and Dan Ariely. 2011. "Building a Better America—One Wealth Quintile at a Time." *Perspectives on Psychological Science* 6 (9): 9–12.

Obama, Barack. 2011. "Remarks by the President on the Economy in Osawatomie, Kansas." White House press release, December 6. http://www.whitehouse.gov/the-press-office/2011/12/06/remarks-president-economy-osawatomie-kansas/.

_____. 2012. "Remarks by the President in State of the Union Address." White House press release, January 24. http://www.whitehouse.gov/the-press-office/2012/01/24/remarks-president-state-union-address.

Perlstein, Rick. 2001. *Before the Storm: Barry Goldwater and the Unmaking of the American Consensus*. New York: Hill and Wang.

Pew Research Center. 2011. *Frustration with Congress Could Hurt Republican Incumbents*. Washington, DC: Pew Research Center.

Reagan, Ronald. 1981. "Inaugural Address." Washington, DC, January 20. http://www.reagan.utexas.edu/archives/speeches/1981/12081a.htm.

Rosenblum, Harvard. 2011. *Choosing the Road to Prosperity: Why We Must End Too Big To Fail—Now.* Federal Reserve Bank of Dallas, 2011 Annual Report.

Said, Carolyn. 2013. "A Rescue for Richmond's Underwater Mortgages?" *San Francisco Chronicle,* June 16.

Schwartz, Nelson, and Shaila Dewan. 2012. "States Negotiate $26 Billion Agreement for Homeowners." *New York Times,* February 8.

Shiller, Robert J. 2012. "Reviving Real Estate Requires Collective Action." *New York Times,* June 23.

Sidney, Mara. 2003. *Unfair Housing: How National Policy Shapes Community Action.* Lawrence, KS: University Press of Kansas.

Skocpol, Theda. 2004. *Diminished Democracy: From Membership to Management in American Civil Life.* Norman, OK: University of Oklahoma Press.

Sorkin, Andrew Ross. 2009. *Too Big to Fail: The Inside Story of How Wall Street and Washington Fought to Save the Financial System—and Themselves.* New York: Viking.

Sorkin, Andrew Ross, and Mary Williams Walsh. 2013. "U.S. Accuses S. & P. of Fraud in Suit on Loan Bundles." *New York Times,* February 4.

Stiglitz, Joseph. 2009. *Freefall: America, Free Markets, and the Sinking of the World Economy.* New York: W. W. Norton.

Stiglitz, Joseph, and Mark Zandi. 2012. "The One Housing Solution Left: Mass Mortgage Refinancing." *New York Times,* August 12.

Suskind, Ron, 2011. *Confidence Men: Wall Street, Washington, and the Education of a President.* New York: HarperCollins.

Teixeira, Ruy. 2011. "Public Opinion Snapshot: Americans Favor Action on Inequality." *Center for American Progress,* November 14. http://www.americanprogress.org/issues/public-opinion/news/2011/11/14/10586/public-opinion-snapshot-americans-favor-action-on-inequality/.

"The Debt Economy." 1974. *Business Week,* October 12.

Vanden Huevel, Katrina. 2008. "Moving Obama." *The Nation,* November 25.

Contributors

Shanti Abedin
Senior Project Coordinator, National Fair Housing Alliance
sabedin@nationalfairhousing.org

Shanti Abedin is the Senior Project Coordinator for lending with the National Fair Housing Alliance (NFHA). In this role, she manages NFHA's education and outreach and investigations on the maintenance and marketing of real estate owned properties. She also provides data analysis and mapping expertise for many of NFHA's other projects and enforcement actions. Prior to joining NFHA, Abedin worked with the New South Wales Department of Planning in Sydney, Australia, as a research editor with the Department of Special Projects, issuing four publications in the Connecting Cities series on key urban planning issues for the Metropolis Congress in 2008.

Katrin B. Anacker
Assistant Professor, George Mason University
kanacker@gmu.edu

Katrin B. Anacker is Assistant Professor at George Mason's School of Public Policy. Her research interests are in housing, urban policy, inequality, real estate markets, research methods, and research design. She is the review editor of the *Journal of Planning Education and Research*. Her work has been published in the *Journal of Urban Affairs*, *International Journal of Urban and Regional Research*, *Housing Policy Debate*, *Housing Studies*, *Urban Geography*, *International Journal of Housing Policy*, and *Housing and Society*. Before joining George Mason University, she was a Research Assistant Professor at Virginia Tech, where she served as coeditor of the academic journal *Housing Policy Debate*.

David Berenbaum
Chief Program Officer, National Community Reinvestment Coalition
dberenbaum@NCRC.org

David Berenbaum serves as the Chief Program Officer of the National Community Reinvestment Coalition (NCRC). He has frequently testified before Congress on fair lending, consumer protection, and valuation issues, and is responsible for implementing NCRC's policy, National Neighbors, and national housing counseling initiatives, as well as related compliance, fair lending, and Affirmatively Furthering Fair Housing programs. He is often featured in the media, including *Dateline NBC*, *48 Hours*, *CBS Evening News*, Bloomberg TV, CNBC, CNN, and others. He previously served as Executive Director of Long Island Housing Services in New York and the Equal Rights Center in Washington, DC.

Saqib Bhatti

Senior Researcher, Service Employees International Union
saqib.bhatti@gmail.com

Saqib Bhatti is a Senior Researcher and Campaigner with the Service Employees International Union (SEIU) and a Fellow at the Nathan Cummings Foundation. He works closely with unions and community organizations across the country to develop strategic campaigns to hold banks accountable for their role in creating and profiteering off the economic crisis. Bhatti plays a critical role in analyzing complex financial issues and then demystifying and translating those issues in order to connect them to grassroots campaigns. He has also written numerous reports, including *Riding the Gravy Train: How Wall Street Is Bankrupting Our Public Transit Agencies by Profiteering off of Toxic Swap Deals* (2012) and *The Win/Win Solution: How Fixing the Housing Crisis Will Create One Million Jobs* (2011).

Janis Bowdler

Director, Wealth-Building Policy Project, National Council of La Raza
jbowdler@nclr.org

Janis Bowdler is the Director for the Wealth-Building Policy Project at the National Council of La Raza (NCLR). She conducts policy and legislative analysis, research, and advocacy on issues that promote the financial security and advancement of Latino families through asset ownership and wealth creation. The Wealth-Building Policy Project has targeted issues such as wrongful foreclosures, neighborhood preservation, financial access, and fair housing for immigrants. Bowdler is an active blogger with regular posts on *Shelterforce*, *Mom's Rising*, *Univision*, and *Huffington Post*, and she also serves on the boards of the Raza Development Fund, Poverty & Race Research Action Council, and Fair Mortgage Collaborative.

James H. Carr

Senior Fellow, Center for American Progress
jim@jameshcarr.com

James H. Carr is Senior Fellow with the Center for American Progress and Distinguished Scholar with the Opportunity Agenda. Previously, he served as Chief Business Officer for the National Community Reinvestment Coalition; Senior Vice President of Financial Innovation, Planning, and Research for the Fannie Mae Foundation; and Assistant Director of Tax Policy with the US Senate Budget Committee. Carr has also been a Visiting Professor at Columbia University. He has published and lectured extensively and has served on research or policy advisory boards at Harvard University, University of California-Berkeley, and University of Pennsylvania. He has testified on several occasions before Congress and has appeared on CNN, Fox News, CNBC, Bloomberg TV, MSNBC, and PBS.

Peter Dreier
E.P. Clapp Distinguished Professor of Politics, Occidental College
dreier@oxy.edu

Peter Dreier is the E.P. Clapp Distinguished Professor of Politics and Chair of the Urban and Environmental Policy Department at Occidental College. He formerly served as Director of Housing for the Boston Redevelopment Authority and as Senior Policy Advisor to Boston Mayor Ray Flynn. His most recent book is *The 100 Greatest Americans of the 20th Century: A Social Justice Hall of Fame* (2012). He is coauthor of *The Next Los Angeles: The Struggle for a Livable City* (2006), *Place Matters: Metropolitics for the 21st Century* (2nd edition, 2005), and *Regions That Work: How Cities and Suburbs Can Grow Together* (2000). He writes regularly for *The Nation, American Prospect, Los Angeles Times*, and *Huffington Post*.

Katrina S. Forrest
Compliance Manager, National Neighbors, National Community Reinvestment Coalition
KForrest@NCRC.org

Katrina S. Forrest serves as a Compliance Manager at the National Community Reinvestment Coalition (NCRC). She is responsible for investigating, developing, and filing systemic fair lending, consumer protection, and mortgage scam complaints. Additionally, Forrest is responsible for managing a variety of federal fair housing and fair lending contracts through the US Department of Housing and Urban Development. Prior to joining NCRC, Forrest worked for the City of Chicago's Department of Law-Collections and Ownership Division, where her professional duties included enforcing violations of the Municipal Code of Chicago that involved the health and safety of Chicago's residents by determining property owners and responsible parties in preparation for litigation.

José A. Garcia
Wealth-Building Policy Fellow, National Council of La Raza
jgarcia@nclr.org

José A. Garcia is a Policy Fellow at the National Council of La Raza (NCLR). He is responsible for developing and executing a project plan and agenda for evaluating and analyzing relevant housing and banking public policies that affect the Latino community, with an emphasis on housing finance and the secondary mortgage market. Prior to working at NCLR, Garcia was the Associate Director for the Economic Opportunity Program at Demos, where he authored dozens of reports on household debt and coauthored the book *Up to Our Eyeballs: How Shady Lenders and Failed Economic Policies are Drowning Americans in Debt* (2008).

George Goehl
Executive Director, National People's Action Campaign
George@npa-us.org

George Goehl is the Executive Director of National People's Action Campaign and National People's Action. He has orchestrated successful national campaigns on housing, banking, and immigration issues. Under his leadership, National People's Action moved more people into the streets in support of financial reform in the three years following the financial crisis than any other organization in the country. Goehl has appeared on Bill Moyers, MSNBC, and CNN, and has been quoted in the *New York Times, Washington Post*, and *Los Angeles Times*, among others. Goehl is a cofounder of the New Bottom Line, a national alliance of community organizing networks working to advance a vision of a new economy in the United States.

Debby Goldberg
Special Project Director, National Fair Housing Alliance
dgoldberg@nationalfairhousing.org

Debby Goldberg is the Special Project Director at the National Fair Housing Alliance (NFHA). She is the point person for NFHA's public policy work on a variety of housing finance issues, including foreclosure prevention, housing finance reform, access to mortgage credit, and others. Goldberg has over thirty years of experience working on public policies to promote fair housing, fair lending, access to insurance, and community reinvestment in communities of color and low-income neighborhoods. Her work also includes extensive training and technical assistance for community-based organizations in those neighborhoods. Prior to joining NFHA, she spent a number of years at the Center for Community Change.

Chester Hartman
Director of Research, Poverty & Race Research Action Council
chartman@prrac.org

Chester Hartman is the Director of Research at Poverty & Race Research Action Council and founder and former Chair of Planners Network. He has taught at several universities, including Harvard University, Yale University, Cornell University, Columbia University, University of North Carolina, University of California-Berkeley, American University, and George Washington University. Among his twenty-two books are *Poverty & Race in America: The Emerging Agendas* (2006) and *A Right to Housing: Foundation for a New Social Agenda* (coedited with Rachel Bratt and Michael Stone, 2006). Among the organizations for which he has been a consultant are the US Department of Housing and Urban Development, US Civil Rights Commission, and Southern Poverty Law Center.

Sandra Hinson
Chief Policy Analyst, Grassroots Policy Project, Research Consultant,
Commonwealth Institute
shinson@grassrootspolicy.org

Sandra Hinson is the Chief Policy Analyst for the Grassroots Policy Project (GPP). Since 1994, she has served GPP in several capacities, including Curriculum Designer, Editor, Researcher, and, between 1999 and 2003, Executive Director. Hinson has worked closely with local organizing groups and statewide coalitions affiliated with U.S. Action, Gamaliel Foundation, National People's Action, Jobs with Justice, and other national and regional networks, providing support on issues related to housing, health care, taxation, budgets, corporate subsidies, racial justice, and environmental justice. Prior to joining GPP, Hinson worked on health care issues with the Communications Workers of America's Health and Welfare Trust.

Donald L. Kahl
Executive Director, The Equal Rights Center
dkahl@equalrightscenter.org

Donald L. Kahl is Executive Director of the Equal Rights Center (ERC). Prior to joining the ERC, Kahl served as Senior Counsel to the Washington Lawyers' Committee for Civil

Rights and Urban Affairs, one of the leading public interest and civil rights law firms in the country. In addition to his nonprofit service, Kahl has more than twenty-five years of legal and management experience. Prior to focusing exclusively on civil rights issues, he was a Senior Litigation Partner and Director of a large private-practice law firm, where he specialized in complex federal litigation for more than twenty years.

Stephen Lerner
Kalmanovitz Initiative for Labor and the Working Poor Fellow, Georgetown University
Stephenklerner@gmail.com

Stephen Lerner is a Fellow at the Kalmanovitz Initiative for Labor and the Working Poor at Georgetown University. He has been a union and community organizer for thirty years and is the architect of Service Employees International Union's Justice for Janitors campaign. Lerner is currently working with community and labor coalitions on campaigns to challenge the economic and political dominance of big banks and Wall Street and the role they played in crashing the housing market and economy.

Douglas S. Massey
Professor of Sociology and Public Affairs, Princeton University
dmassey@princeton.edu

Douglas S. Massey is the Henry G. Bryant Professor of Sociology and Public Affairs at Princeton University's Woodrow Wilson School of Public and International Affairs. He is coauthor of *American Apartheid* (1993), which won the Distinguished Publication Award of the American Sociological Association. His most recent book, *Climbing Mount Laurel: The Struggle for Affordable Housing and Social Mobility in an American Suburb* (2013), analyzes the effects of affordable housing on the surrounding community and on the lives of the project's tenants. He is Past-President of the Population Association of America and the American Sociological Association and current president of the American Academy of Political and Social Science.

Mike Miller
Executive Director, ORGANIZE Training Center
MikeOTC@aol.com

Mike Miller is Executive Director of the ORGANIZE Training Center and has more than fifty years of experience as a community organizer. He directed a Saul Alinsky organizing project, and was a Student Nonviolent Coordinating Committee "field secretary." He has initiated neighborhood, citywide, and statewide organizing projects, consulted widely with community organizations and their sponsor committees, led intensive six-day workshops in the field, and trained organizers. He has lectured extensively and taught urban politics, political science, or community organizing at numerous universities, including the University of California-Berkeley, Stanford University, San Francisco State University, and University of Notre Dame. Miller is the author of *A Community Organizer's Tale: People and Power in San Francisco* (2009) and *Community Organizing: A Brief Introduction* (2012).

john a. powell
Robert D. Haas Chancellor's Chair in Equity and Inclusion and the Director
of the Haas Diversity Research Center, University of California-Berkeley
poweloo8@yahoo.com

At the University of California-Berkeley, john a. powell is Professor of Law and Professor
of African American Studies and Ethnic Studies. He is also Director of the Haas Diversity
Research Center and holds the Robert D. Haas Chancellor's Chair in Equity and Inclusion.
He was recently the Executive Director of the Kirwan Institute for the Study of Race and
Ethnicity at Ohio State University, where he held the Gregory H. Williams Chair in Civil
Rights & Civil Liberties at the Moritz College of Law. He is an internationally recognized
expert in the areas of civil rights and civil liberties and on a wide range of issues including
race, structural racism, ethnicity, housing, poverty, and democracy.

John P. Relman
Managing Partner, Relman, Dane & Colfax PLLC
JRelman@relmanlaw.com

John P. Relman is the founder and Managing Partner of Relman, Dane & Colfax PLLC, a
public interest law firm specializing in civil rights litigation. From 1989 to 1999, Relman headed
the Fair Housing Project at the Washington Lawyers' Committee for Civil Rights. Relman has
written and lectured extensively in the areas of fair housing and fair lending law and practice,
and has provided numerous training classes and seminars for plaintiffs' lawyers, fair housing
organizations, the real estate industry, and lending institutions. He is the author of *Housing
Discrimination Practice Manual* (1992) and has served as an Adjunct Professor at Georgetown
University Law Center and the Washington College of Law at the American University.

Lisa Rice
Vice President, National Fair Housing Alliance
LRice@nationalfairhousing.org

Lisa Rice is Vice President of the National Fair Housing Alliance (NFHA), where she oversees
the communications, resource development, public policy, and enforcement initiatives of the
agency. She is responsible for helping to achieve the organization's goal of addressing the crisis
of segregation in America and the ultimate goal of realizing a truly open society. Under Rice's
leadership, NFHA played a major role in helping to establish the Consumer Financial Protection Bureau, which was formed under the Dodd-Frank Wall Street Reform and Consumer
Protection Act. Rice joined NFHA after serving as CEO of the Toledo Fair Housing Center
and the Northwest Ohio Development Agency. While serving at these organizations, she
developed and implemented Ohio's first predatory lending remediation program.

Robert G. Schwemm
Ashland-Spears Professor, University of Kentucky College of Law
schwemmr@uky.edu

Robert G. Schwemm is the Ashland-Spears Professor at the University of Kentucky College of
Law. He began his legal career with Sidley & Austin in Washington, DC, and then was Chief
Trial Counsel for the Leadership Council for Metropolitan Open Communities in Chicago.

His writings on fair housing law include the major treatise in the field, *Housing Discrimination: Law and Litigation* (1990 and annual updates), and numerous articles in leading law reviews throughout the country. He has been plaintiffs' counsel in several landmark housing discrimination cases, including three in the US Supreme Court. From 1986 to 1990, he was Vice-Chair of the Kentucky Commission on Human Rights and, in 1991, served as Special Attorney and Scholar-in-Residence with the Civil Rights Division of the Department of Justice.

M William Sermons

Executive Vice President and Research Director, Center for Responsible Lending
bill.sermons@reesponsiblelending.org

M William Sermons is Executive Vice President and Research Director of the Center for Responsible Lending (CRL). He is responsible for advancing a policy research agenda into abusive lending practices and works to ensure the delivery of CRL's programs and activities in the areas of research, California advocacy, litigation, and communications. In addition to his work at CRL, he teaches cost-benefit analysis to students in the Carnegie Mellon University's Heinz College Master in Public Policy program. He is the former Director of the Homelessness Research Institute, where he directed both the research and communications functions of the National Alliance to End Homelessness.

Shanna L. Smith

President and CEO, National Fair Housing Alliance
ssmith@nationalfairhousing.org

Shanna L. Smith is President and CEO of the National Fair Housing Alliance (NFHA) and has been engaged in fair housing and fair lending enforcement, education, and research for thirty-six years. Prior to joining NFHA, Smith was Executive Director of the Toledo Fair Housing Center for fifteen years, where she developed groundbreaking cases that successfully challenged discriminatory policies and practices, including the denial of loans to African American and white borrowers because of minimum mortgage loan amounts, private mortgage insurance minimum home value amounts, discriminatory appraisal practices, and homes located in racially integrated neighborhoods.

Gregory D. Squires

Professor of Sociology and Public Policy and Public Administration,
George Washington University
squires@gwu.edu

Gregory D. Squires is a Professor of Sociology and Public Policy and Public Administration at George Washington University. Prior to joining the faculty at George Washington University, Squires taught at the University of Wisconsin-Milwaukee and served as a Research Analyst with the US Commission on Civil Rights. His recent books include *The Integration Debate: Competing Futures for American Cities* (with Chester Hartman, 2010), *There Is No Such Thing As a Natural Disaster: Race, Class, and Hurricane Katrina* (with Chester Hartman, 2006), *Privileged Places: Race, Residence and the Structure of Opportunity* (with Charis E. Kubrin, 2006), *Why the Poor Pay More: How to Stop Predatory Lending* (2004), and *Organizing Access to Capital* (2003).

Acknowledgments

S EVERAL PEOPLE CONTRIBUTED to this volume who we want to thank, and no doubt we will miss a few—to those, we apologize up front. First, we want to thank all of the authors for their contributions to this book and for the work they do every day. Each and every one of them is deeply engaged in the struggles this book is about; these are not simply academic interests for any of them. Second, we want to express our great appreciation to Michael Seng, who brought most of us together in Chicago at the John Marshall Law School to share ideas that led to the completion of this book. As will become evident to every reader, each one of us has learned and benefited from the many who came before us. Some, though certainly not all, are noted in the references and bibliographies in each chapter. We also want to thank the Columbian College of Arts and Sciences and the Department of Sociology at George Washington University for their support. Teri Grimwood did her usual stellar job creating the Index. Finally, we want to express our gratitude to our editor at New Village Press, Laura Leone, who went way above and beyond the normal call of duty in putting all of this together. We have made many friends in the production of this volume and, hopefully, we did not lose too many! We thank you all.

Chester Hartman & Gregory D. Squires

Index